DISTURBED STUDENTS

DISTURBED STUDENTS

Characteristics and Educational Strategies

H. Lyndall Rich, Ph.D.
Professor
Department of Special Education and Rehabilitation
Memphis State University

University Park Press
Baltimore

UNIVERSITY PARK PRESS
International Publishers in Science, Medicine, and Education
300 North Charles Street
Baltimore, Maryland 21201

Typeset by Maryland Composition Company, Inc.
Manufactured in the United States of America
by Universal Lithographers, Inc.

Library of Congress Cataloging in Publication Data

Rich, H. Lyndall.
Disturbed students.
Includes bibliographical references and index.
1. Mentally ill children—Education.   2. Problem
children—Education.   3. Mentally ill children.
4. Problem children.   I. Title.
LC4165.R5   371.94   81-19758
ISBN 0-8391-1708-6   AACR2

Contents

Preface

This book is an introductory text to the characteristics and education of emotionally disturbed and behaviorally disordered children and youth. The approach to these topics is both traditional and innovative. It is traditional in that the characteristics and educational strategies have been previously included in numerous publications; it is innovative in that theoretical and practical connections are made between characteristics, including developmental behaviors, and educational strategies. Although the innovative aspect is not a "cookbook," per se, the final product is a "matching" model whereby practical classroom decisions can be made by special and regular classroom teachers based upon the consistency between characteristics and educational strategies.

Because the matching model requires a multitheoretical orientation, the content of this book is eclectic in nature. It is eclectic in that biological, behavioral, psychodynamic, and environmental theories are used to describe, assess, and identify emotionally disturbed and behaviorally disordered children and youth. In short, no one theory or strategy is considered the most appropriate without considering the characteristics of the children and youth; instead, the most appropriate theory or strategy is the one, from those available, that is congruent with the characteristics of the children and youth.

In order to communicate the proposed content within the space of a single book, certain limitations in scope were imposed. The most significant of these limitations include: 1) focusing on the mildly and moderately emotionally disturbed and behaviorally disordered, thus minimizing the space devoted to children and youth with severe characteristics; 2) providing an overview of theories and strategies, rather than an in-depth discussion; and 3) emphasizing intervention with the behavioral and psychological aspects of disturbance, as opposed to academic or cognitive procedures.

These content limitations, particularly the emphasis on mild to moderate disturbance, were imposed for statistical, legal, and pragmatic reasons. Statistically, more than 75 percent of the children and youth identified as disturbed and disordered fall within the mild to moderate range. This amounts to 1,100,000 children and youth, of which 800,000 are *not* being appropriately served (Kirk & Gallagher, 1979). The numbers alone dictate an urgent need for implementing educational strategies that will increase the probability that these children and youth achieve the greatest possible degree of human potential.

Recent litigation and legislation affecting education has required that handicapped students be served in the "least restrictive environment." Translated into educational practice, mildly and moderately handicapped students are generally being educated in the regular classroom, with or without resource services. This shift in educational placement has created additional responsibilities for educators, particularly the regular classroom teacher. Because of this influx of the emotionally disturbed and behaviorally disordered into the mainstream, there is an increased priority for educational strategies that can be incorporated in the regular class, as well as the special class and the resource room.

The physical space of this book simply precludes a detailed discussion and analysis of all the major characteristics and educational strategies. Instead, referenced overviews are provided for those readers who desire additional information about specific theories or strategies. However, the information contained in this book should be of sufficient quality and quantity to enable the preservice or practicing teacher to understand the basic concepts involved for implementing the various educational strategies.

In addition to the content limitations, a technical problem surfaced that requires explanation. The numerous repetitions of the term "emotionally disturbed and behaviorally disordered children and youth," it was anticipated, would consume an inordinate amount of time and space. Therefore, a shorthand reference to this population has been used: "disturbed students." "Disturbed" was selected as the descriptor even though related terms such as "troubled children," "children in conflict," and "children with behavior problems" have been used synonymously in the literature. "Disturbed," in the context of this book, refers to those children and youth whose behaviors are unacceptable in educational settings, or whose emotional condition is such that it interferes with their personal mental health, or who would otherwise be labeled emotionally disturbed or behaviorally disordered.

"Students" is used in lieu of "children and youth." Because the emphasis of this book is on the education of school-aged children and youth, the term "students" encompasses both the role and age span of the disturbed population. The term students also conveys the belief that the disturbed are primarily learners, rather than patients, clients, or "sick" individuals.

The content of this book is organized into four parts: Background, Characteristics, Educational Strategies, and Synthesis. Even though each of the individual parts and most of the chapters may be read and understood independently, there is an implied sequence. That is, Section I consists of background chapters on history and theories that lead into a discussion in Section II of characteristics, including definitions, classification systems, developmental behaviors, and assessment. Similarly, Educational Strategies, the subject of Section III, contains chapters on intervention, teaching-learning, and management strategies that have partially evolved from the history, theories, and characteristics of disturbance. Section IV, Synthesis, includes a matching model and future directions in the education of disturbed students. The chapter on the matching model, more than any other chapter, is dependent upon an understanding of the preceding chapters. In summary, the book flows from the past, to the present, to the future.

Acknowledgments

I would like to express my sincere appreciation to Drs. Robert M. Anderson, Sara J. Odle, and Anne C. Troutman, all of the Department of Special Education and Rehabilitation, Memphis State University, Memphis, Tennessee, for their enthusiastic assistance in the preparation of this book. Specifically, Dr. Anderson supported me in submitting my ideas for a book to University Park Press; Dr. Odle meticulously corrected numerous manuscript errors; and Dr. Troutman not only read the manuscript for suggested content changes, but co-authored the chapter on Intervention Strategies.

A special note of thanks goes to Ms. Barbara Horrice who efficiently typed and retyped the manuscript.

I would also like to express my gratitude to the editors and publishers who graciously consented to the revised use of materials previously published by the author:

"Behavioral Disorders and School: A Case of Sexism and Racial Bias," *Behavioral Disorders*, 1977, *2*, 201–204.
"Managing Interfering Behavior" and "Establishing the Learning Climate" in J. W. Schifani, R. M. Anderson and S. J. Odle (Eds.), *Implementing Learning in the Least Restrictive Environment*. Baltimore: University Park Press, 1980.
"A Matching Model for Educating the Emotionally Disturbed and Behaviorally Disordered," *Focus on Exceptional Children*, 1978, *10*, (whole number 3).

Last, appreciation is expressed to numerous unnamed individuals—students, colleagues, friends, and family—who indirectly but significantly contributed to this book.

To Shirley Anne, Susan, and Nancey

Section I
BACKGROUND

1
Historical Developments

History is a chronological record of significant events that usually includes an explanation of causes. This chapter uses this definition of history and briefly addresses the events and their causes that have implications for the education of disturbed students. Some professional educators may question the need for a review of historical developments, arguing that "what is past, is past." Although the argument is literally true, a more practical position is that many of the values and beliefs held today regarding the causes of disturbance and their treatment are a product of historical events. In fact, many current social attitudes, diagnostic procedures, and educational techniques are based solely upon historical precedents that may or may not have empirical support. Through a more complete knowledge of related historical events, educators of the disturbed can better understand the process that links past events with current practices. The argument in favor of a historical review is that "what is past, influences the present."

Emotional disturbance is a rather recently labeled handicapping condition, totally absent from the literature before the eighteenth century (Kanner, 1962). However, because individuals were not then identified as disturbed does not mean that emotional and behavioral problems did not exist. More probably, disturbances among the young were masked by social treatment, such as indifference, abandonment, and severe discipline, that denied the existence of the particular handicapping condition. Because of the lack of early historical data regarding the disturbed, it is necessary to examine events relating to other handicapping conditions.

Differential treatment of the handicapped is as old as the recorded history of mankind. Although the historical documents from ancient times until the early 1800s are relatively silent regarding children in general, there is sufficient evidence to reveal a progressively more humanitarian philosophy regarding the handicapped over the past 3,000 years. Hewett (1974) described this progressive pattern in terms of four primary historical determiners: survival, superstition, science, and service.

> The first determiner is the threat of *survival* due to harsh treatment by the physical and social environment. Second, the determiner of *superstition* in relation to the appearance and behavior of the handicapped is of major significance. Our third determiner, *science*, the direct opposite of the second, refers to the natural, lawful, and objective approach to exceptionality. Fourth is the determiner of *service*, the direct opposite of the first, . . . [it] encompasses the care, humane treatment, and societal acceptance afforded the handicapped (p. 10).

Each of these historical determiners or treatment eras is discussed here in terms of the treatment philosophy and the influence of past events on current practices. It should be noted that historical accounts are often unreliable and incomplete, leading to some degree of inference. In addition, the treatment eras discussed do not follow a continuous progression; different cultures at different times have vacillated on this treatment continuum. What may seem to be a specific treatment chronology is a generalized philosophy during a broadly defined period of time.

SURVIVAL ERA (to 500 A.D.)

In ancient cultures, physical fitness was a characteristic that was essential to survival. Not only did individuals have to engage in physical labor in order to secure food and shelter, but they had physically to defend themselves and their territory from destruction, invasion, and pilfering. Life in general required great physical stamina for relatively few life-sustaining rewards. Under these basic conditions, courage, strength, and agility were the required survival skills.

Because of the great demand for physical normality or even supernormality, infants born with physical anomalies were unwelcomed members of the family. The physically disabled were considered a liability because they would not be able to feed or defend themselves. If such infants were permitted to survive, assuming they would under extremely harsh conditions, additional labor on the part of other family members would be required, when most families were barely able to feed and defend themselves. Consequently, infanticide was an accepted practice during the survival era. Infanticide took the form of killing infants, especially by the father, or exposing infants to conditions such as abandonment that eventually led to death.

An excessive number of children, particularly females, created a similar problem, namely, too many mouths to feed. So, in most survival-oriented cultures, only a few physically healthy children, mostly males, were the preferred family constellation (Despert, 1965). Thus, the list of children subjected to infanticide included not only the physically handicapped, but many females and infants in general who enlarged the family size beyond its survival capabilities.

The number of infants that were killed is unknown. Although estimates range from infrequent employment of infanticide to large-scale killing (e.g., "every son that is born ye shall cast into the river," Exodus 1:22), it is generally believed that, on the average, every family subjected at least one child to infanticide during the survival era. The emotional effect of infanticide on the families is similarly unknown. One would suspect that the harshness of the survival era calloused family members to the point of detachment, indifference, and, at the very least, a sense of survival.

About the feelings of all parties concerned—that is, the parents, and in particular the mother—we find no trace outside poetry and the drama. But maternal love has existed through the ages, and it takes little ingenuity to reconstruct the anxiety of the mother during pregnancy and at the time of delivery, when she anticipated the possibility of the barbarian destruction of her child. Surely there was a carryover in her relationship to her remaining children, the ones who had been allowed to live (Despert, 1965, p. 46).

The treatment of disturbance, as opposed to physical handicaps, among children during the survival era is only speculative, because accounts do not exist in the historical records. There were a few writers (e.g., Aretaeus and Soranus) who described the unusual behaviors and secluded treatment of adults who were probably disturbed. However, these writers represented a minority whose ideas were suppressed for almost 2,000 years. One can assume that the behaviors of children that were marginally different were brought into compliance by strict, often harsh, punishment and discipline. Children whose behaviors were grossly different were exiled, tortured, and even destroyed. At any rate, childhood was short, ending at about 7 or 8 years of age, when the children were turned out of the home to live on their own, to perish or survive.

Infanticide reached its apex during the survival era and continually decreased in the succeeding centuries. Today, infanticide has been largely abandoned as an acceptable practice, except in a few underdeveloped countries. However, remnants of the survival era are identifiable in the twentieth century, but in different forms and in different contexts. For example, abortion, sterilization, and euthanasia (killing for reasons of mercy) are considered by many to be forms of infanticide. Whether or not these practices technically constitute infanticide, the underlying rationale is basically the same today as it was in the survival era, that is, to prevent unwanted children, decrease the reproduction of children with undesirable characteristics, eliminate the suffering of children whose death is inevitable, and reduce the family and state burden for caring for children whose capabilities are so limited that they cannot care for themselves. These reasons are not of a twentieth-century origin, but can be traced back to the beginnings of civilization when physical productivity was the measure of human worth.

SUPERSTITION ERA (500–1600 A.D.)

Superstition was not new to the Middle Ages, but irrational explanations of socially unacceptable behaviors did flourish during this era. Founded in pagan religious doctrine and perpetuated by zealous theologians, superstition provided the single most accepted explanation of unusual behavior. Although superstition took many forms, the most prevalent had a religious connotation which held that the child or adult was "possessed" by a spirit that was associated with Satan (Despert, 1965).

This belief in demonology was different from, however akin to, the superstitious beliefs of the earlier survival era. The more primitive societies believed that unusual behaviors were caused by good or evil spirits, and the affected persons were often worshipped, appeased, and even placed in high status positions. The theological leadership in the superstition era, on the other hand, took a more punitive approach regarding those who were possessed. Torture, burning, flogging, and a variety of similarly painful techniques were used to cast out the devil that had taken possession of the individual. Unfortunately, many so-called witches, heretics, and devils lost their lives in the process of treatment.

In those cases in which behavior deviation was less severe, such as hiding, fear, and disrespect, particularly among children, the treatment was typically less severe than that employed with adults. Physical isolation, harsh discipline, and mandatory church attendance were among the more popular forms of treatment. In those cases when the child failed to improve, specialized techniques were required. Among them, the process of exorcism was often employed. Exorcism was a procedure of purification or purging the soul of satanic spirits. The actual ceremony, which had innumerable variations, was conducted by a minister who shouted slogans, quoted scripture, and recited incantations, often supported by such props as knives, candles, water, and instruments for producing noise.

The role of the clergy in the treatment of disturbance is evident throughout the superstition era, but particularly after the fifteenth century. Sporadic accounts have surfaced that provide exemplary evidence of the "professional" treatment afforded disturbed children.

This 7-year-old girl, the offspring of an aristocratic family whose father remarried after an unhappy first matrimony, offended her "noble and god-fearing" step-mother by her peculiar behavior. Worst of all, she would not join in the prayers and was panicstricken when taken to the black-robed preacher in the dark and gloomy chapel. She avoided contact with people by hiding in closets or running away from home. The local physician had nothing to offer beyond declaring that she might be insane. She was placed in the custody of a minister known for his rigid orthodoxy. The minister, who saw in her ways the machinations of a "baneful and infernal" power, used a number of would-be therapeutic devices. He laid her on a bench and beat her with a cat-o'nine-tails. He locked her in a dark pantry. He subjected her to a period of starvation. He clothed her in a frock of burlap. Under these circumstances, the child did not last long. She died after a few months, and everybody felt relieved. The minister was amply rewarded for his efforts by (the girl's) parents. (G. Keller, 1713, in Reinert, 1980, p. 9).

There is little doubt that the children thus subjected to superstitious ceremonies and treatments would be considered disturbed by today's standards for behavior. Certainly, the children so treated in the superstition era violated a socially accepted pattern of behavior and therefore were referred to the primary therapeutic agent within the community—the minister. Treatment was harsh and punitive in most cases, and the signs of cure were obedience, respect, and church attendance.

Many of the historical threads from the superstition era continue to thrive in the education and treatment of disturbed students. Not only are behaviors such as disobedience and disrespect still considered symptoms of disturbance, primarily because they violate an expected behavioral code, but the treatment is often reminiscent of that employed in the superstition era. This treatment includes physical isolation (e.g., exclusion) and harsh discipline (e.g., corporal punishment) with the outcome dependent on evidence that the disturbed student is willing to submit to the requirements of authority. Similarly, the role of religion has not been lost in this historical development. Today, numerous facilities for delinquents are administered by members of the clergy, or, at the very least, the clergy play a prominent role in the treatment program. As late as the 1940s it was observed that:

this method of treating the mentally ill—first putting them in the hands of a physician and then turning them over or leaving them to the good graces of a minister of the church—has survived till our days, as has the old and worn tradition of considering neuroses inseparably within the province of the church and its alleged psychotherapeutic wisdom (Zilboorg & Henry, 1941, p. 83).

Civilization's inability to explain disturbance reasonably created a dependence upon irrational, pseudoreligious superstition. These superstitious beliefs were so deeply ingrained in the Middle Ages that witch burning, demonology, exploitation, and neglect continued for over a thousand years. According to Hewett (1974), "the sixteenth and seventeenth centuries saw an emerging trend toward scientific explanation" (p. 25) that brought new light to the understanding of disturbance.

SCIENCE ERA (1600–1900)

The science era can be characterized as a period of time in which lawful explanations of natural events began to replace the superstitious explanations of the previous era. The discoveries, observations, and theories of Galileo and Newton, for example, propelled the mentality of the world out of the dark ages of mystical reasoning and into an era of classification, categorization, and experimentation. Originally, this scientific process was used to explain physical events, whereas the study of human behavior, including mental illness, moved more slowly into the science era. This initial discrepancy between the emphasis on physical events and behavioral inquiry delayed the understanding of human behavior. This situation established the conditions for two distinct "scientific" explanatory theories regarding human behavior: the astrological and the biophysical.

Scientific interest in astrology was accelerated with the invention and development of technological instruments (e.g., the telescope) with which the celestial bodies could be studied. The moon, in particular, was directly linked to disturbance. Since it was established that there were causative effects between lunar conditions and physical events on earth, it was concluded that humans were subjected to the same lunar influence. Consequently, early in the science era human disturbances were attributed to lunar cycles, and persons affected were committed to lunatic asylums, intended as a refuge from the moon. It is comprehensible that fabled notions of werewolves, jack-o-lanterns, and the like are a product of this early explanation of human behavior that combined scientific and superstitious reasoning. Even though the causative effects of celestial conditions on extreme forms of human behavior have not been supported by modern scientific inquiry, the belief persists that certain personality and behavioral traits may be inferred from celestial conditions, including astrological "signs."

The biophysical theory of behavior, on the other hand, emerged from the science era as the primary explanation of disturbance. This is mainly attributable to the fact that the medical profession became a dominant and influential discipline during this period of time. As a result, there is little doubt that the medical orientation, with its emphasis on biological dysfunction, is the oldest scientific approach to explaining human disturbance (Mahoney, 1980). The biophysical theory is a general theory with a number of specific interrelated theories that were hypothesized by medical researchers during the scientific era: heredity, poisoning, chemical imbalance, glandular dysfunction, disease, and brain damage were among the most prominent. Each of these explanations, in some form, has withstood the test of time and continues to be used to explain disturbance as well as related handicapping conditions such as retardation and learning disabilities. It was not until the twentieth century that nonphysiological theories, particularly psychodynamic, behavioral, and environmental theories, made an impact upon the understanding of disturbed behavior.

In addition to the biophysical causative explanations, the medical profession had an influence on the treatment of the disturbed. Superstition era medical practices such as bloodletting and assorted herb mixtures gave way to antibiotics and tranquilizers. More practical solutions in the form of prevention were also suggested: selective breeding, elimination of masturbation, prudent use of "spirits" (alcohol), and avoiding contact with those prone to fits (epileptic seizures). Interestingly, the ancient practice of trephining (chipping a hole in the skull to permit evil spirits to escape), a forerunner to psychosurgery, was practiced sparingly toward the end of the science era (Hewett, 1974). Since a small percentage of the disturbed were cured by means of these treatments, the older practices of physical protection, isolation, and abuse continued during the science era. These older practices consisted of "idiots, epileptics, and insane . . . bound with galling chains, bowed beneath fetters and heavy, iron balls attached to drag chains, lacerated with ropes, scourged by rods and terrified beneath storms of cruel blows" (D. Dix, 1848, in Zilboorg & Henry, 1941, p. 583).

It was not until the last century of the science era that disturbance among children began to be examined with any degree of seriousness. Before this time, disturbance among children was viewed with suspicion; the emphasis was on adults. After all, children did not have the necessary years of experience, the required physiological development, or sufficient contact with the undesirable elements of society in order to qualify them for mental illness (Coleman, 1964). In short, the underdevelopment or elasticity of the organism meant that the true nature of the child could not be determined, except in those cases in which heredity predetermined the behavior of the child.

The classification and categorization functions of the science era resulted in closer examination of children. Whereas handicapped children tended to be lumped together into a relatively few broad classifications (e.g., idiots, deaf-and-dumb, blind, and incurables), descriptive data were beginning to reveal differences within these categories. Not only was retardation broken down into separate classifications (idiot, imbecile, and moron), but disturbance was beginning to be viewed as a separate syndrome. Howe, in 1852, for example, coined the term "simulative idiocy" for disturbed children who appeared to be retarded, because they exhibited similar behavioral characteristics, but were apparently functioning on a higher level. The distinction between retardation and disturbance was so disguised that "it was not until 1886 that there was a legal separation between insanity and feeblemindedness" (Kauffman, 1977, p. 46).

This scientific process of classification and categorization has continued into the twentieth century. Numerous labeled handicapped conditions, each theoretically reflecting a unique set of characteristics, have evolved from this nineteenth-century practice of categorically differentiating children. Interestingly, this medical model of classifying pathology was adopted by educators, even though children so labeled may have demonstrated relatively minor, if any, unique characteristics, and these had minimal educational relevance.

SERVICE ERA (Twentieth Century)

It was prophetically claimed by the now famous sociologist, Ellen Key, in 1900 that the twentieth century would be the "century of the child." From all indications, this prophecy is becoming a reality. Children today, compared with the centuries before, have a more humane lifestyle, both physically and psychologically, are protected by law, and are provided with more appropriate services, including education. However, educators and society in general cannot be content with what has been accomplished; a great deal is yet to be done. As Kauffman (1979) has warned, "we have made progress—but less progress, I think, than we would like to believe" (p. 49).

The historical road to the twentieth century has been a long and difficult one for disturbed children. They have traveled the road as objects that were physically expendable, as victims of superstitious beliefs, and as subjects of scientific classification. The twentieth century has not witnessed an end to these historical determiners, but they have assumed less importance in an era of service. This change in the direction of more humane treatment appears to be the result of four significant historical threads that were drawn together in the 1970s.

The four historical threads include: 1) the development of alternative classification systems to describe disturbance; 2) the emergence of nonmedical theories explaining the causes of disturbance; 3) the development of specialized educational strategies appropriate for the disturbed; and 4) litigation and legislation enacted to protect and serve the handicapped, including the disturbed. The following summary of the four historical threads serves as an introduction to the remainder of the book. Although the information is limited in this chapter, additional, more detailed explanations are contained in subsequent chapters.

Classification of Disturbances

"Classification refers to the act or process of arranging or grouping objects or facts by classes, based on similar attributes or relations" (Prugh, Engel, & Morse, 1975). The earliest probable classification of disturbance, based on the demonstration of unusual behavior, was that of being possessed. During the science era this superstitious classification eroded in favor of medical terminology that had a disease or biological orientation. Late in the nineteenth century, psychiatry, a branch of medicine, emerged to assume the primary role in the classification of disturbance. Emil Kraepelin, a physician, published a book in 1883 that established the basis for the present psychiatric classification system (Reinert, 1980). "Today we are . . . heirs to a history of control by the medical profession over how disorders are dealt with when they are manifested" (Kauffman, 1979, p. 50).

By the twentieth century, children with severe disturbance were being classified as having mental diseases, insanity, and dementia praecox. Unfortunately, these global classifications provided little information beyond identifying a child as disturbed. As a result, new terms such as psychosis and schizophrenia were developed; these suffered from the same limitation of the earlier classification terms. Even so, references in the literature to psychoses, for example, are pervasive. The extent to which these global medical classifications were used caused Kanner (1961) to observe that "it is strange, indeed, that a historical review of emotional disturbances should occupy itself predominantly, or almost exclusively, with psychosis and, more specifically, with schizophrenia" (p. 4).

This dependence on global medical classifications caused Kanner to conclude that "a historical survey teaches us that progress has always consisted of a breaking down of diffuse generic concepts into specific categories" (p. 4). Following his own advice, Kanner described the syndrome of early infantile autism, whereas Mahler identified symbotic infantile psychosis and Bender defined schizophrenia as a maturational lag. By the 1960s more specific classifications could be found in the literature, including such terms as "hyperactive," "overanxious," "shy withdrawal," and "aggressive" (e.g., American Psychiatric Association, DSM-II, 1968). Clearly, the medical-psychiatric classification systems were moving in several directions: from generic to specific terms, from severe to mild conditions, and from adult to child syndromes.

Even with the apparent changes in medical classifications of disturbances, educators became increasingly dissatisfied with the medical influence. Consequently, educators almost spontaneously began to use labels and categories such as "behavior problem" and "conduct disorder," that were intended to be more useful descriptors in education settings. This well-meaning intent to become independent of medical classifications has resulted in another series of superficial, loosely defined, and educationally irrelevant terms to describe the disturbed. In fact, over 20 different terms have been used during the last decade to describe the disturbed population (Wood & Lakin, 1979).

During the transition from medical to educational classifications, the disturbed population experienced increased services. The movement away from medical classification, which virtually excluded educational responsibility because of its unavailability, excessive costs, and medically restricted treatment, resulted in increased responsibility for schools and other social institutions. No longer equipped with the excuse that a student is a "psychiatric problem," school personnel had to deal with disturbance as a function of the emerging education classifications. To effectively increase appropriate services for disturbed students, however, professional educators must develop an effective classification system, not to label the student, but to plan and implement appropriate educational strategies.

Theories of Causality

The potential causes of disturbance are innumerable. The frequent expression of conceptually simple, intuitive, and narrow explanations for behavior (Jackson, 1968) reflects a range of possibilities: "He learned that from his father"; "She's lived with failure all her life"; "He hangs around with the wrong crowd"; "She was just born that way" and so on. Each of these statements may contain an element of truth, but they do not offer any consistent evidence or organization for specifying the cause of the disturbance.

Rhodes and Tracy (1972a), in an effort to sort through the major explanations, concluded that there were five basic theories of causality that could "be grouped into explanatory systems which are logically related ideas and observations about disturbance" (p. 15). These five identified theories, which have emerged over the past century, are: biophysical, behavioral, psychodynamic, sociological, and ecological. Before continuing it should be noted that a number of educators (e.g., Neill, 1960) have rejected this scientific, therefore "dehumanizing," approach to the understanding of behavior. This diverse group of so-called "countertheorists" have objected to the concepts of labeling and normality, maintaining that individuality should be encouraged, not categorized (Rhodes & Paul, 1978).

The *biophysical* theory, an outgrowth of the biophysical explanation of the science era, maintains that disturbed behavior is a "form of mental disease, a pathological condition that exists because of (physiological) deficiences in the individual" (Newcomer, 1980, p. 24). These deficits may include one or a combination of neural, genetic, biochemical, or developmental conditions. Students diagnosed as brain-damaged, for example, would fall within the biophysical theory of causality.

The *behavioral* theory assumes "that all behavior (adaptive and maladaptive . . .) is the result of lawful application of principles of reinforcement and extinction" (Kameya, 1972, p. 165). Originating from the work of Pavlov and stimulus-response learning theory, the behavioral theory has undergone numerous refinements by such theorists as Watson, Thorndike, and particularly B. F. Skinner, who emphasized operant conditioning. Disturbed behaviors, according to this theory, are "modeled" (Bandura, 1971) or elicited through the introduction of planned or unintentional reinforcement (Skinner, 1953). In short, disturbance is learned.

The *psychodynamic* theory considers disturbance to be a function of maladaptive psychological processes. Brought to world attention by Sigmund Freud, the psychodynamic (also called psychoanalytic) theory has its roots in the medical concept of mental illness. According to this theoretical position, a combination of biological predeterminers and interactions with the environment creates the conditions in which disturbed students develop a conception of self that results in internalized feelings of guilt, anxiety, fear, inadequacy, and so forth. On the simplest level, the psychodynamic theory emphasizes that disturbance is a function of psyche (mental) processes that has resulted in inadequate ego development. This ego inadequacy is manifest in the inability to regulate behavior in accordance with demands of the environment.

The *sociological* theory explains disturbed behavior as a "function of implicit rules governing ordinary social interaction" (Des Jarlais, 1972, p. 263). Therefore, a student who violates these rules is labeled as a social deviant—a role or position in the social system that has certain institutionalized expectations, including rights and obligations. Within the sociological context, disturbed behavior, then, is not a function of behavior itself, but a labeling process exercised by those who have the authority to establish and enforce rules of social interaction. This theory is a clear departure from the three previous theories in that they maintain that the locus of the problem is within the student, whereas the sociological theory maintains that the problem is a function of social expectancies.

The *ecological* theory is based upon the interaction between the organism and its environment. In short, ecologists do not see disturbed behavior as within the individual or within the environment, but that it is "the interaction between the idiosyncratic individual and his unique environment . . . which produces the disturbances" (Feagans, 1972, p. 332). Thus, the ecological theory incorporates all of the theories previously discussed and goes beyond their limitations, maintaining that it is a combination of all the theoretical explanations within the ecosystem that accounts for disturbed students.

These five theories reportedly account for disturbance among students. The sequence presented was not random, but a logical progression from the first theory (biophysical) "representing the most individual and physical focus" to the last theory (ecological) "representing the most universal and complex focus" (Rhodes & Tracy, 1972b, p. 5). Figure 1 is a representation of this logical progression; that is, the theories become sequentially more cumulative, but less specific in their explanation of disturbance.

Each of the theories of causality is a product of historical investigations of behavior that are being applied to the understanding and, consequently, the education of disturbed students. Service to disturbed students is being improved by the increased recognition of multiple explanatory conditions that lead to the diagnostic decision that a student is disturbed.

Educational Strategies

The historical development of specialized educational strategies for the disturbed consists of two primary but interrelated concepts: the

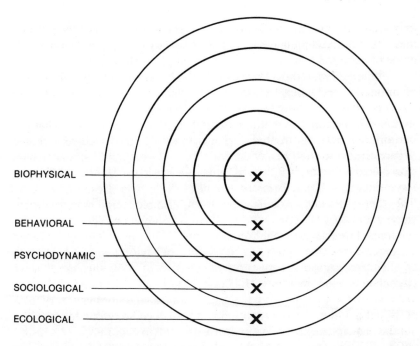

BIOPHYSICAL

BEHAVIORAL

PSYCHODYNAMIC

SOCIOLOGICAL

ECOLOGICAL

Figure 1. Representation of the progression of theories. Adapted from Rhodes and Tracy, 1972b.

implementation of a variety of intervention strategies and changes in the administrative placement of disturbed students. These two conceptual developments will be discussed separately even though they have often affected each other; that is, intervention strategies were often implemented to be consistent with administrative placement, and administrative placement was often employed to accommodate intervention strategies.

Intervention Strategies The survival and superstition eras were discussed with the conclusion that disturbed children were harshly treated by parents with the approval of society. "It was not until the period following the American and French revolutions in the closing years of the eighteenth century that kind and effective treatment of the *insane* and *idiots* . . . made their appearance. In that era of political and social revolution, emphasis on individual freedom, human dignity, philanthropy, and public education set the stage for humane treatment and education of the handicapped" (Kauffman, 1979, p. 43).

In this new humanitarian climate, several mental health pioneers emerged advocating treatment and education concepts that would have impact on the twentieth century. As might be expected in the science era, most of these pioneers were physicians by training, but envisioned treatment beyond the scope of purely biophysical intervention.

Philippe Pinel, the administrator of a French mental hospital, took a dramatic step when he ordered the chains removed from chronic mental patients. It was his contention that the insane would respond better when treated with kindness and respect. Pinel reported that the majority of patients treated in this manner demonstrated remarkable improvement in their behavior. This "moral treatment" spread across Europe and to America, where Benjamin Rush and Dorothea Dix continued to press for reforms on behalf of the insane (Despert, 1965).

One of Pinel's students, Jean Itard, also pioneered new treatment techniques that are consistent with twentieth-century educational procedures. His efforts to teach Victor (the wild boy of Aveyron) consisted of procedures that approximate modern behavioral-educational techniques, including the sequential acquisition of skills through the use of behavior modification. "His book remains a fascinating and moving classic in the education of the handicapped, and contemporary educational methods for the retarded and disturbed are grounded in many of the principles expounded by Itard almost two centuries ago" (Kauffman, 1977, p. 44).

From these rather meager beginnings a number of intervention strategies have emerged. The strategies, listed in this section, are a culmination of past practices that have their roots in the theories of causality. The list is not inclusive, but does contain the major strategies that have been employed with disturbed students. Since the strategies are a product of the theories, they are listed in the same progressive sequence. It should be noted that a primary objective of each strategy is to intervene with the student's disturbance in a way that is theoretically appropriate to the cause of the disturbance.

The *structured* strategy (Cruickshank et al., 1961) was designed for students "defined as hyperactive, with or without the diagnosis of brain damage" (p. 9). The essential features of the strategy include sensory reduction, that is, the removal of all unnecessary stimuli so that the student will be able to focus on that which is essential to the learning process. "It is hypothesized that, if the learning environment can be simplified and highly structured, the hyperactive child will have greater opportunity for success experience . . . Hence, it is proposed that initially the educational program of the school day be completely teacher-directed with little or no opportunity for choice on the part of the child" (p. 18). The strategy is reported to be most effective for those students believed to have a central nervous system dysfunction (biophysical cause).

A *behavioral* strategy may use any one of three primary methods: respondent conditioning, modeling, and operant conditioning (Blackham & Silberman, 1980). The first two models have been used routinely in education; that is, educators have traditionally employed respondent conditioning (eliciting a behavior by introducing a particular stimulus) and modeling (providing behaviors for the student to imitate). Operant conditioning or "behavior modification," on the other hand, was not systematically employed on a large scale until B. F. Skinner popularized the strategy during this century. Based on the behavioral premise that disturbed behavior is a function of positive reinforcement or absence of punishment following a behavior, the intervention strategy employs the same concept to alter the behavior of disturbed students.

The *psychoeducational* strategy "postulates a circular, interacting relationship between thoughts and feelings such that cognitive experience affects emotional experience . . ." (Fagen, Long, & Stevens, 1975, p. 52). The strategy, then, emphasizes such concepts as personal relationships, coping with feelings, dealing with psychological crises, and developing positive feelings of self. The psychoeducational strategy, as opposed to the behavioral orientation of the first two strategies, emphasizes procedures to deal with the feelings, emotions, and social relations of the disturbed student.

Environmental strategies that are a product of the combined sociological and ecological theories have achieved prominence only in the last two decades. Increasing emphasis is being placed on the role of the environment in contributing to disturbance. Therefore, significant aspects of the learning/living environment are considered a prerequisite to education per se. The physical classroom space, the composition of the classroom group, and the instructional style of the teacher, for example, are analyzed in light of students' ecosystems (Proshansky, 1974).

Other strategies, such as reality therapy (Glasser, 1965), the engineered classroom (Hewett, 1968; Hewett & Taylor, 1980), open education (Holt, 1967), and the alternative approaches of the countertheorists constitute variations of the strategies summarized in this section and will be discussed in later chapters. Table 1 illustrates the hypothetical relationships among the theories of causality and the corresponding intervention strategies.

The variety of strategies has increased service to the disturbed primarily because of the availability of instructional/managerial options that have achieved a wide degree of acceptance. No longer limited to the medical model and the stimulus-response approach, educators have been able to employ strategies that are more consistent with the needs of disturbed students and the teachers' personal teaching styles.

Table 1. Primary hypothetical relationships among the theories of causality
and intervention strategies

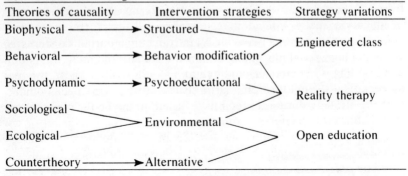

Theories of causality	Intervention strategies	Strategy variations
Biophysical ⟶	Structured	
		Engineered class
Behavioral ⟶	Behavior modification	
Psychodynamic ⟶	Psychoeducational	
		Reality therapy
Sociological		
	Environmental	
Ecological		Open education
Countertheory ⟶	Alternative	

Administrative Placement   Little is known about the administrative
or social placement of the disturbed before 1800. On the basis of the
prevailing practices of the survival and superstition eras one would
suspect that the severely and profoundly disturbed were typically
abandoned, whereas the mildly and moderately disturbed remained at
home, subjected to harsh discipline. There are some records to indicate
that a few children were placed in the custody of a minister for treatment, but this practice was probably limited to a relatively few wealthy
families.

Midway through the science era, institutions for the insane,
amounting to prisons, began to flourish throughout Europe. Most of
these facilities were for adults with severe problems; however, because
childhood was short, many children as young as 7 or 8 years old were
committed along with the adults. Institutions for delinquents, modeled
after adult prisons, were also founded in the latter part of the science
era.

Educationally, the severely and profoundly disturbed were excluded from services in the early part of this century. Most disturbed
children were confined in isolated circumstances such as the home, or
were to be found in state institutions, especially for the retarded. The
mildly and moderately disturbed, on the other hand, fared somewhat
better. To the extent that children in general attended school, the mildly
and moderately disturbed were afforded the same opportunity. However, these children quickly saw much of their educational opportunity
evaporate because of rather strict discipline and, ultimately, exclusion
from school. This was particularly the case because disturbance was
not viewed as a handicapping condition, but as a symptom of disrespect, disobedience, and insolence that was not tolerated within the
rigid rules of education.

The twentieth century has witnessed a number of sequential changes in the placement of disturbed students. Spurred by the medical treatment and scientific classification of disturbance, the development of measurement techniques (e.g., intelligence tests), the passage of compulsory attendance laws, and general humanitarian concerns of society, educational placement changed from segregated to integrated settings. The sequence was one of gradual approximations to the regular class for the mildly and moderately disturbed: from special school, to the special class, to resource services, and finally to the mainstream.

Segregation of the handicapped into special classes was originally viewed by proponents of the eugenics movement in the early 1900's as a means of improving society. . . . However, the development of special classes was part of a broader transformation of the American School. For example, the segregation of handicapped children into special classes closely paralleled the trend toward general-ability grouping in the schools. Some thought that these children would receive a more individualized education in a special class than in the regular class where "their needs could not be adequately met." A common rationale for the administrative arrangement of segregation during this period appeared to emphasize two themes. First, it was thought that the handicapped child could receive the aid and encouragement needed, when taught by specially trained teachers who could "adjust" the curriculum; second, a popular view was that normal children would be free from the restrictions imposed by the handicapped child in the regular classroom (Semmel, Gottlieb, & Robinson, 1979, p. 225).

These two themes provided the impetus for entrenching the segregationist philosophy until the civil rights movement of the 1960s. As a result of the social forces that questioned the efficacy of prevailing human services, educators also began to investigate the empirical bases and humanitarian philosophy on which the special class was founded (Blatt, 1960; Dunn, 1968). Although most of the public and professional debate centered on special classes for the mentally retarded, the disturbed reaped the benefits of a general philosophical change in administrative placement of handicapped students. This change consisted of placing disturbed students, particularly those with mild to moderate problems, in the regular classroom, frequently with resource services.

To date, it has not been clearly demonstrated that regular class placement is superior to segregated placement in terms of academic achievement. Similarly, it has not been demonstrated that the segregated placement is superior to the regular class (Semmel, Gottlieb, & Robinson, 1979). Given these inconclusive results, other factors have contributed to the implementation of the mainstreaming concept. The process of negatively identifying students, reducing their contact with normal peers, and denying their rights to equal access and due process justifiably came under attack by the public, particularly by parents of handicapped students. Consequently, the product of this social movement of the past two decades was the adoption of a more humanitarian service function facilitated by the administrative placement of disturbed students in the most appropriate education setting, namely, the regular class.

Before terminating this brief discussion on administrative placement, it should be made clear that the assignment of disturbed students to the regular classroom is currently limited to those with mild to moderate conditions. Students with more severe conditions (e.g., autistic characteristics) are *not* being assigned to the regular classroom on a permanent basis. Students with autistic characteristics are still being placed in segregated settings—an institution, special class, and/ or resource service—that constitute the least restrictive environment. This is the situation today; tomorrow may bring another flurry of social, legal, and educational debates that may uphold or reverse the current administrative placement philosophy.

Litigation and Legislation

Any discussion of the service era would be incomplete without the inclusion of the court decisions (litigation) and laws enacted (legislation) that have affected the education of the handicapped. Again, the disturbed were not the focus of these legal activities, but they did directly share the benefits that were afforded the mentally retarded, racial minority children, and non-English speaking students. Legal activity seemed to have been propelled by the 1954 Supreme Court decision (Brown v. Board of Education of Topeka) that ruled that segregation violated the 14th Amendment of the U.S. Constitution. After this decision, numerous cases charging discrimination, denial of rights, and/or deprivation of an adequate education were filed on behalf of handicapped students. Some of the most critical court decisions include:

Covington v. Harris (1969) established the concept of "least restrictive means" for educating the handicapped.

Pennsylvania Association for Retarded Children (PARC) v. Commonwealth of Pennsylvania (1971) established that handicapped retarded children were entitled to a free and appropriate education, due process, and placement in the "least restrictive alternative."

Mills v. Board of Education of the District of Columbia (1972) established the right to an education for all children, including those that had been excluded from educational services.

Diana v. State Board of Education (1970), followed by Larry P. v. Riles (1972), established that traditional IQ tests could not be used with minority group children to justify an intellectual handicapping condition.

Lebanks *v.* Spears (1973) established that no handicapped child may be excluded from the opportunity to receive an education because of a handicapping condition.

Halderman *v.* Pennhurst (1977), along with the earlier Wyatt *v.* Stickney (1971), established the right of institutionalized handicapped persons of any age to an adequate education and/or habilitation in the least restrictive conditions.

Combined, these court decisions have systematically shaped the conditions by which the handicapped are to receive an education. The cumulative effects of the litigation mean that disturbed students are not to be denied an education or their civil rights, and, further, that the education must accommodate their unique needs in the regular classroom whenever possible.

Concurrent with the litigation, a series of legislative acts were passed by Congress that reinforced, refined, and extended the rights of the handicapped established by the courts. Between 1957 and 1975, dozens of federal public laws were enacted that affected the handicapped, including legislation for the training of professional personnel, research and demonstration projects, early education assistance, and the construction of mental health centers. The series of federal legislative acts culminated in the passage of the Education for All Handicapped Children Act of 1975 (Public Law 94-142).

Public Law (PL) 94-142 has been acclaimed as "one of the most significant milestones in the history of American education" (Torres, 1977, p. 1). Although PL 94-142 is a complex assortment of definitions, reimbursement formulas, and directives, the critical features are that handicapped children will be provided a free, appropriate education, including an "individual educational program" in "the least restrictive environment."

The litigation and legislation affecting the handicapped did not occur in a vacuum. The legal activity seems to have been a product of social, scientific, and educational changes that gained momentum in the twentieth century. Combined with the movement toward the educational classification of disturbance, the formulation of theories of causality, and the employment of differential educational strategies, litigation and legislation provided a stronger basis for a service era.

From a historical perspective a great deal has been accomplished with regard to the treatment of disturbed students; however, a great deal is yet to be accomplished. Rather than seek to resolve new, magnanimous challenges, it is time to refine and integrate what has been learned from history. It is time to appraise attitudes toward the disturbed, to develop relevant descriptors of disturbance, and to evaluate the effects of programs for the disturbed. Only after these kinds of functional questions are answered can educators, even society, truly claim to be living in a service era.

SUMMARY

This chapter traced the significant historical developments related to the social treatment, classification, and education of disturbed students. It was emphasized that the treatment of children in general during the survival and superstition eras was severe and dehumanizing by today's standards. Infanticide, deprivation, torture, and harsh discipline were routinely used to create a population of physically able and behaviorally compliant children. During the science era the study of children resulted in a number of medical-psychiatric classifications that were used to identify and explain mental illness. Concurrent with this labeling of children, new treatment and educational concepts emerged that were more humanitarian and more effective.

On the basis of historical developments originating in the science era, the twentieth century witnessed a dramatic increase in service to disturbed children. Intensive efforts to classify disturbance, the conceptualization of theoretical models of causality, and the implementation of a variety of educational strategies evolved with a service-oriented objective. The civil rights movement, strengthened by litigation and legislation, culminated in dramatic changes in the education of the handicapped in general. Today disturbed students are entitled to an appropriate education in the least restrictive environment. However, questions related to the functional classification, education, and placement of disturbed students need to be more adequately answered.

2
Theories
of Causality

The term "theories of causality" refers to the scientifically accepted principles that are used to explain the causes of disturbance. The plural form is used because there is no one generally accepted cause of disturbance, but many causes that form a network of explanatory systems. According to Rhodes and Paul (1978), "different perspectives are available to explain the phenomenon of disturbance. . .each perspective has its own knowledge base and represents a sound view of the problem" (p. 11).

Throughout the history of civilization there have been deliberate attempts to explain human conditions that result in unusual or, at least, socially unacceptable behaviors. Before the science era most of these explanations were founded in superstitious and religious beliefs. Beginning in the science era, however, scientific analysis of physical conditions and their effect upon human behavior became the subject of intense investigation. These early science era investigations did not tend to focus on normal behavior, but on physical conditions that resulted in abnormal behavior. This selective focus originated with the medical orientation and its emphasis on physical symptoms such as fever, pain, and other physical conditions. Because of this early medical influence, the cause of a condition or behavior is called its etiology, meaning the science dealing with the causes of disease. Therefore, disturbance was considered a disease, an illness, or a sickness that had a physical basis.

Toward the end of the science era the medical profession moved rapidly into the behavioral-psychological realm of human conditions. Tenets of this medical-scientific process spread into other scientific areas that were more fully emerging in the twentieth century, including psychiatry, psychology, sociology, and ecology. Each of these scientific areas has developed its own distinctive body of knowledge from which the causes of human behavior can be explained or at least theorized.

Emotional disturbance as a human state, condition, or way of behaving has been particularly fertile in generating widely varying explanatory concepts and partial theories over the last half century. Some of these are mere fragments of theory, fragments which are unrelated to any network or system of concepts. Most, however, can be grouped into explanatory systems which are logically related ideas and observations about disturbance. These clusters are not purely arbitrary or artificial. Many of their authors make it clear that their contribution is part of a central school of ideas and concepts. Many not only identify the body of distinctive theory to which they are contributing, but also specify that their school of ideas is distinct from other schools (Rhodes & Tracy, 1972a, pp. 14–15).

Rhodes and Tracy (1972a), in an effort to order and organize the vast body of theoretical knowledge, established rules for sorting individual theories into clusters or models that explained disturbance:

1. Related theories should employ the same basic methodology for any explorations and constructions [e.g., experimental, clinical, or naturalistic].
2. Related theories should share a common orienting outlook in examining and explaining human behavior [e.g., physical, social, or psychic].
3. Related theories should acknowledge a controlling preemptory principle of behavioral genesis [e.g., conditioning, unconscious motivation, or neurological dysfunction].
4. Related theories should agree regarding basic and ameliorating approaches [e.g., behavior modification, psychotherapy, or medication].
5. Each should have a common ambience [philosophical atmosphere] within its cluster group.

These dimensions come together to form a basic model which places a stamp upon any single, isolated theoretical fragment. While it is possible to identify various combinations and permutations of these schools, each has an overriding identity of its own (pp. 15–16).

These rules for clustering individual theories yielded five basic models for explaining disturbance. The theories of causality introduced in Chapter 1 require repeating at this point:

1. Biophysical
2. Behavioral
3. Psychodynamic
4. Sociological, and
5. Ecological.

It is necessary to emphasize the fact that these five models constitute basic or umbrella theories and that many different specific explanations are contained within each model. For example, the biophysical model contains different explanations of disturbance that include clearly different causes such as genetic inheritance, neurological damage, and so forth. Consequently, there is no one biophysical explanation but a number of biophysical explanations that constitute a theoretical model because they share a basic methodology, a common orienting outlook, a controlling principle of behavioral cause, a basic amelioration method, and a common philosophical atmosphere. Similarly, the behavioral, psychodynamic, sociological, and ecological models each contain distinctly different explanations of disturbance. However, the basic premise of each theoretical model is that disturbance can be explained by the model. In short, all biophysical theories maintain that the cause of disturbance has a biophysical basis, all behavioral theories maintain that the cause of disturbance can be explained by principles of learning, and so forth.

On this theoretical level any given behavior may be explained by all five models. Table 1, for example, lists five different causes of aggression that are presumed from the different theories of causality. Actually, any one cause or combination of causes listed in Table 1, plus numerous other causes within the theories, may account for aggression or any other disturbed behaviors. To identify *the* cause, if that is possible, requires that the teacher and students be provided appropriate support services such as medical examinations, psychological evaluations, social worker visitations, and so forth. A complete case history is required if the teacher is to understand the cause of specific disturbed behaviors and plan an appropriate educational experience. For example, if aggression is a function of an allergic reac-

Table 1. Hypothetical causes of aggression based on theoretical models

Theoretical models	Hypothetical causes of aggression
Biophysical	Neural inflammation due to allergic reaction to food additives
Behavioral	Modeled after and/or reinforced by the life-style of the parent(s)
Psychodynamic	Id domination of the personality due to inadequate ego development
Sociological	Function of social rules and expectations, rather than the behavior per se
Ecological	Dysfunctional interaction between the individual organism and the ecosystem (classroom conditions)

tion, then punishment, rewards, rule changes, and so on, will not bring about a reduction in aggression. Only a biophysical intervention in the form of dietary control will be effective. Thus, there is a direct relationship between the causes and characteristics of disturbance on the one hand and the effectiveness of the educational strategies on the other.

In reality, most teachers will not have available the wide variety of support services necessary to investigate thoroughly the cause of disturbance, but appropriate educational strategies can be planned without knowledge of the specific cause. To do this does require, however, that teachers exercise flexibility in considering and implementing educational strategies for disturbed students. Subsequent chapters will be devoted to the implementation of educational strategies in the absence of knowledge regarding the cause of disturbance.

Because there is a strong relationship among the theories of causality, characteristics of disturbance, and educational strategies, a closer examination of the theories of causality is warranted.

BIOPHYSICAL THEORY

The biophysical theory is characterized by the belief that disturbed behaviors are caused by central nervous system dysfunction. Consequently, the biophysical theory represents a disease model, which emphasizes that the problem resides primarily within the physiological structure of the individual, rather than with external environmental conditions. Belief in the biophysical cause of "madness" has persisted since the science era and has included explanations such as blood abnormalities, malnutrition, infection, bacteria (particularly syphilis), and genetic inheritance. For the extremist, disturbed behavior is a consequence of biophysical abnormalities, and normal behavior is a function of normal biophysical conditions. "Most practitioners, however, take a more moderate view; some behaviors and personality characteristics are caused by physical factors, while others are a result of environment and learning" (Morse, Smith, & Acker, 1977, p. 13).

Educators are often skeptical of the biophysical theory even though there are some physiological conditions that clearly result in abnormal behaviors. Some examples include cerebral palsy, in which damage to the central nervous system causes a variety of motor problems; meningitis, which may cause both mental and motor symptoms; and strokes, which may result in a loss of memory, hallucinations, and paralysis. In general, however, this skepticism is justified, because biophysical evidence regarding neurological dysfunction is not typically available for students who are considered to be disturbed. It is clear that students, disturbed or normal, are biophysically different and that these differences have some effect upon personalities, behaviors, and learning patterns. This potential for biophysical causes requires that teachers consider the characteristics of disturbance in terms of a disease orientation that has direct implications for both identification and educational practices.

The biophysical theory is not limited to one explanation but a number of explanations including genetic, biochemical, neurological, and developmental factors. These divisions are somewhat arbitrary, but they do represent logically related concepts that facilitate the discussion of biophysical causes.

Genetic Factors

Research and discussion on the genetic transmission theory of mental illness has been limited to severe forms of disturbance, especially autism and schizophrenia. However, it should be noted that there is no substantive evidence that serious forms of disturbance are inherited. Arguments in favor of the genetic position depend primarily on research that claims a higher incidence of mental illness among children of mentally ill parents when environmental factors have been eliminated (Buss, 1966).

> Although the capacity to become schizophrenic may well be within all of us, there is no question that certain persons have distinctive genes predisposing them to the condition. Individuals taken from schizophrenic parents in infancy and placed with normal adoptive parents subsequently develop schizophrenic symptoms at a much higher rate than those given up for adoption by unafflicted parents. . . .[These] results show conclusively that a major part of the tendency to become schizophrenic is inherited (Wilson, 1979, p. 60).

Wilson's genetic conclusion is one that is shared by some members of the medical and psychological professions as well as a few educators, particularly Bernard Rimland (1969). The fact that a child with the characteristics of severe disturbance has normal siblings does lead to the speculation that genetic rather than environmental factors are involved. Because of the lack of empirical evidence, however, the role of genetic factors in causing disturbance remains controversial.

Biochemical Factors

"Recent developments in neurophysiology suggest that most interactions between nerve cells (i.e., synaptic transmission) are basically chemical in nature. Thus, all activity of the brain and all behavior of organisms is ultimately reducible to the interconnections and synaptic interactions among neurons" (Thompson, 1967, p. 82). This important relationship between biochemical factors and behaviors has been so well documented that it is probable that some behaviors, including disturbance, are caused by biochemical factors.

Teachers are well aware of the fact that the consumption of excessive amounts of foods such as coffee, sugar, and tea can produce negative effects including irritability, restlessness, and aggression. Similarly, inadequate consumption of critical nutrients, minerals, or vitamins can produce physical reactions that may include drowsy, sleepy, or tired reactions. In more critical cases of biochemical dysfunction, phenylketonuria, diabetes, and mental retardation may result. According to Linus Pauling (1968), "mental disease is for the most part caused by abnormal (chemical) reaction rates, as determined by genetic constitution and diet, and by abnormal molecular concentrations of essential substances" (p. 268).

Pauling's reference to diet has critical implications for understanding some school-related behaviors. Malnutrition, for example, is responsible for restricting the growth of nerve cells that have an effect on both intelligence and behavior. It has been documented that below average intellectual functioning may be at least partially attributable to malnutrition, particularly among students from lower socioeconomic environments (Bakan, 1970). Similarly, behaviors such as hyperactivity and lethargy that are often considered by teachers to be symptomatic of disturbance can be the result of malnutrition. It takes little imagination to conclude that students who are undernourished, or who consume inordinate amounts of junk food, or who are victims of drug habits, including alcohol, tobacco, aspirin, and cola, behave in ways that are partially biochemically induced and that are incompatible with the expectations of behavior in school (Fine, 1980).

Biochemical explanations are not limited to diet, but may also include hormone reactions that are exaggerated among some students, particularly adolescents. For example, "during puberty, a boy's tendency to fight gradually increases over several years as the testosterone level in his blood increases" (Moyer, 1973, p. 36). Girls, too, may respond differentially based upon their levels of estrogen and progesterone that are delicately balanced around the premenstrual period and menstrual cycle. For both boys and girls there is extensive evidence to indicate that biochemical changes in the hormonal levels, particularly during times of stress, influence the sensitivity of the neural systems controlling behavior, especially irritable aggression (Moyer, 1973).

Neurological Factors

The central nervous system is an extremely complex and intricate physiological mechanism. This system has been able to withstand tremendous alterations with no visible changes in behavior, yet what seems to be a minor problem may result in significant behavior changes. For example, a child may be involved in an accident and suffer extensive cerebral damage with no visible effects after a short period of time, whereas another child may incur a mild concussion that permanently alters behavior. Most teachers do not have to be reminded of the fact that neurological damage caused by diseases (e.g., meningitis, encephalitis, and sclerosis) or by direct physical trauma (e.g., accidents, fights, and poisoning) can result in extreme behaviors, even death. However, there are some neurological conditions that teachers do need to be aware of since the behavioral effects may be less severe, leading the teacher to conclude that the student is disrespectful, resentful, or hostile rather than to consider the possibility of neurological cause. Some of the more common neurological causes of disturbed behaviors include allergies, fever, and minor head injuries.

Of these three exemplary causes of neurological dysfunction, allergies have been proposed as a major factor in contributing to disturbed behaviors. In fact, Moyer (1975) expressed the belief that aggression and irritability in some cases can be attributed to allergic reactions that cause swelling in the brain:

> When swelling occurs in the areas of the brain that contain the neural connections controlling aggression, the results can be immediate and dramatic. The pressure of the swelling may make neural areas that produce aggression more sensitive, or deactivate areas that normally inhibit aggressive behavior. Behavioral disturbances are only one of many possible allergic reactions, and not all individuals with allergies show a behavioral alteration. Those who do are usually described in terms such as impulsive, combative, unruly, perverse, and quarrelsome. The descriptions are a veritable thesaurus of irritability. The intensity of the symptoms varies from mild reaction, in which the person is a little more annoyed than usual, to a psychotic aggressive reaction (p. 77).

Fever and minor head injuries may also result in neurological damage or irritation. Fever, resulting from a multitude of causes, and minor head injuries, which may result from physical trauma such as fighting, battering by parents, falls, or even bumping into the door, can produce neurological damage. Often this damage is not evident from the relatively minor external symptoms, although extensive internal neurological damage may result. In those cases in which severe symptoms are evident, teachers are usually sensitive to the fact that immediate medical attention is required. However, in many cases the symptoms, including behavior variations, may be so slight that teachers may not consider the possibility of neurological damage. The point here is not to alarm or to make medical diagnosticians of teachers, but to sensitize teachers to the possibilities of neurological damage as opposed to the unquestioning assumption that students are consciously and willfully violating rules of classroom behavior.

Developmental Factors

This discussion of developmental factors is limited "to that part of the brain, the forebrain, in which the destruction of nerve tissue produces disturbances which are specific for brain-injured children" (Strauss & Lehtinen, 1947, p. 18). This reference to developmental factors could be considered neurological, but, since the theory ultimately suggests that in some disturbed students the central nervous system is not adequately *developed,* differentiation of developmental and neurological factors is required.

> Strauss and Lehtinen's interpretation of the behavior of brain-injured children follows from their understanding of the relationship between the new brain and the old brain. . .The old brain contains cell structures which regulate emotions and expressive movements. In the course of neurological development, the new brain becomes an inhibiting influence on the old brain. If the inhibiting effect of the new brain is impaired (or does not develop), the old brain acts unchecked. The excesses of emotional reaction and hyperactivity of the brain-injured child are the result of such an impairment (Sagor, 1972, pp. 71–72).

Stated another way, the Strauss and Lehtinen theory claims that children are born with innate capacities such as reflex action, motor activity, and oral manipulation that are a function of the old brain. During the process of development (learning, maturation, and physical growth) a new brain emerges that serves to regulate the innate function of the old brain. If the new brain does not develop, then behaviors that are a function of the old brain, such as screaming, impulsivity, and hyperactivity, are the result.

Later Strauss and Kephart (1955) elaborated on this theory by including the influence of gestalt theory:

> Thus, the behavior of brain injured children is related to their inability to adequately combine parts into wholes and the concomitant tendency to respond to details rather than wholes. Because of the deficit, a specific stimulus tends to stand out and gains strength through not being integrated with the total stimulus configuration. Consequently, the brain-injured child may respond explosively to a stimulus that is not apparent to the people around him. The lack of structure in his perceptual field increases the relative intensity of extraneous stimulation, reduces the drive of goal-directed activity, and increases distractibility. The child's responses are intense (disinhibited) because he makes fewer non-overt responses than the normal individual; the energy normally released through these responses is stored, increasing the intensity of the overt response (Sagor, 1972, pp. 72–73).

Because of this deficit in stimulus selectivity the behavior of disturbed students is a function of two gestalt processes. On the one hand, the student may concentrate on a specific stimulus, such as a pencil, a button, or a toy, to the total exclusion of other stimuli, including the math lesson or the chalkboard on which the lesson is displayed. On the other hand, virtually all stimuli may take on undifferentiated or equal importance to the student; for example, a street noise may be as significant as the teacher's instructions, or a fluttering leaf may be as visually seducing as the world globe. In any case, the developmental theory states that there is a biophysical dysfunction that can be used to explain the behaviors of students who are considered disturbed.

In summary, the biophysical theory of causality emphasizes the fact that behaviors are, in part, a function of central nervous system dysfunction. Whether the specific cause is genetic, biochemical, neurological, or developmental, the underlying assumption is that some students demonstrate behaviors that are characteristic of disturbance because of biophysical reasons. Although the actual diagnosis of biophysical problems is the responsibility of the medical profession, teachers sensitive to the possibility of biophysical problems play an important role in the observation, referral, and possible treatment of disturbed students. Certainly many treatment procedures require medical supervision, but there is a mounting belief that specific educational strategies are a significant part of the total treatment of biophysically disturbed students.

BEHAVIORAL THEORY

The basic premise of the behavioral theory is that disturbed behaviors are learned. Even though this theory may also be called learning theory, "the occurrence of learning is inferred from the occurrence of a new behavior or from a change in behavior" (Russ, 1972, p. 100). Therefore, the designation of behavioral theory is used to accentuate the behaviors of disturbed students rather than the more popular application of learning theory to the accomplishment of academic or cognitive skills associated with educational objectives. Not that academic skills are unimportant, but that it is social and classroom behaviors of disturbed students that create the greatest concern among many teachers.

The cause of disturbance is not limited to one behavioral theory, but can be explained by many behavioral theories. Any attempt to describe all of the behavioral theories would be an enormous task that is beyond the scope of this book. Therefore, only those basic behavioral theories that have direct relevance to the understanding and cause of disturbance are included. Regardless of the specific theories, there is general agreement that:

> The behaviors a person emits throughout his lifetime are learned through the environment in which he finds himself. We act in a manner which we feel is most appropriate to (will help us get along best in) that environment. From childhood parents, teachers, peers and even strangers provide *cues* and *reinforcement* for responses to the environment. Even the objects of physiological drives such as the types of food we eat, the people we find attractive and so forth, are learned from our associates and society in general (Buckley & Walker, 1970, p. 3).

This learning process accounts for appropriate (normal) behaviors as well as inappropriate (disturbed) behaviors. In the case of disturbed behaviors it can be assumed either a) that students have not learned the appropriate behaviors or b) that the disturbed behaviors conflict with the appropriate behaviors. For example, students who do not raise their hand when wishing to speak in class either a) have not learned first to raise the hand or b) have learned an inappropriate behavior, talking out. The development and maintenance of hand raising and the elimination of talking out behaviors are dependent upon environmental events. "With changes in events, changes in behavior result. An environmental change can occur as an *antecedent* or as a *consequent* event. In either case, the behavior changes, indicating adaptation to environmental conditions" (Russ, 1972, p. 101).

Disagreement over the functional relationship between behaviors and environmental events has led to two distinct groups of behavioral theories. One group of theorists maintains that the most critical element in learning is in the relationship between the stimulus (S) and the behavior, or response (R). This S-R or contiguity (closely connected) theory is based upon the law of association; that is, stimuli and behaviors experienced together tend to become associated (Hilgard & Bower, 1966). Classical and respondent conditioning are also terms that have been used to describe this theoretical position. The second group of theorists maintains that the reinforcement or consequence that immediately follows a response is the critical element in learning. This latter group, known as reinforcement or operant theorists, believes that an organism will select or discover the response that leads to the best reinforcement. Given these two distinct behavioral theories, the cause of disturbance is briefly examined from each position.

Classical Conditioning

The term "classical conditioning" was introduced by the Russian physiologist Ivan Pavlov. This learning-behavioral theory was based upon Pavlov's now famous experiments in which he trained a dog to salivate at the sound of a bell by simultaneously presenting food. In the United States, John B. Watson demonstrated this same principle when he taught a baby to be afraid (i.e., to cry) of a stuffed animal when it was presented simultaneously with a loud noise. In both experiments, previously neutral stimuli (bell and stuffed animal) were paired with eliciting stimuli (food and loud noise) to produce behaviors (salivation and crying). After several trials the previously neutral stimuli produced the behaviors in the absence of the eliciting stimuli. This principle of classical conditioning is summarized by Mahoney (1980):

> If a formerly neutral stimulus is repeatedly paired with a reflective response, the neutral stimulus will acquire the ability to elicit that response by itself (pp. 99–100).

Explaining disturbed behaviors from a classical conditioning perspective depends on an additional concept: generalization. This higher order mental process refers to the probability that a behavior will be caused by a stimulus that is similar to the original S-R relationship. For example, in the case of the baby who was conditioned to be afraid of the stuffed animal, the baby generalized that fear to other stuffed animals and even some real ones because of their similarity to the original stimulus.

The behavioral principles involved in classical conditioning can be used to explain disturbed behaviors. For example, consider the word "bad." "When this word is first presented to an infant, it elicits no consistent reactions. After it has been paired with slaps on the wrists or spankings, however, the word alone becomes capable of eliciting a variety of responses (crying, withdrawal of the hand, etc.)" (Mahoney, 1980, p. 101). Consequently, the word "bad" in this case is a conditioned stimulus that may even be generalized to other stimulus words such as "not nice," "stop that," or even "school." For the student so conditioned, teacher statements can produce a variety of responses including withdrawal, hyperactivity, and aggression.

Modeling disturbed behavior is a special case of "no trial" stimulus control learning that is often associated with classical conditioning theory. According to Bandura (1965), behaviors are learned by observing the behaviors in parents, peers, and other significant models. It is a well known fact that behaviors such as language accents, hand mannerisms, and diet preference are a modeled reflection of the immediate environment of those individuals who possess those behaviors. This behavioral principle has been applied to the learning of disturbed behaviors. Numerous studies have demonstrated that aggression increased among children after they observed aggression, that cursing increased after observing cursing, and so forth. Thus, classical conditioning, including modeling, emphasizes the closeness of significant stimuli to the responses that are generalized to the classroom and other social settings. If these learned responses are considered inappropriate, the students are often labeled disturbed.

Operant Conditioning

"Every stimulus-response. . . formulation of behavior suffers from a serious omission. No account of the interchange between organism and environment is complete until it includes the action of the environment upon the organism *after* a response has been made" (Skinner, 1969, p. 5). Thus, operant conditioning differs from classical conditioning because of the emphasis on reinforcement or the reward or punishment that follows a behavior.

When a response is followed by a pleasant or "satisfying" state of affairs it will be strengthened. When a response is followed by an unpleasant or "annoying" state of affairs, it will be weakened (Mahoney, 1980, p. 104).

Every teacher is at least vaguely aware of this basic premise of operant conditioning. When students have performed well, teachers give them a pat on the back, verbal praise, or a star as a way of encouraging the continuation of appropriate behaviors; when students have performed poorly, teachers physically punish, provide negative feedback, or give demerits as a way of reducing inappropriate behaviors. Of course, teachers are also aware of the fact that they are not the only source of rewards and punishment. Parents, peers, and even the physical environment can provide consequences that are counterproductive to what the teacher intends to accomplish. For example, teacher punishment for acting-out behavior may be ineffective if the classroom peer group is rewarding the behavior. In fact, the teacher's conception of punishment might be interpreted as a reward by the student if the need for attention is stronger than the consequences of punishment. In short, "the organism acts upon the environment to reach a goal" (Travers, 1963, p. 15).

According to the theory of operant conditioning, disturbance is caused by the introduction immediately following behaviors of rewards or punishment that increase the probability that inappropriate (disturbed) behaviors will continue. In the case of either consequence, disturbed students will therefore demonstrate those behaviors that are reinforcing (goal-oriented) for them, even though the behaviors may be considered inappropriate by teachers. For example, attention-getting behaviors may be more strongly reinforced by the laughter and encouragement provided by the peer groups than by the punishment threatened by the teacher.

Operant theory maintains that in the case of the disturbed student disturbed behaviors are being reinforced, or that appropriate behaviors are being punished. Therefore, the consequences provided by the environment are the cause of disturbance.

PSYCHODYNAMIC THEORY

Psychodynamic theory explains the cause of human behavior through an analysis of internal psychological processes. Because of differences among the psychodynamic theorists, several theoretical terms have been used to reflect these differences. For example, psychoanalytic and intrapsychic theories and humanistic psychology are terms that fall within the broader designation of psychodynamic theory. Regardless of the variance among these subtheories, however, a common feature among all of them is that disturbed behaviors are caused by "internal forces [that] are assumed to motivate behavior" (Morse, Smith, & Acker, 1977, p. 12).

Discussion of the internal, psychological processes must include the contribution of Sigmund Freud to psychoanalysis, the forerunner of the more generic psychodynamic theory. Even though Freud's theory was primarily concerned with the negative aspects of human biological instincts, later psychodynamic theorists such as Erik Erikson, Alfred Adler, Carl Rogers, and Abraham Maslow reconceptualized the psychoanalytic theory into a more inclusive psychological theory for explaining the cause of disturbed behavior. Since the psychoanalytic theory represents a conceptually different explanation than the more generic intrapsychic theories, the latter are discussed separately.

Psychoanalytic Theory

Psychoanalysis owes its origin to Sigmund Freud. However, Freud's psychoanalytic theory has been controversial, primarily because it is reputed to be a pessimistic view of human behavior that revolves around sexual instincts (Newcomer, 1980). This criticism is not altogether justified, however, particularly because "the ideas about infantile sexuality are an early development of psychoanalytic theory and a small part of the present body of psychoanalytic concepts" (Kessler, 1966, p. 3).

Understanding human behavior from a psychoanalytic perspective requires that teachers understand three essential concepts. First, human psychological development is characterized by three different periods in the life span of the child: early childhood, the latency period, and puberty. "A special attribute of the child, or his method of reaction, cannot therefore be judged without reference to the specific period of his life" (Freud, 1935, p. 93). Second, human psychological development is attached to the inner growth of the personality. "The psychoanalytic conception shows you the personality of the child as a three-fold nature, consisting of the instinctual life (id), the ego, and the superego" (Freud, 1935, p. 94). The ego and superego develop later in life (between 2 and 5 years of age) and are considered a sign of inner growth. Third, human psychological development is concerned with the interaction and conflict among the id, ego, and superego. In the mature, healthy personality a reality orientation (ego) must control, transform, or sublimate the instinctual desires (id) and the conscience (superego).

The interplay between the three essential elements of psychoanalytic theory forms the basis for understanding the cause of disturbed behavior:

> Freud traces the growth of personality from birth, when the infant's personality involves only an *id*—Freud's summary term for life, sexual, and aggressive instincts that clamor for satisfaction irrespective of the rights, needs, or wishes of anyone else. Soon the child develops to the point where he has a functioning *ego*, an organized and effective basis for operating in the outside world. Then he is potentially a lethal weapon: a seething cauldron of selfish desires (id) that can be put into effective action (ego). At this point he becomes such a burden to his parents and other members of society that his freedom of expression must be curtailed—in short, he must be socialized. Through punishment for unrestricted expression of the id and more positive instruction in what is acceptable, he develops a *superego*, or conscience, which is the internalized version of society's taboos and sanctions.
>
> The child, then, must find his way out of this dilemma: He faces the possibility of guilt and punishment from the superego for nothing more than free expression of his true nature; he cannot change his true nature—his instincts are set by the terms of his biological inheritance. But society and its internalized representative, the superego, are so powerful that the threat first of punishment and later of guilt is too strong to be faced. He must compromise, and the form of that compromise must be either to inhibit his instincts from expression or to somehow change them into a more socially acceptable form. Such inhibition is accomplished by *defenses*, the most powerful of which is called *sublimation*. Attempting to compromise by wholesale inhibition of instincts constitutes psychopathology, not maturity. What is considered mature is to transform or *sublimate* instinctual desires and expressions into socially acceptable, constructive thoughts and actions (*Developmental Psychology Today*, 1971, p. 453).

Sublimation, or the redirection of infantile instincts into activities that are socially approved, has not been successfully accomplished by many disturbed students. Because of faulty experiences in early childhood, disturbed students characteristically employ a variety of unconscious defense mechanisms that ultimately lead to inappropriate behavior.

For example, students whom teachers "designate as quarrelsome, asocial, and never contented with anything, are putting their school companions in the place of their brothers and sisters, and there, at school, are fighting out with them the conflicts which they were not able to finish in their own homes" (Freud, 1935, p. 34).

Within the psychoanalytic theory, then, disturbed behaviors are a result of an imbalance between the impulse system (id) and the control system (ego). When the impulse system dominates the personality, aggressive, impulsive, and/or hyperactive behaviors may result. When the control system is overdeveloped (superego), then the behaviors are apt to be rigid, compulsive, and/or inhibited.

Intrapsychic Theory

Over the past half century Freud's psychoanalytic theory has been expanded, redefined, and criticized by numerous theorists who believe that the intrapsychic phenomenon is essential to explanation of disturbed behavior. "Intrapsychic theorists recognize that pathological behavior represents, in large measure, an adaptive strategy developed by [students] in response to feelings of anxiety and threat. The bizarre and maladaptive behavior they display is not viewed as functionless or random, but as an intricate, albeit self-defeating, maneuver to relieve oneself of anguish, humiliation, and insecurity" (Million, 1967, p. 198). Intrapsychic theory, also called ego psychology or humanistic psychology, places great emphasis on ego functions and environmental conditions. In short, a student's conception of reality and of self is influenced by the interaction between the student and the environment.

Erik Erikson (1968), for example, has identified eight psychosocial stages that must be successfully resolved for the development of a healthy personality. Unsuccessful or negative resolution at any stage consequently results in intrapsychic development and behaviors that are the core cause of disturbance. The first five of Erikson's psychosocial stages occur during childhood and adolescence:

1. Trust versus mistrust. During the first year of life does the infant develop trust through quality care that conveys meaning, goodness, and predictability, or does the infant develop mistrust because of inconsistency, separateness, and general loss of quality care?

2. Autonomy versus shame and doubt. During the second year does the child develop a sense of an autonomous self through muscular experimentation (e.g., climbing, holding, and exploring), or does the child develop a sense of shame and doubt because he or she is deprived of the opportunity to learn and expects defeat in the struggle with adults?

3. Initiative versus guilt. During the preschool years does the child develop initiative through free activity, insatiable curiosity, and consuming fantasies, or does the child feel guilty (essentially bad) because of the moral values adults place on the efforts to develop initiative?
4. Industry versus inferiority. During the elementary school years does the child achieve recognition, or does the child feel inadequate or inferior because he or she does not receive recognition?
5. Identity versus diffusion. During adolescence does the individual have a strong and positive sense of self, or does the individual perceive self negatively and as a pawn to the pressures of others?

Within the context of Erikson's psychosocial stages, disturbance is caused by the student's failure to resolve successfully each of the five critical life crises. Even though Erikson's theory is not concerned with behaviors per se, negative intrapsychic conditions undoubtedly lead to behaviors that are not valued in society or in school. Regardless of the specific behaviors that result, the critical implication is that the cause is related to intrapsychic conditions that are shaped by environmental interactions occurring during developmental periods.

Discussion of the intrapsychic theory leads to one additional conclusion, namely, that during the process of personality development a concept of self emerges. Further, one of the primary functions of the human organism is to maintain consistency with one's concept of self. If a student considers himself or herself agile, attractive, or smart, the student will engage in behaviors designed to protect and maintain those self-images. Similarly, if a student feels clumsy, ugly, or dumb, behaviors will be evidenced that perpetuate those negative concepts. Efforts to maintain consistency are repeatedly evidenced by behaviors that are designed to counter any threat to one's self-concept, even though such behaviors may seem to be counterproductive. Teachers who convey self-inconsistent messages such as "big boys (or ladies) don't act like that" can expect students to react in order to defend their self-concepts. They may choose to return the verbal abuse, become defiant, get into a fight—anything to recover the damage inflicted upon the self-concept (Rich, 1978a). These exemplary behaviors typically are designated as symptoms of disturbance. The cause of the behaviors is related to the inconsistency between the student's intrapsychic concept of self and environmental factors.

Both the psychoanalytic and the intrapsychic theories provide a comprehensive psychodynamic theory for explaining the cause of disturbance. The emphasis within this theoretical position is that psychological development, whether biologically or environmentally induced, or both, is the primary basis for understanding normal as well as disturbed behavior. Disturbance, then, is considered a symptom of psychological problems that originate during critical developmental stages.

SOCIOLOGICAL THEORY

The sociological theory explains disturbance as a form of deviance, or the breaking of social norms. Norms or rules are standards of behavior that are socially defined and require that members conform. Disturbance, then, is the failure to conform. To understand the cause of disturbance from this deviancy perspective, the answers to two central questions are necessary: 1) what social factors exist that cause conformity or deviance? and 2) what is the relationship between the deviant and the norm enforcers? (Des Jarlais, 1972).

No one sociological theory can be used to answer the two questions adequately. As with the previously discussed theories, sociological theory is an umbrella term that encompasses several theories. The theories that seem particularly relevant to the understanding of disturbance in school include anomie, social disorganization, cultural transmission, functionalism, and labeling theories. Even though these theories represent substantial differences in terms of explaining disturbance, their common denominator is the belief that deviance is a form of rule breaking or rule enforcement.

Before separately discussing these sociological theories of disturbance, the relationship between the institution called "school" and general sociological theory needs some explanation. Many sociologists believe that a primary function of institutions, such as school, church, and family, is to teach, enforce, and espouse social values. Until recently schools seemed to have achieved this objective. During the past few decades, however, schools have enrolled a wider variety of students who represent a culturally pluralistic society. The broad range of student characteristics, attitudes, and acculturation add up to marked differences in socialization—the process by which a student becomes integrated into society by learning and conforming to norms. Today most teachers are aware of the gross differences in socialization evident in classes composed of students who represent different races, socioeconomic status, national origins, and even handicapping conditions. Attempting to socialize such a diverse group by a single set of social norms consequently creates the conditions for deviance.

Given the schools' socialization objective and the pluralistic nature of the student population, the five sociological theories may be used to explain the cause of disturbance. Morse and Smith (1980) have succinctly described these sociological theories particularly as they relate to schools and the society in which they function:[1]

Theory of Anomie

According to Durkheim (1964), social norms serve to define and limit human needs. In some parts of modern society, however, a state of "normlessness" exists, since social change is occurring at a rate greater than that which would allow for the adequate replacement of old norms with new norms. Thus, individual needs are allowed to expand to a point beyond which they can be fulfilled within society, and a state of frustration results. The consequence is social deviance, often demonstrated in the forms of crime and mental illness. The theory offers an explanation for high rates of mental illness in a society, but does not seek to explain individual cases of mental illness or deviant behavior which may occur within a "normal" society with well-defined group norms.

The conditions leading to anomie also hamper the school's ability to socialize children. When there is a rapid social change, cultural norms may have become obsolete in everyday interactions by the time they are institutionalized (e.g., dress codes in schools). Difficult problems arise if, for whatever reason, the rules governing social interaction in society do not coincide with those taught in the schools. . . .

Social Disorganization Theory

When social interaction patterns in a community break down, the psychological needs of community members can no longer be met. Under these circumstances, social disorganization is said to occur, and the traditional institutions (such as the family and church) experience severe stress. This often occurs when immigrant groups enter a culture which differs greatly from their own. This was the situation in the late nineteenth and twentieth centuries where different national groups settled in the United States. As children of those immigrants adopted the values of mainstream American society, they were alienated from their parents and their traditional values. A breakdown of family structure occurred.

Social disorganization theorists suggest that such a breakdown leads to increased rates of deviant behavior in the community. Researchers have found that when a subgroup leaves an area of the community, the social disorganization pattern remains the same in that area, affecting the new occupants rather than remaining with the original subgroup. Thus, the rate of deviance in the area remains the same, even though a different group of people is occupying the area. This is known as the "replacement" phenomenon.

The school plays a central role in intensifying the social disorganization resulting from the entrance of a minority group into a community. The school represents and perpetuates mainstream cultural values, thus

[1] From *Understanding Child Variance*, by William C. Morse and Judith M. Smith, developed under Grant No. G007602984 from the Bureau of Education for the Handicapped, U.S. Office of Education, Department of Health, Education and Welfare. Copyright 1980 by Linc Services, Inc. Published and distributed exclusively by The Council for Exceptional Children. Reprinted with permission.

reinforcing the social conditions which have led to the breakdown of family structure and the resultant increase in crime and other forms of deviance. Children who are confronted with conflicting norms may be forced to choose between home and school. High dropout rates are often the result. In other cases the school may become involved in a struggle with influential groups who, for example, wish to prevent the use of certain text books, or the introduction of certain topics into the curriculum. . . .

Cultural Transmission Theory

In any society, there exist models of both "normal" and "deviant" behavior, which are characteristic of subgroups within the society. An individual learns the model of behavior which is typical of the group with which he/she is affiliated. According to this theory, individuals are not innately normal or deviant, but they learn to behave in ways defined as such by the society. Mental illness does not exist as individual pathology, but only as social pathology. The subgroups which perpetuate deviant behavior vary in size, and need not be any larger than the nuclear family.

As a miniature society, a school contains both deviant and nondeviant groups. Deviant students frequently affiliate with deviant subgroups both in school and outside the school setting. These students have adopted norms different from those of the mainstream culture, and are inevitably in conflict with teachers and administrators, who represent and enforce the school rules. . . .

Functionalism

Society is in a state of dynamic equilibrium between forces which maintain it and forces which disrupt it. Functional forces serve to satisfy human needs within the system. Dysfunctional, or pathological, forces disrupt the social system. Social strain is created by the conflict of these forces, and the result is the breaking of social rules (deviance).

Merton (1957) suggests that anomie exists when the goals approved by society are not in alignment with the means provided by social institutions. An individual may accept society's goals and means (conformity), but deviant behavior results if he rejects one or both. If cultural goals are accepted, but institutional means rejected, "innovation" occurs. In school, one innovator is the student who performs criminal acts such as stealing from lockers, smoking or drinking in forbidden places, etc. Like his counterpart in adult society, the school criminal is excluded from school activities, usually by expulsion or suspension. The "retreatist" rejects both goals and means. He or she is treated as "sick," or simply rejected and isolated from mainstream activities. In school this individual is often placed in special education classes, or may be forced to attend a special school (for the retarded or mentally ill). The "rebel" rejects means and goals and attempts to replace them with new ones. Revolutionary tactics are utilized by the rebel whose struggle involves direct confrontation with the representatives of the established social order. He or she is treated in school as a danger to the social order, and is frequently expelled for his activities. The "ritualist" accepts and exaggerates the means of society, but rejects its goals. Such individuals are not seen as deviant since they behave in accordance with the rules, but are often described as "unmotivated" and "not performing to potential". . . .

Labeling Theory

Deviants and nondeviants are psychologically alike in that both behave in accordance with the expectations of others. In fact, the actual behavior of deviants and nondeviants is very similar: both groups break some social rules and conform to others. The difference is in society's perception of their behaviors.

Thus, deviant behavior is seen as a consequence, rather than as a cause, of being labeled deviant. The source of the pathology is considered to be in the enforcers of social rules, rather than in those who are labeled as deviants. Once an individual is labeled "deviant," it is very difficult, if not impossible, to be relabeled "normal."

Labeling theory is particularly applicable to schools, since they have a long tradition of segregating students by testing, tracking and labeling. Labels are applied to indicate a student's expected or actual level of achievement, and entrance to a particular "track" in school is based on this label. Some labels indicate aberrations in behavior patterns: emotionally disturbed, delinquent, school phobic, truant, etc. Other labels describe differences in learning style: learning disabled, dyslexic, retarded, etc. Some labels are based on expectations only, and are given even before deviant behavior has been directly observed. This is especially likely if the child is from a family with a history of emotional or mental disorders, if the child is raised in a culturally different ("deprived") environment, or if the child speaks a different language or is of a different racial origin.

Students who are given various labels generally fulfill the expectations of the labelers. Thus, a mentally retarded child acts retarded, at least in part, because she or he is expected to act in that way (pp. 46–47).

Sociological theory considers disturbance to be a form of deviance, or nonconformity to social norms or rules. The cause of deviance can be explained from the five different sociological perspectives described by Morse and Smith. However, the different perspectives are similar in that they emphasize the role of social enforcers, such as teachers, and the difficulties in socializing students in a pluralistic society. Even though social norms are rapidly changing and often loosely enforced, schools have developed norms that are more permanent and strictly enforced. Proponents of the sociological theory maintain that the discrepancy between the pluralistic nature of students' life-styles and the standards of behavior in schools has frequently led to the labeling of students as disturbed.

ECOLOGICAL THEORY

Ecology is the study of the interrelationship of organisms and their environments. This scientific approach to the understanding of organisms was originally concerned with plants, but was later extended to include human ecology. Thus human ecology has only recently been used as an explanatory method of understanding the cause of disturbance. Within ecological theory the term "ecosystem" is used to describe the interaction between an individual organism and that organism's physical environment. Thus an ecosystem for a student may include a large geographic area, or the community, or even a classroom. Regardless of the physical limits, an ecosystem is an extensive and complex set of conditions that include "the child and the settings and the individuals within these settings that are a part of the child's daily life" (Hobbs, 1975, p. 114). Ecological theory, then, is an inclusive theory that suggests that students are not disturbed, but that it is the relationship between the individual student and the ecosystem that is disturbed (Curran & Algozzine, 1980).

> From the point of view of the ecological perspective there is no denial that some members of a collective unit may find it difficult to follow prescribed social pathways in daily living. There is no denial that some individuals experience psychic pain. There is no denial that some have physical abnormalities. However, the social, physical, and psychic process by which these factors become a disability is a collective process. It is a holistic phenomena [sic] in which the factors mentioned above are transformed into deviance (Rhodes & Paul, 1978, p. 191).

Rhodes and Paul are saying that the ecological theory of disturbance not only incorporates the explanations provided by the biophysical, behavioral, psychodynamic, and sociological theories, but goes beyond them to include the interface with other physical ecosystem elements. Obviously, this does not identify the specific cause of disturbance beyond declaring that it is a function of the ecosystem. This lack of specificity has caused some professionals to question the effectiveness of the ecological theory to provide a framework for understanding the cause of disturbance. According to Swap (1978), an "ecological network" should be organized "to explicate and integrate the ecological model of emotional disturbance in children" (p. 187). This network should include at least three systems or levels:

1. Behavior setting (e.g., classroom or home). A physical milieu, a program of activities, inhabitants, and a location in time and space.
2. Patterns of behavior across settings (e.g., classroom *and* home). The power of different behavior settings to elicit different behaviors and different interactions from the same student tends to undermine the assumption that a student *is* disturbed.
3. The community and culture. These influence the design and meaning of simple behavior settings and the relationships among them. (Swap, 1978, p. 187)

Although ecologists do not necessarily agree on the specific cause of disturbance, Swap's ecological network does provide a framework for analyzing disturbance. From a teacher's perspective this seems to be particularly important because the behavior setting and the cultural influence, in particular, may be causing disturbance. However, since different students interact with different ecosystems with different results, this discussion can only use examples that infer global, rather than specific, causes of disturbance.

The Behavior Setting

The physical classroom characteristics have been an overlooked dimension of behavior even though ". . .physical settings have their own properties which place constraints on some behavior and facilitate, if not require, others" (Proshansky, 1974, p. 553). Teachers are generally aware that classroom characteristics such as room size, crowded conditions, temperature, and general decor are related to behavior. However, many subtle characteristics such as work space, seating arrangements, and traffic patterns often go unnoticed. When the inhabitants are added to the setting, including "bullies," teachers and their different styles, and the principal and his influence, the complexity of the setting increases, and so does the probability that there will be a misfit between students and their ecosystem. Just as a natural disaster or the lack of food creates disturbance among entire populations, characteristics of the behavior setting can be a cause of disturbance.

Patterns of Behavior Settings

Changes in behavior settings typically result in significant changes in students' behaviors. These behavioral differences suggest that behaviors are, in part, a function of the students' ecosystem interaction rather than within the students alone. For example, Thomas and Chess (1977) found extreme variations of behavior between home and school settings."These varied patterns were functions not only of expectations, standards and values of parents and teachers in relation to the children's temperaments and capabilities, but also of the adaptability of the children to inconsistent adult demands . . ." (Swap, 1978, pp. 191–192). The fact that disturbed behaviors are demonstrated in one setting and not in another suggests that disturbance is not global, but limited to specific ecosystems.

The Community and Cultural Influence

Within all communities and cultures, certain standards of behavior are established to regulate deviance. Further, formal institutions (e.g., the legal system, the mental health system, and schools) have been organized to identify, control, and treat individuals, including students, who are deviant. "Specifically, these institutions, created and maintained to help society ward off and isolate its deviant members, project an image of the *ideal type* or the single standard of normal to which we all should adhere and lead us to denigrate, fear and distance ourselves from those who do not fit this pattern" (Swap, 1978, p. 193). Obviously, teachers as members of the society are greatly influenced by these expectations for behaviors. This influence is reflected in their willingness to consider certain types of behavior disturbed.

Some traditional American views, we conclude, severely hamper our national efforts to help children and parents. They obscure the "ecology of childhood"—the overall social and economic system that exerts a crucial influence on what happens to parents and children. Until policy makers and planners shift their focus to the broad ecological pressures on children and their parents, our public policies will be unable to do much more than help individuals repair damage that the environment is constantly reinflicting (Kenniston, 1977, p. xiii).

The ecological theory explains the cause of disturbance as a misfit between the individual student and the environment (ecosystem). The student has individual characteristics that interact with the setting and community and culture influence in such a way that deviance results. Institutionalized expectations and, consequently, sanctions regarding deviance become the means of identifying disturbance. The cause, then, is a function of both the student and the student's ecosystem.

SUMMARY

This chapter briefly discussed five theories of causality that are used to explain the causes of disturbance. These theories included biophysical, behavioral, psychodynamic, sociological, and ecological explanations of disturbance.

The biophysical theory supports the position that disturbance is a function of organic damage to the central nervous system. This damage may occur as a result of genetic, biochemical, neurological, or developmental factors. Regardless of the specific biophysical cause, disturbance is considered a disease that results in abnormal behaviors.

The central theme of the behavioral theory is that disturbed behaviors are learned. Whether by classical or operant conditioning, including modeling, students' behaviors are a function of environmental events. Consequently, disturbed behaviors are conditioned, reinforced, or modeled by the stimuli, consequences, or models in their environment.

The psychodynamic theory maintains that disturbance is a function of internal psychological processes. Whereas psychoanalytic theory emphasizes the role of biological impulses and the development of ego functions, the more generic intrapsychic theory recognizes that disturbance is an adaptive strategy related to negative feelings and emotions.

The sociological theory considers disturbance to be a form of deviance, or the violation of social norms for behavior. Disturbance, then, is the demonstration of behaviors that are the result of inadequate or inappropriate socialization. Consequently, students that are considered disturbed have been defined and identified by the social rule enforcers, including teachers.

The ecological theory does not consider students as disturbed, but rather the interaction between the students and their environments (ecosystems). On a practical level, disturbance is a function of the behavioral settings that interact with student characteristics and community and cultural influences that establish standards of behavior. Disturbance, then, is caused by a misfit between students and their environments.

These five theories of causality represent a brief overview of generally accepted theories. Consequently, they must be viewed as incomplete, oversimplified, and, in some cases, inexact. Regardless of these limitations, a basic understanding of the various theories is necessary for teachers of disturbed students. Not only do the theories explain the causes of disturbance, but in many cases they individually specify the characteristics of disturbance, the assessment procedures to be utilized, and even the educational strategies to be implemented. Thus, the theories permeate virtually every aspect of the education of disturbed students.

Section II
CHARACTERISTICS

3
Defining Disturbance

There is no one standard measure, classification system, or syndrome of characteristics that is generally accepted as *the* criterion for defining disturbance. The mass of data and innumerable professional debates regarding definitions lead to the conclusion that there are no behaviors or psychological conditions that are inherently signs or symptoms of disturbance. "The normality of any act or pattern is *relative* to many other factors—it does not depend solely on the act itself" (Mahoney, 1980, p. 8). In the final analysis, disturbance is idiosyncratic, that is, peculiar to the individual—peculiar to the student labeled disturbed as well as to the person or persons making the decision about the student. For example, behaviors that for one teacher represent disturbance may be viewed as normal by another teacher, behavior intended by a student to reflect independence may be considered an act of defiance by the principal, and behaviors that are diagnosed as neurotic by a psychiatrist may be pronounced delinquent by a judge. The only generalization that can be made regarding this endless procession of different idiosyncratic perceptions is that disturbance is not a function of behavior itself, but of the value judgment people place upon the behavior (Chorover, 1973).

To emphasize the relative, idiosyncratic nature of disturbance, consider the following anecdote:

> All through childhood K was extremely meditative, usually preferring to be alone. He often had mysterious dreams and "fits" during which he sometimes fainted. In late puberty, K experienced elaborate auditory and visual hallucinations, uttered incoherent words, and had recurrent spells of sudden coma. He was found frequently running wildly through the countryside and eating the bark off trees. K was also known to throw himself into fire and water. On many occasions he wounded himself with

49

knives or other weapons. K believed he could talk to spirits and chase ghosts. He was certain of his power over all sorts of supernatural forces. Question: Is K disturbed?

If K demonstrated these behaviors in the classroom, in all probability referral, diagnosis, and special placement would have been imminent. Similarly, if the behaviors had occurred in most American communities, some official action would undoubtedly have been taken. K, however, was a member of a northern Siberian tribe of fishermen and reindeer herders, and his behaviors were considered prerequisites to his chosen vocation, that of tribal medicine man. Therefore, K was considered an important member of his society and was not considered disturbed.

Since unfamiliar social-cultural values are critical in determining disturbance in the case of K, consider two examples of twentieth-century western civilization:

> Al, in his senior year of secondary school, obtained a certificate from his physician stating that a nervous breakdown made it necessary for him to leave school for 6 months. Al was not a good all-round student; his teachers found him a problem and he had a history of poor school adjustment, including failing mathematics in one grade of elementary school. Al talked late and had no friends. Al had odd mannerisms, made up his own religion, and chanted hymns to himself. His father was ashamed of his son's lack of athletic ability and regarded him as "different."
>
> Tom, age six, had a large head at birth that was thought to have been caused by "brain fever." Three of his siblings had died before his birth. Tom's mother did not agree with the relatives and neighbors that Tom was probably abnormal. Tom was sent to school and was diagnosed as mentally ill by the teacher. Tom's mother became angry and withdrew Tom from school, saying she would teach Tom herself. Tom was obsessed with and devoted extended periods of time to manipulating inanimate objects.

These two abbreviated case examples are biased selections from the life histories of Albert Einstein and Thomas Alva Edison (Goertzel & Goertzel, 1962). "These cases speak to (1) the danger of making snap decisions on the basis of superficial and incomplete evidence, and (2) the difficulties in defining mental health [or disturbance]. Being different does not necessarily mean that one is in poor mental health [or disturbed]" (Clarizio & McCoy, 1976, p. 18). Even though at least one teacher in each case may have considered Einstein and Edison disturbed, the overwhelming evidence indicates that both were gifted, creative individuals, who had difficulty conforming to the requirements of school settings.

Defining disturbance within school settings has been closely related to the perceptions and value judgments of teachers. Even though

Table 1. Examples of teachers' judgments of normal and mildly disturbed student behaviors

Behavior	Normal	Disturbed
Laughing	After hearing a joke	After a teacher direction
Fighting	To protect one's self	To get into line first
Eating	In the cafeteria	In the classroom
Talking	In a discussion group	While the teacher is talking
Silence	While the teacher is talking	In a discussion group
Activity	During playground recess	During seatwork activity
Anger	When lunch box is stolen	When accused of stealing
Defiance	When controlled by a peer	When controlled by the teacher
Reading	An assigned lesson	A comic book

teachers may differ greatly in the judgments and values they place on specific student behaviors, the circumstances under which the behaviors occur clearly contribute to the labeling process. Table 1 lists some typical student behaviors that teachers generally consider both normal *and* mildly disturbed.

Teacher judgments and values regarding normal and disturbed behaviors are a function of expectations at a particular time and in a particular place, and which are consistent with a particular goal. In this context compliance with teachers' expectations is presumed to be normal, whereas noncompliance is an indication of disturbance.

The preceding examples of behaviors have been included to accentuate the difficulty in defining disturbance. Definitions of disturbance do exist; however, their usefulness is dependent upon understanding a number of significant factors that have to do with construction, implications, and actual use. The remainder of this chapter will be devoted to these definitions, including a discussion of the significant issues involved in defining disturbance.

DEFINITIONS

Over the past 20 years numerous definitions have been constructed by educators, psychologists, and other mental health professionals in an effort to facilitate the description, identification, and diagnosis of disturbance among students. As a precaution it should be noted that in most instances, if not all, these definitions of disturbance have such severe limitations that many professionals believe them to be inadequate, irrelevant, and even undesirable (Phillips, Draguns, & Bartlett, 1975). This controversy and criticism primarily stems from the fact that the definitions constructed to date are little more than convenience definitions that enable program personnel to categorize and place students who do not fit into the social-educational system. On the other hand, most definitions were undoubtedly constructed with the well-meaning intent to describe disturbance functionally and operationally. Without a definitional vehicle to initially conceptualize and, consequently, identify students with special needs, many disturbed students would have been denied appropriate services in the current educational and mental health systems.

Types of Definitions

In the area of human behavior, definitions are constructed for a wide variety of reasons. For example, some definitions are limited to categorizing, whereas others may focus on causes, and others on behavior. Because of these narrow perspectives there is no such thing as an inclusive, all-purpose definition of disturbance. Cullinan and Epstein (1979) analyzed existing definitions and concluded that there were three basic types: *research, authoritative,* and *administrative.* Wood (1979) added to this list by hypothesizing the components of an *operational* definition of disturbance.

Research Definitions   Research definitions are constructed primarily for the purpose of replication or duplication. Consequently, these definitions are not concerned with disturbance per se, but with providing descriptors of behaviors that can be reliably (consistently) measured. For example, a research definition may state that a disturbed student is "a male pupil in an intermediate elementary grade who physically strikes classroom peers with his fist at least once per school day." With adequate observational procedures another researcher could use this definition and replicate the study at a future date. However, this can *not* be interpreted to mean that disturbed students are males in intermediate elementary school who hit other students. Nor can any research definition be used as an educational definition of disturbance. Research definitions are critical for conducting research, but they are of limited value and often misleading as a tool for defining disturbance.

Authoritative Definitions   "This kind of position statement can be intended to structure an exposition of behavior disorders from some point of view (e.g., that of the author of a textbook or journal article); it may be meant to be controversial, provoking consideration and thoughtful rebuttal of the author's position; or (it) may simply indicate the author's view of behavior disorders as it has been shaped by his professional training and experience and personal philosophy" (Cullinan & Epstein, 1979, p. 18). Since authoritative definitions represent a wide range of personal beliefs, they tend to focus on specific aspects of disturbance that are frequently founded in the theories of causality.

For example, Rimland (1969), a proponent of the biophysical theory, defined disturbance as a "biogenic mental disorder" (p. 706); Alan Ross (1980), a behaviorist, included "behavior that deviates from a . . . social norm" (p. 14); and Jane Kessler (1966), an advocate of psychodynamic theory, considered disturbance to be an "internalized conflict" (p. 227). Authoritative definitions are similar to research definitions in that they often have a limited scope, reflecting a particular bias regarding disturbance.

Administrative Definitions   Administrative definitions, as opposed to research and authoritative definitions, do not emphasize the characteristics of disturbed students as much as they consider the degree of severity in combination with placement options or service categories. These definitions typically include references to placement options such as "assignment to the regular class," "educated with supplemental services," and "requires special placement." These service options, in turn, may be determined by the degree of severity (e.g., mild, severe, chronic, and pervasive) stated in the definition. This definitional format has been widely adopted by state education agencies that are accountable for legal compliance, expenditure allocations, and general record keeping. Although administrative definitions provide relatively little information regarding disturbance, they do have the advantage of identifying services rather than labeling students.

Operational Definitions   Even though the advocates of most definitions of disturbance claim that they are operational (i.e., practical, programmatic, and effective) they fall short of the desired goal. According to Wood (1979) an operational definition contains the following six elements:

1. The "disturber" element: What or who is perceived to be the focus of the problem? [e.g., parents, students, teachers, etc.?]
2. The "problem behavior" element: How is the problem behavior described? [e.g., disruptive, depressed, aggressive, etc.?]
3. The "setting" element: In what setting does the problem behavior occur? [e.g., classroom, home, community, etc.?]
4. The "disturbed" element: Who regards the behavior as a problem? [e.g., peers, teacher, parents, etc.?]

And the questions that relate to the use that can be made of the definition:

5. The "operationalizing" element: Through what operations and by whom is the definition used to differentiate disturbers from nondisturbers or to assess the needs of disturbers?
6. The "utility" element: Does the definition when operationalized provide the basis for planning activities that will benefit those labeled, such as needs assessment, individual assessment, program evaluation, etc.? (pp. 7–8).

These operational and utility elements go beyond the criteria for defining disturbance (elements 1 through 4) and include provisions (elements 5 and 6) that are "useful to guide whatever action is to be implemented" (Wood, 1979, p. 10). None of the currently available definitions of disturbance contains all of the elements of Wood's operational definition. The absence of operational definitions suggests that there is a need both to refine definition concepts of disturbance and to specify program implementation.

Current Definitions

This section discusses four nationally recognized and exemplary definitions of disturbance. All of the definitions are basically of the authoritative type; research and administrative definitions are not included because they are so restrictive or regionally oriented that none has achieved broad based acceptance.

Seriously Emotionally Disturbed

Seriously emotionally disturbed means a condition exhibiting one or more of the following characteristics over a long period of time and to a marked degree, which adversely affects educational performance:
1. an inability to learn which cannot be explained by intellectual, sensory, or health factors;
2. an inability to build or maintain satisfactory interpersonal relationships with peers and teachers;
3. inappropriate types of behavior or feelings under normal circumstances;
4. a general pervasive mood of unhappiness or depression; or
5. a tendency to develop physical symptoms or fears associated with personal or school problems.
The term [seriously emotionally disturbed] includes children who are schizophrenic or autistic. The term does *not* include children who are socially maladjusted but not emotionally disturbed (PL 94-142).

The PL 94-142 definition has a number of advantages and disadvantages in terms of facilitating the identification of disturbed students. On the positive side, the definition is eclectic; that is, the five conditions represent a mixture of several theoretical positions. For example, references to "feelings," "mood," and "depression" are of a psychodynamic origin; the phrases "inability to learn" and "inappropriate types of behavior" are associated with behavior theory; and "interpersonal relationships" suggests a sociological influence. Eli Bower (1969), who originally proposed this definition, obviously intended to avoid a single theoretical orientation. Since disturbed students may be identified on the basis of one or more of the conditions, the eclectic quality of the definition has made it more appealing, if not more palatable, to a wider variety of professionals with different theoretical orientations.

On the negative side, the definition makes no provision for measuring the five conditions. Therefore, operationalizing the definition is left to the subjective judgment of a multitude of teachers, psychologists, and other professionals throughout the country. The same subjective inference is also necessary to determine the existence and relevance of the opening qualifiers: "over a long period of time" and "to a marked degree." It must be assumed that the time should be of sufficient length to rule out temporary conditions, whereas the degree should be extreme in terms of frequency, intensity, and duration. Again, both qualifiers are without guidelines, leaving their interpretation a matter of subjective inference.

Because PL 94-142 has been, and probably will continue to be, a significant yardstick by which disturbance is determined, the five conditions are considered in greater depth. Bower (1969), in proposing the definition, believed that "whatever methods are employed in identifying [disturbed students], they would have to be initiated by the teacher" (p. 45). Toward this end, Bower elaborated on the five conditions:

1. An inability to learn which cannot be explained by intellectual, sensory, or health factors. An inability to learn is perhaps the single most significant characteristic of emotionally handicapped children in school. Such nonlearning may be manifested as an inability to master skill subjects. The nonlearner seldom escapes recognition. Achievement tests often confirm what the teacher has long suspected. If all other major causative factors have been ruled out, emotional conflicts or resistances can be ruled in.
2. An inability to build or maintain satisfactory interpersonal relationships with peers and teachers. It isn't getting along with others that is significant here. Satisfactory interpersonal relations refers to the ability to demonstrate sympathy and warmth toward others, the ability to stand alone when necessary, the ability to have close friends, the ability to be aggressively constructive, and the ability to enjoy working and playing with others as well as enjoying working and playing by oneself. In most instances, children who are unable to build or maintain satisfactory interpersonal relationships are most visible to their peers. Teachers are also able to identify many such children after a period of observation.
3. Inappropriate types of behavior or feelings under normal conditions. Inappropriateness of behavior or feeling can often be sensed by the teacher and peer groups. "He acts funny," another child may say. The teacher may find some children reacting disproportionately to a simple command such as "Please take your seat." What is appropriate or inappropriate is best judged by the teacher using her professional training, her daily and long-term observation of the child, and her experience working and interacting with the appropriate behavior of large numbers of normal children.
4. A general, pervasive mood of unhappiness or depression. Children who are unhappy most of the time may demonstrate such feelings in

expressive play, art work, written composition, or in discussion periods. They seldom smile and usually lack a *joie de vivre* in their schoolwork or social relationships. In the middle or upper grades a self-inventory is usually helpful in confirming suspicions about such feelings.

5. A tendency to develop physical symptoms, pains, or fears associated with personal or school problems. This tendency is often noted by the school nurse and parent. Illness may be continually associated with school pressures or develop when a child's confidence in himself is under stress. In some cases, such illnesses or fears may not be apparent to the teacher; peers, however, are often aware of children who are sick before or after tests or have headaches before recitations. Speech difficulties which may be the symptoms of emotional distress are usually most visible to the teacher and parent.

The significant characteristics of children indicating a need for closer scrutiny by a teacher are inability to learn, unsatisfactory interpersonal relationships, inappropriate behavior, unhappiness, and repetitive illness (Bower, 1969, pp. 22–23. Reprinted courtesy of Charles C Thomas, Publisher, Springfield, Ill.).

The three definitions listed in the remainder of this section are selected examples that represent basically different theoretical approaches to disturbance. Therefore, these definitions are presented as illustrative without any connotation of preference of efficiency compared with other definitions.

Behavior Disorders

Children with behavior disorders are those who chronically and markedly respond to their environment in socially unacceptable and/or personally unsatisfying ways but who can be taught more socially acceptable and personally gratifying behavior. Children with mild and moderate behavior disorders can be taught effectively with their normal peers (if their teachers receive appropriate consultative help) or in special resource or self-contained classes with reasonable hope of quick reintegration with their normal peers. Children with severe and profound behavior disorders require intensive and prolonged intervention and must be taught at home or in special classes, special schools, or residential institutions (Kauffman, 1977, p. 23).

This definition is consistent with the behavioral theory but with sociological overtones. The emphasis on social expectations of behavior is evident in the identification of disturbance. However, the definition provides no guidelines for determining these expectations, apparently leaving the decision in the hands of the teacher and/or support personnel. Kauffman's definition does contain elements of an administrative definition by equating the degree of severity with appropriate placement options. Finally, "it is an optimistic definition, implying that children are not hopelessly disordered in their behavior and that they can learn to behave appropriately" (Kauffman, 1977, p. 24).

Emotional Disturbance

Emotional disturbance is a state of being marked by aberrations in an individual's feelings about him- or herself and the environment. The existence of emotional disturbance is inferred from behavior. Generally, if a person acts in a manner that is detrimental to him- or herself and/or others, he or she may be considered in a state of emotional disturbance (Newcomer, 1980, pp. 6–7).

This definition is of a psychodynamic origin, because the critical factor in determining disturbance is based upon the individual's internal feelings. As with the previous definitions, no guidelines are provided for implementing this definition. Therefore, it is implied that inferences may be made by the teacher, but that the actual decision must be made on behaviors that reflect negative psychological conditions. This definition, as opposed to the two previous ones, places more responsibility for determining disturbance on the student, rather than upon the teacher's judgment.

Behavioral Problem Children

The child who cannot or will not adjust to socially acceptable norms for behavior and consequently disrupts his own academic progress, the learning efforts of his classmates, and interpersonal relations (Woody, 1969, p. 7).

This definition is primarily sociological, because "norms" play a significant role in defining disturbance. Of the four definitions presented, this one would be the least difficult to put into operation, because the identification of behavior problems would be dependent on teachers' expectations and rules. This relative ease in defining disturbance is misleading because the absence of specific expectations and rules means there would be great variance from teacher to teacher, depending on individual levels of tolerance, attitudes toward students, and sense of standards.

Evaluation of Definitions

Advantages and disadvantages are inherent in all definitions of disturbance. Definitions are considered *the initial step* in the identification and classification of students who are disturbed. The initial step is emphasized because the ultimate labeling of a student as disturbed should include extensive and intensive case history, assessment, and diagnostic and service-oriented data. Dependence upon a definition to carry the weight of identification has caused innumerable students to be misdefined as disturbed or normal. According to Hobbs (1975),

Classification can profoundly affect what happens to a child. It can open doors to a child. It can open doors to services and experiences the child needs to grow into competence . . . On the other hand, classification or failure to get needed classification—and the consequences that ensue—can blight the life of a child, reduce opportunities, diminish his competence and self-esteem, alienate him from others, nurture a meanness of spirit, and make him less a person than he could become (p. 1).

Currently there are only two generally recognized advantages to defining students as disturbed. First, the label does entitle schools to special resources that accompany the special needs of students. That is, the number of students ultimately classified as disturbed enables schools to receive monetary funds, acquire support personnel, and provide special services. Second, defining a student theoretically creates the conditions (e.g., least restrictive environment and an individual educational program) that will enable the individual student better to achieve his or her maximum human potential. Both of these advantages, however, are a function of the legal and educational requirements that are intended to ensure an appropriate education. Ideally, both advantages could be provided without the need to stigmatize students with the label of disturbed.

There are a number of disadvantages inherent in the four exemplary definitions. Since these and other definitions of disturbance are not identical statements, the following listing of disadvantages represents generalizations that are typically, but not always, applicable.

Levels of Severity   Current definitions imply that disturbance can be classified into levels such as profound, severe, moderate, and mild. PL 94-142, for example, titles its definition "seriously emotionally disturbed," whereas Kauffman (1977) differentiates "mild and moderate" and "severe and profound." However, little empirical evidence exists to support such a distinction (Olson, Algozzine, & Schmid, 1980, p. 96). Certainly there are students whose behaviors represent greater deviation than others, such as a 12-year-old who is mute as opposed to a 6-year-old who is somewhat active. In fact, some severe conditions have been given special designations (e.g., autism), whereas less severe conditions are described in general behavioral terms (e.g., disruptive). Numerous other clinical examples could be provided, but these examples would only be appropriate in a limited number of situations.

In practice the level of severity is determined by the educational placement of the students. Students assigned to residential or special class settings are considered severe; students assigned to resource room and special class combinations are considered moderate; and students assigned primarily to the regular class are considered mild.

Bower (1969) has described a continuum of severity, ranging from "normal problems" to "fixed and recurring symptoms" that dictate "possible action by the school":

Emotional handicaps may be displayed in transient, temporary, pervasive, or intensive types of behavior. To complete the definition, it would be necessary to establish a continuum in which the degree of handicap can be perceived and perhaps estimated, especially as it relates to possible action by the school. One could begin such a continuum with (1) children who experience and demonstrate the normal problems of everyday living, growing, exploration, and reality testing. There are some, however, who can be observed as (2) children who develop a greater number and degree of symptoms of emotional problems as a result of normal crisis or stressful experiences, such as death of father, birth of sibling, divorce of parents, brain or body injury, school entrance, junior high school entrance, or puberty. Some children move beyond this level of adjustment and may be described as (3) children in whom moderate symptoms of emotional maladjustment persist to some extent beyond normal expectations but who are able to manage an adequate school adjustment. The next group would include (4) children with fixed and recurring symptoms of emotional maladjustment who can with help profit by school attendance and maintain some positive relationships in the school setting. Beyond this are (5) children with fixed and recurring symptoms of emotional difficulties who are perhaps best educated in a residential school setting or temporarily in a home setting (Bower, 1969, p. 27).

Clearly, educational placement and the degree of severity are logically related, but it is the placement that determines the level of severity. The primary disadvantage of current definitions is that they specify neither the levels of severity nor the most appropriate educational placement.

Categorical Descriptors   The four definitions use three different terms to describe the same population of disturbed students: "emotionally disturbed," "behavior disorders," and "behavior problems." The various descriptors have their origins in the different theories of causality. Advocates of the biophysical and behavioral theories define students from a behavioral base and consequently use the term "behavior disorders" as the primary descriptor. Advocates of the psychodynamic theory, who view behavior for psychological meaning, describe "emotional disturbance." Other descriptors, such as "deviant," "children in conflict," "troubled children," "maladjusted," and others, have found their way into the professional literature. Thus, depending on the author's orientation, the list of categorical descriptors of disturbance could be infinite. It is stated in the preface of this book that "disturbed" would be used as a generic term that included all the common descriptors found with reference to this population of students.

Beyond disturbance there is evidence to suggest that many mentally retarded and learning-disabled students demonstrate similar, if not identical, characteristics (Gajar, 1979). Hallahan and Kauffman (1977) found that "no behavioral characteristics can be found that are associated exclusively with any of the three areas [emotionally disturbed, mentally retarded, and learning-disabled]" (p. 139). On the basis of their investigation, they concluded that traditional descriptors were not functional, and therefore that a noncategorical approach based upon teaching techniques should be used in lieu of categorical terms.

In this light, the disadvantage of different definitions is that they focus on different aspects of the same problem. Disturbed students cannot be divided into "psychological problems," "behavior problems," "deviants," or whatever the particular author has in mind. The definitions perpetuate this sort of categorical thinking, when appropriate services should be the ultimate goal.

Measurement of Behaviors   Definitions do not contain measureable behaviors that enable teachers or other responsible personnel to make valid and reliable decisions. Terms such as "inappropriate behavior" and "socially unacceptable" are critical to the definitions, yet they are so vague that their existence is totally dependent upon personal, idiosyncratic judgments.

On the other extreme, the specific listing of behaviors, including frequency, duration, and so on, seems equally inappropriate since the circumstances involving behaviors are important conditions for defining disturbance. For example, crying behaviors signal different meanings for a student who has had a death or divorce in the family as opposed to a student who similarly reacts to homework or being a few seconds late. Disturbance cannot be totally defined by a quantitative method. Since the sum of a student cannot be measured, behaviors are only one aspect of disturbance. For those aspects of the student that do not lend themselves to measurement, personal and professional inference and human sensitivity are important elements in defining disturbance.

A developmental approach to defining disturbance seems to be the most appropriate compromise to this measurement versus personal judgment dilemma. Literature in human growth and development reveals a number of generalizations regarding the developmental appropriateness of behaviors. Thus, disturbance can be defined by behaviors that reflect lower level functioning compared with chronological counterparts within the normal population. This idea of developmental behaviors is more fully explained in Chapter 5.

Student Input   The decision as to whether or not a student is disturbed is chiefly a unilateral, authoritative process. That is, everyone in contact with the student—teachers, parents, and others—potentially makes the decision of disturbance regarding a student. The student seems to have relatively little influence or input, if any, on the decision. Consequently, a disadvantage of definitions is that they perpetuate this adult prerogative philosophy of defining disturbance. Mechanisms that require student participation need to be included in the process of defining disturbance.

Classroom Settings   Definitions tend to limit disturbance to educational settings, particularly the classroom. For example, reference to "learning," "classmates," and "teachers" clearly identifies the classroom as the primary, almost exclusive, setting in which disturbance is defined. This kind of limitation is chiefly defining students' classroom reactions, not disturbance. Disturbance is a global problem, not a situationally specific one. If a student is depressed, aggressive, or hyperactive in the classroom, but not in other social settings, then the classroom rather than the student may need to be evaluated. Therefore, a disadvantage of definitions is that they do not include estimates of behavior beyond the classroom. Student behaviors in the home and in the community need to be incorporated into the definitions.

This section on the evaluation of definitions has only superficially touched upon a few of the issues that are evident in the definitions of disturbance. However, definitions represent a limited component in the process of identifying disturbance. In fact, it is suspected that the actual definitions of disturbance are less important in the ultimate identification process than are personal perceptions of normal and/or disturbed behavior.

TEACHERS' PERCEPTIONS OF DISTURBANCE

Throughout the discussion on definitions of disturbance it is both stated and implied that "no matter what conceptual framework is employed, classifying a person is an arbitrary process" (Prugh, Engel, & Morse, 1975, p. 261). As a consequence, definitions have often done little more than direct official attention to students who do not behave in ways that are consistent with teachers' expectations. In fact, it may well be that definitions have primarily served to legitimatize administrative actions such as referral, exclusion, and special placement (Rich, 1977).

Observation and evaluation of special education programs, disciplinary actions, and misconduct reports reveal a number of consistent characteristics among the students affected. First, inappropriate school behavior has apparently been conceptualized within educational settings as acting-out behavior, which interferes with the control exercised by school authorities. Second, the vast majority of students who have been identified as demonstrating acting-out behavior have been male, often at a rate of ten to one over female students. The prevalence of acting-out behavior exhibited by males leads to a third characteristic of referrals—the students exhibiting this behavior tend to represent minority groups, particularly blacks and Hispanics. Stereotypically, then, the student who is suspended, sent to the principal, or assigned to a special education program, is male, most often black or Hispanic, and has been referred by a teacher because of his acting-out behavior problem (Lindholm, Touliatos, & Rich, 1978).

Although acting-out behavior may ultimately result in any one of many labeled conditions, such as delinquent or incorrigible, educational institutions have limited their focus and perpetuated the development of a label known commonly as "behavior disorders," which has come to be equated with the PL 94-142 definition of disturbance. Unquestionably, the teaching profession has been the discipline most responsible for the initial screening and referral of students suspected of exhibiting disturbance. The rate with which teachers exercise this referral procedure is related to the teachers' responsibility for and observation of students within controlled environments over sustained periods of time. This fact is accentuated for preschool and primary teachers, who are the most consistent observers of behavior outside the home setting. As a result of this early, direct, and extended contact, educational and mental health authorities have tended to ascribe to teachers a primary role in the early referral of disturbance.

Although the ultimate decision to define a student as disturbed resides with an interdisciplinary team, including teachers, parents, counselors, administrators, and other mental hygienists, it has been demonstrated that the teachers' initial decisions have a significant impact on the ultimate identification of disturbance (Rosenthal & Jacobson, 1968). Teachers, by referring students as potentially disturbed, establish expectations that are routinely supported by subsequent diagnostic decisions.

Unfortunately, the label of disturbance is among the least difficult to attach to children; standardized tests are not required, projective techniques need not be employed, and a medical examination is not considered a prerequisite. In fact, some literature has expressed the need to approach disturbance in public school settings from a purely behavioristic perspective (Pimm, 1967), thereby providing a diagnostic approach that could focus on quantity and quality of behavior.

Within educational institutions, value judgments have developed around expectations for student behavior that is limited to a rather narrow, explicit pattern of behavior, independent of the community, legal, or mental health norms. In essence, schools are operated as passive learning environments, where the maintenance of control within a custodial framework has high priority. In such a setting, the successful student is considered neat, obedient, quiet, and punctual. Conversely, educators attach severe consequences to lying, cursing, tardiness, and distractibility, which are ignored by the legal system and have only moderate consequences in terms of community standards. Similarly, educators and mental hygienists (psychologists, counselors, etc.) have developed different criteria for evaluating the severity of behaviors. Educators, as opposed to the mental hygienists, more readily identify unreliableness and stealing as being most indicative of disturbance, whereas withdrawal, fearfulness, and shyness are regarded by teachers as less serious signs or symptoms of disturbance. Table 2 contains the rankings of behavior problems by mental hygienists and teachers sampled over a 50-year period.

Some obvious differences exist between mental hygienists and teachers, and among teachers over the 50-year period. Most noticeable is the fact that the mental hygienists considered behaviors that are symptomatic of internal psychological problems as the most indicative of disturbance. Teachers, on the other hand, considered behaviors that challenged authority or reflected disrespect as the most significant indicators of disturbance. Teachers did alter their perceptions from the 1928 Victorian sexual ethic to be more consistent with mental hygienists in 1952 and 1973, but the prevailing belief in behavioral conformity was still evident. These results led Ahmann and Glock (1959) to conclude that "just because certain kinds of behavior disrupt the well-oiled machinery of a carefully controlled classroom is no defensible reason for labeling it maladjustment" (p. 426).

The significant differences between the perceptions of mental hygienists and teachers indicate basic disagreement in their respective conceptions of disturbance and normal behavior. Although neither perception is necessarily an accurate portrayal of disturbance, there is evidence to indicate that many teachers fail to recognize normal behavior, and inadvertently label it disturbed. This perception of normality or disturbance is apparently the product of the interaction among individual teacher characteristics, student behaviors, and classroom conditions.

Teachers' Perceptions of Normality

Defining normal behavior is a great deal like defining disturbance; that is, normality is relative. In later chapters normality will be discussed in greater depth, but at this point it is sufficient to say that normal behaviors, from a general cultural standpoint, are those behaviors that are expected to occur and that are positively valued by society. For example, behaviors that express independence, assertiveness, and cooperation are expected to occur and are positively valued; thus they are normal. Conversely, extreme anxiety, fear, and depression are neither expected nor desired and therefore potentially constitute disturbance. These examples of normal and disturbed behaviors tend to arouse ambivalent feelings in teachers, and consequently students receive mixed reinforcement from teachers when they are demonstrated.

Table 2.   Behavior problem rankings by mental hygienists and teachers

Behavior problem	Ranking by mental hygienists	Ranking by teachers		
		1928	1952	1973
Unsocial, withdrawing	1	40	6	4
Unhappy, depressed	2	22	3	17
Fearfulness	3	36	23	28
Suspiciousness	4	37	35	18
Cruelty, bullying	5	8	4	13
Shyness	6	50	34	30
Enuresis	7	19	30	45
Resentfulness	8	29	11	1
Stealing	9	2	2	31
Sensitiveness	10	48	24	20
Dreaminess	11	41	40	38
Nervousness	12	20	18	34
Suggestible	13	28	13	44
Overcritical	14	45	27	15
Easily discouraged	15	23	10	5
Temper tantrums	16	13	16	19
Domineering	17	33	15	14
Truancy	18	6	7	40
Physical coward	19	31	33	42
Untruthfulness	20	5	5	16
Unreliableness	21	12	1	8
Destroying property	22	10	12	32
Sullenness	23	35	32	24
Lack of interest	24	14	22	3
Cheating	25	9	9	26
Selfishness	26	24	17	21
Quarrelsome	27	27	28	12
Heterosexual activity	28	1	14	37
Restlessness	29	49	45	35
Inattention	30	26	36	10
Untidy appearance	31	34	31	39
Tattling	32	46	47	36
Impertinence, defiance	33	7	8	2
Obscene notes, talk	34	4	29	46
Laziness	35	17	20	11
Stubbornness	36	32	37	22
Attracting attention	37	39	43	9
Thoughtlessness	38	38	41	23
Imaginative lying	39	42	46	29
Disobedient	40	11	19	6
Carelessness in work	41	25	25	33
Masturbation	42	3	26	48
Impudence, rudeness	43	16	21	7
Inquisitiveness	44	44	44	47
Disorderliness	45	21	39	25

(Continued)

Table 2.   (*Continued*)

Behavior problem	Ranking by mental hygienists	Ranking by teachers		
		1928	1952	1973
Tardiness	46	30	38	41
Interrupting	47	43	48	27
Profanity	48	15	42	43
Smoking	49	18	49	49
Whispering	50	47	50	50

Adapted from Ahmann & Glock (1959). Results were based on the research of Wickman (1928), Stouffer (1952), and Horton (1973).

Within the family unit, boys, in particular, have been encouraged, verbally or through modeling, to demonstrate assertiveness, physical prowess, and independence. This is accentuated for boys from more deprived environments in which impulsiveness, aggression, and strength are prerequisites to psychological, if not physical, survival. The lifestyle of many male students is very different from that of their teachers, who, particularly in the elementary schools, are usually middle-class females. Sex role expectations for females during the first half of this century facilitated passive, obedient, and dependent behaviors. Although this sex role socialization posture is in the process of change, many middle-class female teachers continue to adhere to the traditional expectations and project these expectations to their students, both boys and girls. Consequently, Victor and Halverson (1976) found that ". . . anxious neurotic, inhibited behaviors are more likely to be characteristic of girls, while the acting-out, rebellious, aggressive behaviors are more often associated with boys" (p. 84). The problem behaviors characteristic of girls tend to be invisible in large classroom groups, yet they ". . . may develop into a pathology of total withdrawal and a life of excruciating loneliness" (Zimbardo, Pilkonis, & Norwood, 1975, p. 70). Because of differences in the sex role and cultural socialization process, teachers often fail to account accurately for normality in children, emphasizing instead the need for sameness in behavior, irrespective of sex, race, or background differences.

This critical distinction between individuality and conformity seems to be the essence of teacher-defined disturbance. For many years educators have maintained that each human is a unique organism, possessing a host of individual characteristics that must be expected, maintained, and even encouraged in the educational process. In practice, however, educators typically expect students to fit a pattern of standardized behavior characterized in many cases by social isolation, respect for authority, and lockstep learning. The teachers' tolerance of differences has often become so minimal that conformity rather than individuality is becoming the measure of normality within the classroom. Yet, as Rhodes (1977) has pointed out, it may be that conformity is actually "an illusion of normality" encouraged by teachers but that is actually a form of disturbance itself.

Teachers' perceptions of normality are also evident in other research on the identification of disturbance. For example, Rubin and Balow (1978) conducted a 6-year longitudinal study in which teachers annually rated the behavior of the same 1,500 students of elementary school age:

> Among subjects who received six teacher ratings, 60% (68% of the boys and 51% of the girls) were considered a behavior problem by at least one teacher. Thus, it becomes apparent that behavior that at least one teacher is willing to classify as a problem is the norm rather than the exception for elementary school children. The finding is all the more startling when one realizes that this sample of children fits quite well the normative distribution . . . (p. 109).

Rubin and Balow offered a number of reasons for the results, including the following:

a. children's behavior problems are highly transient . . . ;
b. children's behaviors remain relatively constant, but teachers vary widely in their . . . perceptions of behavior;
c. children's behaviors remain relatively constant . . . but [teachers] vary widely in their judgments as to what behavior constitutes a problem;
d. teachers vary greatly in the environments they create, which in turn produces . . . problem behavior;
e. teacher-child-environment interactions are of such a nature that different children are involved in problem behavior in different settings; and
f. some combination of the above (pp. 109–110).

It is suspected that the last reason, that is, a combination of all the reasons, accounts for the results. Certainly in selected cases the reason for this overidentification of disturbance is related to the teachers' inability to differentiate normal behaviors from those that are symptomatic of disturbance. Clarizio and McCoy (1976) offered an additional explanation for this high identification rate: "the teacher's low annoyance threshold" (p. 29).

These alarming results are not limited to a single study. Kelly, Bullock, and Dykes (1977) found that teachers perceived over 20 percent of their regular class students to have behavior problems. Similarly, Wood and Zabel (1978), in a review of studies, found teacher estimates of disturbance among students to range from 20 to 28 percent of their classroom group.

Obviously, something must be done to reverse this trend of identifying normal behaviors or even transient problems as signs of disturbance. In all probability any success along this line will have to be accomplished by the teachers themselves. There is not only a need for teachers to increase their competence in discriminating normal versus disturbed behaviors, but also to evaluate their own values, expectations, and even classroom teaching behaviors.

It is indeed difficult to analyze one's own values and expectations as they relate to classroom teaching, particularly in the presence of annoying disruptions. However, if significant progress is to be achieved, teachers must evaluate the effects of their personal and teaching behaviors on their students. In essence, "what is needed is a more personal kind of searching, which will enable the teacher to identify his (her) own concerns and to share the concerns of his (her) students" (Jersild, 1955, p. 3). According to Gordon (1966), "one of the most difficult problems the teacher faces in analyzing the learning situation is assessing his own behavior . . ." (p. 89).

In the final analysis there is a need for professional educators, especially teachers, to evaluate the behavior of students from an individual perspective and in light of their own values and expectations. Although the philosophy of education has espoused "individualized education" for over 50 years, that goal has not yet been achieved. Educators continue to expect all children to fit a behavior pattern characterized by low motor activity, absolute obedience, and respect for authority. Violation of this expected pattern may result in exclusion, failure, punishment, and/or labeling. The old saying that "boys will be boys" tends to be applicable in all social settings, except for school.

Classroom Conditions

Teacher perceptions of disturbance are not necessarily an independent judgment, but they are frequently reinforced by classroom conditions that are beyond the control of teachers. The critical classroom factors that tend to be related to the high incidence of teacher-identified student disturbance include: 1) class size and composition, 2) available support services, 3) administrator characteristics, and 4) legal requirements.

Class Size and Composition   It is generally believed that smaller and more homogeneous classroom groups will enhance the teacher's ability to individualize instruction, foster achievement, and effectively manage behavior (Glass & Smith, 1979). Conversely, large, diversified classroom groups create such a potentially complex and unpredictable situation that teachers "foist a large number of rigid rules and regulations upon students so as to make their behavior far less varied, more uniform, and more predictable'' (Mehrabian, 1976, p. 156). Part of this predictability is also accomplished by defining students as disturbed. Even though mildly disturbed students may remain in the regular classroom, this identification process seems to have been maintained as a way for teachers to justify their lack of progress, their inability to manage, and/or their personal frustration.

In addition, regular classroom teachers with only a few problem students, as opposed to those with many, are more likely to define disruptive students as disturbed. Apparently, a comparison or contrast effect is operating, in which students who are overtly different from the normative behavior of the group are more noticeable (Smart, Wilton, & Keeling, 1980). Combined, large and behaviorally diverse classroom groups increase the probability that teachers will define a higher percentage of students as disturbed. Yet the school administration, not teachers, has primary control over these critical classroom conditions.

Available Support Services   In the past, the classroom teacher had the primary, if not exclusive, responsibility for educating the students assigned to his or her classroom. When a disturbed student was identified within or assigned to the regular classroom, the best the teacher could hope for would be to struggle through the year or have the student referred to a special class. Identifying and educating disturbed students now requires the expertise and services of numerous specialized personnel and facilities.

> The implementation of mainstreaming is a complex educational task which requires a team approach. Many school systems have expected classroom teachers magically to have all the skills and time to accomplish the successful mainstreaming of students representing the full range of educational handicaps—in most cases an impossible expectation for teachers. A sound approach to mainstreaming requires shared responsibility on the part of all educators in the school (Turnbull & Schulz, 1979, p. 66).

Thus, the availability of support services becomes a two-edged sword. When only limited services are available, teachers tend to identify students for the purpose of transferring them out of the regular class, and when services are more plentiful, teachers tend to identify students for the purpose of receiving assistance. In either case, the availability of support services has contributed to the teacher identification of disturbed students.

Administrator Characteristics   Principals are the critical ingredient in both the rate of identification and the provision of services for disturbed students. For mainstreaming and resource programs to be successful, principals must become advocates of both teachers and students. Principals who are advocates "defend the integrity of innovation, recruit supportive members, and secure resources . . . Principals can reduce conflict and assist with the formulation of clearly stated mainstreaming goals" (Sivage, 1980, pp. 16–17).

> Resistance to mainstreaming is natural and normal; mainstreaming requires changes in long-standing attitudes, beliefs and practices regarding handicapped children. Implementation necessitates changes in materials, structure, attitudes, and knowledge by every member of the organization. School principals are positioned to facilitate these changes and reduce the natural resistance (p. 17).

On the other extreme, there are principals who resist, even reject, the concept of mainstreaming. Typically, these principals espouse traditional values that include an absolute standard of behavior for both teachers and students. Under such leadership, teachers are often evaluated on such criteria as the orderliness and quietness of the classroom, the frequency of student referrals to the principal, and the number of requests or complaints registered by the teacher. Some principals boast that "you can hear a pin drop" in their schools, or that there are no students in the hallways, or that their schools do not need expensive special services. In such a climate, teacher-defined disturbance becomes a function of intended segregated placement, rather than mainstreaming. If a teacher is devalued because he or she cannot control a disruptive student, it is little wonder that the teacher prefers that the student be assigned elsewhere.

Legal Requirements Conditions and policies beyond those of individual teachers and principals have contributed to the perpetuation of labeling. The state and federal governments and higher education institutions must share the responsibility. Certification requirements, for example, require college course work and training designated by specific exceptionalities. If teachers are trained and certified to educate students with specific labels, then both teacher and student role behavior expectations have been created which must be fulfilled.

Funding or excess cost provisions additionally encourage the maintenance of categorical labels. In an effort to educate all handicapped students, PL 94-142, for example, will provide millions of dollars to local schools for excess costs. Although the intent of the legislation is to educate the student in "the least restrictive environment" or the regular classroom, if possible, the operational guidelines provide funding for students who are identified as having specific handicapping labels. Thus, because of the need for ". . . statistical maintenance and funding categories . . . labeling will most likely continue despite its limitations and unwanted consequences." (Clarizio & McCoy, 1976, p. 113).

A GUIDE TO DEFINING DISTURBANCE

This chapter has listed several definitions of disturbance followed by a discussion of their operational problems and limitations. Subsequent chapters provide additional definition and operational clarity by describing specific assessment procedures, such as observational techniques, diagnostic instruments, and developmental behaviors. In the meantime, a guide to defining disturbance is introduced (Table 3) as a preliminary or screening procedure for making initial decisions regarding the existence of disturbance.

The guide consists of five decision making levels, each of which should be relatively consistent in the direction of "potentially disturbed" before the labeling of a student is considered. As a note of caution, failure to achieve consistency should not be interpreted to mean that the student does not need special services. To the contrary, *all* students need some sort of special services. Failure to achieve consistency does mean that it is unlikely that the student should be labeled disturbed.

Level 1: Judgment

This level is designed to eliminate the idiosyncratic judgment of an individual teacher. As Rubin and Balow (1978) have pointed out, there is a high probability that one teacher will consider any given student disturbed sometime during the elementary school years. A team, on the other hand, consisting of several professionals, the parent(s), and, it is hoped, the student, can provide information beyond the scope and possible bias of an individual teacher. As an initial action, the team is

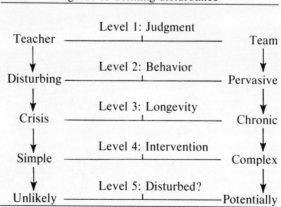

Table 3.   A guide to defining disturbance

responsible for evaluating the accuracy of an individual teacher's judgment of a student.

Level 2: Behavior

Often a particular complaint regarding student behavior is limited to one setting, usually a classroom. In this case the behavior may simply be disturbing to the teacher. If the behavior is evident in other settings, such as other classrooms, the playground, at home, or in the community, then there is greater evidence that the problem is not situationally disturbing, but a more pervasive problem indicating possible disturbance.

Level 3: Longevity

The duration of behaviors has a direct relationship to disturbance. Often students demonstrate normal behavior patterns that were negatively altered by a personal crisis, such as parental divorce, a death in the family, or academic failure. Certainly students need support at such times, but the fact that the behaviors were precipitated by a sudden crisis does not imply that the behavior pattern will continue. Comparatively, chronic behaviors are those that have been demonstrated for an extensive period of time and can *not* be traced to a relatively recent crisis situation. At the very least, the basis for establishing the existence of chronic behaviors should include the last year, and preferably two, of a student's educational and general life experience.

Level 4: Intervention

This level is included in order to reduce the frequency of unnecessarily labeling students as disturbed. Even if the conditions for defining disturbance were met by the three previous levels, it would be pointless to label students unless it was necessary in order to acquire specialized resources. In some cases simple interventions that require minimal time, money, and materials may be sufficient to provide an appropriate education. For example, changing the seating arrangement, class reassignment, or providing a wider range of activities may bring about the desired behavior changes. In those cases in which a more complex intervention is projected, including the need for additional resources, then the next level becomes one of potentially labeling the student.

Level 5: Disturbed?

If a team has judged that a student's behavior is pervasive, with chronic longevity, and that a complex intervention is required, then the student may be defined as disturbed. This, of course, is only the beginning:

extensive assessment and diagnostic data, an individual educational program, and assignment to the least restrictive environment must follow this initial decision. If the team does not agree on the behavior, its longevity, or the need for complex intervention, then labeling is unnecessary and should be avoided.

PREVALENCE

Estimates of the number of disturbed students depend primarily on the definition, the level of severity, and the source of the information. It has been pointed out in this chapter that many of the decisions regarding disturbance are arbitrary, resulting in loosely calculated and global estimates of disturbance that should be interpreted with caution.

In 1969, the President's Commission on the Mental Health of Children reported that disturbance was evident in over 20 percent of the children and youth in the United States. Of this percentage, 0.6 percent were considered seriously disturbed (psychotic), 2–3 percent were considered mildly or moderately disturbed, and the remaining 16–18 percent had temporary emotional problems. In 1975, the Bureau of Education for the Handicapped reported that there were 1,310,000 disturbed students in school, but that only 18 percent were receiving appropriate services. Various states have reported prevalence rates ranging from 0.05 to 15 percent (Schultz et al., 1971). As late as 1979, the President's Commission reported that "for the past few years the most commonly used estimate has been that, at any one time, 10 percent of the population needs some form of mental health services . . . There is new evidence that this figure may be nearer 15 percent of the population" (*Report to the President*, 1979, p. 8).

Estimates independent of government sources also tend to reflect a large range, but overall higher percentage prevalence figures. Morse (1975) analyzed prevalence studies and found that anywhere from 0.1 to 30 percent of children and youth could be considered disturbed. Bower (1969) surveyed schools and found that 10 percent of the students demonstrated signs of disturbance. With regard to the seriously disturbed, the National Society for Autistic Children (1977) estimated that autism occurred in one out of every 2,000 births.

An estimate of 3–5 percent of the school population is generally accepted as the prevalence rate of disturbed students, even though a much higher percentage may need mental health services. To the teacher this estimate may seem unimportant, but in the allocation of finances, long-term planning of specialized facilities, and the training of professional personnel, accurate estimates are critical. An underestimate can create a need for badly needed services, whereas an overestimate can create a waste of specialized resources.

SUMMARY

This chapter emphasized the relative and subjective manner in which disturbance is defined. Several authoritative definitions of disturbance were presented that represented different theoretical orientations. The PL 94-142 definition of "seriously emotionally disturbed" was emphasized because of its legal implications, broad based acceptance, and eclectic nature. All of the definitions, however, contained general descriptors of disturbance without specifying measurable behaviors. This limitation was necessary because disturbance cannot be characterized by a set of absolute and unchanging behaviors.

Because defining a student as disturbed is an arbitrary process that most often begins in the regular classroom, teachers have had a significant impact on the labeling process. Teachers responsible for large and diverse classroom groups tend to define disruptive types of behavior as the most indicative of disturbance. This narrow perspective indicates that many teachers often consider normal behaviors as those that conform to a rather rigid set of classroom rules and expectations. A guide to defining disturbance is provided as a screening procedure for making initial decisions regarding the existence of disturbance.

4

Classification of Disturbance

Classification is the process of grouping concepts into identifying categories based on one or more distinguishing characteristics. Thus, a classification process has been employed when a student is labeled as disturbed. Not only has the student been categorized, but there are theoretical characteristics present that are distinguishable from other special conditions and from the normal population. In fact, any decision that involves a conceptual distinction among behaviors is an act of classification (Achenbach, 1974).

From a scientific perspective the classification of behaviors is an important prerequisite to the understanding of disturbance. "Judgments as to what is wrong with a particular child, what the causes are likely to be, whether he can be helped, and what treatment is appropriate all involve classification . . ." (Achenbach, 1974, p. 61). The alternative to a classification system is the identification and treatment of disturbed students based on intuitive, idiosyncratic, and trial and error choices (Kauffman, 1977). Regardless of the limitations of current classification systems, most professionals are not willing to accept this alternative. Even Carl Rogers (1955), an outspoken critic of dehumanizing systems, explicitly classified personality elements and projected possible treatment outcomes.

Even though selected human characteristics have been categorized since ancient times, the classification of disturbance among students is still in the early stages of development. To date most classification systems involving disturbance have focused on the identification of behaviors or psychological conditions, whereas the potential causes and treatment components have generally not been included in the classification systems. Even the identification function of classification systems is subject to suspicion, insufficiency, and theoretical bias. "Progress in understanding many disorders is hampered by the absence of objective ways of specifying them so that they may be consistently identified by different workers. One of the recurring problems in research on and treatment of childhood autism, for example, is the lack of agreement as to which children are autistic . . ." (Achenbach, 1974, p. 61). These problems only touch the surface of the numerous problems that exist with regard to human classification systems. Some of these problems will be examined in greater depth later in this chapter. In the meantime, selected classification systems of disturbance will be outlined and discussed.

CURRENT CLASSIFICATION SYSTEMS

Because the process of classifying behavior is primarily a scientific endeavor, and because disturbance has historically been viewed as a psychological-medical problem, it is little wonder that the primary classification systems are a product of the psychiatric profession. For example, the American Psychiatric Association (APA) undoubtedly has developed the most widely accepted system currently in existence. However, because the APA system was until recently chiefly devoted to adult classification, an organization known as the Group for the Advancement of Psychiatry (GAP) developed their own classification system, which had greater emphasis on children's mental problems. Both of these classification systems are included in the following discussion. It should be noted that neither classification system addresses the problem of appropriate education. They do, however, include many of the characteristics of students considered disturbed. Therefore, their inclusion is more for their historical value and their importance in communicating with other disciplines than for their practical worth to educators.

It should be noted that some educators have also attempted to develop classification systems for disturbance. To date, these attempts have been little more than global distinctions among a limited variety of primary behavior problems. Educators, as opposed to psychiatrists, have not had the organizational support of a powerful professional association to develop, disseminate, and implement a classification system. Unlike the American Association of Mental Deficiency, which has conceptualized a system for classifying mental retardation, educators of the disturbed have been unable to develop a functional system of disturbance that has educational relevance.

Both the psychiatric and the educational classification systems must be interpreted with caution. The actual use of the systems requires a great deal of student data, input from a variety of professionals, assurance of parental involvement and consent (due process), and the expectation that the classification of a student as disturbed will increase the student's probability of experiencing a more appropriate educational program. Most important, the classification of a student as disturbed has serious implications and consequences that cannot be taken lightly. Therefore, the classification systems are presented for the purposes of increasing understanding of disturbance among educators and effective communication through a common professional language.

American Psychiatric Association

During the first half of the twentieth century the APA made several attempts to establish a standard nomenclature (a system of names) for mental disorders. However, most psychiatrists found that these early attempts were inadequate because, among other things, the defined types of mental disorders were limited to classic conditions, which accounted for only a small percentage of psychiatric patients. After World War II, the APA collected massive amounts of patient data, conducted an exhaustive review of the literature, and catalogued professional suggestions in order to revise the definitions and diagnosis of mental disorders (Knopf, 1979), On the basis of the revised information the APA in 1951 published the *Diagnostic and Statistical Manual of Mental Disorders* (DSM-I).

DSM-I was almost exclusively adult-oriented, because there were relatively few diagnostic categories applicable for the nonadult population. Childhood schizophrenia and adjustment reaction of infancy, childhood, or adolescence were the only diagnostic categories available for the school-aged population. "Although adult diagnosis could also be applied to children, most children seen in psychiatric clinics either were diagnosed as having adjustment reactions or received no diagnosis" (Achenbach, 1974, p. 63). Within the broad category of adjustment reaction to childhood, three subcategories were specified: habit disturbance, conduct disturbance, and neurotic traits. Only the children with the most severe problems were diagnosed as childhood schizophrenic. According to Knopf (1979), the limited differentiation of childhood problems in DSM-I was ". . . reminiscent of the way children were viewed before childhood was discovered" (p. 45).

DSM-II In 1968, a second revision of the *Diagnostic and Statistical Manual* (DSM-II) was published as an updated classification system. DSM-II consisted of 10 major categories of mental disorders.

I. Mental retardation. This refers to general subnormal intellectual functioning that impairs either learning and social adjustment, or maturation, or both. Mental retardation is further categorized by the degree of severity (e.g., mild, moderate) and according to the cause (e.g., rubella, environmental).

II. Organic brain syndromes. This designation refers to disorders caused by the impairment of brain tissue function that results in symptoms such as impairment of orientation, memory, intellectual functions, and judgment.

III. Psychosis. This severe form of mental illness grossly interferes with the individual's capacity to meet ordinary demands of life. Psychosis is typically associated with distortions of reality, hallucinations, delusions, alterations of mood, and/or deficits in perception, language, and memory. Subcategories include a variety of schizophrenic types, affective disorders, and paranoid states. This category contains the classification of childhood schizophrenia, which is described as "a condition that may be manifest by autistic, atypical, and withdrawn behavior; failure to develop identity separate from the mother's; and general unevenness, gross immaturity and inadequacy in development" (DSM-II, 1968, p. 35).

IV. Neuroses. This category of mental disorders is characterized by extreme anxiety as a result of subjective distress. Subcategories of neuroses include, for example, hysteria, phobias, and depression.

V. Personality disorders. This category is characterized by deeply ingrained maladaptive behaviors that resist change, represent lifelong patterns, and are often associated with an absence of remorse or guilt. Exemplary subcategories include paranoid and schizoid personalities, passive-aggressive personality, and a variety of sexual deviations.

VI. Psychophysiological disorders. This group of disorders is characterized by physical symptoms that are caused by emotional factors; this category includes skin, respiratory, musculoskeletal, and intestinal reactions.

VII. Special symptoms. This classification is for individuals with a single specific symptom such as speech disturbance, motor tics, feeding disturbance, or enuresis.

VIII. Transient situational disturbances. This category is reserved for temporary problems that represent a reaction to extreme environment stress during infancy, childhood, adolescence, adult life, or late life. This category is similar to the adjustment reaction classification in DSM-I.

IX. Behavior disorders of childhood and adolescence. This is the only category in DSM-II that is devoted exclusively to non-

adults. Six specific disorders are identified:
1. Hyperkinetic (overactive, restless, distractible, and short attention span)
2. Withdrawn (seclusive, detached, sensitive, shy, and timid)
3. Overanxious (anxious, fearful, and exaggerated motor response)
4. Runaway (tendency to escape from threatening situations; associated with timidity, immaturity, and rejection)
5. Unsocialized aggression (disobedient, quarrelsome, physically and/or verbally aggressive, and destructive)
6. Group delinquent (acquired values and behaviors of a delinquent peer group that may include stealing, skipping school, and staying out late at night).
X. Nonspecific conditions. "This category is for recording the conditions of individuals who are psychiatrically normal but who nevertheless have severe enough problems to warrant examination by a psychiatrist" (DSM-II, 1968, p. 51).

Two concepts are of special interest with reference to DSM-II. First, there is the general assumption that the categories I to X constitute descending degrees of severity. Whereas categories I (mental retardation) and II (organic brain syndrome) represent chiefly nonreversible biophysical disorders, category X (nonspecific conditions) is void of psychiatric disorders. In addition, behavior disorders are more stable, internalized, and resistant to treatment than are transient situational disturbances, but less so than psychoses, neuroses, and personality disorders (DSM-II, 1968, pp. 49–50). In turn, personality disorders "are perceptibly different in quality from psychotic and neurotic symptoms" (DSM-II, 1968, p. 41). Thus psychoses (including childhood schizophrenia) are more severe mental disorders than neuroses; neuroses are more severe than behavior disorders; and behavior disorders are more severe than transient disturbances.

Second, DSM-II places the greatest emphasis on the classification of adult mental disorders. There is reason to believe that many childhood problems continue to be evaluated in light of adult characteristics. "The strong theoretical emphasis, since Freud, upon the continuity between childhood maladjustment and the occurrence of adult disorders has caused childhood problems to be viewed largely in terms of the adult disorders they are believed to culminate in, rather than being studied in their own right" (Achenbach, 1974, p. 65). Even though DSM-II represented a dramatic shift from DSM-I in terms of the classification of mental disorders in children, most professional mental health personnel involved with children were not satisfied with the limitations of this classification system. Because of these limitations, as well as other diagnostic difficulties, the APA developed a third revision of the *Diagnostic and Statistical Manual of Mental Disorders*. **DSM-III** DSM-III, published in 1980, represents a rather dramatic departure from the two previous editions. For the first time an entire section on "disorders usually first evident in infancy, childhood, or adolescence" is included in the diagnostic categories. The text of this section represents at least 20 percent of the material devoted to all diagnostic categories. In addition, various other childhood mental disorders that are presumed to have adult disorder counterparts are scattered throughout DSM-III. "Because the *essential* features of Affective Disorders and Schizophrenia are the same in children and adults, there are no special categories corresponding to these disorders in this section of the classification. For example, if a child or adolescent has an illness that meets the criteria for Major Depression . . . or Schizophrenia, these diagnoses should be given, regardless of the age of the individual" (DSM-III, 1980, p. 35).

The DSM-III classification of disorders among children is comprised of five major groups:

  I. Intellectual
     Mental retardation
 II. Behavioral (overt)
     Attention deficit disorders
     Conduct disorders
III. Emotional
     Anxiety disorders
     Other disorders
 IV. Physical
     Eating disorders
     Stereotyped movement disorders
     Other disorders
  V. Developmental
     Pervasive developmental disorders
     Specific developmental disorders

The following section includes the diagnostic criteria for some of the more common DSM-III childhood and adolescence disorder groups. Several criteria, however, are not included because of their limited value to teachers who are concerned with the classroom behavior of disturbed students. Disorders related to infancy, mental retardation, physical disorders (e.g., tics, enuresis, and sleepwalking), and specific developmental disorders (e.g., reading difficulties, difficulties in learning arithmetic or language) were therefore omitted from the listing of diagnostic criteria. The specific developmental disorders that are related to academic problems were not included because the criteria convey little more than the fact that the student is performing below an expected level given the student's age, intellectual level, and prior education. Each of the diagnostic criteria contained in DSM-III includes two precautionary conditions. First, the behaviors must have persisted for a noticeable period of time, usually 3 or 6 months. Second, the condition must not be due to a more serious form of mental disorder such as mental retardation, schizophrenia, or an adult disorder (if the student is 18 or older).

Interestingly, DSM-III emphasizes that teachers are of critical importance in the diagnosis of an attention deficit disorder. This dependence on teacher data is not evident in the remaining diagnostic criteria of mental disorders.

Selected Diagnostic Criteria for Disorders Usually First Evident in Childhood or Adolescence[1]

Attention Deficit Disorder

Diagnostic criteria Attention Deficit Disorder with [or without] Hyperactivity

The child displays, for his or her mental and chronological age, signs of developmentally inappropriate inattention, impulsivity, and hyperactivity. The signs must be reported by adults in the child's environment, such as parents and teachers. Because the symptoms are typically variable, they may not be observed directly by the clinician. When the reports of teachers and parents conflict, primary consideration should be given to the teacher reports because of greater familiarity with age-appropriate norms. Symptoms typically worsen in situations that require self-application, as in the classroom. Signs of the disorder may be absent when the child is in a new or a one-to-one situation.

The number of symptoms specified is for children between the ages of eight and ten, the peak age range for referral. In younger children, more severe forms of the symptoms and a greater number of symptoms are usually present. The opposite is true of older children.

A. Inattention. At least three of the following:
    (1) often fails to finish things he or she starts
    (2) often doesn't seem to listen
    (3) easily distracted
    (4) has difficulty concentrating on schoolwork or other tasks requiring sustained attention
    (5) has difficulty sticking to a play activity

[1] Reprinted with permission from American Psychiatric Association, *Diagnostic and Statistical Manual of Mental Disorders* (3rd ed., *DSM*-III). Washington, D.C.: American Psychiatric Association, 1980.

B. Impulsivity. At least three of the following:
   (1) often acts before thinking
   (2) shifts excessively from one activity to another
   (3) has difficulty organizing work (this not being due to cognitive impairment)
   (4) needs a lot of supervision
   (5) frequently calls out in class
   (6) has difficulty awaiting turn in games or group situations
C. Hyperactivity. At least two of the following:
   (1) runs about or climbs on things excessively
   (2) has difficulty sitting still or fidgets excessively
   (3) has difficulty staying seated
   (4) moves about excessively during sleep
   (5) is always "on the go" or acts as if "driven by a motor"
D. Onset before the age of seven. . . .

Conduct Disorder

Diagnostic criteria Conduct Disorder, Undersocialized, Aggressive

A. A repetitive and persistent pattern of aggressive conduct in which the basic rights of others are violated, as manifested by either of the following:
   (1) physical violence against persons or property (not to defend someone else or oneself) e.g., vandalism, rape, breaking and entering, fire-setting, mugging, assault
   (2) thefts outside the home involving confrontation with the victim (e.g., extortion, purse-snatching, armed robbery)
B. Failure to establish a normal degree of affection, empathy, or bond with others as evidenced by *no more than* one of the following indications of social attachment:
   (1) has one or more peer-group friendships that have lasted over six months
   (2) extends himself or herself for others even when no immediate advantage is likely
   (3) apparently feels guilt or remorse when such a reaction is appropriate (not just when caught or in difficulty)
   (4) avoids blaming or informing on companions
   (5) shares concern for the welfare of friends or companions . . .

Diagnostic criteria Conduct Disorder, Undersocialized, Nonaggressive

A. A repetitive and persistent pattern of nonaggressive conduct in which either the basic rights of others or major age-appropriate societal norms or rules are violated, as manifested by any of the following:
   (1) chronic violations of a variety of important rules (that are reasonable and age-appropriate for the child) at home or at school (e.g., persistent truancy, substance abuse)
   (2) repeated running away from home overnight
   (3) persistent serious lying in and out of the home
   (4) stealing not involving confrontation with a victim . . .
B. [Same as B. Conduct Disorder, Undersocialized, Aggressive]

Diagnostic criteria Conduct Disorder, Socialized, Aggressive

A. [Same as A. Conduct Disorder, Undersocialized, Aggressive]
B. Evidence of social attachment to others as indicated by at least two of the following behavior patterns: [Same as the five conditions under B. Conduct Disorder, Undersocialized, Aggressive]

Diagnostic criteria Conduct Disorder, Socialized, Nonaggressive

A. [Same as A. Conduct Disorder, Undersocialized, Nonaggressive]
B. [Same as B. Conduct Disorder, Socialized, Aggressive]

Anxiety Disorders

Diagnostic criteria Separation Anxiety Disorder

A. Excessive anxiety concerning separation from those to whom the child is attached, as manifested by at least three of the following:
   (1) unrealistic worry about possible harm befalling major attachment figures or fear that they will leave and not return
   (2) unrealistic worry that an untoward calamitous event will separate the child from a major attachment figure, e.g., the child will be lost, kidnapped, killed, or be the victim of an accident
   (3) persistent reluctance or refusal to go to school in order to stay with major attachment figures or at home
   (4) persistent reluctance or refusal to go to sleep without being next to a major attachment figure or to go to sleep away from home
   (5) persistent avoidance of being alone in the home and emotional upset if unable to follow the major attachment figure around the home
   (6) repeated nightmares involving theme of separation
   (7) complaints of physical symptoms on school days, e.g., stomachaches, headaches, nausea, vomiting
   (8) signs of excessive distress upon separation, or when anticipating separation, from major attachment figures, e.g., temper tantrums or crying, pleading with parents not to leave (for children below the age of six, the distress must be of panic proportions)
   (9) social withdrawal, apathy, sadness, or difficulty concentrating on work or play when not with a major attachment figure . . .

Diagnostic criteria Avoidant Disorder of Childhood or Adolescence

A. Persistent and excessive shrinking from contact with strangers.
B. Desire for affection and acceptance, and generally warm and satisfying relations with family members and other familiar figures.
C. Avoidant behavior sufficiently severe to interfere with social functioning in peer relationships . . .

Diagnostic criteria Overanxious Disorder

A. The predominant disturbance is generalized and persistent anxiety or worry (not related to concerns about separation), as manifested by at least four of the following:
   (1) unrealistic worry about future events

(2) preoccupation with the appropriateness of the individual's behavior in the past
(3) overconcern about competence in a variety of areas, e.g., academic, athletic, social
(4) excessive need for reassurance about a variety of worries
(5) somatic complaints, such as headaches or stomachaches, for which no physical basis can be established
(6) marked self-consciousness or susceptibility to embarrassment or humiliation
(7) marked feelings of tension or inability to relax . . .

Other Disorders

Diagnostic criteria Oppositional Disorder

A. Onset after 3 years of age and before age 18.
B. A pattern for at least six months, of disobedient, negativistic, and provocative opposition to authority figures, as manifested by at least two of the following symptoms:
    (1) violations of minor rules
    (2) temper tantrums
    (3) argumentativeness
    (4) provocative behavior
    (5) stubbornness . . .

Diagnostic criteria Identity Disorder

A. Severe subjective distress regarding uncertainty about a variety of issues relating to identity, including three or more of the following:
    (1) long-term goals
    (2) career choice
    (3) friendship patterns
    (4) sexual orientation and behavior
    (5) religious identification
    (6) moral value systems
    (7) group loyalties
B. Impairment in social or occupational (including academic) functioning as a result of the symptoms in A . . .

Pervasive Developmental Disorders

Diagnostic criteria Infantile Autism

A. Onset before 30 months of age.
B. Pervasive lack of responsiveness to other people (autism).
C. Gross deficits in language development.
D. If speech is present, peculiar speech patterns such as immediate and delayed echolalia, metaphorical language, pronominal reversal.
E. Bizarre responses to various aspects of the environment, e.g., resistance to change, peculiar interest in or attachments to animate or inanimate objects.
F. Absence of delusions, hallucinations, loosening of associations, and incoherence as in Schizophrenia . . .

Diagnostic criteria Childhood Onset Pervasive Developmental Disorder

A. Gross and sustained impairment in social relationships, e.g., lack of appropriate affective responsivity, inappropriate clinging, asociality, lack of empathy.

B. At least three of the following:

(1) sudden excessive anxiety manifested by such symptoms as free-floating anxiety, catastrophic reactions to everyday occurrence, inability to be consoled when upset, unexplained panic attacks

(2) constricted or inappropriate affect, including lack of appropriate fear reactions, unexplained rage reactions, and extreme mood lability

(3) resistance to change in the environment (e.g., upset if dinner time is changed), or insistence on doing things in the same manner every time (e.g., putting on clothes always in the same order)

(4) oddities of motor movement, such as peculiar posturing, peculiar hand or finger movements, or walking on tiptoe

(5) abnormalities of speech, such as questionlike melody, monotonous voice

(6) hyper- or hypo-sensitivity to sensory stimuli, e.g., hyperacusis

(7) self-mutilation, e.g., biting or hitting self, head banging

C. Onset of full syndrome after 30 months of age and before 12 years of age.

D. Absence of delusions, hallucinations, incoherence, or marked loosening of associations . . .

Noticeably, DSM-III does not contain childhood or adolescence criteria for withdrawal. This severe behavior manifestation is implicitly included under "Pervasive Developmental Disorders" and directly identified in other sections of the manual, specifically "Adjustment Disorder with Withdrawal" (DSM-III, 1980, p. 302). It is necessary to point out this omission because social withdrawal is considered to be a pervasive problem that is evidenced by many disturbed students.

Conduct disorders constitute a major portion of the mental disorders of childhood and adolescence. Four categories of conduct disorders are organized according to whether or not aggression and socialization are evident. In general, DSM-III defines aggression as a violent confrontation with other people, whereas nonaggression is characterized by norm or rule violations. Similarly, socialization refers to the existence of emotional bonds or social attachments between the student and other people, whereas the undersocialized student lacks these bonds or attachments. One could make the case that undersocialized students are, in fact, withdrawn and that nonaggression is the equivalent to hyperactive or impulsive behavior (attention deficit disorder).

The separate diagnostic criteria in DSM-III are not a series of totally unrelated mental disorders, but can be organized along a continuum of severity. For this purpose, DSM-III contains several "decision trees for differential diagnosis" as an aid to understanding the hierarchical structure of the classification system. One of the trees (Figure 1) deals specifically with the relationship between mental disorders and academic or learning disorders.

Note that the listing of mental disorders along the left-hand margin of Figure 1 implies a degree of severity in descending order from the top (neurological disorder) to the bottom (identity disorder). If the student shows evidence of "demonstrable signs of focal CNS [central nervous system] disease," then the clinician may tentatively conclude that there is a neurological disorder. If there is no evidence of CNS disease, then the clinician proceeds to the next step, that is, "subaverage intellectual and adaptive functioning." If this step is answered "yes," then the tentative diagnosis would be mental retardation; if "no," then the clinician would proceed to the next step and so on until the appropriate diagnosis was determined.

Even though DSM-III is relatively explicit regarding the diagnostic criteria for childhood and adolescent mental disorders, the probable causes and appropriate treatments are either vague or not specific. In fact, probable causes are only alluded to in terms of the predisposing factors and familial conditions that accompany each identified disorder. DSM-III defines predisposing factors as childhood and adolescent characteristics that precede the actual demonstration of the specific disorder. Familial patterns refer to "whether the disorder is more common among biologically related family members than in the general population" (DSM-III, 1980, p. 32). The emphasis on biological relationship therefore minimizes the effect of the environmental interaction within the family constellation. Table 1 summarizes the predisposing factors and familial patterns associated with each disorder. As a matter of convenience the prevalence and sex ratio (male:female) are included.

An obvious implication of the information contained in Table 1 is that the causes of childhood and adolescent mental disorders are generally unknown ("no information") or that there is only a correlation with predisposing and familial factors. Those causes that are suggested include biophysical (attention deficit and pervasive developmental disorder), psychodynamic (separation anxiety), and a mixture of psychodynamic and behavioral (conduct disorder and overanxious) conditions. It seems therefore that DSM-III makes no substantial contribution toward identifying the causes of mental disorders.

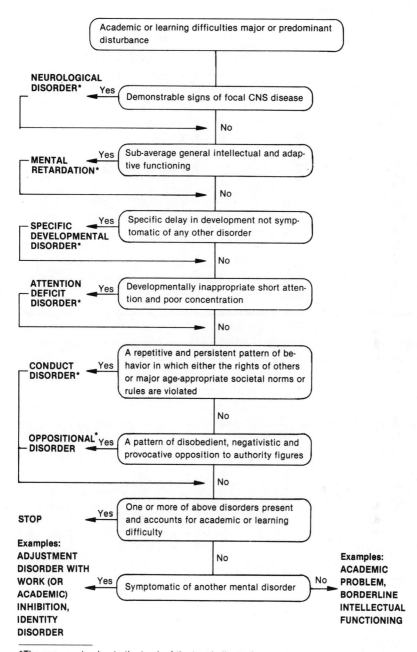

Academic or learning difficulties major or predominant disturbance

NEUROLOGICAL DISORDER* Yes ← Demonstrable signs of focal CNS disease

No →

MENTAL RETARDATION* Yes ← Sub-average general intellectual and adaptive functioning

No →

SPECIFIC DEVELOPMENTAL DISORDER* Yes ← Specific delay in development not symptomatic of any other disorder

No →

ATTENTION DEFICIT DISORDER* Yes ← Developmentally inappropriate short attention and poor concentration

No →

CONDUCT DISORDER* Yes ← A repetitive and persistent pattern of behavior in which either the rights of others or major age-appropriate societal norms or rules are violated

No →

OPPOSITIONAL* DISORDER Yes ← A pattern of disobedient, negativistic and provocative opposition to authority figures

No →

STOP Yes ← One or more of above disorders present and accounts for academic or learning difficulty

No

Examples: **ADJUSTMENT DISORDER WITH WORK (OR ACADEMIC) INHIBITION, IDENTITY DISORDER** Yes ← Symptomatic of another mental disorder → No Examples: **ACADEMIC PROBLEM, BORDERLINE INTELLECTUAL FUNCTIONING**

*The arrows returning to the trunk of the tree indicate the possibility of multiple diagnoses.

Figure 1. Differential diagnosis of academic or learning difficulties. Reprinted with permission from the American Psychiatric Association, *Diagnostic and statistical manual of mental disorders,* third edition (DSM-III). Washington, D.C.: American Psychiatric Association, 1980.

Table 1. Predisposing factors and familial patterns associated with childhood and adolescent disorders (including prevalence and sex ratio)

Mental disorder	Predisposing factors	Familial patterns[a]	Prevalence	Ratio (M:F)
Attention deficit	Mental retardation Epilepsy Neurological disorders	Intrafamily[a]	Up to 3%	10:1
Conduct disorder	Parental rejection Inconsistent management Harsh discipline Shifting caretakers Large family size Father absent	Parents with: antisocial personality alcohol dependence	Common	4:1 to 12:1
Separation anxiety	After some life stress (e.g., death, illness, moving)	Intrafamily	Common	1:1
Avoidant disorder	No information	No information	Uncommon	Unknown
Overanxious	Eldest children Small families Upper socioeconomic strata Demanding parents	No information	Common	3:1
Schizoid	No information	No information	Rare	3:1
Oppositional	No information	No information	Unknown	Unknown
Identity disorder	No information	No information	Unknown	Unknown
Pervasive developmental disorder	Maternal rubella Phenylketonuria Encephalitis Meningitis	Intrafamily	0.003%	3:1

Adapted from DSM-III, 1980.

[a] Intrafamily means more common within the family unit than in the general population.

The prevalence and sex ratio data presented in Table 1 also require comment. Interestingly, several disorders are described as common occurrences particularly among boys. This picture presented by DSM-III is consistent with the incidence of disturbance identified by teachers. However, the high frequency occurrence of some disorders (e.g., conduct problems among boys) is a reason to suspect the existence of a mental disorder. From a statistical perspective, common behaviors are a measure of normality, not mental disorder. Therefore, it may be that normal developmental behaviors are being interpreted as signs or symptoms of disturbance.

Another limitation of DSM-III is the absence of appropriate treatment recommendations. This failure to specify treatment seems to be a function of the different theoretical orientations represented within the psychiatric profession. The introduction section of DSM-III states that the diagnosis of a specific mental disorder represents the initial step in formulating a treatment plan. The treatment plan itself depends on the orientation of the professional implementing the treatment. In this context DSM-III provides four examples of clinical orientations that include psychodynamic, behavioral, family, and somatic (physiological) therapy. Thus, DSM-III begs the question of treatment by referring to professionals with different theoretical orientations.

DSM-III is a classification system that emphasizes the characteristics of mental disorders in the form of diagnostic criteria. Given the wide variety of mental disorders, potential causes, and treatment approaches, it is not surprising that DSM-III is limited to characteristics. This is the case because DSM-III does not constitute a single classification model, but a potpourri of psychological and behavioral deviations that reflect a number of theories of causality and treatment. As a classification system, however, DSM-III does represent clearly defined criteria that are generally accepted as the standard by which mental disorders are classified.

Group for the Advancement of Psychiatry

The GAP system is remarkably consistent with the DSM-II categories; therefore it will not be discussed in detail. The GAP system consists of 10 categories of children's disorders that are ordered from minimal to severe conditions (Knopf, 1979).

1. Healthy Responses
    This category assesses the positive strengths of the child and tries to avoid the diagnosis of healthy states by the exclusion of pathology. The criteria for assessment are the intellectual, social, emotional, personal, adaptive, and psychosocial functioning of the child in relation to developmental and situational crises.

2. Reactive Disorders
    This category is based on disorders in which behavior and/or
    symptoms are the result of situational factors. These disturbances
    must be of a pathological degree so as to distinguish them from
    the healthy responses to a situational crisis.
3. Developmental Disorders
    These are disorders in personality development that may be be-
    yond the range of normal variation in that they occur at a time,
    in a sequence, or in a degree not expected for a given age level
    or stage in development.
4. Psychoneurotic Disorders
    These disorders are based on unconscious conflicts over the han-
    dling of sexual and aggressive impulses that remain active and
    unresolved, though removed from awareness by the mechanism
    of repression. Marked personality disorganization or decompen-
    sation, or the gross disturbance of reality testing, is not seen.
    Because of their internalized character, these disorders tend to-
    ward chronicity, with a self-perpetuating or repetitive nature.
    Subcategories are based on specific syndromes.
5. Personality Disorders
    These disorders are characterized by chronic or fixed pathological
    trends, representing traits that have become ingrained in the per-
    sonality structure. In most but not all such disorders, these trends
    or traits are not perceived by the child as a source of intrapsychic
    distress or anxiety. In making this classification, the total per-
    sonality picture must be considered and not just the presence of
    a single behavior or symptom.
6. Psychotic Disorders
    These disorders are characterized by marked, pervasive devia-
    tions from the behavior that is expected for the child's age. They
    are revealed in severe and continued impairment of emotional
    relationships with persons; loss of speech or failure in its devel-
    opment; disturbances in sensory perception; bizarre or stereo-
    typed behavior and motility patterns; marked resistance to change
    in environment of routine; outbursts of intense and unpredictable
    panic; absence of a sense of personal identity; and blunted, un-
    even, or fragmented intellectual development. Major categories
    are based on the developmental period with subcategories in each
    period for the listing of a specific syndrome, if known.
7. Psychophysiological Disorders
    These disorders are characterized by a significant interaction be-
    tween somatic and psychological components. They may be pre-
    cipitated and perpetuated by psychological or social stimuli of

stressful nature. These disorders ordinarily involve those organ systems innervated by the autonomic nervous system.

8. Brain Syndromes

    These disorders are characterized by impairment of orientation, judgment, discrimination, learning, memory, and other cognitive functions, as well as by frequent labile affect. They are basicially caused by diffuse impairment of brain tissue function. Personality disturbances of a psychotic, neurotic, or behavioral nature also may be present.

9. Mental Retardation

10. Other Disorders

    This category is for disorders that cannot be classified by the above definitions or for disorders to be described in the future (abridged from Group for the Advancement of Psychiatry, 1968).

Most of the 10 mental disorder classification categories include clinical subtypes that parallel DSM-II. However, two GAP categories are different from most classification systems. These categories, Healthy Responses and Developmental Deviations, were included as a precaution against the unnecessary labeling of children and adolescents as mentally disordered. According to Knopf (1979), the category of Health Responses, in particular, "minimize[s] the practice of clinicians to exaggerate minor childhood problems into pathological ones for classification purposes" (p. 52). Similarly, Developmental Deviations provides a category for children and adolescents whose maturational rate or psychological development does not precisely follow a stringent pattern of normal development, but whose deviation is only marginal. With the common prevalence of several disorders contained in DSM-III it is suspected that many of these students could be classified as demonstrating Developmental Deviations according to the GAP classification system.

Both the APA (DSM-II and DSM-III) and GAP systems are clinical approaches to the classification of disturbed students. The systems emphasize the behavioral and psychological characteristics of students who may be diagnosed according to the criteria of several categories of mental disorders. Neither system has effectively addressed the issues of cause or treatment. Despite these limitations, the APA, in particular, and GAP systems are widely recognized and clinically accepted standards by which mental disorders are classified.

Educators' Systems

It is somewhat misleading to say that educators have a classification system of disturbance as such. Instead, a number of educators (e.g.,

Morse, Cutler, & Fink, 1964; Quay & Peterson, 1979) have attempted to classify disturbance by means of a dimensional approach. Dimensions, according to Kauffman (1977), are syndromes or clusters of highly intercorrelated behaviors. Other educators (e.g., Gropper et al., 1968) ignored the dimensional approach and have developed a system for classifying the seriousness of behaviors according to educational criteria.

An early comprehensive study of educational programs for the disturbed (Morse, Cutler, & Fink, 1964) attempted to classify students according to a psychoeducational classification system. This system, which was deeply rooted in psychiatric terminology, included five categories of disturbance.

1. *Neurotic*
   (a) Internalizing (depression, withdrawal, obsessions, phobias, psychophysiological reactions, etc.)
   (b) Externalizing (acting out, counteraggression, negative oppositional attitude, etc.)
2. *Encephalopathic*
   (a) Motor involvement (driven-ness, emotional instability, overreaction to stimulation, perseveration, etc.)
   (b) Language symbolization involvement (dyslexia and related learning problems, orientation deficiency, symbolization difficulty, etc.)
   (c) Convulsive disorders
3. *Schizophrenic*
   (a) Relatively intact intellectual functioning (verbal communication present, accessible to relationships, etc.)
   (b) With retarded intellectual functioning (mutism, marked withdrawal, autism, inaccessibility, etc.)
4. *Primitive-Neglected*
   Relationship capacity relatively intact, but skills and values impaired with resultant behavior problems
5. *Affectionless Personality*
   Capacity for depth relationships severely impaired
(R. D. Rabinovitch, 1963, in Morse, Cutler, & Fink, 1964, pp. 39–40)

Morse, Cutler, and Fink found it difficult to assign students to the different categories because of the lack of creditable diagnostic information and because the information that was available indicated that students could be classified in two or more of the categories. In the end more than half of the students fell into the general neurotic classification. "The largest single group was made up of acting out neurotic boys, a syndrome which appears significantly less often among girls" (pp. 40–41).

The fact that the early educational classification systems relied upon psychiatric data and terminology accentuated the need for a school-based system. In response to this educational need, Gropper et al. (1968) developed a procedure for classifying school-related problem behaviors. This procedure was based on the assumption that teachers could not effectively manage or educate disturbed students unless they could accurately recognize the existence of problem or disturbed behaviors. However, the Gropper et al. system does not classify disturbance according to specific behaviors, but classifies any behavior according to three levels of seriousness: normal, problem, or referable. To assist teachers in judging the level of seriousness, 14 educationally relevant descriptive criteria (e.g., intensity, frequency, duration) were formulated for classifying the behavior of students (Table 2).

The *normal* level refers to problems meeting normal criteria. Their frequency, intensity, duration, potential contagion effects, etc., describe situations in which a generally well-adjusted child can sometimes exhibit a problem. They are problems inherent in being at a given age level, in being exposed to new learning tasks or new or threatening situations. The responses tend to be temporary, short-lived, and generally non-damaging. At the *problem* level, their effects are more disruptive to the child, longer lasting, damaging to others, etc. These are the marks of a child who is maladjusted. At both the *normal* and *problem* levels, the severity of problems is insufficient to warrant referral for professional help. The teacher can handle problems at both levels but is likely to devote more time to those at the *problem* level. Problems that reach the *referable* level (by definition) . . . warrant attention by mental health specialists. The criteria aid the teacher to recognize when problems reach this level (Gropper et al., 1968, pp. 480, 482).

During the decade of the 1970s other educational classification systems began to appear in the educational literature. The most notable of these new systems is the behavioral dimension classification system developed by Quay and Peterson (1979). This system utilizes observational and statistical procedures to classify a constellation or syndrome of behaviors. "First, empirical evidence is obtained showing that the dimension exists as an observable constellation of behavior. Second . . . the objective nature of most of the constituent behaviors permits considerable reliability of judgment about the degree to which the child manifests the dimension" (Quay, 1972, p. 7).

Based upon observational and statistical studies of students' behaviors, four behavioral dimensions were identified (Quay, 1972):

1. Conduct problem. "a pattern involving aggressive behavior, both verbal and physical, associated with poor interpersonal relationships with both adults and peers" (p. 9).
2. Personality problem. "implies withdrawal instead of attack . . . [including] such traits as feelings of distress, fear, anxiety, physical complaints, and open and expressed unhappiness" (p. 11).

Table 2. Summary of criteria for classifying problem behavior

Description of criteria	Normal	Problem	Referable
A. *Intensity* How disruptive of the child's other activities is the problem behavior?	Non-disruptive. Behavior does *not* interfere with the child's other activities	Disruptive. Behavior interferes with the child's other activities	Extremely Disruptive. Behavior completely disrupts child's other activities
B. *Appropriateness* Is the behavior a reasonable response to the situation?	Reasonable. Response is acceptable or expected for the situation	Inappropriate. Response is undesirable for the situation	Excessive. Response is out of proportion to the situation
C. *Duration* How long does the behavior episode last?	Short-lived. Episode lasts only a short time (short time within a class period)	Moderately long. Episode extends over a longer period (some carryover from one class to the next)	Long-lasting. Episodes are long-lasting (greater part of a day)
D. *Frequency* How often does the behavior occur?	Infrequent. Behavior usually is not repeated (rarely repeated in a day; rarely repeated on other days)	Frequent. Behavior is repeated (may be repeated several times a day; may be repeated on several days)	Habitual. Behavior happens all the time (repeated often during day; repeated on many days)
E. *Specificity/ generality* In how many types of situations does the behavior occur?	Occurs in Specific Situation. Behavior occurs in specific type of situation	Occurs in Several Situations. Behavior occurs in more than one type of situation	Occurs in Many Situations. Behavior occurs in many types of situations
F. *Manageability* How easily does the behavior respond to management efforts?	Easily Managed. Responds readily to management efforts	Difficult to Manage. Inconsistent or slow response to management efforts	Cannot Be Managed. Does not respond to management efforts
G. *Assessability of circumstances* How easily can the circumstances that produced the behavior be identified?	Easily Assessed. Easy to identify situation or condition producing behavior	Difficult to Assess. Situation or condition producing behavior difficult to identify	Cannot Be Assessed. Cannot identify situation or condition producing behavior

(Continued)

Table 2. (*Continued*)

Description of Criteria	Normal	Problem	Referable
H. Comparison with maturity level of class How close to the norm of the class is the problem behavior?	No Deviation From Level of Class. Behavior is par for the group	Below Level of Class. Behavior is below the group level	Considerably Below Level of Class. Behavior is considerably below the group level
I. Number of problem behaviors exhibited	Rarely more than one	Usually more than one	Usually many and varied
J. Acceptance by peers Does the child have difficulty being accepted by peers?	Accepted. Is accepted by peers	Has Difficulty Getting Along. May have difficulty with particular individuals	Not Accepted. Unaccepted by group
K. Recovery time How quickly is the situation leading to the episode forgotten?	Rapid. Gets over episode quickly	Slow. Gets over episode more slowly	Delayed. Does not get over episode
L. Contagion 1. Does the behavior disrupt the activities of others? 2. Do others copy the problem behavior?	Little or No Effect on Others. Behavior does not disturb or does not serve as a model for others	Considerable Effect on Others. Behavior disturbs immediate neighbors or neighbors copy behavior	Excessive Effect on Others. Behavior disturbs whole class or whole class copies behavior
M. Degree of contact with reality Does the behavior represent a loss of contact with reality?	No Confusion Between Real/ Unreal.	Some Confusion Between Real/ Unreal.	Confuses Real/ Unreal.
N. Response to learning opportunites How readily does the child respond when learning opportunities are provided?	Responds Positively to Enrichment/Remedial Work.	Responds Slowly or Weakly to Enrichment/ Remedial Work.	Does Not Respond to Enrichment/Remedial Work.

Reprinted with permission from Gropper, G. L., Kress, G. C., Hughes, R. and Pekich, J., Training teachers to recognize and manage social and emotional problems in the classroom. *Journal of Teacher Education*, 1968, *19*, 477–485.

3. Inadequacy/immaturity. "this pattern seems to represent a persistence of . . . behaviors when they are inappropriate to the chronological age of the child . . ." (p. 13).
4. Socialized delinquent. "involves environmental and social factors (e.g., gang activities, delinquent companions) and is comprised of behaviors generally not manifest in institutional settings" (p. 15).

Although Quay and Peterson (1979) provide no indication of severity among the categories, the frequency with which the four dimensions occur is presented in descending order. In terms of sex, boys are more often identified as having conduct problems, whereas girls are more apt to be classified as having personality problems. Relatively few data have emerged that will permit educators to make statements or predictions about the cause, treatment, school performance, or future behavior of students classified according to the four dimensions. According to Quay (1972), these limitations of the dimension approach must be answered in three steps.

> The first step must be to demonstrate that the category of dimension of disorder actually exists . . . The second step is to demonstrate that children can reliably be placed somewhere on the continuum of characteristics defining one or more of the patterns . . . Finally, the relationships between the patterns of deviant behavior and their psychological antecedents and consequences must be demonstrated (p. 2).

Some progress has been made in the development of an educationally relevant classification of disturbance. This progress has been limited, however, to the first two steps suggested by Quay (1972). The third step, that of specifying the "psychological antecedents and consequences" has evaded any general conclusions, probably because of the individualistic and variable nature of the human organism. "Despite the progress described, diagnostic classification of emotional disturbance . . . in children remains a thicket of thorny problems" (Hobbs, 1975, p. 57).

This section has presented a limited number of classification systems that are used to categorize students according to the characteristics of disturbance. Although it is basically agreed that classification systems should do more than simply label students, all of the systems discussed are limited to this single objective. Even in terms of this restricted function, however, numerous critics have questioned the efficiency, effectiveness, and humanitarianism of classification systems in general. After discussion of some of these criticisms or problems, subsequent chapters cover student developmental behaviors and assessment procedures that form integral parts of the classification of disturbance.

PROBLEMS OF CLASSIFICATION SYSTEMS

The construction and repeated revision of the numerous classification systems indicate that neither psychiatrists nor educators have developed "the" system for categorizing human psychological and behavioral conditions. Years of experience with the classification of disturbance have indicated to most professionals that the current systems have not been perfected and, in all probability, may never achieve the state of perfection that is required. The reasons for this imperfection include a number of problems that are associated with human classification systems and even definitions in general.

The Stigmatizing Problem

From a humanitarian viewpoint, the labeling of students typically has a stigmatizing effect. The employment of a classification system represents the initial process in the labeling of students which must be regarded as having potentially grave consequences. Labels used in education, especially those that are negatively valued, such as emotionally disturbed, behaviorally disordered, and mentally retarded, may have impact well beyond the school years into adult life, causing unnecessary and senseless pain, frustration, and dehumanization. At the very least, labels categorizing students during their school-age years may have a negative effect on the way peers and teachers react, the types of programs and activities that are available, and the extent to which educational and personal goals may be achieved. Consequently, many professional educators have "grown increasingly more concerned with the random labeling (of students) . . . and the lack of educational relevance of such labels" (Knoblock et al., 1974, p. 3).

The Whole Student Problem

Classification systems focus on a limited number of negatively valued characteristics, rather than on the whole student. "What must be emphasized is that no classification system can possibly take account of *all* the attributes of a human individual—the function of classification systems is simply to provide explicit principles for grouping individuals with respect to *some* of their attributes that are related in important ways to the goals of the classifier . . ." (Achenbach, 1974, p. 62). The classification of a student as disturbed therefore fails to recognize those characteristics that are normal, desired, or positive. Yet the label is applied to the whole student, and this tends to create the conditions that identify everything about the student as disturbed.

The Theoretical Problem

Chapter 2 discussed five basic theories that explain the causes of disturbance among students. However, these theories go beyond causality and are translated into student characteristics, assessment, and programming. Seldom does a major theoretical proponent (e.g., Sigmund Freud or B. F. Skinner) consider disturbance outside of his or her area of expertise. Consequently, most classification systems represent only one theoretical position, as does the one developed by Quay and Peterson (1979), or they represent a conglomerate of theoretical positions, as does the APA system, that are difficult for a variety of professionals with different theoretical backgrounds to interpret consistently. "Perhaps the poorest method of developing a classification system with logical integrity is through a broadly represented professional committee. History has shown that the products of such committees represent a set of compromises reminiscent of platform statements from smoke-filled caucus rooms" (Hobbs, 1975, pp. 14–15).

The Practitioner Problem

The problem inherent in one's professional role is similar to the theoretical problem. Specifically, practitioners tend to view disturbance from a narrow perspective that relates to one's own responsibility, training, and expectation. Teachers and psychologists, for example, tend to focus on different aspects of the behavior of students when making diagnostic decisions. Whereas teachers, who work with large groups, tend to identify acting-out behavior, psychologists, who usually work on a one-to-one basis, are more apt to consider withdrawn behavior as a symptom of disturbance. In short, the category or subcategory classification of disturbance is frequently a reflection of the practitioner's role, rather than of the characteristics of the student. For example, a student who is aggressive, disobedient, impulsive, and from a lower socioeconomic background may receive various diagnostic labels from various practitioners (Table 3). This diagnostic mosaic is not limited to marginally disturbed students. For example, Carl Fenichel (1966) related the diagnostic sequence of a seriously disturbed student who was labeled by different practitioners as autistic, schizophrenic, brain-damaged, mentally retarded, and aphasic.

The Adult Orientation Problem

Many classification systems, particularly that of the APA, are based on the characteristics of mental disorders as they occur among adults.

Table 3. Practioners' potential diagnostic labels for
the same student

Discipline	Potential diagnostic label
Pediatrics	Brain injury
	Central nervous system disorder
	Minimal brain dysfunction
Psychiatry	Conduct disorder
	Personality disorder
	Transient situational disturbance
	Behavior disordered
Psychology	Emotionally disturbed
	Psychoneurosis
	Overanxious
Sociology	Culturally deprived
	Socially maladjusted
	Disadvantaged
Judiciary	Delinquent
Education	Adjustment problem
	Conduct problem
	Aggressive
	Behaviorally disordered

Although the APA has moved in the direction of nonadult disorders, the fact remains that the terminology, data, prognosis, and so forth have evolved from the study of adults. Therefore, it has not been decided whether many of the mental disorders attributed to adults can be validly attributed to children and adolescents (Achenbach, 1974).

The Developmental Problem

As a general rule, the diagnostic criteria contained in the classification systems represent a still picture of behavior. Very little emphasis is placed on the behavioral events before or after the picture. To compound this static condition, virtually no data are provided that would enable the diagnostician to make a decision based on normal developmental behavior. For example, what is the normal level of motor activity for a 9-year-old? How often do children and adolescents get into fights? Even though DSM-III states that teacher reports are necessary in the diagnosis of an attention deficit disorder "because of greater familiarity with age-appropriate norms," it is assumed that all teachers possess an identical set of accurate developmental norms for all students, whether black or white, rich or poor, male or female, retarded or gifted, throughout the developmental years. Obviously, this is not the case. Therefore, each of the classification systems intuitively depends upon each diagnostician applying his or her own set of idiosyncratic developmental guidelines.

The Statistical Problem

The validity and reliability of any classification system ultimately determine its effectiveness as a diagnostic tool. According to Kauffman (1977), "the extent to which a child or his behavior receives the same classification (a) over a span of time, (b) under different conditions, and (c) with different classifiers using the same methods (i.e., reliability of a classification system) and the degree to which a child's classification by one method corresponds to measurement and prediction of his behavior using other techniques or is predictable from theoretical constructs (i.e., validity of a classification system) are crucial considerations in the evaluation of any categorization schema" (p. 25). In this regard, DSM-II has not achieved an acceptable degree of reliability or validity. Zubin (1967), for example, found that the agreement between two clinicians categorizing the same psychiatric patients was as low as 6 percent, meaning that they agree on the same diagnostic label in only 6 of 100 patients. The more severe the problem, the greater the agreement; the less severe the problem, the greater the disagreement. It should be noted that most of the disturbed students in local education programs would constitute less severe cases and therefore would typify the statistical problems inherent in classification systems. Because of its recent publication, the statistical data have not been compiled on DSM-III (1980).

Classification systems that utilize behaviors, such as the Quay and Peterson (1979) system, rather than inferences about psychological conditions, clearly have an advantage with regard to reliability and validity. However, the behavioral systems suffer from a more limited perspective of disturbance. In fact, it is felt that the behavioral systems represent a statistical diagnosis that is related to disturbance only by definition.

SUMMARY

The classification of behavior into distinguishing categories has existed throughout the recorded history of mankind. It was not until this century, however, that there has been a concentrated effort to classify a broad range of different mental disorders. Psychiatrists have assumed the leadership for classifying mental disorders and have developed the most widely recognized standards (e.g., DSM-III). Because of the clinical implications and limitations of the psychiatric systems, educational classification systems have begun to evolve. These educational classification systems emphasize the diagnosis of school-related behaviors, thus requiring a greater degree of information from teachers.

All classification systems that categorize human behaviors suffer from a number of problems. Both the psychiatric and the educational systems are limited to the classification of student characteristics; neither effectively addresses the causes or treatments of disturbance. In addition, labels that are applied to students are stigmatizing; are based on a limited amount of information; suffer from adult, theoretical, and practioners' biases; and tend to be statistically unreliable and invalid. Consequently, classification systems may be described as a lesser of two evils, for although the current systems are clearly imperfect, most psychiatrists, educators, and others are unwilling to accept a purely personal, idiosyncratic approach to the classification of disturbance.

5
Developmental Behaviors

"What is cute at two, is borderline at six, and delinquent at 12." This axiom implies that adult reactions to behaviors will depend upon the age of the child. What is normal at one age may not be so at another age. For example, adults may be somewhat amused if a 2-year-old pulls his or her pants down while in the yard, or says "pee-pee" in the presence of neighbors, or takes another child's toy. The same behaviors demonstrated by a 6-year-old, however, are generally annoying to adults and will not be tolerated from a 12-year-old. These different adult reactions to the same behaviors convey the belief that behaviors are expected to change as the child grows older (Herbert, 1974).

In education, psychiatry, and psychology, a variety of child and adolescent behaviors have been used to define and classify students as disturbed. One of the critical problems with identifying specific behaviors is that the behaviors are often considered in isolation; that is, there is no frame of reference for evaluating the behaviors beyond the fact that they are not consistent with the expectations of the diagnostician, particularly the teacher. It has been stated in previous chapters that because a student does not comply with the teacher's expectation is no justifiable reason, in and of itself, to label a student disturbed. Although the definitions and classification systems assume that teachers have acquired a set of age-appropriate norms, the variability of behavioral expectations among teachers suggests that this is a faulty assumption. This critical diagnostic problem may be partially resolved if students' behaviors are evaluated from a normative, rather than an individualistic, frame of reference. The most accepted and best available normative standard is the evaluation of behaviors from a developmental perspective.

Developmental behavior refers to the normal sequential process of behavior change (Meyer, 1964). Thus, through the life span, behaviors are expected to change, and they are expected to change in ways that are biologically and environmentally determined. Changes in behaviors are not random or spontaneous, but follow a sequential and progressive pattern. According to Ilg and Ames (1960), "our observations of child behavior have led us to believe that almost any kind of behavior you can think of . . . develops by means of remarkably patterned and largely predictable stages" (p. 13).

The sequential and progressive developmental pattern is generally shared by developmental psychologists and other human growth and development specialists (Havighurst, 1980). In fact, Bloom (1964), in his study of human characteristics, summarized the results of his study with a single graphic model. Figure 1 is a representation of the relationship between the level of developmental behaviors and chronological age. In this graph the heavy single line represents the level of development for any given behavior or characteristic at any given chronological age. The broken lines represent expected or normal variance from the average. Only when behaviors are outside the broken

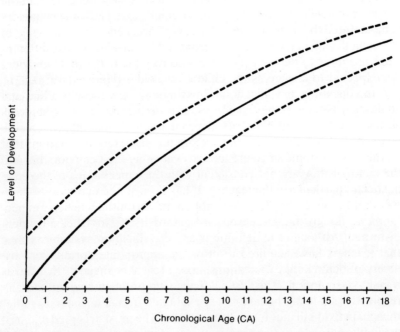

Figure 1.   The general relationship between the level of normal development and chronological age. Adapted from Bloom, 1964.

lines do they constitute abnormal or potentially disturbed behaviors. Thus students diagnosed as disturbed would be behaviorally functioning on a different developmental level from their chronological peers in the normal population. Although disturbed students would be expected to function on a lower developmental level, "different" level is stressed because some students functioning on a higher level may not be understood by teachers, and consequently they may be considered disturbed (Rich, 1978b).

This graphic model is a representation of developmental behaviors. The model is oversimplified, however, and does not totally represent the complex nature of human behavior. In order to interpret behaviors accurately according to the model, the reader should be aware of the major limitations inherent in this simplistic representation.

First, not all developmental behaviors or characteristics can be graphically plotted by means of the same line configuration as that depicted in Figure 1. The line configuration may be significantly different for different behaviors. For example, the acquisition of language would require a positively accelerated line, whereas lines representing most physical characteristics would level off during adolescence.

Second, demographic differences among students, particularly those of sex, socioeconomic status, and physical and intellectual limitations, create subgroups that often cannot be compared with the total population. For example, developmental behaviors such as dependency and hyperactivity must be plotted separately for boys and girls, and not compared with the sexes combined.

Third, the development profile in Figure 1 represents a general pattern; for individual students the pattern is not usually a smooth developmental line from infancy to adulthood. "Scientific studies of normal children have shown this general trend toward 'improvement' in behavior is not steady and uninterrupted" (Ilg & Ames, 1960, p. 16). Thus, individual students typically progress in a predictable manner, but in one that is best represented by an ascending but jagged pattern of development.

Fourth, development occurs both continuously, as represented in Figure 1, and in stages. "The apparent discontinuity in behavioral organization is basic to stage theories of development: there are times during growth when behavioral development appears to advance by means of striking changes in complex patterns of behavior" (Kohlberg, in *Dev. Psy. Today*, 1971, p. 7). Kohlberg has listed five criteria for developmental stages:

1. Change from one stage to another involves change in form, pattern, and organization of an individual's behavior—not just in the frequency and intensity of and individual's responses.

2. Each successive stage involves a new and qualitatively different organization of responses. Not only may the behavior be different and with different emphasis in each stage, but the basic rules governing the behavior differ also.

3. Change from stage to stage is inevitable; except in extremely unusual or damaging circumstances, the individual does not respond in terms of earlier modes. [This criterion has special importance for understanding disturbed behavior because many of the theories state that a disturbed student is one who has stopped on, regressed to, or is delayed in attaining a particular stage of development.]

4. The stages in an individual's development appear in a sequence that is fixed and unvarying from individual to individual. Stages are the universals of every human being's development.

5. Stages involve progress toward increasing complexity—each successive stage integrates critical formal aspects of previous stages into a more articulated organization (Kohlberg, in *Dev. Psy. Today*, 1971, p. 7).

With these limitations in mind, an example of a developmental behavior may serve to clarify the relationship between development and disturbance. In Figure 2, the levels of dependent behavior for three-fourth-grade boys, age 12, are displayed on the developmental model. In this example, dependency, or "seeking affection, acceptance, and emotional reassurance from adults" (Kagan & Moss, 1962,

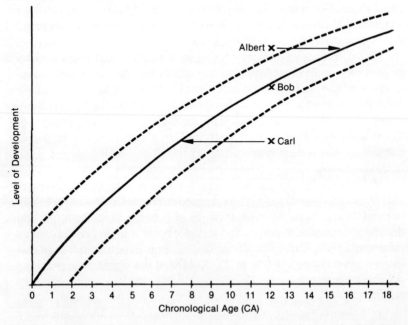

Figure 2.   Relationship between dependency and normal development for three boys.

p. 51), was based on the frequency of observed dependent behaviors. Hypothetical scores have been calculated and plotted for each boy. One boy, Bob, clearly falls within the range of the expected rate for the occurrence of dependency behaviors. The other two boys, Albert and Carl, demonstrate atypical rates of dependency behaviors. Albert's rate of dependency behavior is more like that of a boy 16 years of age, whereas Carl's dependency behaviors approximate those of a 7-year-old. Thus, Carl's level of dependency is symptomatic of a lower stage of development for his chronological age. Without knowing Carl's biological and environmental circumstances, one could speculate that Carl stopped, or fixated, at an earlier stage, or that he had achieved a higher level and then regressed to his present level of dependency development. Of the three boys, Carl is the student most likely to be referred as potentially disturbed, because he is significantly below the normal level of development for dependency. Albert, too, however, may be subjected to referral. Because Albert's dependency development is precocious, his behavior may be interpreted by teachers to be antisocial or oppositional. Thus, students functioning on a different level of development are often subject to referral and ultimate classification as disturbed, even though behavior significantly below the normal level of development is a preferable indicator of disturbance.

The remainder of this chapter focuses on two interrelated aspects of disturbance and developmental behaviors. First, several relevant developmental theories will be discussed, summarized, and translated into student behaviors that are typically considered characteristic of disturbance. Second, selected developmental behaviors suggested by the theories will be discussed and hypothetically ranked along a continuum of severity. The ultimate objective is to produce a normative listing of student developmental behaviors that can be used by teachers to evaluate the relative seriousness of behaviors considered to be symptomatic of disturbance.

DEVELOPMENTAL THEORIES

Developmental theories are concerned with the description and explanation of changes in behavior that are the result of maturation and experience through the life span, particularly during the preadult years (Kohlberg, 1975). There is not one theory, but numerous theories that describe and explain behaviors from different developmental perspectives. For example, Thomas (1979) referenced over 50 different theories covering an array of topics such as intellectual, physical, social, moral, psychological, and motivational development. Given this wide range of developmental constructs, the basic problem is selecting those that are appropriate for explaining disturbance and then integrating them so that the theories will explain disturbed behaviors when considered separately or cumulatively. Alfred Baldwin (1967) examined several developmental theories and concluded that they were not contradictory concepts. "The theories are concerned with different aspects of child development more than they are focused on different explanations of the same behavior. This fact suggests an eclectic integration of the theories provided that they can be reconciled in language" (Baldwin, 1967, pp. 597–598). Several educators (e.g., Andrews & Bartolini, 1964; Swap, 1974) have attempted to accomplish what Baldwin has suggested by synthesizing child development theories and describing behaviors that are representative of the various stages of development.

From the numerous developmental theories available, four have been selected as being the most relevant to the understanding of behaviors that are symptomatic of disturbance among students: 1) Freud's personality theory, 2) Erikson's psychosocial theory, 3) Peck and Havighurst's moral character theory, and 4) Maslow's motivational theory. A number of well known theories (e.g., Piaget's cognitive theory, Kohlberg's moral theory, and Rotter's social learning theory) are not included in this chapter. Although the omitted theories have contributed significantly to the understanding of behavior, the theories that are included more logically lend themselves to the description and classification of disturbed behaviors.

Freud's Personality Theory

Sigmund Freud is a controversial theorist, chiefly because of his early insistence on the importance of instinctual psychosexual development. Certainly some behavioral forms of disturbance may be a function of this sexuality construct (e.g., overt masturbation, sexual aggression, and exposure). However, Freud's most significant contribution to the understanding of disturbance and classroom behaviors is contained within his theory of personality.

According to Freud, the personality of an individual consists of three major systems: the id, the ego, and the superego. In the normal or mentally healthy individual these three systems function harmoniously, but "when the three systems are at odds with one another the person is said to be maladjusted" (Hall, 1954, p. 22). These three systems and their implications were introduced in Chapter 2, but they require elaboration if they are to be translated into behaviors.

Id In the first year of life the only mental function that exists is the id (Lee, 1976). The function of the id is to reduce tension, pain, and discomfort, or to experience pleasure and satisfaction. Freud summarizes this id function with the term "pleasure principle." The id-dominated personality is self-centered and is characterized as demanding, impulsive, irrational, selfish, and pleasure-seeking. "The id is not governed by laws of reason or logic, and it does not possess values, ethics or morality. It is driven by one consideration only, to obtain satisfaction for instinctual needs in accordance with the pleasure principle" (Hall, 1954, p. 26).

The id function is readily evident in an infant who is hungry or in pain. If the tension is not immediately reduced, the alternative is crying, screaming, and extensive motor behavior in the form of kicking, hand flinging, and facial movements. These behaviors are tolerated, even expected, from an infant, but if demonstrated by older children these same behaviors are considered symptomatic of disturbance. Behaviors such as hyperactivity, impulsivity, and temper tantrums are considered to be a function of the id, and thus represent the lowest level of developmental behaviors. These behaviors eventually take one of two courses: they continue or they come under the influence of the ego.

Ego As the child matures the id is out of step with reality. Therefore, the interaction between the child and the external world requires the development of a new psychological system: the ego. The ego, which is regulated by the reality principle, is necessary to prevent or postpone the discharge of energy until a satisfactory solution can be discovered. "For example, the child has to learn not to put just anything into his mouth when he is hungry. He has to learn to recognize food, and to put off eating until he has located an edible object" (Hall, 1954, p. 28).

Although the ego first emerges during the second year of life, its complete development is a rather slow process. During early childhood many id-propelled behaviors are still evident, but these are typically brought under control by the ego in later childhood. This transition from id to ego domination is particularly noticeable when children learn effective use of words rather than physical actions as a solution to satisfying needs (Achenbach, 1974). In the early school years limited hyperactivity, controlled impulsivity, and infrequent temper tantrums are an indication that the reality principle is becoming a more effective mediating process. The ego's job, however, is much more complicated than simply negotiating between the id and reality. It must also contend with the demand of a third personality system: the superego.

Superego Rather than pleasure or reality, the superego strives for the ideal or perfection. The superego develops as a result of the interaction between child and parents (or primary caretakers). In this interactive process the child assimilates parental standards regarding what is good, bad, virtuous, wicked, sinful, and so forth. "The internalization of parental authority enables the child to control his behavior in line with their wishes, and by doing so, secure their approval and avoid their displeasure. In other words, the child learns that he not only has to obey the reality principle in order to obtain pleasure and avoid pain, but that he also has to try to behave according to the moral dictates of his parents" (Hall, 1954, p. 31). Consequently, one of the primary functions of the superego is to regulate behavior in order to maintain a stable society, including that of the school.

Like the ego, the behavioral implications of the superego are complex. In terms of disturbed behaviors, however, three superego courses are likely: underdevelopment, overdevelopment, and inappropriate development. An underdeveloped superego, which may result from inconsistent parental values, is evident in the lack of guilt or remorse when the student violates critical social values. For example, the student may engage in theft, cheating, or destruction as a means of satisfying needs, but has no genuine feelings of regret or even the desire to alter the behavior. An overdeveloped superego may occur when parents strictly and consistently approve or disapprove of behaviors on moralistic grounds. These students are apt to have extreme feelings of guilt, shame, or doubt when they violate, or think they may violate, even minor rules or expectations. For example, the student who misses one test answer or accidentally speaks without permission may be so plagued by guilt that he or she goes into a shell of humiliation, failure, or withdrawal. Last, the inadequately developed superego may be a function of a pluralistic cultural society. In this sense inadequate refers to cultural values of the society, particularly as they are enforced in schools. For example, respect for authority (particularly female teachers) and being on time are values enforced in school, but may not be important values within the students' primary culture. Consequently, specific behaviors cannot be listed, because different cultural values dictate a wide variety of superego-controlled behaviors.

In the mentally healthy personality the ego should control, mediate, or counteract the impulses of the id and the inhibitions of the superego. As an individual matures, the influence of the ego should approximate the developmental profile presented earlier in the chapter. However, "it should come as no surprise that the ego often fails to keep a balance between these two adversaries and the realistic demands of the external environment. The stress on the ego is often extreme, and it may respond to this stress with various *defense mechanisms*" (Mahoney, 1980, p. 79). Defense mechanisms such as those presented in Table 1 are unconscious processes that are employed by individuals to protect the ego, reduce tension, and eliminate conflict among the three systems.

Table 1. Examples of defense mechanisms

Mechanism	Description	Example
Denial	Refusing to acknowledge unpleasant aspects of reality	Denying that parents are getting a divorce
Displacement	Shifting of feelings from one item to another to which it does not belong	Dislike of a peer or of reading may be shifted to the teacher, a pet, etc.
Distortion	Distorting significant aspects of reality	Perceiving oneself as more or less popular than is warranted
Identification	Becoming like the person who threatens oneself	Acting like the teacher or parent who is punitive, aggressive, etc.
Introjection	Incorporating the demands of another person as if they were their own	The teacher demands quietness in the class so the child demands quietness in other environments
Isolation	Mental separation from others after an unpleasant experience	After a difficult experience (a fight, an exam, etc.) there is a marked blank pause or nonresponse
Rationalization	Defense against negative feelings or actions by inventing reasons	Explaining failure on an exam because someone borrowed one's textbook
Regression	Going back to earlier modes of functioning	After a negative experience the child wants to be held as an infant
Repression	Excluding thoughts or feelings from conscious awareness	"Forgetting" about an earlier failure or fight
Reaction formation	Behaving or acting in ways that are opposite to unconscious impulses	Actively supporting school rules when one unconsciously enjoys breaking rules
Sublimation	Channeling instinctual drives into socially approved activities	Expressing aggressive impulses through sports

Mechanisms, descriptions, and examples are taken from Achenbach (1974), Mahoney (1980), and A. Freud (1946).

Defense mechanisms cannot generally be translated directly into developmental behaviors. However, it is important for teachers to recognize that defense mechanisms are necessary if students are to maintain adequate mental health. Attempts to strip away defense mechanisms through moralistic or punitive actions typically serve no purpose beyond reducing the student to a lower developmental level that may result in aggression, withdrawal, or self-abuse. It is only when students use defense mechanisms consistently, even habitually, that mental health solutions should be considered.

As a final note, the reader is cautioned that there are no clear boundaries between the three hypothetical systems. The terms id, ego, and superego are simply shorthand notations that refer to substantively different personality processes that influence developmental behaviors.

Erikson's Psychosocial Theory

According to Erik Erikson, a student's personality and behavior change as a function of adaptive coping skills that are acquired at critical developmental stages. These stages represent eight individual crisis periods that occur over the life span. Each crisis must be successfully resolved before the individual can move to the next crisis stage. If the crisis is not resolved, then the individual will remain at that stage of development until it is conquered (Havighurst, 1980). "There has been a tendency here and there to turn the eight stages into a sort of rosary of achievement, a device for counting the fruits of each stage—trust, autonomy, initiative, and so forth—as though each were achieved as a permanent trait. People of this bent are apt to leave out the negative counterparts of each stage, as if the healthy personality had permanently conquered these hazards. The fact is that the healthy personality must reconquer them continuously . . ." (Erikson, 1965, p. 326).

The successful resolution of a particular crisis stage is a function of the interaction between the individual and the environment. "In acting, a person generates certain environmental consequences. The nature of these consequences is determined by the person's cultural milieu, the nature of the significant people in the environment with whom he or she interacts, the person's age, and the content of his or her actions. Thus, an individual's needs will be met at each point in development only to the extent that he or she can activate appropriate behaviors from the environment" (Lee, 1976, pp. 17–18).

Erikson's psychosocial theory was introduced in Chapter 2 as an intrapsychic theory. Both the introduction and this section limit themselves to the first five of the eight crisis stages. Since the last three crisis stages deal with adults, they are considered inappropriate in understanding the behavior of disturbed students. The first five stages, on the other hand, are concerned with childhood and adolescence.

I. *Infancy* [age 0–1]:   Trust versus Mistrust
    The first "task" of the infant is to develop "the cornerstone of a healthy personality," a basic sense of trust—in himself and in his environment. This comes from a feeling of inner goodness derived from "the mutual regulation of his receptive capacities with the maternal techniques of provision"—a quality of care that transmits a sense of trustworthiness and meaning. The danger, most acute in the second half of the first year, is that discontinuities in care may increase a natural sense of loss, as the child gradually recognizes his separateness from his mother, into a basic sense of mistrust that may last through life.

II. *Early Childhood* [age 1–3]:   Autonomy versus Shame and Doubt
    With muscular maturation the child experiments with holding on and letting go and begins to attach enormous value to his autonomous will. The danger here is the development of a deep sense of shame and doubt if he is deprived of the opportunity to learn to develop his will as he learns his "duty," and therefore learns to expect defeat in any battle of wills with those who are bigger and stronger.

III. *Play Age* [age 3–5]:   Initiative versus Guilt
    In this stage the child's imagination is greatly expanded because of his increased ability to move around freely and to communicate. It is an age of intrusive activity, avid curiosity, and consuming fantasies which lead to feelings of guilt and anxiety. It is also the stage of the establishment of conscience. If this tendency to feel guilty is "overburdened by all-too-eager adults" the child may develop a deep-seated conviction that he is essentially bad, with a resultant stifling of initiative or a conversion of his moralism to vindictiveness.

IV. *School Age* [age 5–10]:   Industry versus Inferiority
    The long period of sexual latency before puberty is the age when the child wants to learn how to do and make things with others. In learning to accept instruction and to win recognition by producing "things" he opens the way for the capacity of work enjoyment. The danger in this period is the development of a sense of inadequacy and inferiority in a child who does not receive recognition of his efforts.

V. *Adolescence:*   Identity versus Identity Diffusion
    The physiological revolution that comes with puberty—rapid body growth and sexual maturity—forces the young person to question "all sameness and continuities relied on earlier" and to "refight many of the earlier battles." The developmental task is to integrate childhood identification "with the basic biological drives, native endowment, and the opportunities offered in social roles." The danger is that of identity diffusion, temporarily unavoidable in this period of physical "take hold" or, because of youth's tendency to total commitment, in the fixation in the young person of a negative identity, a devoted attempt to become what parents, class, or community do not want him to be.[1]

---

[1] Reprinted with permission from Erikson, E. H. Youth and the life cycle. *Children,* 1960, 7, 43–49.

Erikson's theory places great emphasis on the interaction between the individual organism and the social setting. That is, the extent to which the individual can successfully resolve each crisis is largely dependent upon the coordination of psychosocial conditions that are specific to that developmental stage. One of these critical conditions includes overt behaviors. According to Erikson (1963), patterns or modes of behavior that are limited by the individual's capabilities at the time of the specific crisis may result in the negative resolution of that crisis.

The negative resolution of each stage crisis is critical to the understanding of disturbed behaviors. Developmentally, students who have not resolved an earlier stage crisis will demonstrate behaviors that are characteristic of that earlier stage. For example, an adolescent who has not successfully resolved the industry versus inferiority crisis will demonstrate behaviors that are characteristic of students of elementary age. Therefore, the exemplary adolescent would be functioning on a lower developmental level, which is characteristic of disturbance. Table 2 lists some hypothesized student behavioral indicators that are typical for each negatively resolved stage.

The behavioral indicators presented in Table 2 are grouped according to the negative resolution of Erikson's developmental stages. For example, those indicators typical of mistrust are developmentally lower or younger than the remaining indicators listed; guilt indicators are developmentally lower than inferiority and identity diffusion, but higher than mistrust and shame and doubt; identity diffusion indicators are developmentally the highest or most mature of all the indicators listed in Table 2.

Erikson's psychosocial developmental indicators are interpreted to be consistent with the behaviors that correspond to personality theory. Specifically, Freud's description of behaviors associated with id and superego functions correspond respectively with Erikson's mistrust and guilt crisis stages. The emergence of the ego also is consistent with shame and doubt indicators, whereas behaviors associated with the maturing ego seem to be progressively associated with inferiority and identify diffusion. For the adult who is mentally healthy it is suspected that ego development and higher level psychosocial stages maintain a parallel relationship. On the other hand, behaviors that are symptomatic of regression to or fixation on a lower level of personality or psychosocial development are considered to be characteristic of disturbance.

Peck and Havighurst's Moral Character Theory

This theory attempts to classify moral maturity according to a developmental sequence of descriptive terms that "represent a pattern of

Table 2.   Student behavioral indicators typical of
negatively resolved crisis stages

Negative crisis stage	Typical behavioral indicators[a]
Mistrust	Self-destructive
	Hyperactive
	Isolated
	Physically rigid
	Mute
Shame and doubt	Withdrawn
	Hypoactive
	Timid/shy
	Dependent
	"Clinger"
Guilt	Self-defacing
	Compulsive
	Ritualistic
	Anxious
	Moralistic
Inferiority	Negative (about self)
	Defensive
	Socially isolated
	Cautious
	Attentive
Identity diffusion	Cliquish
	Oppositional (toward authority)
	Conduct problem
	Indecisive
	Rule testing

[a] These behavioral indicators should be conceptualized as extreme or continuous forms since all students may demonstrate these on a temporary basis.

acts, rather consistent through time, which may be said to 'characterize' and define the human individual" (Peck & Havighurst, 1960, p. 1). On the basis of the results of an extensive research project, Peck and Havighurst identified five character types that represent successive stages of moral character development: amoral, expedient, conforming, irrational-conscientious, and rational-altruistic. The researchers also concluded that the character types normally correspond to chronological developmental periods. Table 3 depicts both the successive character types and developmental periods in descending order. Note that the successive development takes one of two forms during later childhood; the remaining character types form a linear hierarchy. "This set of character types was intended to: (1) be defined and labeled in terms of the control system the individual uses to adapt his search for satisfaction to the requirements of the social world; (2) include all the possible modes of adaptation; (3) be defined in terms of motivation (so long as it achieves behavioral expression); (4) represent both op-

Table 3.   Descending scale of character types correlated with developmental periods

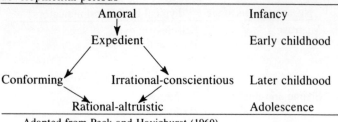

Amoral	Infancy
Expedient	Early childhood
Conforming Irrational-conscientious	Later childhood
Rational-altruistic	Adolescence

Adapted from Peck and Havighurst (1960).

erational patterns of behavior, and the stage of psychosocial development to which each pattern presumably is most appropriate" (Peck & Havighurst, 1960, p. 4). Each of the character types, therefore, represents persistent patterns of motives that result in predictable forms of moral behavior. Although no individual is exclusively one type, each individual is dominated by a motivational and behavioral pattern that is generally consistent with a particular moral character type.

Amoral   The amoral character type is a normal developmental stage of infancy. During the first year of life infants have no moral principles, and therefore no controls over their impulses. Infants consider themselves to be the center of the universe and the object of all activity within that universe. At this age, infants react to their own personal needs without regard to their effects on others. In fact, other people are mere objects that are means of self-gratification. Although this behavior is generally acceptable during infancy, self-centered behavior will not be tolerated indefinitely by society. Therefore, through interaction with others the infant gradually begins to accept prohibitions and sanctions.

If the behaviors of the amoral character type continue into childhood or adolescence, such students will obviously be suspected of being disturbed. Not only will these students be considered impulsive, demanding, and self-centered, but other terms such as emotionally immature, insensitive, and socially oblivious will be used to describe their behavior. "To sum them up, they are poorly socialized, having little liking or regard for people; highly unstable in their self-control; lacking in effective inner principles; and they are decidedly irrational" (Peck & Havighurst, 1960, p. 91).

Expedient   Normally the amoral character type evolves into the expedient type. Although some remnants of the earlier stage are still evident, such as self-centeredness, the child typically behaves in ways that society defines as moral. Thus, expedient children have given up much of their spontaneity and impulsiveness because they have learned to get along with others in order to obtain personal gratification. Early childhood is also a time when children ". . . have learned to respect the reward-punishment power of adults, and to behave correctly when adults are around" (Peck & Havighurst, p. 6).

This picture of external motivation is one that suggests that children go through the motions of moral behavior in order to achieve personal ends. Internally, children continue to view themselves as the only person who is really important, but they are aware of possible social detection and censure that may prevent personal gratification. Thus, they are honest, polite, obedient, and so on, when these behaviors will immediately achieve goals or avoid punishment. The expedient type represents a kind of superficial morality.

Behaviorally, expedient students function well in school even though they are functioning on a lower level of development. Because expedient students recognize the power of the teacher in meeting their needs, they typically respond appropriately to directions, rules, and other social control techniques. "External sanctions are always necessary, however, to guide and control their behavior, and keep it moral. In the absence of such controls, they immediately relapse into doing what they please, even if this involves shoving other children around, taking what they want, or otherwise gratifying their self-centered desires" (Peck & Havighurst, 1960, p. 6).

Conforming   At the next stage of moral character development, a student may develop in one of two directions: conforming or irrational-conscientious. Conforming behavior becomes an extension of the expedient type when students internalize social moral values. Whereas students may have initially gone through the motions of acting moral in the expedient stage, they have now learned, perhaps through habit and reinforcement, to behave and even think in terms of socially prescribed expectations. Conforming students, therefore, are rule-oriented: they behave in ways that significant authority figures or the social code say they should behave. If the student does not live by the rules, he or she may become anxious, uncomfortable, or experience a sense of guilt.

Behaviorally, the conforming student is a compulsive one. These students meticulously attempt to carry out the letter rather than the spirit of the law when teachers implement classroom rules. Moral responsibility, then, is not a function of internalized values, but is defined by the student as acting in accordance with the rules. Peck and Havighurst maintain that students at this stage are ". . . depressed, dull, unhappy, and quite unable to stand up to the world even to express their antagonism toward it" (p. 94).

Irrational-Conscientious   In later childhood if a student does not go the route of conforming, then the irrational-conscientious stage is the alternative. The two stages are similar in that there is a strong standard of right and wrong behavior, but rather than evaluate behavior from a rule base, the irrational-conscientious student has developed an internal code of morality that may be independent of rules or the effects of his or her behavior on others. Thus, a behavior is good or bad because the student has defined it as such, not because the behavior does or does not serve a broader moral purpose for others.

Irrational-conscientious behavior ". . . is characteristic of children who have accepted and internalized the parent rules, but who have not attained awareness that the rules are man-made and intended to serve a human, functional purpose" (p. 7). According to Peck and Havighurst, this stage of moral development can serve either a positive or negative purpose. On the positive side, "if the parents' code fits in well with a moral code which has been produced in the society by long, empirical testing of what is good for people, then it probably contains few seriously defective elements" (p. 8). However, on the negative side, parental codes that do not fit well into the general social morality are apt to produce student behaviors that are ultimately labeled a conduct problem, delinquent, or disturbed. For example, students who are raised in extraordinary home environments that are characterized as impoverished, hostile, or criminal may internalize an irrational-conscientious moral code that conflicts with the social and school-oriented sense of morality. Stealing, fighting, cheating, and sexual behaviors are a few examples of social moral violations that may be committed according to the student's internalized moral code.

Rational-Altruistic   This stage represents the highest level of moral character development. Because Peck and Havighurst identified few, if any, adolescents functioning at this level, the following brief quotation will serve to describe the rational-altruistic student. "Such a person not only has a stable set of moral principles by which he judges and directs his own action; he objectively assesses the results of an act in a given situation, and approves it on the grounds of whether or not it serves others as well as himself . . . In the ideal case he is dependably honest, responsible, loyal, etc., because he sees such behavior is for everyone's well-being" (p. 8).

The terms used by Peck and Havighurst to describe moral character types are noticeably different from the terms used by Freud and Erikson. However, all three theories are consistent in that they support the hierarchical nature of development and that certain characteristic student behaviors can be expected at each stage. These behaviors are often used to make diagnostic decisions about whether or not students are disturbed. If student's behaviors are significantly less developed than those that are normally expected, then there is an increased probability that the students will be considered disturbed.

Maslow's Motivational Theory

Abraham Maslow's theory of motivation does not categorize behaviors as such, but rather human needs that result in a variety of behaviors. Maslow's theory postulates a hierarchy of "prepotent" needs in which "the appearance of one need usually rests on the prior satisfaction of another lower level need" (Maslow, 1970, p. 247). Thus, if there is a deficiency at any hierarchical level, behaviors will be directed toward meeting the need at the particular level.

Maslow's motivational hierarchy consists of five need clusters ranging from the most basic physiological deficiency needs at the foundation to self-actualization needs at the apex (Thomas, 1979):

1. Physiological needs
2. Safety needs
   a. Physical safety
   b. Psychological safety
3. Love (and belongingness) needs
4. Esteem needs
5. Need for self-actualization

This "fixed order" of hierarchical needs "is not nearly so rigid as we may have implied" (Maslow, 1970, p. 259). Even though Maslow contends that most individuals systematically proceed along this hierarchy, there are exceptional individuals who do not follow this need pattern. One critical exception to the hierarchy is the reversal of love and esteem needs. "This most common reversal in the hierarchy is usually due to the development of the notion that the person who is most likely to be loved is a strong and powerful person, one who inspires respect or fear, and who is self-confident or aggressive" (Maslow, 1970, p. 259).

Summary descriptions of each of the need levels are provided in the following paragraphs. In addition, some hypothetical student behaviors are included within the descriptions. However, these behaviors must be considered speculative since there are many determinants of behavior other than needs.

Physiological Needs   Deficiencies in life maintenance substances such as air, food, water, and shelter are considered the most prepotent. If the individual suffers an extreme deficiency in any of these life-sustaining substances, all other needs become secondary. The individual's behavior will be mobilized to fulfill this physiological deficiency. If a student is hungry enough, or cold enough, or thirsty enough, then obeying rules, showing respect, learning, or even attending school is totally irrelevant for that student. Maslow cautions, however, that physiological needs such as chronic hunger are rare in developed countries. Within favorable environments, expressions of hunger are in actuality a temporary physiological inconvenience and not a prepotent need. Teachers, however, should be aware of the fact that some students, particularly those from impoverished homes, may be consistently and chronically deficient in physiological needs.

Safety Needs   If the physiological needs have been reasonably well gratified, then the safety needs emerge (Maslow, 1970). Safety needs can be categorized into two basic types: physical and psychological. Although these two types of safety needs are interrelated, they do represent substantively different threats to the physical and/or psychological well-being of the student.

Physical Safety Needs   This category includes reactions that reflect a fear of physical harm and behaviors that are intended to protect oneself physically. Among infants, reactions to threat or danger are quite noticeable if, for example, "they are disturbed or dropped suddenly, startled by loud noises, flashing lights, or other unusual sensory stimulation . . ." (Maslow, 1970, pp. 251–252). Among children, illnesses seem to threaten physical safety. According to Maslow, illness may have an obvious effect on the child. "Thus a child who because of some bad food is taken ill may, for a day or two, develop fear, nightmares, and a need for protection and reassurance never seen in him before" (p. 252).

Some students consistently demonstrate behaviors that are an indication that they need physical safety. For example, younger students may ask for the teacher's protection from a bully, or may want to sit away from classmates, preferably in a corner, or may exaggerate the symptoms of a minor injury. Among adolescents, behaviors may take the forms of carrying weapons, gang protection, or social isolation. These exemplary student behaviors are characteristic of developmentally low-level motivational functioning. Among preschoolers, behaviors designed to produce physical safety are common, but as children grow older and enter school the prepotency of this need gradually diminishes.

Psychological Safety Needs   This level extends the safety needs to include a preference for structure, limits, or routines that will produce a predictable, orderly world. Maslow maintains that "injustice, unfairness or inconsistency in parents seems to make the child feel anxious and unsafe and makes the world look unreliable, or unsafe, or unpredictable" (Maslow, 1970, p. 252). Consequently, students at this level thrive on environmental guidelines that can be counted on for the present and the future. Students functioning in the psychological safety need level typically engage in behaviors that reduce the complex, thus unpredictable, nature of their environment. Such students may be compulsive, engaging in rigid, routine behaviors; or they may be dependent because they want the predictability of a familiar adult; or they may be possessive because they try to "own," and thus control, their environment. When confronted with a new environment, a new learning activity, or a new social relationship they become extremely anxious, even panic-stricken. Thus, students on this level are reluctant to take an initiative, to do something a different way, or to meet new people. Instead, they prefer doing the same things day after day. In extreme cases of psychological safety needs, such as the behavior of autistic children, the student may want the environment exactly replicated daily; for example, the student may want the same book on the same shelf, the same coat on the same hanger, and the same teacher requiring the same behaviors.

Love Needs   If the safety needs are reasonably well gratified, then the love needs will emerge. Love needs include the desire for friendship, affection, and belongingness, or the need to be emotionally connected to others. Among adults, according to Maslow, a deficiency at the love level is a basic cause of maladjustment. Among adolescents, behaviors are directed toward establishing interpersonal bonds. This need is evidenced by adolescent attempts to achieve group membership such as in clubs, fraternities, gangs, and cliques. On a one-to-one level, dating behaviors, including touching, holding, and sex, are used to achieve love and belongingness needs. Maslow was careful to point out that love and sex are not synonymous, but that many adolescents engage in sex with the belief that it will ultimately lead to love (Maslow, 1970). Children, on the other hand, are attempting to resolve lower level needs and have not yet reached the level of development that emphasizes love and belongingness. Because Maslow restricts his discussion at this level to adolescents and adults, it is entirely possible that children who seem to be seeking love are, in fact, attempting to resolve physiological or safety needs in the form of dependency or protection.

Esteem Needs   If the lower level needs have been resolved, then the individuals become engrossed in a search for a stable, positive evaluation of themselves—for self-respect, adequacy, recognition, and so forth. "These needs may be classified into subsidiary sets. These are, first, the desire for strength, for achievement, for adequacy, for confidence in the face of the world, and for independence and freedom.

Secondly, we have what we may call the desire for reputation or prestige . . . recognition, attention, importance, or appreciation" (Maslow, 1970, p. 256).

Students considered to be disturbed have not reached this level of motivation. Students who are negative about themselves, who are unconcerned about academic and social performance, or who want structure rather than freedom are conveying the message that they are on a lower motivational level. On the other hand, students who are burning the midnight oil to achieve academic excellence, who are concerned with their reputation or social popularity, or who are trying to prove to themselves and others that they have skills, may well be attempting to develop self-esteem.

Need for Self-actualization   The number of people who have satisfied the physiological, safety, love, and esteem needs, and are now seeking self-actualization, is a limited group. Self-actualization means that what a person *can* do, the person *must* do (Maslow, 1970). It represents striving to become the ideal parent, the ideal teacher, the ideal doctor, and so forth. Because of the limited number of individuals functioning at this level, Maslow (1965) confesses that he does not know much about self-actualization. Therefore, it is reasonable to conclude that there are no disturbed students who are functioning at this level.

Summary and Behavioral Conclusions

The four theories discussed in this chapter represent somewhat different views of human behavior, yet they are remarkably similar. Even though the differences are evident in the terminology, the theoretical bases, and the stages related to human behavior, each theory considers normal behavior to be a function of a hierarchical pattern of progressive and predictable development. An analysis of each theory suggests that specific behaviors can be deduced from the stage descriptions. Because the theories are compatible, a behavioral synthesis can be projected as a function of the hierarchical stage development. Thus, the following behaviors, representing normal development, constitute a behavioral synthesis:

Unsocialized behavior is behavior that is driven by the need to achieve immediate gratification, but without regard for others. This level of behavior is characteristic of autism and includes extreme forms of hyperactive and impulsive behaviors.

Protective behaviors are intended to defend oneself, physically and/or psychologically, from environmental threats. This level includes withdrawn, dependent, and ritualistic behaviors.

Table 4. Relationships among developmental theory stages and the behavioral synthesis

Freud's stages of personality	Maslow's motivational hierarchy	Erikson's psychosocial crises	Peck and Havighurst's character types	Behavioral synthesis
Id	Physiological needs	Trust vs. mistrust	Amoral	Unsocialized Hyperactive
Ego[a]	Safety needs Physical	Autonomy vs. doubt	Expedient Irrational-conscientious[d]	Impulsive Protective
Superego	Psychological	Initiative vs. guilt	Conforming[d]	Withdrawn Dependent Ritualistic
Ego[b]	Self-esteem[c]	Industry vs. inferiority		Defining (testing) Negativistic
	Love[c]	Identity vs. role diffusion	Rational-altruistic	Aggressive Assertive Self-controlled

Adapted from Rich (1978b), pp. 1–11.

[a] Ego as the emergence of a limited reality orientation and ego control.
[b] Ego as higher level functioning and regulating stage of personality.
[c] Self-esteem and love are frequently interchangeable in hierarchical development.
[d] Irrational-conscientious and conforming are separate rather than hierarchical developments.

Defining or testing behaviors are attempts to determine the competence of oneself and/or the environmental requirements. This level includes negativistic, aggressive, and assertive behaviors.

Self-controlled behavior indicates ownership of self accompanied by positive and productive environmental interaction. This level is occupied by students who are essentially free from external control and lower level needs, and who can direct and regulate their own behavior in accordance with a mature perception of reality.

These behaviors are discussed in greater detail in the next section. In the meantime it is appropriate to point out the relationships among the four theories and the behavioral synthesis. Table 4 is a representation of these relationships. Table 4 contains a number of horizontal and vertical relationships that have implications for understanding disturbed behavior from a developmental perspective. Vertically, the theories and behaviors represent stages of development in descending order from basic to advanced. These stages are closely related to chronological age, which determines normal behavior, but for the disturbed student, behavior characteristic of a younger individual tends to be more applicable. Horizontally, the theory stages and behaviors match across the columns in Table 4. For example, the id personality stage, mistrust crisis resolution, physiological needs, and amoral character type are compatible descriptors of unsocialized behavior that is characteristic of normal infants. However, this horizontal proximity should be interpreted with caution and flexibility. This is particularly important because the theoretical stages are not equally amenable to rigorous comparison, nor does such a continuum account for individual variance. Therefore, the continuum represents a generalization that may not be an accurate developmental assessment for an individual student.

BEHAVIORAL SYNTHESIS

The behavioral synthesis or developmental ranking of selected student behaviors is consistent with the four theories and other authoritative sources. Numerous research projects (e.g., Bloom, 1964; Kagan & Moss, 1962; MacFarlane, Allen, & Honzik, 1954) have documented the fact that different student behaviors normally occur during different developmental periods. The behavioral synthesis derived from the theories is consistent with the exemplary research projects and can be plotted on a developmental profile (Figure 3). The behavioral positions on the profile indicate the approximate typical age at which these behaviors are most evident. Although all students demonstrate some degree of all of the behaviors throughout their life spans, the position on the profile indicates when the behaviors most dramatically but nor-

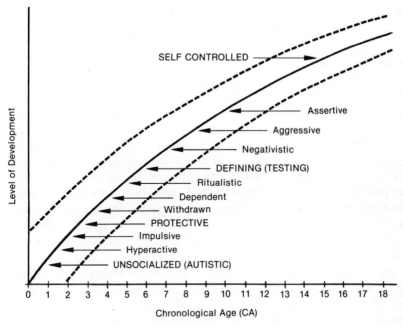

Figure 3.   Developmental profile of the behavioral synthesis.

mally occur. For example, impulsive behavior that is infrequently evidenced by a 12-year-old does not mean the student is developmentally
2 years old. Although this example may represent temporary regression, the totality of the student's behavior must be considered, including the frequency, duration, and circumstances surrounding the
behavior. "The expanding knowledge of children indicates that 'abnormal' behavior among normal children is plentiful. We now recognize
that no child is completely free from emotional difficulties. The prevalence of problems is, in fact, so widespread that some psychologists
doubt that these deviations should be regarded as abnormal" (Clarizio
& McCoy, 1976, p. 4). Consequently, only those students who demonstrate relatively extreme and consistent forms of more basic behaviors during later developmental periods should be considered as potentially disturbed.

Reference to some disturbed behaviors, particularly immaturity
and inadequacy, are not included in the synthesis since they infer a
developmental problem. For example, to say that a 10-year-old student
has developmentally regressed to the impulsive or withdrawn stage is
also saying that the student is immature. Therefore, immature and
inadequate behaviors are implied throughout the behavioral synthesis.

Unsocialized Behaviors

This behavior type, evidenced by self-centeredness, the lack of social awareness, self-stimulation, and extraordinary hyperactivity and impulsivity, represents the most basic or youngest developmental level. Behaviors of this type are characteristic of infants who are operating on a self-fulfilling, demanding pattern, wherein the behavior is an attempt to achieve immediate, even irrational, gratification. During the later stage of infancy, however, these unsocialized behaviors should begin to diminish. If a child continues to demonstrate behaviors characteristic of an infant, then the diagnosis of severe disturbance such as autism or childhood schizophrenia is a possible consequence. These two exemplary categories of severe disturbance are difficult to distinguish except on the basis of historical data. "This refers to the view held by many clinicians that the childhood type of schizophrenic reaction represents a regression from some higher level of development, while . . . autism involves grossly atypical development from birth" (Herbert, 1974, p. 215).

Autistic Behavior   Unsocialized behaviors are similar to the characteristics of autistic children that have been clinically described by Kanner (1973). Although great variations may be observed among autisitic students, the following characteristics, including one or more behavioral manifestations, are typically evident.

1. Relationship with people
   Little or no eye contact
   Withdrawal from people (extreme self-isolation, unresponsiveness)
   Parallel play
   Lack of affect (little or no visible emotional reaction)
2. Speech (communication)
   Excessive response to sounds
   Echolalia (repeating what someone has said)
   Mutism (no language)
   Inappropriate or bizarre speech
   Misuse of personal pronouns
   Articulatory defects
   Vocal peculiarity (e.g., sing-song or monotonous tone of voice)
3. Motor phenomena
   Hyperkinesis (high level of motor activitiy)
   Hypokinesis (low level of motor activity)
   Stereotyped, repetitive movements (e.g., walking on tiptoe; hand flapping)
   Temper tantrums

4. Ritualistic and compulsive phenomena (preoccupation)
   Abnormal attachments to objects
   Abnormal preoccupation with objects or ideas (idiot savant)
   Headbanging, headrolling, and body bouncing
   Nonadaptable and resistant to change (e.g., must have same cup
   to use)
   Ritualistic behavior, desire for sameness (e.g., always walks on
   line)
5. Perceptual abnormalities
   Lack of response to sound
   Failure to show response to pain
   Attending to self-produced sounds
   Smelling and tasting objects, including people
   Covering, flickering, and banging ears and eyes
   Staring

Generally, these characteristics of autism are described as self-stimulation. Students with autistic characteristics have not and probably
will not be assigned to the regular classroom. However, a limited
number of such students who have progressed developmentally, academically, and socially through special education services have been
mainstreamed. Even in these cases, however, some characteristics of
autism are still evident, particularly hyperactive, impulsive, and protective behaviors.

Hyperactive Behaviors Excessive motor activity among students
is called hyperactivity or hyperkinesis. Hyperactive students are those
described by teachers and parents as constantly on the move, exploring
their environments, climbing over chairs, running around the room,
and so on. Typically, hyperactive behavior is also associated with other
classroom learning problems such as short attention span and distractibility. The variability of motor activity among students appears to be
diverse. In fact, in a study of normal infants the most active ones were
300 times as motor-active as the least active ones (Bakwin & Bakwin,
1972). Autistic infants tend to maintain a high level of motor activity
that has been described as rhythmic, repetitious, and purposeless.
Hyperactivity in the absence of other autistic characteristics constitutes the next level of developmental behaviors.

The concept of hyperactivity is a greatly debated issue. The literature available on teacher perceptions of motor activity among students, for example, does not present a clear or consistent pattern.
Some researchers maintain that students identified by teachers as hyperactive do not generally demonstrate motor activity levels that are
significantly different from normal students (Pope, 1970). On the other

hand, there is reported evidence that supports a quantitative difference in motor behavior between hyperactive and normal students as judged by teachers (Victor & Halverson, 1976). These different results may be due to the fact that hyperactivity is imprecisely defined and difficult to measure. Consequently, hyperactivity as seen by teachers tends to be in the eye of the beholder, particularly when students are creating other classroom behavior problems. In one research study (Rich, 1978c), teachers tended to identify hyperactive students as those who also engaged in acting-out, noncompliant behaviors, whereas students who were engaged in solitary but nondisruptive motor activity, such as foot shaking and rocking, were unobserved by the teachers.

Developmentally, hyperactivity must be evaluated in light of the student's chronological age and sex. Younger students are more motor-active than older students; boys are more motor-active than girls. Figure 4 clearly illustrates that higher levels of motor activity can be normally expected among younger students, or that motor activity normally decreases with age. In over 50 percent of the cases in which

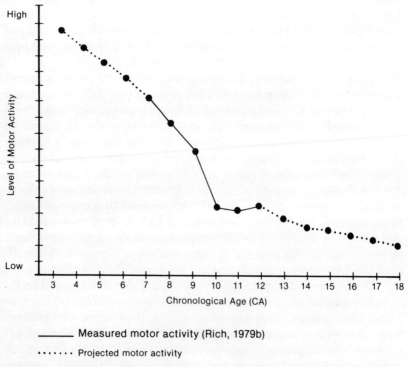

——— Measured motor activity (Rich, 1979b)

• • • • • • Projected motor activity

Figure 4.   Relationship between levels of motor activity and chronological age.

teachers identified students as hyperactive, they were also identifying the youngest students in the class (Rich, 1979b).

The data on hyperactivity suggest that teachers should develop differential expectations of motor behavior given the age and sex of the students. Teacher development of age-appropriate norms seems to be particularly important during the elementary school years. Figure 4 shows, for example, that the level of motor activity dramatically decreases between the ages of 7 and 10, so that a difference of a few months could be the primary factor in identifying a student as hyperactive or normal. If, on the other hand, a student's level of motor activity approximates that of a much younger student or a preschool child, it is an indication that the student is hyperactive.

Impulsive Behavior   The phrase "inability to delay gratification" is often used synonymously with the behavior characterized by impulsivity. This term implies that students act without thinking in order to gratify their wants or needs. That is, they grab, shove, take, steal, or do whatever is necessary to satisfy a need immediately. In the final analysis, impulsivity is an extension of unsocialized behavior that also includes hyperactivity. Sanford (1962) maintains that the degree of impulse control and ego development are highly related and that both adhere closely to the developmental profile. Impulsivity has also been associated with aggression (Kauffman, 1977), but it is suspected that many acts against people are incidental and not a deliberate socialized aggressive behavior. Impulsivity in its extreme form does represent a basic, infant-like developmental behavior.

The continued demonstration of impulsivity among students has been primarily attributed to two conditions aside from the theories of causality: environmental deprivation and limited verbal skills. Students from deprived, lower socioeconomic environments are noticeably more impulsive than students who are from more enriched environments. One explanation is that for deprived students there is no payoff for waiting. To hesitate means that the food, or the bed, or the money will have gone to someone else. In short, the great number of needs and the limited number of resources in deprived environments have taught students to be impulsive if they are to survive. Certainly, within the orderly, controlled classrooms of most schools such behavior would be considered a symptom of disturbance.

Limited verbal skills are also a cause of impulsivity. Students raised in deprived, repressive, or verbally restrictive environments often do not possess the verbal skills necessary to fulfill needs in a social manner. Whereas most students have found that words are the key to meeting needs, some less verbally skilled students are more action-oriented. Since classrooms are highly verbal settings, students with limited verbal skills tend to be more obvious to teachers. However, the degree to which they are obvious is not related to what they say, but what they do. The exception to the last statement is when students curse. Cursing behaviors may have many causes, but one in particular is the lack of verbal skills. Such students may not know how socially to express frustration, anger, or even feelings, so they impulsively react—they curse. Student behaviors that are associated with the lack of verbal skills are often labeled impulsive. Unless these students are able socially to meet needs and develop verbal skills, they are apt to remain at a basic developmental level and ultimately be labeled disturbed.

Protective Behaviors

This group of behaviors, which are normally experienced during early childhood, consists of behaviors that are intended to protect oneself against potentially threatening environmental conditions. The intense effort to socialize children at this age, that is, to eliminate unsocialized behaviors, creates conflict between the impulse for self-gratification and externally enforced reality. Young children are no longer able spontaneously to act as they have in the past because they are now subjected to adult control techniques such as punishment, moral messages, and the removal of love. At this age most children begin to perceive themselves as externally controlled when consequences are ". . . typically perceived as the result of lack, chance, fate, as under the control of powerful others" (Rotter, 1966, p. 3). Students, in order physically and psychologically to deal with this new set of living conditions, engage in protective (withdrawn, dependent, and ritualistic) behaviors.

Withdrawn Behaviors   This behavior is characterized by movement away from people or ". . . behavior that keeps people at a distance physically and emotionally" (Kauffman, 1977, p. 207). Unlike withdrawal associated with autistic children who may be unaware of others, the young child at this level of withdrawal recognizes the existence of others, but chooses to reduce social contact. Consequently, withdrawal may be given other labels such as timid, shy, or isolated.

Among nonautistic students extreme withdrawal is considered the lowest developmental level of behavior. However, it should be remembered that all students are withdrawn from time to time, particularly when they are confronted with a personal crisis. In fact, Bakwin and Bakwin (1972) maintain "that most shy, withdrawn children allowed to develop in their own way and at their own pace adjust satisfactorily in adult life" (p. 467). On the other hand, withdrawal ". . . may arise from, or at least be exacerbated and maintained by, the constraints of overrestrictive parents, punishment for social approach responses, inadvertent reinforcement of isolate play, or lack of opportunity to learn and practice social reciprocity" (Kauffman, 1977, p. 212). Thus, continued withdrawal among students through the school years, reinforced by teachers who require passive, quiet, and orderly classrooms, may result in a pattern of behavior that is symptomatic of disturbance.

Dependent Behaviors   Students who maintain a high level of attachment, seek affectionate contact, desire physical closeness, or frequently seek help, especially from adults, are said to be dependent. This behavior pattern, which first arises from the mother-infant bond, is believed to be the basis of the socialization process (Clarizio & McCoy, 1976). Thus, dependency is appropriate during the first few years of life, but after that the child should move toward independent behavior. Too much dependency, or overdependency, has been generally attributed to two child-rearing practices: overprotection and rejection. In the case of overprotection the child does not develop autonomy, or independence, and is reinforced for dependent behaviors. The rejection theory states that "the child's dependency needs are frustrated with the result that the child, lacking sufficient support and nurturance, is unable to progress successfully through the experiences culminating in independence" (Clarizio & McCoy, 1976, p. 41).

Boys and girls differ dramatically on this developmental behavioral dimension. Whereas girls tend to demonstrate a significant degree of dependency throughout childhood and even adolescence, boys are typically expected to show demonstrable signs of independence at a much younger age. For both boys and girls, however, this is a gradual transition from dependence to independence.

Among students, a high level of dependence on adults is an indication that such students have not adequately developed a sense of independence and thus require the protection of significant others. The high frequency continuation of dependency behaviors, compared with the rate among students of similar age and sex, is an indication that a student is functioning on a lower developmental level.

Ritualistic Behavior   This behavior pattern, often designated as "compulsive" in psychodynamic terminology, is characterized by stringent compliance with rules, norms, and social expectation. Ritualistic students comply with a system of literal rules in order to protect themselves from potential consequences. They are always on time, they follow every classroom rule, and they always turn in assignments as requested. They are rule-oriented. Noticeably, ritualistic students are intimidated by rapidly changing transition times, new students, substitute teachers, and inconsistent rule enforcement. Their physical and psychological protection is based upon ritualistic behavior that avoids the temporary, inconsistent, and unpredictable nature of dependency. Such students often annoy teachers because they do exactly what is requested, they want rules clarified, and they persist in defining expectations.

Students who are developmentally functioning on the ritualistic level are demonstrating behaviors characteristic of young children. Often these behaviors may be confused with withdrawal or dependency because the students restrict social contacts and appear to want directions from the teacher. However, ritualisitic behaviors emphasize rules, norms, and expressions, and not people. Ritualistic and dependent behaviors represent an evolution from withdrawal in that the student's developmental level shifts from noninteraction to stringent compliance with norms, or subservient association with people. The distinction between ritualistic and dependent behaviors may be only in terms of the objective of the behavior. At any rate, behavior that is primarily characterized by ritualistic compliance with norms is developmentally inappropriate and is symptomatic of disturbance.

Defining (Testing) Behaviors

These behaviors are intended to test the environment for limits and determine the relative power and control possessed by the student. In effect, the student is emerging as an internally controlled individual (Rotter, 1966), perceiving consequences as a result of his or her own actions. Developmentally, students at this level have passed through the unsocialized and protective stages of behavior and are now defining their environments in order to predict the consequences of future behaviors. They want to know what they can do, when they can do it, where they can do it, and so forth. Defining behaviors are considered developmentally higher than the behaviors previously discussed because they require some independent action in the form of risk taking behaviors.

Negativistic Behavior   This behavior is not synonymous with an oppositional disorder (DSM-III) in which students challenge authority, but focuses on the perceived negative aspects or limitations of the students themselves. Negativistic behavior is symptomatic of a lack of trust or confidence in oneself. This behavior tends to maintain the potential performance and credibility of oneself by projecting the belief that one cannot succeed. Behaviors typical at this level include declining an invitation to be on a team, saying "I can't (or won't) do it" before trying, and an unwillingness to state personal opinions. In short, the student must know what he or she can do before being willing to display competence or lack of it publicly. There is the general feeling that "It is better not to try, than to try and fail." Thus, when a student says "I won't do it," he or she may be saying "I don't want to try until I know I can succeed."

Negativistic behavior is a necessary link between protective and self-controlled behaviors. Each student must begin to develop an understanding of his or her own competence, initiative, and self-worth before moving to the next developmental level. However, if a student continues to be plagued by inner doubt, self-defeat, or inadequacy, it is a sign that the student is fixated on the negativistic level.

Aggressive Behavior   Aggressive behaviors of later childhood involve a confrontation between the student and another student(s), teachers(s), or other person(s). This behavior is associated with conduct disorders and is responsible for the majority of students being identified as disturbed. Aggressive behavior is goal-oriented; that is, it is a controlled response to conflict, frustration, and the like. Uncontrolled aggressive behavior, on the other hand, is more consistent with the developmental level of the unsocialized student. This distinction is reflected in the socialized and undersocialized types of conduct disorders described in DSM-III. Controlled or socialized aggression, then, is considered to be an indication that the student is attempting to define further the limitations of the environment in terms of personal power, control, and resolution of conflict. Obviously, aggressive behavior cannot be tolerated indefinitely within the classroom.

Kauffman (1977) warned that two points need clarification:

> First it must be recognized that perfectly normal, emotionally healthy children perform aggressive behaviors, including temper tantrums, verbal assaults, hitting, teasing, stealing and other acts which are a part of the aggressive child's repertoire. The point is that aggressive children perform such onerous deeds at a much higher rate and at a much later age than normal children . . . Second, aggressive behavior is frequently observed to be a component of other facets of disordered behavior, e.g., delinquency, faulty moral judgment, impulsivity . . . Under some circumstances aggression may be interpreted to represent immaturity or developmental lag (p. 173).

The frequency of aggressive behaviors among students is a significant indicator of both disturbance and normality. For example, Patterson et al. (1975) found that aggressive students engaged in two to five times as many noxious behaviors as did normal students (Table 5). Thus, occasional aggressive behaviors do not typify disturbed students, since aggressive acts are also characteristic of normal students. However, the high frequency occurrence of such behaviors as shouting, attacking, and destroying property must be reduced, if not eliminated, in the classroom. It is significant to note that teachers typically perceive aggressive behaviors to be symptomatic of disturbance, whereas lower

Table 5. Selected noxious behaviors, their descriptions, and the average time elapsing between their occurrences in aggressive and nonaggressive students

| Noxious behavior | Description | Average time between occurrences (minutes) | |
		Aggressive students	Nonaggressive students
Noncompliance	Not doing what is requested	11	20
Yell	Shouting, yelling, or talking loudly	18	54
Tease	Teasing that produces displeasure, disapproval, or disruption	20	51
Negative physical act	Attacking or attempting to attack another with enough intensity to inflict pain (e.g., biting, kicking, slapping)	24	108
Destructive	Destroying, damaging, or trying to destroy or damage any object	33	156

Adapted from Patterson et al. (1975), p. 5.

level behaviors, particularly dependency and ritualistic acts, go relatively unnoticed in the classroom. All developmentally regressive or delayed behaviors should be the subject of teacher concern; referral and intervention should not be limited to aggressive students. In fact, it is possible that the student frustration experienced in an overcontrolled classroom precipitates aggressive behavior.

Assertive Behavior This behavior represents a higher developmental level of socialization than does aggressive behavior. Although assertiveness also represents a person-environment defining technique, it consists of more appropriate expression of previously aggressive behaviors. Even though assertive behaviors such as demanding, coercion, and intimidation may constitute inappropriate classroom behaviors, they are not an immediate or obvious threat. Students who are bullies or gang leaders often display a considerable degree of assertiveness. Although aggressive acts sometimes accompany these social roles, reliance upon assertive behaviors is the primary feature at this developmental level.

In addition, there is normal assertiveness, for example, telling others what to do, pushing one's way through a crowd, and demanding one's rights. In fact, teachers routinely exercise assertive and, to a lesser extent, aggressive behaviors in the performance of their teaching responsibilities (Parsons, 1951). The type and degree of assertiveness will vary among individual students, but the underlying purpose of this behavior is to define more clearly one's place in the environment. To know what one can do, when, why, how, and so on, is a prerequisite to the final developmental step: self-controlled behavior.

Self-controlled Behavior

The developmental apex of the behavioral synthesis consists of independent, internally controlled, self-regulated behaviors. Self-controlled behaviors are essentially void of the lower level developmental behaviors such as dependency, ritualism, aggression, and assertiveness. Self-controlled students have satisfactorily resolved the psychosocial crises appropriate for their chronological age, their personality is regulated by their ego, their safety needs have been positively resolved, and their behavior is regulated by a sense of cooperation. In short, their behavior is positively self-directed within a framework of morality, unselfishness, and reality.

Developmentally, self-controlled students cannot be disturbed. However, teachers should be aware of the fact that some self-controlled behaviors are frequently misinterpreted within the classroom, particularly when student behaviors and teacher expectations conflict. If the teacher is unjust, inconsistent, or incorrect the self-controlled student will attempt to clarify and remedy the situation. The teacher may respond to the student's intervention negatively by saying, for example, "Keep quiet," or "It's none of your business." Such confrontations lead some teachers to begin to suspect the self-controlled student of disturbance. Fortunately, most teachers have the capacity to recognize their own inappropriate behaviors and are not threatened by the reality intervention of a self-controlled student.

STABILITY AND CHANGE AMONG BEHAVIORS

Predicting behavior change among disturbed students is, in general, a difficult, complex, and, at best, an imprecise task. The research on the persistence or stability of disturbed behaviors from childhood to adolescence and early adult life is contradictory and incomplete, and thus inconclusive. "Put bluntly, there is no research evidence yet available indicating that clinical analysis of the child's emotional status or dynamics leads to any more effective prognosis of adult mental health or illness . . ." (Kohlberg, LaCrosse, & Ricks, 1972, p. 94).

The results of research on disturbance within school settings are somewhat encouraging, yet puzzling. Both Glavin (1972) and Stennett (1966) found that 60 to 70 percent of the students diagnosed as disturbed could not be reidentified after 3 years, even though most of the students did not receive any special services. This spontaneous remission, or behavior change without treatment, suggests, among other things, that developmental behaviors were inappropriately diagnosed as symptoms of disturbance.

There is some literature that indicates that selective behaviors are more persistent. For example, Kagan and Moss (1962) concluded that aggressive behavior was more stable for men, whereas dependency and passivity were more stable for women. This persistence, however, was partially attributable to the fact that social expectations reinforced these perceived sex-related behaviors. Kauffman (1977) expressed the belief that "hyperaggressive behavior in childhood is a discouraging indicator of adult adjustment," but he does not believe that withdrawal, dependency, and shyness are predictors of serious adult problems (p. 173). On the other hand, DSM-III ranks conduct disorders and oppositional disorders as less severe, thus less stable, than other developmental problems, including social isolation and noncommunication. Beliefs regarding the predictability of behaviors seem to be related to the theoretical orientations of those persons making the predictions. That is, behaviorists generally view acting-out behaviors as the most serious and stable symptoms of disturbance, whereas psychodynamic authorities emphasize the seriousness and stability of internalized psychological conditions that include such behaviors as withdrawal, shyness, and dependency.

Even though there is considerable disagreement over the stability of disturbed behaviors, there are two conclusions that are generally accurate regarding the predictability of behavior change: 1) the more severe the behavior, the greater the probability that the behavior will persist; and 2) to the extent to which the student's environment remains unchanged, the greater the probability that the behavior will remain unchanged. First, severe behaviors of any type (e.g., self-injurious behavior, extreme withdrawal, and destructive aggression) seem to have lasting effects throughout students' lives. Severe behaviors that are diagnosed at age 6, or 10, or 15 are usually still evident in adult life. Autism, for example, is considered a life long disability, because many of the behaviors that characterize autism are continously present, even though the students may develop some adaptive skills. Behaviors that are symptomatic of mild or moderate disturbance, however, are not accurate predictors of adult behaviors. This conclusion reinforces the likelihood that educators may be using identification procedures such as personal perceptions, behavioral expectations, and so forth that very narrowly define disturbance in classroom settings, but that ignore normal developmental behaviors.

Second, the predictability of any behavior change is related to changes that occur in the student's environment (Bloom, 1964). If there is no substantive change in a basically negative environment (e.g., punitive or deprived), then the behaviors that characterize disturbance will persist. If, however, the environment supports the basic needs of the student, the behaviors will tend to progress through the developmental sequence. It seems to be true that "the environment is a determiner of the extent and kind of change taking place in a particular characteristic" (Bloom, 1964, p. 209).

Thus, the stability and change among behaviors is related to the severity of the behavior and the influence of the environment. When the behavior constitutes severe disturbance and/or the environment is nonsupportive, then one may predict that the behavior will continue; when the behavior constitutes a mild or moderate form of disturbance and/or the environment is supportive, then one may predict that the behavior will progressively change. These conclusions have critical implications for educators, particularly because behavior change is partially a function of the educational environment, including instructional strategies, teacher behaviors, management techniques, and so forth that influence the behavior of disturbed students.

SUMMARY

On the basis of selected developmental theories a behavioral synthesis was constructed as an alternative to the definitions and classification systems used to determine the characteristics of disturbance. The primary advantage of a developmental approach is that age-appropriate norms for selected behaviors can be hierarchically constructed, with significant negative variance potentially constituting disturbance. The disadvantage of the developmental approach is the hypothetical nature of the selected behaviors that does not account for individual, yet normal variance (Phillips & Kelly, 1975).

The basic assumption of the development theories and behavioral synthesis is that disturbance is a function of behaviors that are chronologically younger or developmentally lower than would be normally expected given the chronological age of the student. Thus, disturbed students are those who have fixated on, or regressed to, or who are delayed in achieving behaviors that are typical of their chronological counterparts in the normal population of students. The behavioral synthesis included the following progressive hierarchy of behaviors: unsocialized (hyperactive and impulsive), protective (withdrawn, dependent, and ritualistic), defining or testing (negativistic, aggressive, and assertive), and self-controlled. The more severe the behavior and/ or the more nonsupportive the student's environment is, the greater the probability that the behavior will persist at a lower level of development.

6

Assessment of Characteristics

School counselors, clinicians, and particularly teachers daily evaluate and interpret some aspects of students' behaviors—their homework, their punctuality, their peer relations, and a host of other tasks and responsibilities related to school performance. The process that school personnel use to acquire information about students is called assessment. Whether the assessment is formalized and systematic, or spontaneous and intuitive, the information acquired is used to make decisions about students. On the basis of assessments, students are instructed, graded, disciplined, assigned, placed, and even labeled. Unquestionably, school personnel spend a great deal of time assessing students.

Because the types of assessments that teachers use are extensive, ranging from standardized tests of academic achievement to the single observation of an incident, this chapter is limited to the assessment of student behavior and personality characteristics and the significant classroom environmental conditions that are associated with disturbance. Certainly the assessment of other student characteristics such as academic skills, intellectual functioning, and physical traits is critical to the development of an effective educational program and for the identification of handicapping conditions (e.g., learning disabilities and mental retardation). In fact, a frequently used criterion for determining disturbance is that students must have average or above average intelligence. PL 94-142 goes beyond this intellectual criterion and implies a complex assessment that will explain "an inability to learn which cannot be explained by intellectual, sensory, or health factors." Therefore, the identification of disturbed students necessitates a multidimensional assessment approach. Alone, the assessment of behavior, personality, and environmental conditions does not constitute a sufficient procedure, but information regarding these characteristics is critical to the identification of disturbance. When other handicapping conditions have been ruled out as the cause of school problems, then the assessment of behavior, personality, and environmental characteristics becomes necessary.

TYPES OF INFORMATION

An effective assessment procedure requires several types of information. Salvia and Ysseldyke (1978) identified six types of information that can be classified according to "the time at which the information is collected (current or historical) and how the information is collected (from observations, tests, or judgments)" (p. 6). Table 1 includes examples of the different types of information that should be included in an assessment.

Current and Historical Information

Assessment procedures should include longitudinal data regarding students, that is, information collected over a time span from the earliest

Table 1.   Types of assessment information, classified according to the time the information is collected and the type of information

Current	Historical
Observations	
Frequency count of occurrence of a particular behavior	Birth complications
	Record of childhood diseases
Antecedents of behavior	Anecdotal records
Major incidents	Observations by last year's teacher
Tests	
Results of a standardized personality test administered during the assessment	Results of a standardized achivement test battery administered at the end of the previous year
Results of in-class academic tests administered by the teacher	Results of first-grade school readiness tests
Judgments	
Parent's evaluations of how well the child gets along in family, with friends, etc.	Previous medical, psychological, or educational diagnosis
Rating scales completed by teachers	Previous report cards
Teacher's reason for referral	Parents' recall of developmental history, childhood illnesses and accidents, etc.

Adapted from Salvia & Ysseldyke (1978), p. 7.

known data to the present situation. Even though teachers are primarily concerned with the present functioning of students, information from past observations, tests, and judgments is necessary to place the students' current situation into perspective. For example, a history of withdrawn behavior is an indication that the behavior represents a chronic condition, whereas only recently demonstrated withdrawn behavior may indicate the possibility of a crisis reaction rather than disturbance. Most of the definitions and classification systems specify a need for some sort of historical data. In fact, PL 94-142 states that disturbed characteristics must be exhibited "over a period of time," and the DSM-III criteria for mental disorders include the provision that the condition must have a duration of at least 3 to 6 months.

Of the two kinds of time-oriented assessments, current information is much more frequently used to classify the characteristics of students and to diagnose disturbance. This preference for current information is due to the fact that it is much more easily obtained, the specific type of assessment can be preplanned, and the information can be verified. Historical information, on the other hand, tends to be limited, permanent, and often biased. "School diagnosticians cannot go back in time to observe previous characteristics, behaviors, and situations. A diagnostician who wishes to incorporate a student's history into the assessment procedure must rely on previously collected information or the memory of individuals who know the student" (Salvia & Ysseldyke, 1978, pp. 7–8). Regardless of the problems inherent in collecting historical data, the information that is available should be included in the assessment.

Observation

A teacher sees a fight, checks homework, counts the number of students who arrive late, and hears a student curse. Each of these examples is a form of teacher observation of student behavior, yet such observations are of little value unless the teacher conscientiously looks for and records specific behaviors for the purpose of making decisions (Cartwright & Cartwright, 1974). Thus, observation is the act of intentionally and systematically viewing and recording particular behaviors for some specific purpose.

Creditable observation also implies that certain conditions are maintained (Johnson, 1968):

1. A representative or typical sample of students' behaviors must be obtained.

This means that teachers should establish a schedule for observing specific behaviors throughout the school day. Observations that are made under extraordinary conditions frequently are distorted views of students' behaviors. For example, a teacher who observes the frequency of fighting behavior during free time, recess, or transition periods is apt to encounter a disproportionate number of fights compared to the remainder of the school day. Similarly, some students may demonstrate more inappropriate behaviors during a math period, or on Mondays, or at the beginning of the school year. This is not to say that fighting or other inappropriate behavior should be permitted, but rather that unrepresentative behaviors should not be generalized to describe the students' total school behaviors. A systematic schedule of observation that focuses on specific behaviors across time and settings is more representative than a spontaneous or convenience schedule.

2. An accurate record of observed behaviors must be made.

Wright (1960) has classified the most common observational procedures into two systems: open and closed. Open systems are narrative recordings of continuous behavioral sequences. In essence, the coverage of the open systems includes everything about the student, the behavior, and the situation. Open systems are primarily used by researchers, but they tend not to be efficient observational procedure for classroom teachers because of the extensive amount of time required to observe and record behaviors.

Closed systems of observational behavior assessment are more frequently used by classroom teachers. According to Hall, Hawkins, and Axelrod (1975), the closed systems fall into two general classes: a) measurement of lasting products, and b) direct observation of transitory behaviors.

(a) Measurement of lasting products. This strategy is presented first because it is the closest to the present practice of teachers. Many classroom academic behaviors, such as computing arithmetic problems, writing a report, painting a picture, erasing an error, or constructing a manual arts project, result in a lasting product that can be measured readily after the behavior occurs. In addition, various nonacademic behaviors, such as writing on bathroom walls, littering the playground, washing hands, or cleaning the desk, also produce changes in the environment which can be measured at a later time. The primary advantage of measuring lasting products is that the teacher can usually accomplish the measurement at a convenient time rather than watching continuously for the behavior to occur (p. 197).

(b) Direct observation of transitory behaviors. Behaviors such as hand raising, talking out, being courteous, giving correct oral answers, and being out-of-seat are transitory. They leave no product that can be measured subsequent to the occurrence. In order to obtain a record of such behaviors, they must be observed [and recorded] when they happen. . .The choice of measurement procedure depends on the duration of the behavior under study, how obvious it is, the number of different behaviors being recorded consecutively, the magnitude of behavioral change expected, the precision of measurement desired, and the amount of time and attention which can be devoted to the recording (p. 199).

Whether teachers are interested in assessing permanent products or transitory behaviors, an observational record must be maintained. On the simplest level a frequency count of selected behaviors may be kept by recording tallies or check marks when the defined behaviors occur. For example, a teacher may be interested in the frequency of social contacts (i.e., physical or verbal communication) initiated by a particular withdrawn student. The teacher could keep a record by tallying the frequency of social contacts. An example of such a record is presented in Figure 1. If more dimensions of social contacts are added, such as duration and quality, then the recording becomes more complex. Other behaviors, such as time out of seat, fighting, cursing,

---

Student   _George R._

Behavior   _Social Contacts_

Setting   _Regular Classroom_

Date(s)   _March 16-21, 1981_

Observer   _Ms. Jones, Teacher_

Time   Frequency by Days

Time	Monday	Tuesday	Wednesday	Thursday	Friday
8 – 9:	/	0	/	//	0
9 – 10:	Resource – No Observations				
10 – 11:	//	///	//	0	/
11 – 12:	Lunch – No Observations				
12 – 1:	/	/	/	0	/
1 – 2:	/	/	//	0	0
Total	5	5	6	2	2

Figure 1. Example form for recording behavior.

minutes late, and temper tantrums can be defined, observed, and recorded by teachers. The specific system for recording student behaviors will depend upon the individual teacher. A wrist counter, an abacus, and paper-and-pencil techniques, to name a few, have been used to record behavior. Regardless of the technique, teachers should select student behaviors that are related to the assessment of disturbance, that can be directly observed, and that can be accurately recorded.

3. The record must be analyzed or scored faithfully.

The observation condition implied by this statement is not so much the mathematical manipulation (e.g., adding frequencies) as the bias that often exists in the collection of data. For example, a teacher who has "had it" with a student is more apt to record a high frequency of negative behaviors, whereas a teacher who believes a student is good, conscientious, and so on is more apt to overlook behavior that is to be recorded. Consequently, the faithfulness of observation is a matter of consistent recording that is an accurate record of actual behavior.

A second implication of faithfulness has to do with the interpretation of observation data. Since any behavior may be the result of many causes, and any cause may lead to different behaviors, teachers and other clinicians must be extremely careful about drawing conclusions from closed behavior records. Interpretations cannot take the place of good descriptions. Vague statements such as "He wants attention," "She's lazy," and "He daydreams" are interpretations of students' behaviors, *not* descriptions of behavior. Similarly, teacher generalizations such as "He's never on time," "She's always in trouble," and "He never does what I tell him" are patently incorrect assessments of behavior. In order to analyze and score behaviors faithfully, both vague terms and generalizations must be defined as observable behaviors that can be recorded.

The observation of behavior is probably the most common source of information for the assessment of disturbance. Professional educators, however, are reluctant to depend exclusively on this method, or any one assessment method, because of the bias, weakness, and fallibility that is inherent in any single assessment technique (Rich et al., 1981). According to Gordon (1966), "no observer can ever fully overcome his own perceptual orientation. The word 'objective' then, is used as a desired goal, rather than a reality. It is possible to record what one sees objectively, but it is a mistake to assume that it is seen objectively" (p. 65).

Tests

"Tests are a predetermined collection of questions or tasks to which predetermined types of behavioral responses are sought" (Salvia &

Ysseldyke, 1978, p. 9). This predetermined nature of tests assumes that students' responses are correct or incorrect, appropriate or inappropriate, even normal or abnormal. In terms of cognitive information (e.g., math, history), this assumption may be justified because cognitive information generally can be factually verified. Consequently, tests designed to measure students' cognitive knowledge are the most widely used type of test in education (Dizney, 1971).

Tests that require students' responses regarding values, affect, feelings, attitudes, and other intrapersonal characteristics, as opposed to cognitive information, are critical in the assessment of disturbance. The intrapersonal characteristics of students usually cannot be inferred from the observation of classroom behaviors or the results of cognitive tests. Therefore, tests used in the assessment of disturbance must go beyond the overt or surface level of behaviors and provide information about students' inner characteristics, particularly personality traits.

Tests that assess intrapersonal characteristics often suffer from a lack of validity and/or reliability; that is, the tests may not be measuring the intended characteristic or the tests may not be consistently measuring the characteristic over time or between students. Even with these limitations the results of tests are frequently accepted, without question, as an accurate assessment of students' intrapersonal characteristics. The American Psychological Association (1966) warns against the rigid practice of blindly accepting test results:

> Psychological and educational tests are used in arriving at decisions which may have great influence on the ultimate welfare of the persons tested, on educational points of view and practices, and on development and utilization of human resources. Test users, therefore, need to apply high standards of professional judgment in selecting and interpreting tests . . . (p. 1).
> Almost any test can be useful for some functions and in some situations, but even the best test can have damaging consequences if used inappropriately. Therefore, primary responsibility for improvement of testing rests on the shoulders of test users (p. 6).

The test items used to assess intrapersonal characteristics are typically developed through two distinct but interrelated procedures: ideal concepts and standardization. Ideal concepts refer to predetermined characteristics such as "happy," "sociable," and "beautiful" that are presumed to be positively valued within the students' culture. Therefore, students who respond in ways that indicate that they are "depressed," "isolated," and "ugly" are assumed to be demonstrating symptoms of disturbance.

Standardization is another way of saying that there are predetermined or standard answers to predetermined questions. In test development, questions are given to a large number of normal students, and their answers are analyzed by means of a variety of statistical procedures (e.g., factor analysis). By this process, specific high frequency answers become the norm or standard by which subsequent students are evaluated. Thus, if most students answer a question in a particular way, then the few students who answer the question another way are considered somehow different, deviant, or even disturbed.

Tests do provide assessment information about intrapersonal characteristics that observation cannot provide. It is important, however, to emphasize the fact that test results are a tentative and temporary assessment of students' intrapersonal characteristics and should not be treated as absolute or permanent data. The credibility given to the results of any one test, or even series of tests, should be tempered by the consistency with and appropriateness to other assessment procedures, including observations and judgments.

Judgments

The assessment of students' characteristics cannot be totally measured by means of a quantitative approach, that is, through observations and tests. For those aspects of students that do not lend themselves to measurement, professional inference and human sensitivity are important ingredients in the assessment process. Therefore, assessment must go beyond the science of measurement and include the art of human judgment (Rich et al., 1981).

In the final analysis, all assessment ultimately requires human judgment. "Judgments represent both the best and the worst of assessment data. Judgments made by conscientious, capable, and objective individuals can be an invaluable aid in the assessment process. Inaccurate, biased, subjective judgments can be misleading at best and harmful at worst" (Salvia & Ysseldyke, 1978, pp. 9–10).

When a teacher, counselor, or other school personnel decides which behaviors to observe, which tests to administer, which students to refer, or which students will be labeled disturbed, personal judgment has been exercised. Unfortunately, educators' judgments are often clouded by expectations of students' behaviors. It is difficult to analyze one's own values and expectations; thus it is difficult to analyze one's own judgments, as they relate to classroom teaching, particularly in the presence of annoying disruptions. However, if "conscientious, capable, and objective" judgments are to be made, then "what is needed is a more personal kind of searching, which will enable the teacher to identify his own concerns and to share the concerns of his students" (Jersild, 1955, p. 3). Clearly, "one of the most difficult problems the teacher faces in analyzing the learning situation is assessing his own behavior" (Gordon, 1966, p. 89).

Together, current and historical information in the form of observations, tests, and judgments constitute a comprehensive assessment process. Each of the six kinds of information is vital for reaching professionally responsible decisions regarding disturbance among students. Data that have been collected but that are limited to only one or even a few kinds of information should be regarded as screening data—not a complete diagnostic assessment (Long, Morse, & Newman, 1976).

The remainder of this chapter is devoted to examples of different kinds of assessment procedures that emphasize students' behavior, personality, and environments. The decision to include certain assessment procedures and omit others is arbitrary; however, the procedures included are representative of those available, are supported by substantial research, and are extensively documented in the professional literature.

BEHAVIOR ASSESSMENT

In the final analysis all assessments are based on behavior. Students' responses to self-concept instruments, parents' answers to interview questions, and teachers' ratings of students all constitute behaviors. But behavioral responses to assessment procedures are qualitatively different from the naturalistic, unsolicited student behaviors that occur in the classroom. It is the behavior of the first type that is the subject of behavior assessment.

Behavior assessment generally falls within one of two assessment types: observation and judgment. Observation, which was initially discussed in an earlier section of this chapter, is undoubtedly the most common source of behavior information. Formalized judgments, as opposed to intuitive, spontaneous, or reactionary judgments, typically do not occur until later in the assessment process.

Behavior assessment via observation should be guided by a number of generally accepted principles. First, what behaviors will be observed? All behaviors cannot be directly observed; therefore the observer must select well defined "target" behaviors. In terms of disturbance, behaviors that bring negative attention to students are a logical starting point. Second, how will the behaviors be recorded? It was indicated earlier that some type of closed system is preferable for teachers assessing temporary behaviors. (If an outside observer is available then other systems may be considered.) For example, the frequency of behaviors such as fights, cursing, and asking for directions may be recorded with tallies, checks, or tokens, whereas the duration of behaviors such as crying, temper tantrums, and being out of seat additionally requires some sort of timing device (Cooper, 1974). Third, why is the behavior being observed? Generally, assessment "provides information that can enable teachers and other school personnel to make decisions regarding the children they serve" (Salvia & Ysseldyke, 1978, p. 4). Thus, the specific reasons for behavioral assessment are numerous, but the underlying rationale should be based on effective decision making on behalf of the student. For example, one teacher may want to compare the behavior of a student with other students to determine whether significant differences exist; another teacher may want data to find out whether a particular intervention is effective; a third teacher may want data to support referral for special services; and a fourth teacher may want to find out whether a student is disturbed in order to secure additional resources. After the what, how, and why questions have been answered, then it is necessary to answer the procedural questions regarding behavioral assessment—who, when and where. Who will do the observing and recording—the teacher, an aide, another student? When will the observations be made—hourly, daily, weekly? Where are the settings for the observations—the regular classroom, academic periods, the resource room?

The questions relating to what, how, why, who, when, and where need to be concretely answered before one attempts to observe student behaviors. Without a definitive, systematic observation approach the behavior assessment data are of little, perhaps even negative, value. On the other hand, accurate data can be a valuable resource in the decision making process, particularly regarding the diagnosis of disturbance and the effectiveness of treatment. As an illustration, consider the behavior of George R. tabulated earlier in this chapter (Figure 1).

George's teacher, Ms. Jones, suspected that he was withdrawn and, if the suspicion was verified, planned to implement strategies designed to improve his social behavior. Ms. Jones in conjunction with a guidance counselor had decided that a behavior that was indicative of withdrawal was a significantly reduced frequency of social contacts (verbal or physical interaction with peers). Ms. Jones observed and recorded the frequency of George's social contacts for 1 week; she also observed and recorded the number of social contacts of three other randomly selected boys in the classroom. These baseline (before treatment) assessment data yielded 20 social contacts for George and 86, 102, and 111 for the other three boys. Thus, the preliminary or screening observation data indicated that the frequency of George's social contacts was significantly less than the number that would normally be expected among boys in her class. On the basis of these results, Ms. Jones decided to implement two different strategies or treatments: first, to place George in a small discussion group 2 hours per day for 1 week, and second, to praise George verbally each time he made a social contact during a 1-week period.

On successive weeks Ms. Jones collected the frequency of social contacts during baseline, the first strategy, no strategy intervention, the second strategy, and again no strategy intervention. Ms. Jones counted the frequency of George's social contacts and plotted them on a line graph (Figure 2). Tentatively, Ms. Jones could conclude that verbal praise, rather than small group experiences or no treatment, was most effective in increasing the frequency of George's social contacts. Thus, behavior assessment via observation did contribute to Ms. Jones' understanding of George, which subsequently enabled her to make educational decisions. The data do *not*, however, answer questions about the diagnosis of disturbance or even of withdrawn behavior. To answer these questions a more extensive assessment procedure is required.

Behavior assessment also consists of judgments. Judgments take many forms, including report card grades, conduct remarks, disciplinary requests, anecdotal records, and even statements made about students in the teachers' lounge. Judgments that are permanently recorded (e.g., notes, report cards) tend to be of greater value than temporary judgments (e.g., verbal statements, unrecorded observa-

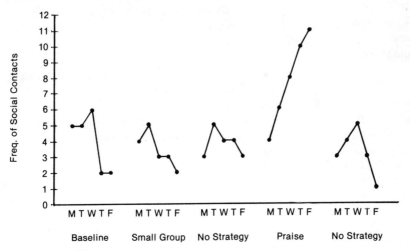

Figure 2.   Frequency of George's social contacts during different strategy and no strategy weeks.

tions) in the assessment process because they can be evaluated, replicated, and verified. Unfortunately, many judgments, both permanent and temporary, are idiosyncratic, that is, a function of the individual teacher's method of recording, personal beliefs and values, and so forth. Although these idiosyncratic judgments may never, and perhaps should never, be eliminated from the assessment process, two procedures have been routinely used both to provide a permanent record and to reduce the variability of teachers' judgments: behavior rating scales and structured interviews.

Behavior Rating Scales

This type of assessment has become popular among educators over the past few decades. This popularity is probably the result of the increased emphasis on the behavior theory in explaining disturbance, the simplicity of administration, and the fact that rating scales provide permanent records that theoretically identify behavior problem areas. The scales themselves represent an uncomplicated, straightforward approach to the assessment of behavior. Beyond knowledge of the general instructions, no specialized training is necessary to administer, score, or interpret rating scales. Teachers should not be misled, however, by this simplistic quality of behavior rating scales. At least three critical limitations of these scales should be considered. First, teachers' judgments are a significant factor in the rating of behaviors, even though there is an attempt to standardize the responses. Second, literally hundreds of scales have been published, but very few have sufficient normative data to justify the screening of disturbed students. Third, the scales should not be used alone to assess disturbance; the results are only another piece of information that can be used in the diagnostic process.

Behavior rating scales list a series of different student behaviors, usually 25 or more, that the teacher is to rate (judge) on a scale of severity. Through a statistical process (e.g., factor analysis) the scales cluster or group related behaviors into different problem areas. Table 2 lists some exemplary behavior rating scales, including the number of different behaviors that are rated, the severity scale (e.g., 1 to 5), and the behavior problem areas or clusters identified.

Probably the best known and most widely used behavior rating scale is the Behavior Problem Checklist (BPC). The extensive use of the BPC is undoubtedly related to the uncomplicated scoring procedure, the focus on school-related problem behaviors, and the extensive amount of field testing data on the instrument that has been accumulated over the past 20 years. According to Quay (1977), the most useful

Table 2.   Example of behavior rating scales

Checklist	Items	Scale	Behavior problem areas
Behavior Problem Checklist (Quay & Peterson, 1979)	55	0–2	Conduct problem Personality problem Inadequacy/immaturity Socialized delinquent
Pupil Behavior Inventory (Vinter et al., 1966)	34	1–5	Classroom conduct Academic motivation and performance Social-emotional state Teacher dependence Personal behavior
Devereux Child Behavior Rating Scale (Spivack & Spotts, 1966)	97	1–5[a]	Distractibility Poor self-care Pathological use of senses Emotional detachment Social isolation Poor coordination Incontinence Messiness/sloppiness Inadeqate need for independence Unresponsiveness Proneness to upset Need for adult contact Anxious-fearful ideation "Impulse" ideation Inability to delay Social aggression Unethical behavior
Ottawa School Behavior Checklist (Pimm & McClure, circa 1969)	100	1–2[b]	High-risk problem behavior
Walker Problem Behavior Identification Checklist (Walker, 1970)	50	1–4	Acting-out behavior Withdrawal Distractibilty Disturbed peer relations Immature/dependent behavior

[a] Most of the behaviors are rated on a 1–5 scale; however, some behaviors require a 1–7, 1–8, or 1–9 scale rating.
[b] This is a "yes" or "no" rating as to the existence of each behavior.

purposes of the BPC are "the identification of, and differentiation among, dimensions of deviance in children and adolescence" (p. 285).

The sample behaviors from the BPC presented in Table 3 represent different behavior problem areas that are rated by the teacher for individual students. Each behavior item is rated as constituting no problem (0), a mild problem (1), or a severe problem (2).

Table 3.   Sample student behaviors on the Behavior Problem Checklist

Behavior problem area[a]	Sample student behavior item
Conduct problem	Restlessness; inability to sit still
	Disruptiveness; tendency to annoy others
	Negativism; tendency to do the opposite of thing requested
Personality problem	Shyness; bashfulness
	Hypersensitivity; feelings easily hurt
	Depression; chronic sadness
Inadequacy/immaturity	Preoccupation; "in his own world"
	Short attention span
	Passivity; suggestibility; easily led
Socialized delinquent	Steals in company with others
	Belongs to a gang
	Truancy from school

[a] The behavior problem areas were defined in Chapter 4 as an educators' classification system.

The results obtained from the BPC and other checklists must be interpreted with caution, particularly because teachers tend to judge students in general as having several mild or severe behavior problems. Werry and Quay (1971) found that teachers of "normal" kindergarteners and first and second graders rated a significant number of their students as demonstrating problem behaviors. In fact, Werry and Quay found that teachers rated 49.7 percent of all boys as having problems with restlessness, and 41.4 percent of all girls as demonstrating "shyness; bashfulness." The overall rating of 1753 normal students on the 55 behavior items revealed that teachers judged boys to have an average of 11.4 problems (mild and severe combined), mostly of the conduct problem type. Girls were rated as having fewer problems, with an average of 7.6, and their problems were typically of the personality problem type. Thus, it must be assumed that most students will be rated as having some problems. It is only when the frequency and severity of these problems significantly differ from the average that behavior checklists can be used as a screening assessment indicating the possibility of disturbance.

Structured Interviews

Aside from the observation of behavior, interview approaches are among the most widely used assessment procedures. Routinely teachers interview students regarding inappropriate behavior and possible motivation, with questions such as: "What did you say?" "Where are you going?" "Why did you do that?" "How do you feel about what you did?" and so on. Interviews of this type, however, tend to be spontaneous and emotional; they rarely provide useful information because such interviews are usually intended to blame, monitor, or otherwise disapprove of students or the behavior. On the other hand, a planned assessment interview potentially provides information that can only be obtained from students or their parents in a face-to-face inquiry session.

Structured interviews with the students being assessed and their parents often take the form of specific questions designed to obtain specific information; hence the term "structured." The specific interview questions should be designed to obtain information that will enable the teacher or clinician to understand the behavior and personality of students in order to reach a diagnostic decision and plan an appropriate program. From the practical, legal, and humanitarian points of view, both students and their parents must be involved in the program planning when a handicapping condition is verified; therefore, it makes sense that the persons ultimately affected should be involved in the assessment process.

Most interviews have a definite psychodynamic flavor that is evidenced by the emphasis, among other things, on psychological problems, motivating causes, and psychiatric terminology. Therefore, interviews typically go beyond the assessment of behavior and probe the personality realm. Jane Kessler (1966), for example, has provided a model "diagnostic guide" that includes observation, test, and judgment assessment procedures, but which has a definite emphasis on interviews, particularly with parents:[1]

I. *From the Parents*
    (In interviewing parents, one is concerned with obtaining factual information about the child, but also with assessing, if possible, the parents' attitudes and feelings. The best method is to start with general inquiries and follow up with specific questions.)
    A. *General inquiry*
        1. "What is the problem which concerns you?" The parents may be specific and well-informed about this, or vague and perplexed, or even so indifferent that they are there only because they were told to come.
        2. "When did you first learn of the difficulties? What were you told? Have you done anything about this before?" The parents may seem astonished that a problem exists, and insist that they were never informed of it. If their account of what has been said to them is inaccurate, the distortions they introduce will be helpful in understanding them.
        3. "Have you any ideas what the possible causes of the school problem might be?" The parent may blame the school,

---

[1] From Jane W. Kessler, *Psychopathology of Childhood,* Copyright 1966, pp. 221–223. Reprinted by permission of Prentice-Hall, Inc., Englewood Cliffs, N.J.

themselves, or some physical defect, or they may intuitively sense a psychological cause.
4. "Were there any problems before he started school? Did you anticipate his having difficulties?"
5. "What has been said to the child about his school failures? How does he feel about them?" One hopes to get an indication of the parents' closeness to the child and of their ability to communicate with him.

B. Specific inquiry
1. Current behavior
   a. Other symptoms: Enuresis, thumb sucking, lip licking, sleep problems, feeding difficulties, fighting, dawdling, and so on.
   b. Peer relationships: Choice of playmates, role usually taken by the child, interest in seeking companionship, close friendships, teasing, being teased, and so on.
   c. Physical activity: Degree of interest and form it takes. . .reaction to instruction in sports involving physical contact with other players.
   d. Family relationships: Acceptance of parental authority, of criticism, restrictions, requests, and punishment. Responsibility for self-care and for helping in home. Relationship to siblings, patterns of dominance, bickering, jealousy, and so on.
   e. Expressed feelings about going to school: History of reluctance to attend, differences in mood during school and vacation periods, comments about work, successes and failures.
2. Pre-school history
   a. Birth and early development: Abnormalities. . .worries during the first years. Age of walking, development of speaking.
   b. Feeding: Usual appetite, food preferences, history of force feeding, present attitudes, age of weaning from bottle.
   c. Toilet training: Time if recalled, parents' recollection of relative easiness, history of constipation, history of force, participation by the parents.
   d. Early discipline: Easy or difficult to control, means used, manner of handling early aggression (e.g., biting and kicking), manner of handling verbal aggression.
   e. Mental development: Verbal development, intellectual curiosity (i.e., questions asked), expression of curiosity about sex differences, birth of babies, death, God, and so on. Nursery school.
   f. Medical history: Previous illnesses, operations, accidents, present defects (e.g., allergies, visual defects).
3. Family history
   a. Family illness or crises: When, how explained to the child, his reactions.
   b. Chronic tensions in home: Financial, marital difficulties, in-laws, crowding and so on.

    c. Separations from parents: When, how long, reasons, how explained, child's reaction.

    d. Parents' educational experiences: Schooling. Was it easy, enjoyable, difficult, or what? Their current occupations and attitudes toward them.

    e. Parental handling of current school problem: Degree of interest, what has been said and done, degree of accord between parents about handling of the problem, evidences of interplay between parents or parent and child.

    f. Indications of identifications: Father-son, mother-daughter, father-daughter.

II. *From the Child*

No attempt is made here to describe the diagnostic usefulness of psychological procedures or to recommend any special battery of tests; this would require extensive presentation and a critique of the voluminous literature available. None is foolproof, and even those tests which differentiate diagnostic groups (e.g., organic versus functional) overlap to an embarrassing extent. In studying an individual child, one must evaluate the tests in the light of his history and behavior.

A. *Attitudes*

    1. Child's awareness of the problem: Evaluation of his expressed feelings about the difficulty, particularly in terms of anxiety and involvement.

    2. His self-concept: How does he see himself—as a top student, a bad child, or a foreordained failure?

    3. Reactions to success and failure: Level of aspiration, realistic understanding of his limitations, pleasure in success, reactions to difficult questions, admission of lack of knowledge, and so on.

B. *General behavior*

    1. Patterns of withholding and blocking: Kinds of situations which arouse these reactions.

    2. Response to examiner: Degree of openness, readiness to establish a relationship, eagerness to confide, ability to verbalize reactions and experiences, tolerance for work involved in taking tests.

    3. Special preoccupations: Aggression, violent ideas, intimations of catastrophe or danger, self-devaluation, intrusion of fantasy into tests.

    4. Activity or passivity: Extent to which he is governed by a wish to be liked, to avoid trouble, and so on. What awakens spontaneity? Frequency with which he asks questions. Degree to which he resents being told what to do.

Kessler readily conceded that the accuracy of interview information, particularly that of a historical nature, is often questionable; therefore, the information must be interpreted with caution. In addition, Achenbach (1974) warned that "unless the interviewer is thoroughly familiar with the range of behavior typically displayed by children of

various ages, intelligence, and socioeconomic levels in interview settings, he may mistake normal withdrawal, anxiety, fear, or boister-
ousness for pathological conditions" (p. 578). Therefore, interview
data must be collected by a competent, sensitive interviewer, asking
specific and relevant questions that are designed to become a part of
the total assessment package.

PERSONALITY ASSESSMENT

Personality characteristics may be assessed from the observation of
behavior, the information collected during interviews, and the results
of tests. However, none of these techniques provide a direct assessment of students' inner thoughts, feelings, attitudes, and so on. The
data obtained are all indirect assessments of personality that are judged
to reveal certain personality characteristics by the examiner. Thus,
judgment, interpretation, and inference play a significant role in the
assessment of personality and, consequently, the decision to label a
student as disturbed.

By far the most frequently used procedure for assessing personality takes the form of tests. Numerous personality tests, which may
be roughly categorized as standardized or projective, are currently
being used to assess students who are suspected of being disturbed.
Table 4 lists some exemplary tests that are widely used for the purpose
of personality assessment by educators and other mental health professionals. Noticeably most of the personality tests were developed between 1950 and 1970, a period of time when the emphasis on psychological implications of disturbance reached its apex. According to
Salvia and Ysseldyke (1978), the emphasis on new personality assessment techniques is part of the movement away from psychological
assessment toward a more objective study of behavior.

> Along with a shift in orientation and an increased skepticism about the
> adequacy of personality devices and the relevance of information ob-
> tained, we have witnessed an increased concern for the privacy of the
> individual. Not long ago, congressional hearings debated the extent to
> which personality assessment constituted invasion of privacy. Schools
> are now required by law to gain informed consent from parents before
> assessing children and may only maintain and disseminate *verified* infor-
> mation about a child. It has been increasingly difficult to convince parents
> that personality assessment *should* take place, and there is no way to
> verify the information gathered by personality tests (Salvia & Ysseldyke,
> 1978, p. 378).

Contrary to the belief of many behaviorists, personality assessment should not be categorically dismissed as irrelevant, unverifiable,
or an invasion of privacy. Certainly, great care must be exercised in

Table 4. Examples of personality tests

Bender Visual Motor Gestalt Test (Bender, 1938)[a]
Blacky Pictures Technique (Blum, 1967)[a]
California Psychological Inventory (Gough, 1969)
California Test of Personality (Thorpe, Clark, & Tiegs, 1953)
Children's Apperception Test (Bellak & Bellak, 1965)[a]
Children's Personality Questionnaire (Porter & Cattell, 1959)
Draw-a-Person (Urban, 1963)[a]
Early Childhood Personality Questionnaire (Coan & Cattell, 1970)
Edwards Personality Inventory (Edwards, 1966)
Evanston Early Identification Scale (Landsman & Dillard, 1967)[a]
General Anxiety Scale for Children (Sarason et al., 1960)
Holtzman Inkblot Technique (Holtzman, 1966)[a]
House-Tree-Person (Buck & Jolles, 1966)[a]
Human Figure Drawing Test (Koppitz, 1968)[a]
Junior-Senior High School Personality Questionnaire (Cattell, Coan, &
  Belloff, 1969)
Lipsitt Self-Concept Scale (Lipsitt, 1958)
Minnesota Multiphasic Personality Inventory (Hathaway & McKinley, 1967)
Piers-Harris Childrens' Self Concept Scale (Piers & Harris, 1969)
Personality Adjustment Inventory (Rogers, 1961)
Rorschach Ink Blot Test (Rorschach, 1966)[a]
Tennessee Self Concept Inventory (Fitts, 1965)
Thematic Apperception Test (Murray, 1943)[a]

[a] Projective-type test.

the administration, scoring, and interpretation of personality tests. Personality assessment is but one part of an effective assessment package; no single test or observation or judgment can stand alone in the assessment of disturbance. Both standardized and projective tests, in conjunction with other assessment procedures, can contribute to the understanding of students, the diagnosis of disturbance, and effective educational planning.

Standardized Tests

Standardized, or norm-referenced, personality tests are more frequently used than tests of the projective type chiefly because they may be administered to large groups with a minimal amount of specialized training. Standardized tests typically consist of a series of printed questions, usually from 50 to 200, that require a multiple-choice, scaled, or weighted response. For example, the following items and the response choices are common among standardized personality tests:

I am happy: yes or no
I am afraid: always, often, sometimes, rarely, never
I cry easily: true or false

How I feel about myself:

I would rather play by myself □ or with friends □

The specific test items are chosen by the test author because he or she believes that particular answers or patterns of answers will distinguish personality characteristics. The instrument is then administered to a large sample of students, whose answers are statistically analyzed in order to determine the pattern of normal responses. The responses of a particular student are compared with the responses of the normative sample on which the test was standardized. This statistical comparison, which is made using the tables in the test manual, reveals whether or not the student produced responses consistent with the normal population. Significant variation is often judged to be an indication of disturbance or at least a personality problem.

Choice of the specific test to be administered should be determined by the kind of personality information desired. According to Walker (1973), five areas of personality are measured by the various tests: attitude, behavior traits, interests, self-concept, and emotional development. These general areas are further broken down into numerous subareas. For example, the Piers-Harris Children's Self-Concept Scale claims to assess several components of self-concept, including intellect, body image, social position, and self-satisfaction.

It is suggested that any professional educator interested in utilizing a standardized personality test first consult the *Seventh Mental Measurements Yearbook* (Buros, 1972), which devotes almost 400 pages to a review of personality tests. This review discusses the critical aspects of tests, including administration functions, cost, personality areas assessed, and, most importantly, the extent to which the tests measure what they are supposed to measure (validity).

Projective Tests

Projective tests typically consist of ambiguous or neutral stimuli (e.g., inkblots, designs, or pictures) that students are to describe or reproduce in an individual testing situation. Theoretically, students *project* certain aspects of their personality into their responses, thus the term "projective." This type of test is an outgrowth of psychodynamic theory, which maintains "that there are internal causes of behavior and that the identification of these causes will facilitate both an understanding of behavior and behavior change" (Salvia & Ysseldyke, 1978, p. 373).

Even though some aspects of projective tests have been standardized, the narrative and open-ended nature of this type of test requires a greater degree of clinical training in order for diagnostic decisions to be made. Consequently, projective tests are an assessment of a student's personality that is not determined solely on how other students may respond to the same stimuli, but more on the needs, motives, desires, and so on expressed by the student in the testing situation.

For nonpsychometric personnel, particularly teachers, there is a mystique that surrounds the projective test process. Often teachers of disturbed students receive a psychological assessment report simply stating that a student was administered a certain test that indicated certain results. Unfortunately, most teachers have only a vague notion about the particular tests and even less knowledge about how the results were determined. In order to eliminate some of this mystique, the following discussion will focus on two of the most frequently used projective tests: the Visual Motor Gestalt Test and Human Figure Drawings.

Visual Motor Gestalt Test   This test, commonly known as the Bender Gestalt (Bender, 1938), consists of nine geometric designs (Figure 3) that are presented to the student on individual cards one at a time. The student is asked to copy each design on a blank piece of standard size paper. Student reproductions of the Bender Gestalt designs have been used to diagnose a wide variety of handicapping conditions, particularly mental retardation, learning disabilities, brain in-

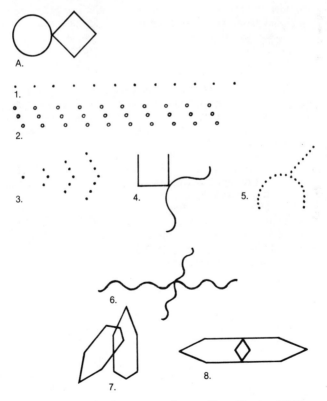

Figure 3.   A visual motor gestalt test. (From Bender, 1938).

jury, and emotional disturbance. Even though the Bender Gestalt was introduced over 40 years ago, it is still widely accepted as a personality and psychological assessment technique.

In assessing personality disturbance, the student's reproductions of the Bender Gestalt designs are scored according to 10 primary criteria, or "emotional indicators," that are directly related to the assessment of disturbance. According to Koppitz (1964) the emotional indicators and their implications for mild or moderate disturbance include:

1. Confused order (i.e., figures scattered arbitrarily on paper without logical sequence or order). This indicator is associated with poor planning, mental confusion and/or an inability to organize material.
2. Wavy line (i.e., two or more abrupt changes [angles] in the direction of the line of dots or circles in designs 1 and 2). This indicator is associated with instability in motor coordination and personality; or poor coordination and personality; or poor coordination and poor integrative capacity; or poor motor control.
3. Dashes substituted for circles (i.e., at least half of all the circles on design 2 are replaced with dashes). This indicator is associated with impulsivity and lack of interest or attention; or preoccupation with personal problems; or an attempt to avoid doing what is required.
4. Increasing size (i.e., dots and circles in designs 1, 2, and 3 increase progressively in size until the last ones are three times as large as the first ones). This indicator is associated with low frustration tolerance and explosiveness.
5. Large size (i.e., one or more designs are drawn one third larger in both directions than the design on the stimulus card). This indicator is associated with acting-out or aggressive behavior.
6. Small size (i.e., one or more designs are drawn half as large as the design on the stimulus card). This indicator is associated with anxiety, withdrawal, constriction, and timidity.
7. Fine line (i.e., line so thin or light that it requires effort to see the completed design). This indicator is associated with timidity, shyness and withdrawal.
8. Overwork or reinforced lines (i.e., total design or part of it is redrawn or reinforced with heavy, impulsive lines). This indicator is associated with impulsive, acting-out, or aggressive behavior.
9. Second attempt at drawing designs (i.e., abandoning a design before or after it has been completed and a new drawing is made). This indicator is associated with impulsivity and anxiety.
10. Expansion* (i.e., using more than one sheet of paper to complete the nine designs). This indicator is associated with impulsive acting-out and aggressive behavior.
    Indicators 1, 4, and 10 normally occur among younger children in kindergarten and the primary elementary grades (adapted from Koppitz, 1964).

The generalizations that may be made regarding personality assessment and the Bender Gestalt are: 1) that large drawings indicate acting-out behavior such as impulsivity and aggression, and 2) that small drawings indicate withdrawn behavior including shyness and timidness. Of course, these 10 criteria are grossly simplified indicators of marginal disturbance; the assessment of severe disturbance such as schizophrenia and other forms of psychosis requires a much more detailed analysis and sophisticated interpretation of design deviations. However, Koppitz (1964) maintained that all of the "children with five or more emotional indicators were among those referred for psychological evaluation because of serious emotional maladjustment" (p. 131).

Human Figure Drawings   Personality assessments that involve the drawing of a person include the Human Figure Drawings (HFD; Koppitz, 1968), Draw-a-Person (DAP), Evanston Early Identification Scale, and House-Person-Tree tests. These tests are remarkably similar in that assessment is based on the absence or alteration of critical body characteristics at different developmental ages. All of the test authors maintain that artistic skill or drawing ability is unrelated to personality assessment.

Koppitz (1968) interpreted and scored HFDs from two different types of objective signs. "One set of signs on the HFDs is believed to be primarily related to children's age and level of maturation; these signs are called *Developmental Items*. The second set of signs is thought to be primarily related to children's attitudes and concerns; these signs are designated *Emotional Indicators*" (p. 7).

Developmental Items   The inclusion of certain characteristics in the HFD is reported to be a function of developmental age. Koppitz (1968) identified 30 HFD characteristics that differentiated the developmental maturation of elementary school-age students. For example, it was generally found that head, eyes, nose, mouth, body, and legs were present on most of the HFDs by the age of 5; feet were added by age 6; dimensional arms and legs (as opposed to a single line) and hair were expected by age 7 or 8; neck was included by age 9; and arms down and arms attached at shoulders were expected by age 10 or 11. Boys were typically 1 year older than girls before arms, feet, hair, and arms down were included. Students who do not include the expected items for their chronological age are considered developmentally delayed.

Emotional Indicators   Koppitz (1968) analyzed the results of several HFD studies and found that certain emotional indicators occurred most often among students who had been diagnosed as having certain kinds of personality characteristics or problems (Table 5). For example, students diagnosed as shy produced HFDs that were small, with no nose or mouth, and with the hands cut off. The information in Table

Table 5.   Summary of findings on emotional indicators on HFDs of children

Emotional indicators	Personality characteristics					
	Shy	Aggressive	Psychosomatic	Stealing	Brain injury	Poor school achiever
Integration		O			×	×
Shaded body	O			O		
Shaded hands				O		
Asymmetry		×			×	
Slanting figure				O	×	×
Tiny figure	×				×	
Big figure		O		O		
Transparency		O		O	×	
Tiny head				O		
Teeth		×				
Short arms	O		×			
Long arms		×				
Big hands		×		×		
Hands cut off	×				×	
Legs together			O			
Genitals		×				
Monster						O
Clouds			×			
No nose	×		×			
No mouth	×		O			O
No body				O	×	×
No arms		O		O		×
No feet	O					
No neck				×	×	

Adapted and abridged from Koppitz (1968). ×, item occurs significantly more often on HFDs of personality groups indicated. O, item occurs more often, but not significantly, on HFDs of personality groups indicated.

5 represents a general summary of the relationship between personality characteristics and emotional indicators evidenced by students completing a HFD. This kind of "cookbook" cannot be used to make diagnostic decisions; rather, it should only be considered as an introduction to the assessment implications of the HFD as a projective test.

There appears to be a consensus among the experts on HFDs that no one-to-one relationship exists between any single sign on HFDs and a definite personality trait or behavior on the part of the boy or girl making the drawing. Anxieties, conflicts or attitudes can be expressed on HFDs in different ways by different children or by one child at different times. This writer can only underscore what others have emphasized again and again: It is not possible to make a meaningful diagnosis or evaluation of a child's behavior or difficulties on the basis of any single sign on a HFD. The *total* drawing and the combination of various signs and indicators should always be considered and should then be analyzed on the basis of the child's age, maturation, emotional status, social and cultural background and should then be evaluated together with other available test data (Koppitz, 1968, p. 55).

Koppitz's warning about the uses and misuses of the HFD is equally applicable to all personality tests, both standardized and projective. Certainly, personality tests can contribute to a comprehensive, effective assessment of students, *if* assessment decisions take into account not only the test results but also other significant circumstances or conditions that affect the behavior and personality of students.

ENVIRONMENTAL ASSESSMENT

This chapter is primarily concerned with the assessment of the behavior and personality of students. However, it is necessary to point out the fact that a complete assessment must go beyond individual students and assess significant components of their environments. "Astute diagnosticians are presently well beyond the point of focusing their assessment efforts exclusively on the child" (Smith, Neisworth, & Greer, 1978, p. iii). This is another way of saying that behavior and personality are rarely a function of the individual student alone, but are caused, influenced, or at least supported by innumerable environmental factors. In short, behavior and personality are a function of the person *and* the environment.

Within the classroom there are at least four critical environmental factors that affect student behavior and personality: the physical setting, social relations, curricular experiences, and teacher behaviors. This section does not attempt to discuss assessment procedures for each of the factors, but simply calls attention to the fact that data regarding these environmental factors should be included in the assessment of students.

The Physical Setting

The physical properties of the classroom can produce physiological effects that are often mistakenly considered symptomatic of disturbance. For example, when the classroom is too hot, or overcrowded, or lacks the necessary personal space, the frequency of negative student behaviors such as aggression, frustration, and irritability usually increases. When assessing students, the physical setting must therefore also be assessed in order to shed light on the role of the environment and the occurrence of disturbed behaviors.

According to Smith, Neisworth, and Greer (1978), the following physical properties of the environment influence behavior:

Illumination (i.e., is there sufficient, nonglare lighting?)
Noise (i.e., is the noise at a tolerable, nondistracting level?)
Temperature (i.e., is the temperature at a comfortable level?)
Personal space (i.e., is there sufficient individual space or separation between students?)
Crowding (i.e., is the room size sufficient for the number of students?)
Furnishings (i.e., is the furniture sufficient and flexible enough to accommodate different activities?)
Other (i.e., is the room appropriately decorated, uncluttered, organized, clean, etc.?)

Social Relations

It is generally believed that students who have good friends enjoy better mental health than students who have relatively few friends or who are actively disliked (Fox, Luszki, & Schmuck, 1966). The extent to which students are accepted, supported, or reinforced by the classroom peer group has definite implications for disturbance. Unfortunately, many mainstreamed students have felt isolated, intimidated, or unaccepted in the regular classroom. This atmosphere of rejection occurs when classroom peer groups treat students as different, as scapegoats, or as otherwise unwelcome in the classroom. Of the four environmental factors, inadequate or inappropriate social relations constitute one of the most significant contributors to disturbance. In fact, most of the definitions of disturbance include a criterion that has to do with the lack of satisfying relationships.

Data collected from observations, tests, and interviews often provide information regarding students' status in the class. Observation, for example, may reveal that the classroom group employs negative nicknames, is unwilling to share, congregates into selective cliques, or engages in frequent dominant or submissive roles. These behaviors are indicators that the social relationships within the classroom do not support good mental health and, consequently, contribute to disturbance. Also, sociograms, in particular, are useful assessment techniques for determining friendship patterns and social distances among class members. An analysis of students' social choices can readily reveal whether the class has definite "stars" or isolates, whether friendship patterns are polarized or evenly distributed, or whether disturbed students are accepted or rejected. In short, the assessment of social relations is a necessity if teachers are to be effective in interpreting the characteristics of disturbance and promoting a mentally healthy classroom climate.

Curricular Experiences

Of all the environmental factors, curricular experiences are the most difficult to assess. Obviously, that which is to be learned by students must be appropriate, that is, individually relevant in terms of their needs, skills, objectives, and so forth. One thing is patently clear: disturbed students have generally been unsuccessful learners in school (Bloom, 1976). Each year they have typically fallen further behind in their expected amount of achievement. These unsuccessful years of school experience have resulted in academic retardation, feelings of inadequacy, and negative attitudes toward school. This negatively spiraling experience has contributed significantly to the demonstration of disturbed behaviors in the classroom. For example, students who are required to complete tasks that are well above their functional skill levels or that are affectively inappropriate are apt to act-out, become hyperactive, or withdraw.

Thus, in addition to behavior and personality assessment, academic and intellectual data are necessary to plan and evaluate curricular experiences. The individual education program (IEP) required by PL 94-142 is an effort to design an appropriate education for each mainstreamed student. Although the specific information on an IEP will probably differ for each student, the following minimum information is required:

1. Statements indicating the child's present level of performance.
2. Annual goals indicating anticipated progress during the year.
3. Intermediate (shorter term) instructional objectives.
4. A statement of the specific special education and related services to be provided, as well as the extent to which the student will participate in regular education programs.
5. The projected date for initiation of services and the anticipated duration of services.
6. Evaluation criteria and procedures for measuring progress toward goals, on at least an annual basis. (Odle & Galtelli, 1980, p. 248).

The requirements of an IEP clearly establish the need for the assessment of curricular experiences. The completion of items 1 and 6, in particular, must be supported by assessment data that go beyond disturbance and include information regarding learning.

Teacher Behaviors

Today's schools are accommodating a wider variety of students with a wider variety of characteristics, including attitudes, skills, and behaviors. Consequently, routine teaching behaviors of the past, such as prolonged lecturing to large groups, are inappropriate for a large percentage of students. Research on teaching has produced one significant conclusion: different teachers with different instructional styles have different effects on different students.

While we are not at all certain what combination of events makes a good lesson or what combination of qualities makes a good teacher, the potentially better teacher is one who is able to plan and control his professional behavior—to teach many kinds of lessons, to reach many diverse learners, to create different social climates, and to adapt a wide range of teaching strategies to constantly changing conditions. The reason the teacher must possess a range of teaching strategies is simply because different styles or patterns of teaching behavior are useful for different educational purposes, and every teacher seeks educational ends that demand more than one way of teaching (Joyce & Harootunian, 1967, p. 94).

The assessment implication, then, is that each teacher must evaluate the effects of his or her teaching behavior on different students, particularly those who are failing, disruptive, unmotivated, or otherwise disturbed. For example, how do particular students respond to lectures, demonstrations, tutoring, rewards, empathy, control, freedom, and so forth? The most effective educational program cannot be implemented until these kinds of questions are answered.

Environmental assessment is a necessary ingredient in the assessment of the characteristics of disturbed students. Although the focus is not on students per se, information regarding the environmental conditions with which disturbed students interact provides a more comprehensive diagnostic picture, enabling educators more effectively to define or classify students and, ultimately, plan and implement more effective educational programs. This section of the chapter is included to increase teacher awareness of the role of environmental factors and their relationship to disturbance, rather than identify specific assessment procedures. The instruction and management implications of the physical setting, social relations, curricular experiences, and teacher behavior will be discussed in Section III.

SUMMARY

This chapter emphasized the assessment of the characteristics of disturbed students. Since school personnel are continuously evaluating the academic status of all students, there has been relatively little emphasis on the assessment of nonacademic characteristics. Therefore, this chapter included a discussion of the types of assessments and the specific assessment of students' behavior and personality, and of their environments.

The kinds of information were classified according to the time of the assessment (current or historical) and how the information is collected (from observations, tests, or judgments). Current information on students, or data regarding their present functioning, tends to be more useful, easily obtained, and valid, and therefore more frequently used as an assessment. Historical data, on the other hand, tend to be limited and biased, but such data are necessary to evaluate the longevity or chronic nature of the particular characteristic.

Observation, or the act of intentionally and systematically viewing and recording behavior, is probably the most common source of assessment information used to identify disturbed students. However, observation is limited to an assessment of overt behavior. In order to assess internal or personal characteristics, personality tests that consist of predetermined questions are used to understand better the meaning of behaviors or to categorize characteristic traits. Professional judgments, although representing the best and the worst of assessment, are necessary to interpret, analyze, and utilize the observation and test information.

Observations, tests, and judgments are used to assess three critical dimensions of disturbance: behavior, personality, and the environment. Specific exemplary behavior and personality assessment techniques and instruments, including their advantages and disadvantages, were emphasized. Environmental factors that cause, influence, or support disturbance also must be assessed in order for educators effectively to diagnose disturbance and plan education experiences. A complete assessment of students should include all of the kinds of information about the three critical dimensions of disturbance.

Section III
EDUCATIONAL STRATEGIES

7

Intervention Strategies

Intervention strategies are specific educational and/or treatment procedures that have been designed to intervene into the lives of disturbed students. "Intervention is a mediational process which enters into the variant reciprocity between a child and his or her world, to affect that reciprocity, and to promote a different outcome than would have been expected without such interposing" (Rhodes & Tracy, 1972b, p. 27). In short, the intervention strategies are intended to alter the biophysical, behavioral, psychological, and/or environmental circumstances of students to reduce disturbance by increasing appropriate behavior and positive mental health. The different intervention strategies consist of different instructional methodologies, management techniques, objectives, and so on that deal with different aspects of disturbance. None of the strategies can be considered inclusive; the emphasis of each is on different aspects of disturbance rather than the whole student.

During the mid-twentieth century a number of intervention strategies emerged claiming to be "the" approach for educating or treating disturbed students. Individually, the intervention strategies are based on fundamentally sound principles of methodology, human growth and development, learning, and so forth, that are derived from a specific theory of causality. From the variety of interventions available, classroom teachers have frequently accepted a single strategy and implemented it on a unilateral and wholesale basis regardless of the students' characteristics, behaviors, problems, or needs. Observation of classes

---

This chapter was co-authored by H. Lyndall Rich and Anne C. Troutman.

that contain disturbed students, however, reveals that no one theory or intervention strategy is universally accepted (Rich, 1978b).

In order to resolve at least partially the question as to which intervention is most appropriate, it is first necessary to provide succinct operational descriptors of the different strategies. Once the strategies have been differentiated on methodological grounds, then the task becomes one of matching disturbed students with the particular strategy that is most appropriate. This chapter concentrates on the methodological descriptors of the major strategies; matching of strategies and students, based on the characteristics of disturbance, is discussed in Chapter 10.

CLASSIFICATION OF INTERVENTIONS

One of the earliest efforts to analyze and classify the different educational interventions used with disturbed students was reported by Hollister and Goldston (1962). Their analysis of different classroom operations resulted in a "preliminary taxonomy" that organized "procedures and considerations involved in conducting these classes" (p. i). Hollister and Goldston concluded that there were 12 different criteria that represented fundamental differences among interventions that included administration procedures, student selection and study, classroom methodology, and supportive operations. Six of the criteria dealt specifically with classroom methodology:

1. The relationship building process; that is, the extent to which the teacher established a climate of emotional understanding and support, including interpersonal and group relationship building procedures.
2. The motivation development process; that is, the extent to which the teacher specifically guided students toward realizing their potential, including their motivation to learn and to effect social adjustment.
3. The perceptual retraining process; that is, the extent to which the teacher utilized diagnostic findings to formulate an educational program to train or retrain the intact mental abilities.
4. The classroom behavior management processes; that is, the extent to which the teacher provided structure and knowledge of individual and group functioning to control maladaptive behavior.
5. The behavior re-education process; that is, the extent to which the teacher provided corrective learning experiences through a gradual, planned process of unlearning inappropriate behavior while maximizing acceptable behaviors.

6. The academic education process; that is, the extent to which the teacher developed an individualized cognitive based curriculum, including tutoring, remedial education, and special methods and materials (abridged and adapted from Hollister & Goldston, 1962, pp. 10–20).

For any given classroom, each of the six criteria could be expressed as a continuum from "no evidence" to "frequent demonstration" of the classroom condition. Significant differences in the continuum positions therefore represent different methodological interventions. Table 1 is a hypothetical example of the differences between two teachers (A and B) on the six criteria. On the basis of the differences between teachers A and B, it may be said that the two classroom conditions are substantively different. In the example presented in Table 1, A represents a teacher who apparently places high priority on the psychological and social implications of behavior and is primarily concerned with relationships and motivation within a minimally controlled classroom environment. In addition, teacher A places a lower priority on educational methods that are designed to develop cognitive or academic skills among students. The emphasis of teacher B, on the other hand, is on structured and sequential cognitive and behavior learning methods, with relatively less concern for the psychological and social implications of behavior.

Of course, the number of possible classroom conditions that can be represented by the six criteria are too numerous to identify and discuss individually. Therefore, the classification of interventions must be a global estimate that reflects the general emphasis of the different classroom conditions. Besides, teachers and classroom conditions are

Table 1. Different classroom operations demonstrated by two teachers A and B

Classroom operations criterion	No evidence of existence		Frequently demonstrated
Relationship building process	B (near left)		A (far right)
Motivation development process	B (left)		A (right)
Perceptual retraining process	A (left-center)	B (center)	
Behavior management process	A (left-center)		B (right)
Behavior re-education process	A (left-center)	B (center-right)	
Academic education process	A (center)	B (right)	

not precisely the same day after day. Not only is there human variability, but one expects that students will progressively change, making
it necessary to alter the classroom methods and procedures.

Morse, Cutler, and Fink (1964) utilized the Hollister and Goldston
(1962) taxonomy of classroom conditions and further analyzed classes
for disturbed students. This analysis included the categorization of
classroom methodological types into specifically labeled intervention
strategies. The researchers warned, however, that "it was obvious that
a multitude of dimensions ran through the complex characteristics of
the several programs [interventions], and that no single dimension or
set of categories sufficed for their description" (p. 28). Nonetheless,
a "rough classification scheme" was developed that organized the
interventions according to seven types. Three of the types, "naturalistic," "chaotic," and "primitive," could not be classified as bona
fide strategies because they operated under a spontaneous, often inconsistent philosophy that was without an organized approach or any
specific preplanned design. The remaining four program types represented different interventions that consistently adhered to both theoretical and methodological classroom operations:

1. Psychiatric Dynamic
   Major emphasis was on dynamic therapy and pupil acceptance, with
   educational aspects played down or secondary. Individual therapy
   was expected or required. Parental therapy was stressed. There was
   heavy psychiatric involvement in diagnosis, decision making, treatment processes, consultation, and evaluation. Emphasis was on acceptance, use of interpersonal relationship, and overall tone.
2. Psycho-Educational
   Psychiatric and educational emphases were balanced with joint planning and interweaving-equality of two emphases, educational and
   clinical. Educational decisions were made with a consideration of
   underlying and unconscious motivation. Educational aspects stressed
   creative, project type work, individual differences, and a benign but
   not permissive atmosphere. Clinical participation was apparent, but
   not omnipresent or decisive in day to day actions.
3. Psychological Behavioral
   This series was based in systematic psychology of learning theory,
   with emphasis on diagnosis of learning potential capacities and relationship to specific remediation techniques. It involved the use of
   associative learning and formal habit. It contained a nonpunitive
   structure with emphasis on changing symptomatic responses through
   specific techniques on a planned, ego level.
4. Educational
   Emphasis was on formalized, accepted educational procedures such
   as routine drills, work books, inhibition of symptomatic behavior,
   and attention to skill training and drill. Little use was made of group
   processes. Emphasis was on control with restrictive handling seen
   as corrective. Atmosphere was nonhostile. These classes relied

largely on extension of traditional educational procedures without much systematic attention to the theoretical design (Morse, Cutler, & Fink, 1964, pp. 28–29).

In addition to these specific intervention differences, Morse, Cutler, and Fink polarized the interventions on theoretical grounds. The psychiatric dynamic and psycho-educational interventions were considered to have a general "dynamic" orientation, whereas the psychological behavioral and the educational interventions represented a "specific learning or conditioning theory" orientation. These two orientations may be roughly equated with the psychodynamic and behavioral theories of causality and philosophies of education.

Rhodes and Tracy (1972b) expanded on the previously cited studies and further classified dozens of interventions that ranged from genetic engineering to "ecological interface" (i.e., reducing the conflict inherent in a mismatch of students and their environments). Many of the interventions are only indirectly related to education per se. For example, several medical or biophysical interventions involve education or teachers only peripherally, if at all, in the form of benign responsibilities such as checking a student's medication schedule or observing the behavioral effects of drugs. On the other extreme, some interventions are virtually the total responsibility of teachers within educational settings. Interventions that primarily represent a cognitive or academic orientation, such as remedial and re-education interventions, are examples of more exclusive teacher responsibility. Many of the interventions, however, suggest a multidiscipline approach that includes teachers, parents, counselors, psychologists, pediatricians, and so forth.

Rhodes and Tracy (1972b) believed that the best means of conceptual organization of the interventions was to anchor them in the theories of causality (Chapter 2). "In an intervention, the conceptual framework directs and channels the action, by providing an analysis of the nature of the problem which dictates the intervention, and by suggesting the outcome toward which the intervention is directed" (Rhodes, 1972, p. 23). Consequently, Rhodes and Tracy classified the numerous interventions according to a predetermined theoretical framework that encompassed the biophysical, behavioral, psychodynamic, sociological, and ecological theories. In addition, they "tried to take into account current voices of dissent and reform" and included a grouping called "countertheoretical."

Numerous professionals involved in the education of disturbed students have subsequently used the Rhodes and Tracy framework to organize and describe intervention strategies (e.g., Newcomer, 1980; Morse & Smith, 1980; Reinert, 1980; Shea, 1978; Swanson & Reinert,

1979). This chapter is consistent with that conceptual framework. The remainder of this chapter will be devoted to the practical classroom applications of the different interventions. In addition, a number of supportive intervention strategies such as physiological and psychoanalytic interventions will be briefly discussed. It should be noted that wholesale or across-the-board application of the interventions has not proven to be a desirable or effective approach. Instead, selected aspects of the interventions are recommended with selected students. This concept of matching interventions with the needs or characteristics of particular students holds true in segregated settings such as the special class and resource room as well as the regular class.

THE INTERVENTION STRATEGIES

This section contains methodological descriptors of some of the major educational intervention strategies that have directly evolved from the theories of causality. The intervention strategies included are structured (biophysical), behavior modification (behavioral), psychoeducation (psychodynamic), environmental (sociological and ecological), and countertheory alternatives. These intervention strategies and the major variations or supportive strategies discussed later do not constitute all of the available interventions. However, these interventions do represent specialized approaches that are the most frequently referenced strategies for educating and treating disturbed students.

Structured Strategy

A teaching method based on the work of Strauss and Lehtinen (1947) and described by Cruickshank et al. (1961) has become known as the structured strategy. This method was designed primarily to remediate academic and social problems of students who were hyperactive, either because of some brain injury or malfunction or because of emotional disturbance. Cruickshank et al. (1961) hypothesized that these students fail academically because of certain specific characteristics associated with their hyperactivity. These characteristics include:

Distractibility   This is "an inability of the patient [student] to control his attention to stimuli which are immediately significant, the inability . . . to adapt negatively to unessential stimuli, and an apparent hyperawareness of visual, auditory and tactual stimuli within the perceptive field of the observer" (p. 4). The students are unable to screen out stimuli in the environment that are not essential or even related to the task at hand. They respond equally to relevant and irrelevant things they see, hear, or touch, and are thus unable to focus their attention on assigned tasks. Such students are often described as having short attention spans.

Motor Disinhibition   An aspect of distractibility which includes an inability to refrain from responding to stimuli that elicit movement is termed motor disinhibition. For the hyperactive child, holes seem to require that fingers or pencils be poked into them, objects on walls were put there to be picked at, and desks were made to be jiggled.

Dissociation   The inability to see stimuli as wholes, but instead to respond to isolated aspects of them, is defined as dissociation. The student may copy a design including interlocking geometric shapes as if the shapes were entirely separate and unrelated.

Figure-Background Disturbance   The tendency of students to confuse or reverse figures and their backgrounds may result in an inability to determine what part of their environment is of primary importance. This difficulty may be particularly marked when a student is reading from materials that include colorful illustrations or when trying to determine which material on a blackboard is necessary for him or her to copy.

Perseveration   Perseveration is defined as an inability to shift easily from one activity to another. The student who perseverates gets stuck on one response or behavior. The student may repeat words or phrases several times when reading or make the same error repeatedly when attempting to spell a word, even though he or she is aware that it is wrong. When given a worksheet of mixed addition and subtraction problems, if the first problem is addition, the student may add all the problems. This characteristic may also be demonstrated in motor movements; for example, the student may open and shut a ring binder notebook over and over until it is taken away.

Body Image Concept   Hyperactive students often appear to have little concept of their body image. This may lead to lack of appropriate self-concepts, which in turn results in impairment of many types of learning.

Consideration of the characteristics described above led Cruickshank and his colleagues to design interventions intended to provide successful learning experiences for these students. Many of the behavioral problems displayed by the students were believed to result from continuous failure experiences, and therefore the provision of successful experience should minimize these behavioral problems. In designing this environment, a number of other factors were considered, including the authors' belief that these students had disorders of perception—that they somehow did not correctly interpret information received through their senses. The teaching method is based upon an acceptance that the defect within the student cannot be removed, that a normal educational environment is not suitable, and that a different environment must be created which teaches "directly to the disability" (Cruickshank et al., 1961, p. 14).

The environment designed comprises four basic elements:

1. Reduced environmental stimuli
2. Reduced space
3. A structured school program
4. An increase in the stimulus value of teaching materials.

Reduced Environmental Stimuli   One way in which to mitigate the hyperactive student's distractibility is to minimize the available distractors in the classroom. Normally, classrooms, particularly those for elementary students, are colorful, exciting places. There are learning centers, bulletin boards, mobiles, displays, pets, and 30 other students. Pencil sharpeners, intercoms, traffic noises, and sounds from group work keep the noise level at what teachers often call a "busy hum." Such an environment, although fully appropriate for most learners, makes learning impossible for the hyperactive student. The structured classroom for these children must be made devoid of such extraneous stimuli. Windows should be made opaque, and walls and floors painted or carpeted in neutral colors similar to that of the classroom furniture. The furniture itself should be limited to that which is absolutely necessary. No decorations should be on walls or furniture; all equipment and teaching materials should be kept in closed cabinets so as to be out of sight. The number of students should be kept small, as this will also minimize distractions. The teacher should avoid wearing jewelry or other potentially distracting ornaments.

The distraction of noise may be minimized by locating the classroom in an area of the school away from major traffic patterns. Carpeting on the floor and soundproofing around doors and windows will also cut down on sound. Pencil sharpeners and intercoms should be removed or disconnected.

Reduced Space   The larger the space in which a student is located, the greater the potential for distraction. The classroom itself should be smaller than the average classroom, with perhaps an adjacent storage and work area for the teacher. A central feature of the structured classroom environment is the provision for each student of a cubicle in which to do all individual work. This cubicle should be just large enough for the student's desk and chair, with walls that extend beyond the student. The desk is placed against the back wall of the cubicle so that the student's back is to the classroom. No decoration of the cubicle is allowed, and the desk should be firmly fastened to the floor or wall to minimize motor responses such as moving, rocking, or jiggling the desk. Nothing is allowed on the desk except the task on which the student is working, thus enhancing the probability that he will attend to that task.

A Structured School Program   A stable, predictable routine must be established. At the beginning of the program, all decisions must be made by the teacher. Because the students have not had successful experiences with choices, the teacher should eliminate all choices. The students should not even decide upon which hook to hang their coats, or where to put their lunch boxes. As the children become more successful, the teacher may gradually introduce structured choice situations.

The daily schedule should be completely predictable. Routines should be firmly established and adhered to without deviation. The establishment of routines may be facilitated by enrolling students in the program one at a time and ensuring that each one works well within the routine before another is admitted. Social interaction among the students should be as carefully structured as other activities, perhaps beginning with group viewing of filmstrips or listening to music.

Stimulus Value of Materials   Enhancing the stimulus value of teaching materials decreases distractibility and minimizes perseveration. Materials should be free of extraneous illustrations or decoration, and the important features should be highlighted, using color or size to increase their attention value. Only one assigned task is permitted on the student's desk. It may be placed on a brightly colored mat to enable the student to differentiate the task from the background of the desk or table.

Materials used in the classroom emphasize visual and auditory perceptual training as well as academics. Individualized work is emphasized, with group instruction occurring only after the students have experienced much individual success.

A program closely related to that developed by Cruickshank and his colleagues, but applied exclusively to students classified as disturbed, has been described by Haring and Phillips (1962) and Gallagher (1979). Haring and Phillips advocated interfering with the disturbance by replacing inappropriate or maladaptive habits with those that will result in the student's successful adjustment at school and at home. Consequently, more emphasis is placed on the need for the student to change maladaptive behavior patterns and less emphasis on a presumed pathology within the student.

In addition to the four basic elements previously discussed, Haring and Phillips (1962) proposed additional guidelines for the teacher of the structured classroom:

Limited dilution: Reduction of academic demands at first, but there should be a continued emphasis on basic skills.

Concreteness: Avoidance of abstraction to facilitate completion of assignments.

Developmental stages: Assigned work must be consistent with students' developmental stage and/or readiness level to perform the assigned tasks.

Immediate scoring: The provision of rapid feedback on all assignments.

Achievement: Making the student aware of accomplishment; i.e., the student should be shown continually that he or she is making progress.

Teaching approach: Provide a stabilizing influence by consistently reacting to behavior, thus helping the student to discriminate appropriate from inappropriate behavior.

Expectations: Making clear to the student what is expected.

Follow-through: Ensuring that students live up to expectations.

Consequences, not punishment: Using preferred activities, not punishment, to increase motivation and task completion.

Reduced verbalization: Avoid unnecessary talking by showing students what to do, rather than telling them.

Response to misbehavior: Immediate interference with inappropriate behavior.

Make-up work: Expect that students will complete work missed because of absence.

The following case study illustrates the progress made by an individual student in a structured classroom:

Billy was an emotionally disturbed youngster in the fifth grade. He was prone to picking fights in class and on the playground. He had been "talked to" by teachers and principals almost every week of his four-and-one-half years of school. He always resolved to do better but never seemed to keep his word for more than a week or two. Consultation with parents, although the parents tried to be helpful, seemed to lead nowhere.

Billy entered a special class at the beginning of the second semester of his fifth year in school. By the end of the school year, he had gained an average of one full year of achievement in each of the subject-matter fields measured above—about four times his typical gain and twice the normal gain—and wanted to go on to summer school in order to catch up completely with his regular class as soon as he had caught up with their level of work. The teacher and principal agreed with Billy in this objective but added that he had to learn to control himself and settle his problems more constructively before he could return.

An additional year found Billy under excellent control socially and emotionally, up to his class level or ahead in all subjects. He was ready to go back to his regular school and class and take his rightful place among his peers in a renewed and mature manner.

In the special classes Billy experienced a more detailed, structured set of requirements. He knew what he was supposed to do, how to do his work, and he learned the consequences of doing or not doing his work. He was respected, and he learned to respect himself and others more fully. He gained achievement in the manner that it is predicted children will gain, both in achievement and in social-emotional living, when the opportunity is presented in small, regulated, structured classroom settings where fairness, firmness, consistency, and respect are the uppermost considerations (Haring & Phillips, 1962, pp. 96–97).

Behavior Modification

Behavior modification is an intervention procedure based on behavioral principles established by Thorndike (1911), Watson (1924), and Skinner (1935, 1938). The approach taken by behavior modifiers is that underlying causes of behavior, if they exist, are unobservable, unprovable, and thus not of interest to those attempting to change behavior. The behavior modifier deals only with that which is observable. Whereas professionals with another point of view might say that a student has a poor self-concept or is depressed, behavior modifiers confine themselves to statements like "Johnny keeps saying that he hates himself," or "Harold hasn't smiled in days." Observations are further refined by being quantified; the behavior modifier would count the number of Johnny's self-deprecating statements or Harold's smiles so that an exact description of the current behavior could be given.

Behavior modifiers believed that behavior is controlled by its consequences. What happens after a specific behavior is emitted determines whether or not the behavior will be repeated. Behavior modification is based on the premise that human behavior is learned from past experiences, and that inappropriate behavior can be unlearned by changing the consequences that occur when it is emitted. New behavior may be learned by the systematic application of consequences. Behavior modification is essentially an optimistic way of looking at the behavior of disturbed students; no assumption is made that there is any internal defect in the student. Disturbed behavior is viewed as either the failure to learn appropriate responses or as the result of past learning of inappropriate responses. When the disturbed behavior is changed, the student is no longer disturbed.

The cornerstones of behavior modification are several basic principles of learning. These include:

1. Positive reinforcement
2. Negative reinforcement
3. Extinction
4. Punishment

Positive Reinforcement The principle of positive reinforcement describes a relationship between two environmental events. An event is termed a reinforcer if the behavior that precedes it is strengthened upon its occurrence. Suppose, for example, that a toddler begins to make sounds that approximate the word "cookie." Whenever he makes those sounds, his mother gives him a cookie. If the child then makes the sounds more often, positive reinforcement has occurred and the cookie can be said to be a positive reinforcer. It is important to note that the cookie is defined as a positive reinforcer only after its effect on behavior is determined. If giving the toddler cookies did not increase his making "cookie" sounds, then cookies are not positive reinforcers. Many behaviors, both appropriate and inappropriate, are learned through positive reinforcement. Consider the following instances:

Marvin cleans his room and his mother thanks him. He begins to clean his room every day before going to school.

Suzie begins screaming in the supermarket. Her mother quickly gives her a cookie. Suzie soon begins screaming as soon as she and her mother enter the supermarket.

Several types of positive reinforcers have been identified. Primary reinforcers are those that have biological significance, including food and water. Secondary or conditioned reinforcers are those that have acquired their reinforcing properties through being paired with primary reinforcers. These include social reinforcers such as praise or attention from adults or peers, tangible objects such as toys, and activities such as the opportunity to play games. Changing students' classroom behavior involves making access to primary or conditioned reinforcers contingent upon appropriate behavior. The teacher of severely disturbed students might give students small pieces of cereal when they looked at her. Less severely disturbed students might earn small toys for completing academic tasks and behaving appropriately.

By far the most commonly used forms of positive reinforcement, particularly for students in regular classrooms, are social reinforcement and activity. Social reinforcement in the form of teacher attention and praise is effective for most students and many teachers find that they use no other form. Some teachers supplement social reinforcement with activities, which students earn by performing appropriately. Premack (1965) described the use of activities as reinforcers in a statement which has since become referred to as the Premack Principle. This principle simply states that any activity in which students frequently choose to engage may be used as a reinforcer for any other activity in which students do not choose frequently to engage. Thus, free time may be used as a reinforcer for doing math facts for students who do not like math, but do like to play. On the other hand, math facts may be used as a reinforcer for engaging in social activities if students are withdrawn and prefer academic tasks to social interaction.

The use of either tangible or activity reinforcers may be supplemented with token reinforcement procedures (Kazdin, 1977). Tokens are generalized reinforcers whose value depends on their exchangeability for something of value. Money is the best known token reinforcer; it has little or no intrinsic value, but serves as a powerful reinforcer because it can be exchanged for many things. Classroom teachers may use tokens in the form of points, stars, chips, or other items. Students earn tokens for appropriate behavior and exchange these tokens for activities or tangible reinforcers.

Negative Reinforcement   Another relationship between environmental events is negative reinforcement. This relationship exists if the removal of an item or event results in an increase in the behavior that precedes it. Suppose that Marvin's mother, finding that thanking Marvin for cleaning his room was ineffective, required him to remain in it on Saturday morning until it was clean. If Marvin then cleaned his room, the relationship between cleaning and confinement is one of negative reinforcement. Marvin behaves appropriately because an unpleasant event is removed when he does. Teachers use negative reinforcement when they keep students inside during playtime until work is finished.

Extinction   Extinction occurs when reinforcement is withdrawn from a previously reinforced behavior. This results in a decrease in the behavior. If Suzie's mother stopped giving Suzie cookies when she cried in the supermarket, Suzie would eventually stop crying. Teachers most commonly use the principle of extinction when they ignore behavior that occurs because it has previously been positively reinforced by teacher attention. Many disturbed behaviors will disappear if ignored; the teacher should, however, be aware that there will almost certainly be a temporary increase in the inappropriate behavior before extinction occurs.

Punishment   Behavior modifiers use the term punishment in a slightly different manner than it is normally used. Punishment does not necessarily refer to such traditional procedures as spanking or keeping students after school. Punishment, like positive reinforcement, refers to a relationship. An event that results in a decrease in the behavior preceding it is termed a punisher. If a toddler who is spanked for running into the street stops doing so, then spanking is a punisher. If, one the other hand, he continues to run into the street, spanking is not a punisher. Teachers frequently think they are using punishment when they are not. Such procedures as paddling or detention may actually positively reinforce inappropriate behavior because of peer admiration or increased teacher attention. In general, the effects of punishment are less reliable than those of positive reinforcement (Azrin and Holz,

1966), and punishment is not often recommended for changing classroom behavior.

The effectiveness of behavior modification in the classroom has been thoroughly documented (O'Leary & O'Leary, 1972). In general, some combination of positive reinforcement for appropriate behavior and extinction of inappropriate behavior is recommended (O'Leary et al., 1969). The following example illustrates the use of behavior modification:

> Larry was an 8-year-old student who spent part of his day in Ms. Wilson's resource room for disturbed students but most of his time in Ms. Jackson's second-grade class. He worked well in the resource class, where tokens were given for completing assignments and behaving properly. However, he did no work in the regular classroom and was extremely noisy and disruptive.
>
> Ms. Wilson and Ms. Jackson talked together and devised a strategy to help Larry behave in the regular class. Ms. Jackson agreed to ignore Larry's noises and attempts to get her attention and to give him five points for each academic task completed. The points were to be added to the total he earned in the resource room and were exchangeable for a variety of reinforcing activities. Soon Larry began completing the majority of his schoolwork. His behavior also improved to the point that it was acceptable to Ms. Jackson.

Psychoeducational Strategy

The psychoeducational intervention strategy is an educational extension of the psychodynamic theory. However, behavioral, sociological, and ecological theories are also evident in the methodology. For example, the psychoeducational strategy places emphasis on the internal psychological causes and treatment of disturbance, yet appropriate behavior, peer group influence, and environmental conditions are important intervention factors. Educationally, "the basic function of a psychoeducational curriculum is to provide for planned learning situations which stimulate two major personal developments: constructive expression of affective experiences, and integration of facts and feelings" (Fagen, Long, & Stevens, 1975, p. 56). Thus, the psychoeducational strategy is designed to intervene with the negative psychological conditions of disturbed students (e.g., feelings, emotions, and self-concept) and promote better mental health that is evidenced by appropriate social behavior, academic achievement, and so forth. Academics are initially, at least, relatively unimportant educational objectives that are delayed until the disturbed student is psychologically and behaviorally ready to learn math, reading, and other cognitive skills.

The methodology of the psychoeducation strategy is guided by several basic assumptions (Long, Morse, & Newman, 1971, p. 330):

1. "An educational milieu [environment] must be developed in which careful psychological attention is given to everything that affects the pupil as he interacts with the school, staff, peers and curriculum." According to Redl (1959b), some of the most important milieu factors include the classroom social structure, values that the teacher projects, the behavioral regulations, and the physical classroom properties. If the classroom is to have therapeutic properties, then the teacher must be aware of how these and other factors affect disturbed students and be prepared to alter the milieu when it does not facilitate personal adjustment.

2. "An understanding of the teacher-pupil relationship is important." A basic premise of the psychoeducational strategy is that psychological-behavioral change primarily evolves because of people, not the curriculum, the architecture, or other physical properties. Therefore, the relationship between the teacher and the disturbed student is of vital importance. Teacher characteristics such as empathy, sensitivity, and positive regard are prerequisite personal attributes, whereas interpersonal communication skills, firmness, and involvement are important interpersonal attributes. The disturbed student should view the teacher as a person who is sincerely interested in his or her personal adjustment.

3. "All learning must be invested with feelings to give it interest, meaning and purpose." The standard curriculum in most classrooms is relatively void of materials that generate feelings. Calculating abstract math problems, memorizing facts, and reading standard texts may create frustration or anger, but they typically lack "interest, meaning and purpose" for many disturbed students. Thus, materials and activities that capitalize on students' interests faciliate learning.

4. "Conflict can be used productively to teach new ways of understanding and coping with stress." Crisis intervention (Morse, 1976) is a process whereby psychoeducational teachers use negative student experiences such as fights, loneliness, and fear to help students to cope with their feelings and develop appropriate behavior. The goals are frequently accomplished with a technique called "life space interviewing" (Redl, 1959a). This kind of interview centers around a specific crisis, when and where it occurs. Moralizing, blaming, and authority-oriented statements are avoided. Instead, the teacher aims at helping the student to gain insight into the problem and to develop more positive alternatives for dealing with the situation that led to the crisis.

5. "The teacher must have the ability to collaborate with other members of the school and community." Educating disturbed students should not be the exclusive responsibility of the teacher. Rather, the teacher should be able to organize and call upon the resources of

numerous individuals, such as a medical doctor, a psychologist, a speech therapist, and parents. Because academics represent a limited psychoeducational goal, the teacher requires assistance in planning programs that meet the needs of the whole student.

Concepts such as "coping," "crisis," "relationships," and "feelings" are so vital to the psychoeducational intervention strategy that specialized curricula have been developed. The most notable of these is Fagen and Long's "psychoeducational curriculum approach to teaching self-control" (Fagen & Long, 1979; Fagen, Long, & Stevens, 1975). "Through a process of classroom observation and analysis of disruptive behavior in both special and regular school settings, a core of eight skill-clusters [areas] were identified. Four of these skill-clusters rely heavily on intellectual or cognitive development, while the other four are more related to emotional or affective development" (Fagen & Long, 1979, p. 70). The self-control curriculum consists of 175 learn-

Table 2.   An overview of the self-control curriculum

Area (definition)	Unit
Selection (ability to perceive incoming information accurately)	1. Focusing and concentrating 2. Mastering figure-ground discrimination 3. Mastering distractions and interference 4. Processing complex patterns
Storage (ability to retain the information received)	1. Visual memory 2. Auditory memory
Sequence and ordering (ability to organize actions on the basis of a planned order)	1. Time orientation 2. Auditory and visual sequencing 3. Sequential planning
Anticipating consequences (ability to relate actions to expected outcomes)	1. Developing alternatives 2. Evaluating consequences
Appreciating feelings (ability to identify and constructively use affective experience)	1. Identifying and accepting feelings 2. Developing positive feelings 3. Managing feelings 4. Reinterpretating feeling events
Managing frustration (ability to cope with external obstacles that produce stress)	1. Accepting feelings of frustration 2. Building coping resources 3. Tolerating frustration
Inhibition and delay (ability to postpone or restrain action tendencies)	1. Controlling actions 2. Developing part-goals
Relaxation (ability to reduce internal tension)	1. Body relaxation 2. Thought relaxation 3. Movement relaxation

Adapted from Fagen and Long (1979), pp. 70 and 72.

ing tasks that are spread among the eight skill-clusters or areas and 23 units (Table 2).

The first four curriculum areas consist chiefly of cognitive skills, whereas the last four consist primarily of affective skills. The distinction between cognitive and affective skills is often only semantic, however, because both skill types interact throughout the curriculum. "For example, *storage* pertains to memory processes, traditionally regarded as a cognitive ability, but memory may be disrupted by anxiety or emotional stress even to the point of amnesia. *Appreciating Feelings*, on the other hand, clearly aims at affective experience but at the same time requires retention of verbal concepts (e.g., sadness, joy, resentment) if feeling states are to be correctly identified. Our contention is that cognitive performance is enhanced by the mastery of affective experience, which is likely to be enhanced by intellectual mastery" (Fagen & Long, 1979, p. 70).

Fagen and Long (1979) provided several examples of how the curriculum can be used to help students develop self-control. One of their examples includes a student who aggressively acts out negative feelings.

John: From Upset to Attack

John is a large 10-year-old boy with a reputation for physically acting out against other children. One day, the class is hard at work on a science project. . . . All of a sudden someone screams loudly. Larry, a thin little boy with glasses, has been smacked in the face by John. . . . John is cursing violently and is about to grab Larry again, when the teacher intervenes and directs him out of the room.

In the corridor John says, "That little bastard better stop giving me the finger sign or I'll break all of his fingers."

Analysis of John's Problem

John needs to learn to manage negative feelings without being destructive, and to express feelings through words, not just raw physical outbursts.

Managing Frustration—John can be taught to understand that upsetting feelings occur when one's needs are thwarted and that strength can mean enduring frustration, as well as saying how you feel about being upset (Unit 1. Accepting Feelings of Frustration; Unit 2. Building Coping Resources; Unit 3. Tolerating Frustration). For example, present situations where John hears and shares with others things that "bug" people his age and how negative emotions can be handled without hurting himself or others.

Appreciating Feelings—The teacher can assist John in recognizing when he is getting angry and using verbal or non-verbal signals to allow for "cooling off" (Unit 1. Identifying and Accepting Feelings). For example, role playing may be used to give John practice in acceptably expressing himself when feeling mad . . . (Fagen & Long, 1979, p. 76).

Other students may have different kinds of self-control weaknesses and therefore require a different curriculum emphasis. For example, students who have test anxiety may need to develop relaxation skills; impulsive students may need to be able to inhibit and delay; students who feel incompetent or unhappy may need to appreciate feelings; and students who blame others may need to anticipate consequences.

The self-control curriculum does not represent the totality of the psycho-educational intervention strategy. However, the curriculum is an operational strategy that can be implemented by regular and special classroom teachers. The difficulty in operationalizing the more inclusive assumptions of the psychoeducational intervention is that they tend to represent methodological guidelines rather than "how to" techniques. "A major concern of . . . psychoeducational theory continues to be its complexity. It is not an approach that can be learned in a one-week workshop or one-semester course. Rather, it is a technique that requires continued study and personal and professional growth throughout one's career" (Swanson & Reinert, 1979, p. 273).

The psychoeducational methodology is tempered by the teacher's attitude, values, and sensitivity as well as training and experience. The essence of the psychoeducational intervention is not to ignore feelings and authoritatively control behavior, but to promote positive feelings and to assist students in developing internal control over their own behavior. These are accomplished through a therapeutic milieu, positive teacher-student relationships, a "feeling"-oriented curriculum, and crisis management with the assistance of a resource team.

Environmental Strategy

Environmental intervention can be restricted to the classroom (e.g., milieu therapy) or include the total community. This range of living environments includes a potentially infinite number of individuals, rules and regulations, expectations, social systems, and so on that form a complex but interrelated network of conditions that contribute to the concept called "disturbance."

> The disturbed child can be viewed as a collective object of a microcommunity who becomes both a generator and receptacle of reverberating emotions and behavior. He becomes the focus of collective dynamics which flow and ebb around him. Intervention should take into consideration the reciprocal nature of the phenomenon and should not treat the child as the sole possessor of the disturbance (Rhodes, 1970, p. 309).

Rhodes is saying that disturbance is not a function of the individual student, but of the interaction between the student and the community in which the student lives. In fact, Rhodes and Head (1974) have identified several major social systems that contribute to both the cause and elimination of disturbance: education, mental and physical health, the legal-correctional system, social welfare, and religion. Whereas nonresponsive systems (i.e., those that are inhumane, irrelevant, or incompetent) contribute to disturbance, "caring" systems reduce the frequency of disturbance. Thus, effective environmental intervention requires that the individuals, institutions, and systems in the student's environment effectively respond to the needs of the student.

On a practical level, some educational programs are utilizing a limited community intervention approach. For example, Project Re-ED (Hobbs, 1967), a semiresidential program, focuses on the behavior of students and the contribution of the peer group in the maintenance of inappropriate behavior. However, an equally important part of the Project Re-ED program goes beyond the traditional boundaries of the school. Specialized personnel such as liaison teacher-counselors or social workers also work with the students' families and regular teachers in order to create a more responsive, appropriate, and generally "caring" network of support systems. The counselors also frequently reach out "to community agencies, and to individuals—to any reasonable source of help for a child in trouble . . . The goal is to make the system work, not simply to adjust something inside the head of the child" (Hobbs, 1967, p. 1109).

The case for environmental intervention is illustrated in the following example:

> Harry was an aggressive 14-year-old who was frequently in trouble at school. He had developed a reputation for fighting, talking back, and truancy. The approach of the school personnel was to "get tough" and not hesitate to use corporal punishment and suspension.
>
> The school guidance counselor investigated Harry's situation and discovered several contributing conditions.
>
> First, Harry's parents worked at night, and when they were home they tended to be hostile toward Harry when he interrupted their routine. Second, Harry's friends, all of whom lived in a deprived neighborhood, placed a high value on toughness, independence, and "not letting adults mess over them." Third, Harry's reading behavior, which included squinting, holding the book close, and so on, indicated that he may have a vision problem. Fourth, Harry's formal educational career had been dominated by direct, controlling, and authoritarian teachers.
>
> On the basis of these pieces of information it seemed that Harry's living environment was contributing to, if not reinforcing, his aggressive behavior. The counselor talked with the school's family services department about family therapy to reduce the hostility and increase understanding among the family members. An eye examination revealed that Harry did need corrective lenses in order to read effectively. Harry and his peer group were enrolled in a temporary group therapy program that emphasized "positive" independence. Harry's teachers were asked to eliminate unnecessary control, avoid direct confrontation, and refrain from punitive retaliation.

Environmental intervention in this case produced positive results. When Harry's environment stopped contributing to his aggression there was a marked reduction in his disturbed behavior.

On a smaller scale the example of Harry has implications for classroom environmental intervention. Innumerable factors such as the teacher, the classroom group, the physical classroom, and the curriculum in some way contribute to disturbance. Therefore, intervention must involve the manipulation of the classroom environment, not just the disturbed student. If someone or something must be "blamed" for creating disturbance it must be the student *and* his or her environment, of which the teacher is a significant part.

> The time has come to begin to concentrate attention upon changing the ecological [environmental] conditions under which children have to live and grow, and thus reduce the number of occasions of disturbance and the number of children who are extruded or alienated from their living units. This is the only way in which our society can hope to come to terms with the magnitude of the problem called emotional disturbance (Rhodes, 1970, p. 314).

Countertheory Alternative

Countertheory is not a theory, but a philosophical humanistic position that is radically different from, and in most ways opposed to, the interventions that are based on the theories of causality. Countertheory does not represent an organized body of knowledge, nor does it include a specific educational intervention. Consequently, there is some disagreement among the countertheorists over the goals and methods of education. Countertheory seems to be whatever different countertheorists such as Illich (1973), Kozol (1975), and Reimer (1971) say that it is. However, this diversity among countertheorists is not considered a liability, but rather a desirable condition, because individuals are unique and cannot be pigeonholed according to a preconceived theory or intervention (Rhodes & Paul, 1978).

On what issues, then, do countertheorists tend to agree?

1. That no one standard of behavior is more desirable than another. "They hold that the variety of human experience should be celebrated rather than eliminated, and that education should serve to expand awareness of the full range of human potential" (Morse & Smith, 1978, p. 3).

2. That labeling students is a dehumanizing process that alienates disturbed students from other students, teachers, and normal life experiences. "Labelling usually justifies unequal treatment or segregation [socially, educationally, and/or psychologically] and is frequently based on racism, sexism, or class prejudice" (Burke, 1972, p. 579).

3. That traditional schools, including the curriculum, teaching behaviors, and regulations, must be radically changed. "When we put together in one scheme such elements as a *prescribed curriculum, similar assignments for all students, lecturing* as almost the only mode of instruction, *standard tests* by which all students are externally evaluated, and *instructor chosen grades* as the measure of learning, then we can almost guarantee that meaningful learning will be at an absolute minimum" (Rogers, 1969, p. 5).

On the issue of methodology, countertheorists again seem to represent a diverse set of opinions. One basic theme, however, tends to be replicated throughout the literature: self-determination (Gross & Gross, 1969). This means that students are free to decide for themselves their mode of behavior, what they will learn, and how they will learn it. Paul Goodman (1969), speaking for the countertheorists, stated: "We can, I believe, educate the young entirely in terms of their free choice, with no processing whatsoever. Nothing can be efficiently learned, or, indeed learned at all—other than through parroting or brute training, when acquired knowledge is promptly forgotten after the examination—unless it meets need, desire, curiosity, or fantasy" (p. 99). However, most countertheorists do not conceptualize this as an absolute freedom, but as freedom that is tempered by a recognition of the rights of others and the natural consequences that follow any self-determined behavior.

Whereas most traditional educators are convinced that most students will not learn the necessary living skills unless they are directly instructed, countertheorists believe that students are naturally motivated to learn and that it is direct instruction that negatively affects achievement, emotional development, and behavior. Because of this different view about education, numerous "alternate" schools, that is, alternatives to traditional education, have been established and are operated on the belief that they are more relevant. Relevance typically is interpreted to include the following goals or methods:

Increased emphasis on affective experiences
Personalization of the teacher's role
Improved teacher-student relationships
Loosening of school structure and regulations
Accommodation of a variety of learning styles
Acceptance of human variance (Morse & Smith, 1980, p. 68).

The underlying methodology, then, is governed by the students' decisions to learn, or not learn, whatever is meaningful to themselves. This is accomplished in an atmosphere of personal involvement, positive relationships, and unconditional acceptance. Gross and Gross (1969) reported that such alternative schools are successful not only with normal students, but with the "unteachable" delinquent, disturbed, and ghetto students as well.

A. S. Neill (1960) provided an example of how freedom to learn affected one student at Summerhill:

> Winifred, aged thirteen, a new pupil, told me that she hated all subjects, and shouted with joy when I told her she was free to do exactly as she liked. "You don't even have to come to school if you don't want to," I said.
>
> She set herself to have a good time, and she had one—for a few weeks. Then I noticed she was bored.
>
> "Teach me something," she said to me one day; "I'm bored stiff."
>
> "Righto!" I said cheerfully, "what do you want to learn?"
>
> "I don't know," she said.
>
> "And I don't either," said I, and I left her.
>
> Months passed. Then she came to me again. "I am going to pass the college entrance exams," she said, "and I want lessons from you."
>
> Every morning she worked with me and other teachers, and she worked well. She confided that the subjects did not interest her much, but the aim did interest her. Winifred found herself by being allowed to be herself (Neill, 1960, pp. 30–31).

Even though the countertheory alternative intervention has generally been limited to segregated settings, particularly special alternative schools, the methodology can be used within the regular class to some degree. Alternative approaches "challenge the creative and courageous teacher to explore new dimensions in interpersonal relationships, self awareness, expressive mediums, and to increase the relevance of education" (Morse & Smith, 1980, p. 70). However, the countertheory intervention is but one of many strategies that are available to educate disturbed students. The countertheory alternative is no different than the structured, behavior modification, psychoeducational, and environmental intervention strategies in the sense that the one employed should be appropriate for the disturbed students who are involved.

PREVALENCE OF INTERVENTIONS

The number of educational programs that employ the different intervention strategies is difficult to determine, or even to estimate with reasonable accuracy. It is suspected that most regular class teachers, with their emphasis on academic achievement and behavioral compliance, use basically the same procedures that they used before the introduction of disturbed students to the regular class. This would typically include external control methods with a behavioral orientation. Problems with prevalence estimates have been accentuated by the fact that the number of teachers responsible for the education of disturbed students has astronomically increased since the enactment of PL 94-142 and the "least restrictive environment" provision for mainstreaming mildly and moderately handicapped students. Consequently, the only reliable data regarding the prevalence of different intervention strategies have been derived from analyses of special classes for disturbed students.

Three special class prevalence studies (Morse, Cutler, & Fink, 1964; Fink, Glass, & Guskin, 1975; and Kavale & Hirshoren, 1980) have produced data that are probably consistent with the intervention prevalence among regular class teachers. The data in Table 3 indicate that currently the most common type of intervention is behavioral. This represents a very definite shift from the 1964 study, which revealed that the greatest emphasis was on psychological intervention (i.e., psychodynamic and psychoeducational). Noticeably, Table 3 contains no reference to the structured or countertheory intervention strategies. Since there are relatively few programs that use the structured or countertheory interventions exclusively, program components of these particular strategies are included in the "other" category. In addition, the structured methodology has been incorporated within major intervention variations, particularly Hewett's (1968) engineered classroom, and programs for brain-injured and learning-disabled students.

The interventions that are contained in Table 3 also require comment. First, "psychodynamic" was listed as an educational intervention strategy separate from "psychoeducational." Even though these two interventions are somewhat different, it is suspected that the educational methodology is more similar than dissimilar. Besides, a purely psychodynamic intervention is a supportive strategy that is

Table 3. Prevalence of different intervention strategies identified by three studies

Interventions	Morse, Cutler, & Fink (1964)		Fink, Glass, & Guskin (1975)		Kavale & Hirshoren (1980)	
	N	%	N	%	N	%
Behavioral	18[a]	33	21	36	33	62
Psychodynamic	7	14	4	7	7	13
Psychoeducational	14	26	16	27	ND	ND
Ecological	ND	ND	ND	ND	3	6
Other	15[b]	27	17[c]	30	10[c]	19
Total	54	100	58	100	53	100

ND, no data.

[a] Includes behaviorally oriented "educational" intervention strategies.

[b] Includes "naturalistic", "primitive", and "chaotic" interventions.

[c] Includes primarily eclectic interventions, i.e., combinations of different interventions.

rarely found in traditional educational institutions, but is used primarily in specialized mental health facilities. Second, the reference to behavioral interventions is not limited to behavior modification. The behavioral theory of causality also includes variations of classical conditioning and modeling. Thus the data on behavioral interventions include a wide variety of strategies that focus on the behavior of disturbed students. Third, the ecological interventions could probably be better described as environmental interventions. Since ecological theory goes well beyond the resources and responsibility of schools, it is doubtful that the programs could be technically classified as ecological.

The data in Table 3 reinforce the observation by Salvia and Ysseldyke (1978) that there is an educational trend away from the psychological treatment of disturbance and toward behavioral intervention. Whether or not this trend will continue is debatable. Certainly there is a need for behavior-oriented interventions, but there is also a need for other interventions including psychological, environmental, and medical strategies. Whatever trend develops in the future should be based on the needs of disturbed students and not on popularity or convenience.

INTERVENTION VARIATIONS

Very few intervention strategies exclusively adhere to the methodology derived from a single theory. Many of the intervention strategies, including those discussed earlier, rely heavily upon a single theory, but they frequently employ methods that are borrowed from other theories. However, some intervention strategies clearly are based upon two or more theories. The engineered class, reality therapy, and open education are three exemplary eclectic interventions that constitute major variations for educating disturbed students.

Engineered Classroom

The engineered classroom described by Hewett (1968) and Hewett and Taylor (1980) combines a structured approach, similar to that previously described, with systematically applied behavior modification. These authors have conceptualized emotional disturbance in a unique manner. Rather than describing such students in terms of psychopathology, they state that emotional disorders are a result of failure on the part of students to attain certain levels of learning competence. These levels of competence, from lowest to highest are:

1. Attention
2. Response

3. Order
4. Exploratory
5. Social
6. Mastery

Failure to achieve competence at any one of these levels results in behavior that leads to a child's being labeled emotionally disturbed. Table 4 shows typical behaviors displayed by students who have not achieved a given level of competence. The classroom program described by the authors is designed to enable students to achieve appropriate levels of competence through careful choice of curriculum, conditions, and consequences. These three factors are considered as three sides of a learning triangle, all of which must be considered in planning a program for a particular student.

Curriculum   Curriculum is chosen according to the level of competence at which the student is deficient. Curriculum may vary from procedures designed simply to demand attention from the student to complex academic tasks. A "thimbleful" approach is recommended, in which small forward steps are programmed and small gains rewarded. Specific curriculum areas at each level of competence include:

I. Attention Level
   A. Vision and Visual Perceptual Skills
   B. Hearing and Auditory Perceptual Skills
   C. Task Attention Skills
II. Response Level
   A. Motor Coordination Skills
   B. Verbal Language Skills
   C. Nonverbal Language Skills
   D. Task Response Skills
III. Order Level
   A. Direction-following Skills
   B. School Adjustment Skills
IV. Exploratory Level
   A. Degree of Active Participation
   B. Knowledge of Environment
V. Social Level
   A. Relationships with Others
   B. Self-concept
VI. Mastery Level
   A. Self-help Skills
   B. Health and Hygiene Skills
   C. Reading Skills
   D. Written Language Skills
   E. Computation Skills
   F. Vocational and Career Development Skills (Hewett & Taylor, 1980, p. 134–135).

Table 4. Negative variance from the six levels of optimal learning competence

Too little	Optimal	Too much
Disturbances in sensory perception Excessive daydreaming Poor memory Short attention span	Attention	Selective attention Fixation on particular stimuli
Immobilization Passivity Clumsiness Depression	Response (motor)	Hyperactivity Self-stimulation
Failure to develop speech Failure to use language for communication	Response (verbal)	Extremely talkative Uses profanity Verbally abusive
Self-injurious Destructiveness Disruptiveness Attention seeking Irresponsibility Disobedience	Order	Overly conforming Resistance to change Compulsive
Bizarre or stereotyped behavior Anxiety Preoccupation Shyness	Exploratory	Plunges into activity Tries to do everything at once
Extreme self-isolation Inability to relate to people Social withdrawal Alienates others Acts bossy Fighting Temper tantrums	Social	Hypersensitivity Overly dependent Jealousy Inability to function alone
Uneven or fragmented intellectual development Lacks basic school skills Laziness in school Dislike for school	Mastery	Preoccupation with academics Overintellectualizing

Abridged from Hewett and Taylor (1980), pp. 100–101.

Conditions   Consideration of the conditions under which learning is to take place is an important facet of the engineered classroom. Such conditions include "when, where, how, how long, how much, and how well" (Hewett & Taylor, 1980, p. 109).

Consequences   An important aspect of the engineered classroom is the consequences that are provided for appropriate and inappropriate behavior. Hewett and Forness (1977) have identified six types of positive consequences:

1. Acquisition of knowledge and skill
2. Knowledge of results
3. Social approval
4. Multisensory stimulation and activity
5. Task completion
6. Tangible rewards

Emotionally disturbed children often need tangible rewards on a temporary basis. As these children become more and more successful, the teacher may depend more heavily upon intrinsic rewards. In the engineered classroom, tokens or points are used which may be, at first, exchanged immediately for candy or other treats. Later, the points may be exchanged only after a certain number have been earned. As the students become less dependent on material rewards, points may be exchanged for free time and gradually eliminated completely.

Negative consequences are also used in the engineered classroom. These may include response cost (the removal of points), time outside the classroom, and sending the student home for a day if behavior continues to be inappropriate.

Carefully considering all sides of the learning triangle leads to what Hewett and Taylor (1980) call the orchestration of success. The harmony thus created in the classroom is based also on rewarding small increments in growth and in making school in general less fear-inducing for the student.

Two important aspects of the engineered classroom are the physical arrangement of the room and the scheduling of activities. The physical arrangement of this classroom does not emphasize the reduction of environmental stimuli, although cubicles are provided for students who are very distractible. The classroom is colorfully decorated and includes several learning centers, including an order center, an art center, a communication center, and an exploratory center, each designed to provide tasks at the appropriate level of competence. Students are provided with large (2' × 4') tables in lieu of standard desks. This provides a large surface so that clutter may be avoided and also automatically provides separation among the students. In addition, the large table enables the teacher to sit near a child to help him with a task without getting too close. Extreme closeness may be troubling for some emotionally disturbed students. Areas within the classroom are also provided for small group instruction and storage of materials.

The classroom schedule will vary according to the students' ages and according to whether a self-contained or part-time (resource) program is provided. The schedule will always begin with an "order task," a paper-and-pencil activity designed to promote following instructions, getting down to work, and an immediate success experience. Table 5 presents a sample schedule for an elementary self-contained class. Each 1-hour instructional period is divided into three 15-minute work periods, with a 5-minute segment after each period during which work is corrected and points are given. Thus, students are given immediate feedback on all academic work and behavior.

The following example illustrates the development of social interaction skills in a group of disturbed students in an engineered classroom at a psychiatric hospital:

> One Christmas season the teacher of ten junior high students in the NPI School decided he would attempt a class drama project, using a radio script version of Dickens' *A Christmas Carol*. . . . Two students with serious response problems claimed they would have no part in it since they would have to perform in front of an audience, but these were the only strong dissenters. The teacher was particularly concerned about one child who had a serious reading problem and who was unable to read the script. This boy, he decided, could work on sound effects, where accurate reading would not be necessary. One of the reluctant response problems was assigned as "engineer" to control the volume on the loudspeaker. He was assured he could perform his duties off stage, away from the audience. The other children were assigned parts in the play which they practiced, and the whole class was "standing by" when the show went "on the air". . . . The performance was flawless. . . . The class had functioned as any group of junior high children in a public school setting might have been expected to. The success of this project was largely due to the enthusiasm and extreme patience of the teacher, as well as his skill in viewing each child as a candidate for "doing something" and in making wholly individual assignments based on the child's readiness for participation on the social task level (Hewett and Taylor, 1980, p. 205).

Reality Therapy

William Glasser (1965) coined the term "reality therapy" to describe a specialized learning process by which disturbed students can become behaviorally responsible students. According to Glasser, students who cannot fulfill their basic identity needs (i.e., love and self-esteem) deny the reality of the world around them and go the route of delinquency or withdrawal. Reality therapy, then, is designed to help disturbed

Table 5.   Sample elementary daily schedule: engineered classroom

	Mon/Wed/Fri		Tues/Thurs	
8:45	Order task			
9:00	Individual reading Word study Skill development	Reading	Motivation for story writing Story writing Sharing	Story writing
10:10	Recess			
10:25	Practice in basic facts Arithmetic instruction Skill development	Arithmetic		
11:25	Language instruction (phonics, spelling, handwriting, language development)			
11:50	Lunch			
12:40	Listening (teacher reads to class)			
1:00	Art tasks Science tasks Communication tasks Order tasks	Exploratory		
	(Two exploratory tasks are selected daily. The students are divided into two groups, the teacher supervising one, the aide, the other. Both groups spend 25 minutes on each task.)			
1:50	Recess			
2:00	Physical education			
2:20	Group and individual activities (music, current events, sharing, group discussion, individual tutoring)			
3:00	End of school day			

From Hewett and Taylor, 1980, p. 246.

students face reality and learn to fulfill responsibly their basic identity needs.

The methodology of reality therapy has a distinctive psychodynamic orientation, yet the objectives are clearly behavioral and sociological. This blend of separate but intimately interwoven theoretical concepts is evident in the general methodological principles that serve as a guide for implementing reality therapy.

Get Involved   The teacher must quickly build a firm relationship with the student. The disturbed student "is desperate for involvement and suffering because he is not able to fulfill his needs. . . . [The student] is looking for a person with whom he can become emotionally involved, someone he can care about and who he can be convinced cares about him . . . (Glasser, 1965, p. 21). To accomplish this involvement step, the teacher must be firm, interested, and sensitive, and, perhaps above all, be able to share some of his or her "own struggles so that the [student] can see that acting responsibly is possible though sometimes difficult" (p. 22).

Emphasize the Present   Unlike psychoanalysis, reality therapy deals with the present. Reminding students of past failures interferes negatively with the involvement process and reduces the possibility of success in the present and future. Do not reinforce failures, but expect success in the future.

Deal with Behavior   The purpose is not to search for *why* a student is behaving in a particular way or *how* the student feels about the behavior. Rather, reality therapy is interested in *what* behavior is occurring and how the behavior is contributing to the student's failure. Thus, an important part of this strategy is to describe to the student in nonpunitive terms his or her behavior and how it is related to failure. The emphasis on behavior is also reinforced by the fact that responsible behavior can be developed much more quickly than positive attitudinal changes.

Reflect on the Behavior   Give the student an opportunity to reflect on and make a value judgment about his or her behavior. The value of this experience of responsible self-evaluation and direction cannot be overemphasized. This is usually best accomplished by asking questions, not making statements such as moral judgments and other teacher values (Hawes, 1969).

Make a Plan   This step is important because it should specifically identify responsible behaviors. This is the student's plan, *not* the teacher's. Although teachers are often tempted to tell a disturbed student what to do, the student must come up with a plan of his or her own. For example, a student may plan to talk (rather than fight) with peers who get him or her angry, or prevent a teacher conflict by getting homework in on time, or increase social acceptance by complimenting peers (rather than ridiculing them). Thus, the plan defines the behaviors that will meet personal needs and develop responsibility.

Getting a Commitment   It is not enough for a student to develop a plan; he or she must be committed to it. This is a commitment made to the teacher by the student. Questions again are important, rather than statements or directions. For example, "How long will you follow your plan?" "Will you talk to Harry, rather than hit him, if he gets you angry?" and "How will this plan make you more responsible?"

No Punishment   Punishment does not teach responsible behavior, but that adults have the power to inflict pain. Teaching responsible behavior takes a great deal of time and effort; there are no instant solutions. Reality therapy is based on the belief that the natural and realistic consequence of misbehavior, not arbitrary punishment, is the best discipline.

Don't Accept Excuses   It may take a long time for a student to fulfill his or her commitment. In fact, many students may try to make excuses for not keeping their commitments. Teachers who care, however, do not accept excuses. Accepting excuses does not teach responsible behaviors; it proves that the teacher doesn't really care and the old failure patterns begin to reoccur (Hawes, 1969).

Although reality therapy is primarily an individual teacher-student process, Glasser (1969) has translated the principles of teaching responsible behavior into a "classroom meeting" format. "There are three types of classroom meetings: the *social-problem-solving* meeting, concerned with the students' social behavior in school; the *open-ended* meeting, concerned with intellectually important subjects; and the *educational-diagnostic* meeting, concerned with how well students understand the concepts of the curriculum" (Glasser, 1969, p. 122). The conditions for conducting a classroom meeting are spelled out by Glasser: the teacher and all of the classroom group should be included, the group should sit in a close circle, the meetings should be scheduled on a regular daily basis (10–30 minutes), and the discussions should always be directed toward solving a problem.

Of the three classroom meeting types, the social-problem-solving meeting seems to have the greatest relevance for disturbed students, since inappropriate behaviors affect the objectives of the other two classroom meeting types. Glasser provides an example of such a classroom meeting which, it should be remembered, utilizes reality therapy principles:

> We discussed at some length what they gained by cutting school and what problems it was causing. We also discussed the school's methods of handling truancy and their parents' reactions to these methods. The students maintained that school was dull and that they saw little sense in what they were learning. They gave the impression that their lives were so full of interesting things to do outside of school that they didn't feel they could attend regularly. They rationalized their position by saying that this year was the last time they would have a chance to cut because next year, when they entered high school, they would have to toe the mark. Questioning their rationale, I said that I doubted that they would attend high school any more regularly. I added that I did not believe that the things they complained about in the eighth grade would be much different in high school. As we continued to talk, most of the students admitted that the reference to high school was rationalization; from their experience with sisters, brothers, and friends, truancy was just as common in high school as in the eighth grade.
>
> At this point we had accomplished what in Reality Therapy would be called exposing the problem for open, honest discussion. My warm and personal attitude helped the class to open up. Talking only about the present problem, we got it out on the table for everyone to examine. Getting this far probably would have been sufficient for the first of a series of meetings aimed at a real solution to the truancy problem. Because the meeting was a demonstration, however, I wanted to go further, and

I started pressing the class for a solution. I asked them if they would talk to the absent students to try to get them to stop cutting and to attend school regularly. I knew that unless the students made a value judgment that going to school is worthwhile, they would not attend regularly. It was clear that the statements they made about the value of school were merely lip service. Unless their attitude toward school could be changed, I or anyone else faced an impossible task in trying to get them to come regularly. . . The relevance of the school work must be taught, and where too much irrelevant material is in the curriculum, it must be replaced by material more meaningful to the children.

I attempted, nevertheless, to get from the students present a commitment to attend school the next day. Their wariness toward me and toward anyone who suggested change was apparent in their refusal to make this commitment. The refusal was also a perfect example of the difficulty we have in getting students to participate in irrelevant education. They gave every reason they could think of why they might not be in school the following day. To end the meeting and to help the students understand the importance of making a commitment, I introduced a technique that sometimes works even when a value judgment has not been made: I asked the class to sign a statement promising to come to school the next day. About one-third of the twenty-nine students were willing to sign the statement. The others were very leery about it, giving all kinds of excuses such as that they might be run over on the way to school. They did not want to do anything as binding as signing a piece of paper saying they would attend school. To the nonsigners I said, "If you won't sign a paper stating you will come to school tomorrow, will you sign a paper stating that you won't sign a paper? In other words, will you put your lack of commitment in writing?" After much heated discussion, about one-third more said they would sign the second paper. Although signing this paper did not commit them to come to school, it might still help them to understand the commitment process. One-third of the students remained who refused to sign either paper. I asked them if they would sign a paper stating that they would sign nothing, but they were too smart for me and still refused to sign. I said, "Under these circumstances, will you allow your names to be listed on a piece of paper as students who refuse to commit themselves in any way regarding truancy?" I would put their names on the paper; they would not have participated in the commitment process in any way. To this they agreed, and we obtained the three lists at the end of the meeting.

One meeting with little involvement, no real value judgment, and weak commitment produced, as I expected, no improvement in attendance. There was, however, much discussion not only among these students but also in the entire seventh and eighth grades concerning the class meeting. I had set the stage for a series of meetings to attack the problem of truancy. If this first meeting could have been followed with regular meetings several times a week, the students could have discussed the importance of attending school and been led toward value judgments, plans, and commitments (Glasser, 1969, pp. 125–127).

Open Education

The concept of open education can refer either to a physical learning environment that has very few interior walls or to a program that provides students with a wide range of choices regarding learning goals and activities (Gump, 1974). Even though this double meaning has created some confusion, most educators (e.g., Rathbone, 1971) believe that the essence of open education is in the human element rather than in the architecture. "Regardless of the name, there is an overriding belief in the growth potential of children . . . called emotionally disturbed. There is a strong humanistic component to open education—the child is valued for what is already inside him and is not seen from the perspective of a deficiency model" (Knoblock, 1973, p. 359). The educational experiences are not only "open" to the students, but to everyone who participates, including teachers, administrators, and parents. In short, everyone has something to say about what is to be learned, why it is to be learned, and how it is to be learned.

Knoblock (1973) considered open education to be an extension of the psychoeducation intervention, because both strategies share many methodological approaches including an integration of affective objectives with academic content, responding to feelings as well as behaviors, and developing interpersonal relationships and self-worth. However, open education goes beyond the psychoeducational intervention to emphasize the dimension of self-determination or freedom that is characteristic of the countertheory alternative strategy. Consequently, open education is similar to humanistic education, which represents "a commitment to educational practice in which all facets of the teaching/learning process give major emphasis to the freedom, value, worth, dignity and integrity of persons" (Combs, 1981, p. 446).

Combs (1981) elaborated on the philosophy of teaching/learning shared by open and humanistic educators:

1. [it] accepts the learner's needs and purposes and develops experiences and programs around the unique potential of the learners;
2. facilitates self-actualization and strives to develop in all persons a sense of personal adequacy;
3. fosters acquisition of basic skills necessary for living in a multicultured society . . .;
4. personalizes educational decisions and practices (to this end it includes students in the processes of their own education via democratic involvement at all levels of implementation);
5. recognizes the primacy of human feelings and uses personal values and perceptions as integral factors in educational processes;
6. develops a learning climate that nurtures learning environments perceived by involved individuals as challenging, understanding, supportive, exciting, and free from threat; and
7. develops in learners genuine concern and respect for the worth of others and skill in conflict resolution (Combs, 1981, p. 446).

Open education represents a philosophy rather than a specific methodology. Whatever is done methodologically must be guided by such concepts as freedom, involvement, and feelings, whereas the roles of

authority, structure, and predetermined objectives are virtually eliminated. Two examples of open education serve to illustrate these concepts. The first example comes from a student, whereas the second
represents a teacher's experience.

A student:

> The freedom of this project to me means an acceptance of each person—
> student or staff—for what he is, where he is and where he wishes to go.
> There seems to be an implicit trust in each of us that we know what is
> best for ourselves—and that there are people around to help us figure it
> out, to give us a lot of feedback on our thinking, acting, relating, behaving,
> etc.; that this kind of feedback is given and asked for freely—there are
> no strings attached (e.g., grades) nor pressures to do or be a certain
> way—that with this kind of freedom we will come to trust ourselves and
> be more ourselves and that this is learning and growing (Knoblock, 1973,
> p. 364).

A teacher:

> One day Danny . . . , one of my colleagues, and I brought a hundred feet
> of blank film leader to class and showed it to the children. They picked
> up thin magic markers and paints and inks and made a film of colors and
> shapes. There was no need for instruction. Before we could say a word
> about how to make a film, the children were already making one. Before
> we had a chance to talk about the product of their work we were over-
> whelmed by their desire to see it—and to dance to their sound track, and
> to play the film on their bodies while they were dancing, and to flick the
> lights in the classroom on and off while all of this was happening. In a
> few hours these kindergarten children had developed their own "mixed
> media" technology. We had just stepped aside and let them learn and
> teach us (Kohl, 1969, pp. 61–62).

SUPPORTIVE INTERVENTIONS

Intervention strategies that are implemented in school settings are primarily the responsibility of educators. Education, however, is not the
only profession that is involved in the treatment of disturbed students.
Professions such as medicine, psychiatry, social work, and the judiciary also intervene with students who are considered to be brain-
injured, psychotic, culturally deprived, and delinquent. Even though
the labels are different, each refers to students whose behaviors are
socially unacceptable and/or whose mental health is less than adequate.
Since educators generally have the earliest, most sustained, and greatest responsibility for intervening with disturbed students, other human
services professions are considered to be supportive. In addition, supportive professions typically serve a limited number of students with
more severe problems, whereas their involvement with mildly or moderately disturbed students tends to be relatively temporary, specialized, and consultative.

Whereas educators are largely responsible for the intervention strategies discussed earlier in this chapter, the role of educators in the following supportive interventions is more restricted. This is not to say that educators have no responsibility, but rather that educators have more benign roles such as observing, monitoring, and evaluating the performance of students who are involved in supportive interventions. The exemplary supportive interventions, or noneducational alternatives, include physiological, psychoanalytic, and expressive therapy, and other intervention strategies.

Physiological Intervention

Direct physiological intervention involves the manipulation of the human organism (Morse & Smith, 1980). Direct psychological manipulation includes medical intervention, particularly drug, orthomolecular (megavitamin), and diet therapy. Of course there are other physiological interventions such as psychosurgery and electroconvulsive therapy (shock treatment). The latter two interventions have been publicly and professionally criticized to the point that it is generally believed that such interventions are rarely used, at least with children.

Historically and legally, physiological interventions have been the exclusive responsibility of the medical profession and other licensed specialists. "Under no circumstances are teachers ethically or legally permitted to perform medical diagnosis, to administer drugs or other medical procedures, or to recommend the use of drugs" (Morse & Smith, 1980, p. 27).

Drug Therapy   The use of drug therapy in the treatment of disturbed students is a controversial issue. Some medical professionals maintain that hyperactivity and other learning and behavior problems are physiologically based and therefore can be treated with drugs (e.g., Gadow, 1979), whereas others believe that the behaviors characteristic of disturbance have a psychological origin and that drugs only mask the problem (e.g., Sroufe, 1975). Most professionals take a middle ground on this issue, recognizing that some "forms of psychological experience may precipitate (or 'cause') psychiatric disorders in those who are biologically predisposed to them" (Wender & Klein, 1981, p. 28).

According to Gadow (1979), there are two major drug types that have significant effects on the behavior of disturbed students: antiepileptic and psychotropic. Antiepileptic or anticonvulsant drugs such as diphenylhydantoin (trade name Dilantin), methsuximide (Celontin), and phenobarbital (Luminal) are less controversial than psychotropic drugs (Morse & Smith, 1980), probably because antiepileptic drugs have a history of effective control over many types of seizures and convulsions that have a proven physiological basis and that constitute a dangerous condition for individuals so affected. Psychotropic drugs, on the other hand, remain a center of controversy, particularly when they are prescribed for younger children. In general, the opponents of psychotropic drugs argue that:

1. Disturbance is a social, psychological, and environmental problem, not a physiological condition.
2. Drugs temporarily conceal or suppress symptomatic behaviors, thereby reducing the need for interventions that will produce more permanent behavior change.
3. The existence of disturbed behavior constitutes a subjective judgment (expectation), when in fact the behavior may be relatively normal.
4. Drugs produce side effects that are often more serious than the symptoms being treated.

Of course, the advocates of drug therapy recognize the antidrug arguments and recommend a carefully administered drug therapy program when the physiological evidence indicates that such an intervention is warranted. The position of drug therapy advocates is expressed by Wender and Klein (1981): "We now know that even some disorders believed to be 'neurotic' are biologically based—and that drugs offer the closest thing to a long-term cure" (p. 27).

Psychotropic drugs are classified according to their primary function: stimulants, antipsychotics (major tranquilizers), sedative/antianxiety agents (minor tranquilizers), and antidepressants.

Stimulants [e.g., methylphenidate (Ritalin), dextroamphetamine (Dexedrine), and pemoline (Cylert)] are among the most frequently prescribed psychotropic drugs for children and are used primarily for the management of hyperactivity. . . .

Major tranquilizers [e.g., thioridazine (Mellaril) and chlorpromazine (Thorazine)] are typically administered to control hyperactivity, aggressivity, self-injurious acts and stereotyped behavior and to facilitate in general management. . . Surveys show that major tranquilizers are used more frequently to control behavior disorders in mentally retarded and emotionally disturbed children in special education programs. . . .

Minor tranquilizers [e.g., diazepam (Valium) and chlordiazepoxide (Librium)] are much more aptly named sedative-antianxiety agents because one of their primary uses is in the management of anxiety. All have anticonvulsant properties, but Valium (the most frequently prescribed drug in the world) . . . has hypnotic properties and, therefore, may be administered to induce sleep. . . .

The name antidepressant [e.g., imipramine (Tofranil) and phenelzine (Nardil)] is misleading when one considers the variety of disorders for which these drugs are used. In children, Tofranil is the most frequently prescribed tricyclic drug . . . in the treatment of enuresis [bed wetting] and occasionally for hyperactivity (Gadow, 1979, p. 6–7).

All drugs have negative side effects. Zbinden (1963) categorized negative drug reactions into three groups:

1. Functional; i.e., changes in the function of the organism that result in thirst, headaches, slurred speech, dizziness, nausea, insomnia, irritability, etc.
2. Biochemical; i.e., changes in the chemical composition in the organism that are evidenced by alteration in hormone levels, lack of blood coagulation, urinary difficulties, etc.
3. Structural; i.e., a physiological change in the organism such as cataracts, liver damage, tissue deterioration, etc.

Functional and biochemical reactions tend to cease when the drug intake is stopped.

The role of drugs in the treatment of disturbed children is a controversial issue. "Only future research by the medical profession and allied disciplines can answer questions of the value of medications and the dangers inherent in their use" (Kaufman, 1977, p. 151). In the meantime, teachers can be of invaluable assistance to disturbed students, their families, and the medical profession. By carefully monitoring and reporting the behavior of students on prescribed drugs, the teacher can be instrumental in the success of the drug therapy. "Remarkable sensitivity to drug effects on the part of the teacher has been replicated regularly in our laboratory. . . We recommend strongly that monitoring of drug effects must include reports from the teacher if the physician hopes to effectively treat school children with learning and/or behavior disorders" (Sleator & Sprague, 1978, p. 579).

Orthomolecular (Megavitamin) Therapy   During the past few years there has been a growing emphasis on megavitamin therapy (i.e., large doses of multiple vitamins) as an effective biophysical intervention (e.g., Cott, 1972). There is the general belief among megavitamin theorists that drugs interfere with the metabolism of the body, whereas vitamins facilitate normal metabolism (Rimland, 1979). "Some biophysical practitioners believe that large doses of specific vitamins and minerals can be used to correct existing biochemical imbalances and, consequently, to relieve behavioral and learning problems" (Morse & Smith, 1980, p. 27).

Even though it is not known how vitamins specifically affect the physiology of disturbed students, Rimland (1979) has maintained that megavitamin therapy is beneficial in over half of severe disturbances, including autism. Consequently, Rimland advocated massive doses of vitamin B complex, particularly B_6, and vitamin C, along with mineral tablets that include magnesium and zinc.

Morse and Smith (1980), however, warned teachers that "some vitamins can actually be harmful when taken in excessive quantities. As in drug therapy, a teacher's role is to be alert for possible problems initially (screening and referral), to observe the effects of treatment (monitoring), and to report these observations to parents" (p. 27).

Diet Therapy   It is generally known that certain nutritional deficiencies create unhealthy physiological conditions such as brittle hair, skin disorders, and skeletal abnormalities. In extreme cases of malnutrition, mental retardation and even death may result. In less severe cases, behaviors that are considered symptomatic of disturbance, such as inattentiveness, irritability, and withdrawal, may be partially attributed to deficiencies in iron, thiamin, protein, niacin, or sodium (Springer, 1977). On the other extreme, the consumption of excessive amounts of non-nutritional foods such as sugar, caffeine, and food additives may produce reactions ranging from skin disorders (e.g., hives) to behavioral symptoms (e.g., depression, fatigue, or hyperactivity).

The above statements emphasize that what students eat is important not only to their physiological health, but also to their learning ability and behavioral normality. Thus, diet therapy is an important intervention strategy for some disturbed students. Since specially designed diets are used to treat physiological conditions such as hepatitis, phenylketonuria, and diabetes mellitus, it seems reasonable to conclude that diet therapy would have an effect on some classroom behaviors (Morse & Smith, 1980).

The effects of food additives are directly related to diet therapy. Feingold (1976), for example, maintained that one of the primary causes of hyperactivity is related to the consumption of food additives including flavors, colors, and preservatives, particularly salicylates, and tartrazine (the yellow No. 5 dye). Feingold reported that 30 to 50 percent of the children on the Feingold K-P Diet of reduced food additives not only improved behaviorally, but were able to discontinue drugs and other medications after only a few days. However, Baker (1980) and Johnson (1981) could not locate any research studies that supported Feingold's exorbitant claim. The most optimistic estimate is that approximately 5 percent of the hyperactive children benefited from the additive-free diet (Levy, 1978).

The emphasis on the nutritional aspects of learning and behavior has caused schools, school systems, and the federal government to evaluate school meal programs and the availability of junk foods such as colas and potato chips. Certainly the coin machines that dispense junk foods in schools provide a lucrative economic return, but perhaps at the cost of causing learning and behavior problems. Regardless of the pros and cons, "if a child is receiving diet therapy, for whatever reason, the teacher's role is to be aware of the dietary requirements and to follow the physician's recommendations" (Morse & Smith, 1980, p. 28).

Psychoanalytic Intervention

Psychoanalytic intervention is a specialized treatment process that is guided by the basic principles of psychodynamic theory. Of critical importance is the fact that many classical psychoanalysts believe that disturbance is the result of faulty environmental experiences particularly involving parents during infancy and early childhood. These experiences create an imbalance among the three personality systems (id, ego, and superego) and accelerate the use of unconscious defense mechanisms, resulting in psychological trauma and inappropriate behavior (Hartman, 1959). Because psychoanalytic intervention necessitates going back into the past life experiences of the student rather than focusing on the present, the treatment setting, qualifications, and objectives of the psychoanalysts are substantively different from those of the teacher.

The psychoanalytic treatment setting typically involves scheduled sessions in an office or small group meeting room that is designed to be physically comfortable and free of irrelevant distractions, and to increase bilateral communication. This picture of the therapy setting is quite different from most regular classrooms, in which large groups gather in physically uncomfortable settings and are bombarded with distractions, and where bilateral communication is restricted. Consequently, even if teachers had the skill and interest, psychoanalytic intervention would be difficult to accomplish in the regular classroom.

Aside from the setting, psychoanalytic intervention has a strong emphasis on the inner life of the student. "Cognitive processes (e.g., insight and awareness) and affective processes (e.g., identification and transference) are interfaced in an effort to facilitate externalization of feelings, awareness of repressed conflicts and attitudes, and the development of new patterns of behavior" (Cheney & Morse, 1972, p. 331). Thus, psychoanalytic intervention requires that the student go back in time, recognize and understand the faulty environmental experiences, and produce new, more acceptable behaviors, based upon this knowledge and awareness. This process requires a long-term intervention that typically does not produce an immediate cessation of problem behaviors (Morse & Smith, 1980).

The relationship between educators and psychoanalysts should be a mutually collaborative one, with the welfare of the disturbed student as the primary objective. Unfortunately, in the past both educators and psychoanalysts have created a climate of suspicion, mistrust, and irrelevance. Whereas many educators feel that therapy is a "joke," many psychoanalysts have perpetuated a condescending relationship. Regarding the latter point, Anna Freud (1935) perpetuated the communication difficulties between educators and psychoanalysts:

> I maintain that even today psychoanalysis does three things for pedagogy [teaching]. In the first place, it is well qualified to offer a criticism of existing educational methods. In the second place, the teacher's knowledge of human beings is extended, and his understanding of the complicated relations between the child and the educator is sharpened by psychoanalysis. . . . Finally, as a method of practical treatment, in the analysis of children, it endeavors to repair the injuries which are inflicted upon the child during the process of education (p. 106).

Anna Freud's three points may be applicable to some teachers who are insensitive taskmasters and who inflict injury upon students. Also, some psychoanalysts may be in a position to criticize educational methods, extend the teacher's knowledge, and repair the damage caused by education. However, as a generalization Anna Freud's statements do not facilitate communication between the two professions, nor do they recognize the unique role of the teacher, nor do they give credit to teachers for having a specialized knowledge of students. Certainly, some disturbed students may profit from psychoanalytic intervention, but other students may not. If the source of a student's problem is in the past, and if the educational intervention is ineffective, then psychoanalytic intervention is a possible supportive alternative. However, psychoanalytic intervention should be considered a collaborative endeavor among the teacher, psychiatrist, and parents, with the welfare of the disturbed student as the primary objective.

Expressive Therapies

Specific expressive therapies such as play, drama, art, and music therapy have generally evolved from the same theoretical framework as psychoanalytic intervention. Briefly, expressive therapies, regardless of the particular mode, are intended to permit students to express themselves in a nonthreatening manner so that the student and/or the treatment specialist can better understand the internal forces that motivate behavior. According to Newcomer (1980) the different therapies have somewhat different purposes:

> Play therapy is a method that permits children to air their feelings through the medium of play. It is presumed that children . . . are most natural and comfortable when at play. . . . It connotes a method by which a child is given the freedom to act out and say what he or she thinks and feels (p. 349).

Drama therapy is based on the assumption that an individual may gain greater understanding of the dynamics influencing his or her behavior if he or she is permitted to act out various aspects of his or her life (p. 367). Art and music therapy are distinct therapeutic tools that share the goal of producing desirable changes in an individual through media. Both artistic techniques provide a unique adjunct to the therapeutic milieu as non-verbal forms of communication . . . they are often regarded as projective techniques through which an individual may express the unconscious forces that motivate his or her behavior. Theoretically, they enable an individual to creatively and spontaneously act out feelings (p. 391).

Expressive therapies can be invaluable supportive interventions. Although they originated from and are used in connection with psychoanalytic intervention, they need not be limited to clinical settings. In fact, teachers have discovered that expressive therapies are appropriate for the classroom (Reinert, 1980). However, teachers must be careful not to overgeneralize their observations during expressive therapy sessions, or to clinically analyze students' behaviors or feelings beyond their level of competence. If expressive therapies *are used as vehicles* for students to express themselves in the classroom and to provide teachers with insight into the personal realm of students, they serve well as supportive interventions.

Other Interventions

This broad, nondescriptive "other" category is included as a reminder that interventions other than those discussed in this chapter are currently being employed with disturbed students. For example, other interventions include:

Genetic counseling
Orthomolecular psychiatry
Aversive therapy
Community intervention
Parent and/or family counseling
Institutional residence
Remedial education
Group therapy, and
Individual counseling.

Any discussion of these exemplary interventions is probably impractical for the classroom teacher and certainly impossible within the limitations of this book. However, if information is desired, Rhodes and Tracy (1972b) is a recommended starting point.

SUMMARY

This chapter has provided brief descriptions of intervention strategies that are employed to intervene into the lives of disturbed students in order to educate, treat, or otherwise promote a positive outcome. The interventions discussed included the primary strategies (structured, behavior modification, psychoeducational, environmental, and countertheory alternatives), major variations (engineered class, reality therapy, and open education), and supportive, or noneducational interventions (physiological, psychoanalytic, and expressive therapy).

The organization of the intervention strategies followed a pattern consistent with the theories of causality; that is, they commensurately progress from a specific to a complex account of disturbance. Table 6 illustrates the relationship between the theories and the intervention strategies.

Table 6 indicates that the different intervention strategies are based on different theories of causality and that both the theories and strategies progress from specific to complex explanations and interventions. The term "specific" refers to a narrowly defined, measurable cause of disturbance and an intervention that is similarly defined and measurable, usually including controlled, preplanned methods that are designed to intervene with the cognitive, behavioral, and/or physiological aspects of disturbance. Conversely, "complex" refers to a more globally defined, inductive cause of disturbance and an intervention that is more comprehensive, usually including variable, interpersonal methods that are designed to intervene with the affective, psychological, and/or environmental aspects of disturbance.

Table 6.   Theories of causality and interventions

Continuum	Theory	Intervention
Specific	Biological ────────────→	Physiological[a] Structured
		Engineered[b]
	Behavioral ────────────→	Behavior modification
		Reality therapy[b]
	Psychodynamic ──────────→	Psychoeducational Psychoanalytic[a] Expressive therapies[a]
	Sociological/ecological ──────→	Environmental
		Open education[b]
Complex	Countertheory ──────────→	Alternatives

[a] Supportive interventions.
[b] Multitheoretical interventions.

The research on intervention types indicates that behavioral strategies, rather than psychological ones, are more frequently used in educational settings. This is at least partially attributable to the fact that behavioral methods are more consistent with the training, skills, and expectations of most teachers. However, the variety of intervention strategies available indicates that there are methodological options available that go beyond behavior and include intervention with a broader spectrum of disturbance. The type of intervention employed must be based on the needs of students and not on the convenience of educators.

8
Teaching-Learning Strategies

If a visitor walks down the hall of a typical elementary or secondary school, briefly looking into each classroom along the way, a number of rather obvious differences can be observed. In one classroom, students are seated in a rather orderly fashion, watching and listening to the teacher lecturing from the front of the class. In a second classroom, the noise level is much greater, clusters of students are scattered around the room, and the teacher is moving around from group to group. In a third classroom, the teacher is working on records, while the students read or write individually at their own desks. In a fourth classroom, the teacher is severely reprimanding a student, while the rest of the classroom group watches the disciplinary process. Of course, these four classroom examples represent only a small portion of an infinite number of teaching-learning behaviors that can be routinely observed.

Assuming the brief observations are representative of each teacher's behavior, the four teachers typify 1) an authoritarian information giver who teaches as if education is a one-way communication process; 2) a facilitator of student interaction who places priority on informality and involvement; 3) an uninvolved or laissez-faire teacher, who places emphasis on the record-keeping aspects of classroom organization; and 4) a disciplinarian who is inordinately concerned with the managerial aspects of teaching.

Among the students, the observed behaviors will range from motionless, quiet, obedient students to students who are active, loud, and defiant. Some will be completely involved in a lesson; others are virtually asleep. Some students usually comply with teacher expectations, whereas other students pursue their own interests regardless of the classroom situation. Most important, some students like school and succeed in learning whereas others, who do not like school, often succeed in failing. Individually and collectively, students have an effect on classroom teaching-learning conditions.

The curriculum experiences also have an effect on the behavior of both teachers and students. In particular, the educational objectives to be achieved, the content that is covered, and the learning process employed by teachers and students produce significant classroom differences. For example, objectives that require rote recall, obtained from a textbook, typically emphasize visual skills demonstrated in a quiet, orderly classroom, whereas higher-level objectives that require a new communication produce substantially different teaching-learning conditions.

Finally, the composite effect of different teaching behaviors, different curriculum experiences, and different student and group influences is primarily responsible for producing different learning climates. Of course, every teacher would like to have a classroom climate that is free of personal conflict, where students learn in a free, pleasant, and cooperative environment. Such a climate is difficult to achieve, however, and is never attained by many teachers. Conflicts between students erupt, unmotivated students may waste their time, and teachers may serve primarily as behavioral censors. Over the past few years a number of terms have evolved that have been used to identify, study, or describe classroom climates, such as environmental psychology, social psychology, therapeutic milieu, social climate, and learning atmosphere. Although the terms are not synonomous, they infer that the learning climate includes ". . . the surrounding conditions and influences that affect personal development" (Dale, 1972, p.16).

A chapter on teaching-learning strategies separate from intervention strategies is not meant to imply that they are unrelated concepts. To the contrary, teaching-learning and intervention strategies are intrinsically interwoven and interdependent. In fact, teaching behaviors and curriculum experiences largely define or differentiate the interventions, whereas the interventions typically dictate the teaching behaviors and curriculum experiences. This interdependence is in part the subject of a matching model discussed in Chapter 10. In the interim, teaching-learning strategies are treated separately from interventions, as well as from behavior management (Chapter 9), chiefly for the purposes of discussion, analysis, and ultimately synthesis. This chapter includes some of the most critical aspects of teaching-learning strategies, namely, teaching behaviors, curriculum experiences, group dynamics, students' affective needs, and learning climates. Individually or in combination, these teaching-learning factors can have a significant effect on the education of students in general, and disturbed students in particular. Consequently, the use of teaching-learning strategies cannot be left to chance, but must be analyzed, planned, and implemented in order to maximize the educational opportunities of disturbed students.

TEACHING BEHAVIOR

There seems to be little question that the teacher is the single most critical factor in determining the conditions for learning in the classroom (Smith, Neisworth, & Greer, 1978). The teacher, as an adult with both the power and the responsibility to educate the students assigned to the classroom, occupies a commanding and influential position. According to Mehrabian (1976), an obvious feature of schools is that ". . . a small number of people occupy positions of great dominance— persons who command resources enabling them to reward greatly or punish severely" (p. 153).

Thus, the character of the classroom is largely dependent upon the teacher's use of personal, professional, and legal influence on the students within the classroom. How a teacher exercises this influence, then, becomes a critical factor in prompting different classroom conditions. The direction and extent to which teachers influence classrooms seems to be chiefly dependent upon 1) instructional behavior and 2) leadership behavior, or teaching style.

Instructional Behavior

How a teacher teaches makes a difference. Not only are instructional methods related to student achievement, but they are associated with the rate of deviant behavior as well. Student achievement, time at task, attitude toward school, and behavior form a syndrome of characteristics that tend to be inseparable. Therefore, teaching behaviors that promote achievement also tend to reduce deviant behavior. The opposite is also true: teaching behaviors that do not promote achievement, involvement, or positive attitudes are associated with higher rates of deviant behavior (Coker, Medley, & Soar, 1980).

Because of the instructional relationship between student behavior and other educational factors, this section discusses several critical instructional behaviors that are associated with teaching effectiveness. Although teaching is a complex variety of multidimensional functions that must be considered in totality for an accurate assessment of teaching, there are several instructional behaviors that are reported to reduce or increase specific student behaviors. The instructional behaviors discussed in this section include teacher behaviors that 1) provide clarity, 2) affect movement, and 3) convey expectations. Most of the research and literature on these aspects of instruction has focused on normal student populations; there is, however, substantial information to support the belief that disturbed students in the regular class would be similarly affected.

Instructional Clarity   In an effort to quickly bring about behavioral and academic compliance, teachers frequently use vague references to deviant behavior and nonacademic performance. General statements, such as "Stop that!" "What is the class supposed to be doing?" and "What did I say yesterday?" tend to produce anxiety, create distractions, and generate confusion. Students who are busy at tasks and are behaviorally compliant shift their attention to the teacher's intervention; students who were the intended target of the intervention are often oblivious because they are not clearly identified in the communication. Typically such vagueness creates more deviance than it reduces. Instructional clarity could eliminate the unnecessary side effects. Directed statements, such as "George, keep your feet on the floor," "Class, you are to be working your math problems," and "Talking is not permitted during quiet time," provide more clarity by specifically identifying expected behaviors.

Academic behaviors are also affected by teacher clarity. Bush, Kennedy, and Cruickshank (1977) found that teacher clarity involves ". . . explaining concepts and directions in a manner which is understandable and at a pace which is appropriate" (p. 10). Examples of teacher clarity in this context include taking sufficient time to explain concepts and tasks and emphasizing difficult problems and ideas. A second dimension of clarity includes the teacher's use of frequent demonstrations, examples, and illustrations.

Failure to provide clear communication regarding behaviors and academic tasks creates deviance. Compliant students become distracted witnesses to the intervention, and deviant students lack the information necessary to perform appropriately. Conversely, instructional clarity provides specific information to both the compliant and deviant students, conveys a clear message of teacher expectations, and prepares students to complete academic tasks more satisfactorily.

Instructional Movement   The transition from one activity to another is critical to both academic and behavioral intervention. For example, the shift from math to reading, from individual activities to group projects, or from recess to the classroom are transition times that are highly susceptible to the development of off-task behavior. The success with which the teacher can terminate an old activity and initiate a new one is related to the frequency of inappropriate student behavior.

According to Kounin (1967), a smooth transition between activities increases the teacher's instructional success. On the other hand, deviance increases when the transition reflects jerkiness. This transition problem is created by "(a) dangles (initiating an activity without immediate follow through); (b) flip-flops (stopping an old activity and initiating a new one and then engaging in an action such as a question about the old one); (c) thrusts (bursting in with the initiation of a new activity without engaging in any action to ascertain the target group's readiness to receive the induction)" (Kounin, 1967, p. 226.).

Clearly, students with learning and behavioral problems are adversely affected by jerky types of instructional movements. This transition problem is often fostered by the fact that many teachers use individual key students to determine the group's readiness to shift activities. Unfortunately, the brighter, more compliant students are used by the teacher as a cue to alter activities; the disturbed student is rarely considered in a large group of regular students. To reduce deviance, however, the teacher must employ smooth instructional movement techniques that consider individual readiness for the transition.

Instructional Expectations   The extent to which teachers reward and punish is a critical dimension of teacher influence. This complex pattern of approval and disapproval is often a function of teacher expectations and attitudes toward individual members of the classroom group. Unfortunately, students with handicapping conditions, students who are members of different racial or ethnic groups, and even students who are male may receive proportionately more punishment and fewer rewards than other students in the classroom. Although most teachers probably do not intentionally demonstrate such bias, the fact remains that teachers in general have a lower expectation of success for students who do not fit the teacher's preferred pattern of behavior for successful students.

Even though many teachers maintain that they treat all their students the same, that is, with impartiality and equality, the evidence does not support this claim. For example, Rosenthal and Jacobson (1968) report a strong relationship between teacher perceptions of students and students' success in the classroom. When teachers perceived students positively, those students were more successful; when teachers perceived students negatively, those students were less successful. However, the degree of student success is not a function of teacher perception, but of teacher behaviors that are consistent with those perceptions. Teachers respond differently toward different students. This difference in teacher responses may account for a great deal of the success and failure of individual students.

Certainly, differences in instructional expectation may be minimal, but they do exist. Brophy and Good (1974) have collected and synthesized data that support the position that teachers translate different expectations into instructional differences. Unfortunately, disturbed students most often constitute "lows" in the following research summary of teachers' instructional expectations.

1. Waiting Less Time for Lows to Answer: Teachers have been observed to provide more time for high achieving students to respond. . . .
2. Staying with Lows in Failure Situations: Teachers have been found to respond to lows' . . . incorrect answers by giving them the answer or calling on another student. . . .
3. Rewarding Inappropriate Behavior of Lows: Teachers have been found to praise marginal or inaccurate student responses. . . .
4. Critizing Lows More Frequently than Highs: Teachers have been found to criticize lows more frequently than highs when they provide wrong answers. . . .
5. Praising Lows Less Frequently than Highs: When lows provide correct answers they are less likely to be praised. . . .
6. Not Giving Feedback to Public Responses of Lows: Teachers . . . have been found to respond to lows' answers (especially correct answers) by calling on another student to respond. . . .
7. Paying Less Attention to Lows: Teachers attend more closely to highs . . . [e.g.,] smile more often and maintain greater eye contact. . . .
8. Calling on Lows Less Often: Teachers have been found to call on high achieving students more frequently. . . .
9. Differing Interaction Patterns of Highs and Lows: In elementary classrooms, highs dominate public response opportunities. . . . In secondary classrooms highs become even more dominant. . . .
10. Seating Lows Farther from the Teacher: Seating pattern studies have sometimes found that lows tend to be placed away from the teacher. . . .
11. Demanding Less from Lows: This is a broader concept suggesting such activities as giving these students easier tests (and letting the students know it) or simply not asking the student to do academic work.... (Abridged from Brophy & Good, 1974, pp. 330–333).

Other teachers demonstrate more obvious negative attitudes and low expectations for the handicapped, including the disturbed. Turnbull and Schultz (1979) provide an example of teacher behavior that conveys a negative attitude toward a mentally retarded student:

Kate, a third grader, has been classified as educable mentally retarded [EMR] on the basis of formal diagnostic tests. Kate goes to the resource room for one and one-half hours every day. Her classroom teacher tends to exclude her from almost all activities on the basis that 'no child with her limited development can effectively participate in the regular classroom.' When other students in the class fail to achieve according to the teacher's expectations, the voiced threat by the teacher is, 'If you cannot do your assignments, you will have to go with Kate to work with the other EMRs in the resource room.' Both Kate and her peers get the message (p. 340).

The differences in expectations that Brophy and Good (1974) and Turnbull and Schulz (1979) have translated into instructional expectations have implications for teaching-learning strategies. If disturbed students are considered "lows" in the regular class and teacher communication is consistent with many of the differences listed, disturbed students will be less successful and they will constitute behavior problems. In addition, the differences in teacher instructional behavior violate most of the intervention strategies previously discussed. Individually, teachers need to be aware of the differences in their instructional expectations, and consciously and intentionally communicate with disturbed students in terms of an intervention, education, and management plan based upon knowledge of individual students.

The personal characteristics of the teacher, rather than knowledge of subject matter, are critical in shaping expectations and developing teaching-learning strategies (Hamachek, 1969). Teachers, like students, have affective needs that are reflected in their classroom behavior. Although numerous personal or personality characteristics are evident among teachers, a positive self-concept, sensitivity, and flexibility, in particular, contribute significantly to their behavior and consequently to student growth.

It has been demonstrated that teachers with positive self-concepts have more positive views of others (students, administrators, parents, and fellow teachers) and are optimistic regarding the success of others. The implications of teacher self-concept are pervasive in terms of classroom interaction and promoting student development. Rather than expecting failure and observing inappropriate behavior, teachers with positive self-concepts expect success and observe appropriate behavior. In short, they highlight accomplishments both academically and behaviorally.

Sensitivity, or perceptiveness and empathy, is important for a teacher to identify and predict accurately how a student will feel and what the student will do within the classroom (Smith, 1966). Teachers with high levels of accurate sensitivity are person-oriented, honest with themselves, and are motivated to understand their students. A sensitive teacher can recognize subtle cues, either in terms of body language or verbal communication, to know that a student has positive or negative affect regarding the classroom experience. Kounin (1967) used the term "withitness" to convey a similar concept, namely, the teacher's awareness of the total classroom and the ability to identify students who are not responding adequately to the instruction and provide appropriate intervention.

The personal freedom or flexibility to pursue options and alternatives in the teaching process has direct implications for the teaching-learning strategy. Many teachers doggedly move through an activity to accomplish specified objectives at the expense of losing the student, cognitively and affectively, along the way. Flexible teachers recognize that more than one activity or set of materials may be appropriate for accomplishing an objective. Flexibility in teaching is also relevant to student affective development. Whereas some students require freedom in the pursuit of objectives, others need direction and structure. However, such flexibility is not spontaneous but planned, based on the needs of the students.

Teacher self-concept, sensitivity, and flexibility are personal characteristics considered prerequisites to appropriate teaching behaviors. Obviously, the list is only partial; however, they are considered priority teacher characteristics for promoting student growth. Specifically, the characteristics indicate the capacity and willingness to adapt teaching behaviors, including expectations, to the cognitive and affective needs of the individual student.

Teacher Style

The characteristic manner in which the teacher fulfills the classroom leadership role in an educational environment is referred to as teaching style. The construct traditionally used to describe teaching style has been described as a continuum leading from teacher-centered to student-centered behaviors. In the final analysis, this teaching style dimension can be described as representing a control continuum. Although the descriptive nomenclature may vary (e.g., authoritarian-democratic, direct-indirect, or controlled-reflective), the critical factor is the exercise of power by the teacher. "In essence, the . . . continuum involves the extent to which the teacher makes decisions for the child" (Kauffman & Lewis, 1974, p. 281). Because teacher style is reported to be relatively permanent for a given teacher, and because teacher influence on student behavior is relatively great, a more fruitful conception of teacher style is warranted.

Direct, dominant, and authoritarian styles are reported to be characteristic of *external* control approaches in which the interaction, objectives, and so forth are more exclusively regulated by the teacher.

Indirect, reflective, and democratic styles have been associated with *internal* control approaches in which students assume intrapersonal and interpersonal regulation. Thus, internal teaching styles are characterized by a limited exercise of control and more facilitative interaction patterns.

Examples of teacher style behaviors characteristic of the external-internal control continuum are identified as direct-indirect by the Flanders (1965) Interaction Analysis system. In the Flanders system, direct teacher style behaviors consist of lecturing, information giving, providing directions, criticizing, and justifying authority. These behaviors restrict student freedom and set limits or focus attention. Indirect teacher style behaviors, on the other hand, increase student freedom and reduce limits by asking questions, building on student ideas, responding to feelings, praising, and encouraging. Although the two extremes provide a clear distinction on the direct-indirect continuum, a teacher rarely demonstrates behaviors from only one extreme and excludes the other. More often, teachers demonstrate a blend of direct-indirect behaviors, relying more heavily upon style behaviors in one direction.

Mosston (1972) refers to this external-internal continuum of teacher control as a spectrum of teaching styles that range from "command to discovery." The spectrum consists of seven sequential styles, each of which represents a particular approach to the teacher-student transaction (Table 1). The spectrum is not limited to the teacher's classroom instructional behavior, however, but also includes decisions regarding instructional preparation and the evaluation of students. The

Table 1.   Spectrum of teaching styles

| Teaching style | Teacher and/or student instructional decision | | |
	Preparation	Execution	Evaluation
1. Command	Teacher	Teacher	Teacher
2. Task	Teacher	Teacher and student	Teacher
3. Reciprocal	Teacher	Teacher and student	Teacher and student
4. Individual program: teacher design	Teacher	Teacher and student	Student
5. Guided discovery	Teacher	Student	Student
6. Problem solving	Teacher and student	Student	Student
7. Individual program: student design	Student	Student	Student

Adapted from Mosston (1972).

teacher who decides what will be taught, how it will be executed, and what evaluation standards will be used represents the most direct, external, or command style. The extent to which the teacher relinquishes the responsibility for these unilateral decisions and involves students in the instructional process determines the teaching style position on the spectrum. The indirect or internal style extreme (individual program-student design) represents minimal teacher control accompanied by maximum student decision making regarding the instructional experience.

Simply because the teaching styles are listed on a hierarchical teacher control spectrum does not mean that any one style is preferable to another. According to Mosston (1972), "the teacher who is familiar with a variety of teaching styles is ready to cope with new conditions and to interact successfully with various forms of student behavior. . . . The spectrum seeks to provide the teacher with a rational basis for selecting a style appropriate to each particular group of students in each particular setting" (p. 6). Thus, the preferable teaching style is the one that is the most appropriate for the student, the instructional objective, the behavior, the setting, and the teacher at a particular time.

Several studies have demonstrated that the teacher's leadership behaviors, specifically teaching styles, influence the behavior and performance of students. The clearest evidence of leadership effect comes from a classic study by Lewin, Lippitt, and White (1939) that dealt with three distinctly different leadership styles: authoritarian (external control), laissez-faire (no control influence), and democratic (internal control). Brophy and Good (1974) have provided an excellent summary of this classic study:

> Laissez-faire leadership tends to create chaos and confusion. Authoritarian leadership achieves efficient productivity but at the cost of frustration and a generally negative group atmosphere leading to outbreaks of aggression when the leader is absent. In contrast to both of the above, democratic leadership appears to be successful in enabling groups to reach productive goals but without the cost of frustration and aggression. In fact, it seems to have the advantage of teaching the group to function more maturely, cooperatively and independently in the leader's absence as well as in his presence (p. 245).

Research conducted over the past 40 years has not refuted these conclusions. Given these results, one may therefore wonder why authoritarian rather than democratic teacher leadership styles are so prevalent in schools. Although there may be as many reasons as there are teachers, there seem to be at least two global explanations for the continued reliance upon the external control teacher style. These explanations are related to the perceived role of the teacher in the classroom: to promote academic achievement and teach in complex environments.

Academic Achievement Undoubtedly, most elementary and secondary teachers place the highest priority on students' ability to perform academically. This emphasis is reinforced by the fact that academic achievement must be consistent with educational, community, and even legal guidelines that specify the measurement of students' academic performance through standardized competency and proficiency tests. Unfortunately, academic testing of this type tends to be limited to specific basic skills such as rote recall information, memorized facts, and simple principles. Thus, schools are being conceptualized as academic institutions that tend to disregard the whole student in an effort to perpetuate the "three Rs" and other basic cognitive skills.

Within this limited academic climate, the authoritarian, external control teacher style is reported to be generally the most effective leadership behavior. Anderson (1959) summarized the research on external and internal leadership styles, emphasizing differences in educational performance. "Democratic leadership is associated with high morale when the primary group goal is social . . . [but] authoritarian leadership is most effective when the task is simple and concrete" (p. 204).

The research results indicate that the external control teaching style is preferable in assisting students in achieving test-measured academic or cognitive objectives. Such a priority is certainly within the role and scope of educational institutions, but it cannot be the singular concern of teachers. The development of an appropriate teaching-learning strategy requires that the teacher alter style behaviors toward a more internal control style when the classroom objectives are more social, affective, or interpersonal in nature.

Unless educators, parents, and the community begin to place greater emphasis on the affective needs of students (i.e., feelings, emotions, acceptance, self-concept, etc.) then the authoritarian, external style will undoubtedly continue as the predominant teacher style. Of course, teachers have long known that students' academic performance cannot be separated from their affective needs (Wirth, 1977). Nevertheless, many teachers have been reluctant to deal with this "sacred," personal area and have chosen to ignore affective education. Instead, educators have taught as if students experience home, school, and community situations that adequately promote positive feelings and emotions. For many students, however, the available evidence indicates that social institutions are not promoting affective development. The increasing frequency of school truancy, classroom disruptions, academic failure, personal isolation, anger, and apathy are visible indicators that the affective component is lacking.

Without a planned, systematic approach for dealing with affective needs, educators have typically provided spontaneous affective experiences. Teachers who praise students, fail them, or express social-moral values are providing affective experiences. Unfortunately, these teaching-learning experiences tend to be a reflection of teachers' preconceived ideals and personal values, which are applied unilaterally. They are rarely used individually in light of students' affective needs.

The important responsibility of developing the whole student, cognitively and affectively, cannot be left to chance. Educators must assume greater responsibility and take a more active and positive role in the creation of educational experiences that will facilitate personal affective growth (Maurer, 1977). This does not mean that academic performance should be relegated to second place, but that alternative goals and methods, including teaching styles, should be employed. This is particularly important for disturbed students, whose primary problem is not academic achievement, but inappropriate behavior and/ or poor mental health. Of course, the shift toward affective education would mean that teachers would have to evaluate and possibly modify traditional external control styles in favor of styles that would promote internal control among students.

Complex Environments.   Harvey, Hunt, and Schroder (1961) hypothesized that individuals, including teachers, can only assimilate so much stimulus bombardment. When their capacity is reached, they develop interpersonal techniques for coping with the situation by reducing the environmental complexity. For teachers, this coping procedure frequently takes the form of an external control style, which emphasizes order, lecturing, and individually focused interaction.

Mehrabian (1976) reached a similar conclusion: "confronted with a potentially complex and unpredictable situation, teachers and school administrators foist a large number of rigid rules and regulations upon students so as to make their behavior far less varied, more uniform, and more predictable; in short, to achieve low-load [low information rate] classrooms" (p. 156).

An example of stimulus bombardment and high information load resulting in an external control style is evidenced in the following anecdote:

> After a particularly difficult examination, the teacher, desiring to show the class her sense of fair play, decided to hear reactions from students regarding their scores. Within a matter of seconds most of the students were complaining about questions, challenging answers, making excuses,

and so on. What was before a quiet, orderly classroom became a mass of noise and movement. The teacher, unable to answer one question before being asked several more, backed away from the students who began to crowd around her. "All right," she yelled, "Everyone sit down and keep quiet. If you raise your hands, I will answer one question at a time."

In the above anecdote, the environment became so loaded with stimuli that the teacher was unable to cope with the situation. Consequently, she reestablished her authoritarian style in order to reduce the information load or environmental complexity.

With thirty children per classroom, some of them demonstrating exceptional learning and behavioral problems, it is easy to understand why teachers may have an information overload and attempt to reduce the classroom information rate. The frequency of interaction alone is remarkably illustrated by different leadership styles. For example, it has been estimated that teacher-student and student-student interactions occur every five seconds in democratically oriented classrooms and every eighteen seconds in more controlled classrooms (Adams & Biddle, 1970). In a six-hour school day, this amounts to 4,332 interactions in the democratically oriented classrooms as opposed to 1,200 interactions in the more controlled classrooms—a significant difference in information load. Unquestionably, the quantity of interaction is a significant factor in establishing the classroom climate (Randhawa & Fu, 1973). Since high rates of interaction reduce teacher awareness of individual differences, the withdrawn or ritualistic student is apt to be overlooked in the classroom (Brophy & Good, 1974).

Although the external style reduces the information rate for teachers, it also reduces the stimulation for students. "The children, in contrast, are going to feel confined and bored, and end up trying to generate arousal and pleasure by interacting amongst themselves" (Mehrabian, 1976, p. 156.). Unsanctioned student interaction typically leads to more external control teacher behaviors, including an increase in the number of rules and disciplinary actions.

Both the academic achievement orientation and stimulus reduction explanations for external control teacher style have significant implications for establishing a teaching-learning strategy. It seems reasonably clear that no one style is appropriate for all students, personally or academically. Therefore, the exclusive reliance upon external or internal styles can create a negative educational experience for a substantial portion of the classroom group.

The extent to which the teacher controls the classroom, or makes decisions for the student, correlates with both intervention strategies and educational objectives. The operation of a structured or behavior modification strategy, which requires stringent time and behavioral schedules measured in small hierarchical increments, is more consistent with the external teacher style. Teachers using behavior modification, however, provide verbal praise for appropriate behavior—a technique that falls within the internal teacher style. Similarly, dynamic strategies that emphasize feelings, freedom, and reflection are more consistent with internal teacher styles, but when limits are set or information is provided, internal style teachers demonstrate external style behaviors. Teachers within the psychoeducational strategy demonstrate a relatively even mixture of external-internal behaviors, with the direction determined by the feeling-behavioral level of the students and the objectives to be accomplished.

Initially, it would be useful for the teacher to determine which students need internal style teaching. Disturbed students in the regular classroom may require either style, or even a blend of teaching styles. For example, an external control teaching style may be required for students whose behavior is characterized as unsocialized, hyperactive, or impulsive. In short, students functioning on the basic personal and academic levels are ". . . lacking important basic skills, [and] need direction or protection until they can acquire them" (Joyce & Harootunian, 1967, p. 95). Students functioning on the higher levels require a different teaching style. Students who are independent, or are assertive, or are attempting to meet higher level needs, such as self-control, are best facilitated by a more open environment with an internal teaching style (Rich, 1978b). Teaching behaviors that are not consistent with the planned intervention strategies, curriculum experiences, and student influences will result in learning climates characterized by frustration, deviance, and failure. The teacher who insists on teaching one way is ignoring the complexity of the curriculum and the variability of human behavior. Students and the curriculum cannot be forced to fit teachers' preferred behaviors. Instead, teaching behaviors should be conceptualized as a variety of expectations and styles that must be analyzed and employed in terms of the needs of students within the educational setting.

CURRICULUM EXPERIENCES

The curriculum, traditionally defined as the educational experiences planned for students, is a persistent influence on the learning behavior and mental health of students. Unlike the variable influence exercised by different teacher behaviors, the curriculum tends to have a more long-term but subtle impact on students and climate. Although curriculum influence may not be obvious, the cumulative effects on academic achievement or failure are profound. The curriculum factors that influence the learning climate include the educational *objectives* to be attained by students, the *content* of the material to be learned and the *process* that is employed to facilitate that learning. Even though the objectives, content, and process components of teaching-learning strategies are here discussed separately, in reality they are intricately interrelated and inseparable. The individual treatment of objectives, content, and process can serve, however, to identify and describe critical curriculum factors and their relationship to teaching-learning strategies, particularly as they relate to disturbed students.

Objectives

The nature of the educational objectives to be achieved by students is a significant part of any well designed teaching-learning strategy. Educational objectives, such as those constructed by Bloom (1956), Krathwohl, Bloom, and Masia (1956), and Dave (1970) have been presented in the form of taxonomies or hierarchies of educational outcomes. In the main, the three taxonomies identify major classes of cognitive, affective, and psychomotor outcomes that form a cumulative hierarchy from basic, simple, and concrete objectives to advanced, complex, and abstract objectives (Table 2).

In general, the hierarchical arrangement of the objectives implies that the more basic objectives must be mastered by the student before

Table 2.   Major classes of cognitive, affective, and psychomotor objectives

Level	Objective	Description
		Cognitive objectives
Basic (low)	Knowledge	The learner can recall information, i.e., bring to mind the appropriate material.
	Comprehension	The learner understands what is being communicated by making use of the communication.
	Application	The learner uses abstractions (e.g., ideas) in particular and concrete situations.
	Analysis	The learner can break down a communication into its constituent elements or parts.
	Synthesis	The learner puts together elements or parts so as to form a whole.
Advanced (high)	Evaluation	The learner makes judgments about the value of material or methods for a given purpose.

(Continued)

Table 2. (*Continued*)

Level	Objective	Description
		Affective objectives
Basic (low)	Receiving (or Attending)	The learner is sensitized to the existence of certain phenomena or stimuli.
	Responding	The learner does something with or about the phenomenon beyond merely perceiving it.
	Valuing	The learner believes that a thing, behavior, or phenomenon has worth.
	Organization	The learner arranges internalized value into a system of priorities.
Advanced (high)	Characterization (or Value complex)	The learner organizes the value hierarchy into an internally consistent system.
		Psychomotor objectives
Basic (low)	Imitation	The learner begins to make an imitation (i.e., copy) when exposed to a behavior.
	Manipulation	The learner performs an act according to instructions.
	Precision	The learner performs an act independent of a model or instructions.
	Articulation	The learner coordinates a series of acts by establishing appropriate sequence and harmony.
Advanced (high)	Naturalization	The learner acts automatically and spontaneously with the least amount of energy.

Adapted from Bloom (1956), Krathwohl, Bloom, & Masia (1956), and Dave (1970).

the next objective level can be successfully accomplished. For example, before a student can cognitively judge the meaning of a poem (evaluation), the student must be able to recall the meanings of words (knowledge); to understand what the words are communicating (comprehension), to supply meaning to the words (application), to break the poem into elements or parts (analysis), and to see the parts of the poem as a whole (synthesis). Many educational tasks involve two or even all three of the taxonomies. For example, when a teacher instructs a student to sit quietly, the teacher is assuming that the student has mastered all of the objectives necessary to complete the task. In other words the teacher believes that the student *received* the instruction, can *recall* and *comprehend* the meaning of the words, is capable of *responding* appropriately, can *manipulate* with *precision* the physical act of sitting quietly, and, perhaps most critical of all, *values* the instruction. Certainly, most students have mastered the objectives for sitting quietly, but disturbed students often do not fall within that broad, normal range of "most" students. Therefore, teachers of disturbed students need to determine which objectives have and have not been achieved with regard to any particular educational task.

Hewett's engineered classroom intervention strategy, particularly its developmental tasks, utilizes the cognitive and affective taxonomies. This intervention strategy is based on the premise that achievement and mastery (higher-level objectives) cannot be accomplished unless attention, response, and so forth (lower-level objectives) have been successfully achieved. Although there has been controversy over the validity of these hierarchical arrangements, research generally supports a direct and cumulative link between the levels of objectives (Madaus, Woods, & Nuthall, 1973).

In terms of teaching-learning strategies, the critical issue is to determine which teaching behaviors or styles are most effective for enabling which students to achieve which objectives. The research on teaching styles tends to support the position that external control styles are more effective when students are to accomplish lower-level objectives, such as recalling specific information and locating specific answers (Bennett, 1976). This conclusion is consistent with the research that supports the contention that students experiencing authoritarian teachers perform better on tests that emphasize low-level objectives such as knowledge and comprehension. Stern (1962), in a review of studies dealing with teaching styles, found that only one study actually demonstrated that the internal control style resulted in significantly greater mastery of knowledge-level subject matter. McKeachie (1962) similarly concluded that students achieved lower scores on content examinations when they experienced teachers with internal control styles, which indicated a "weakness, at least in achieving lower-level cognitive goals" (p. 328). On the other hand, an internal control style is more effective for promoting self-discovery learning, personal adjustment, and higher-level cognitive objectives (Bills, 1956). Stern (1962), who favors the strategy of external style and subject matter, reaffirmed the finding that internal styles are associated with more positive personal adjustment on the part of the students.

Research involving both normal and disturbed students experiencing a variety of interventions and teaching styles has yielded some consistent patterns. Structured, or authoritarian, or external control methods have demonstrated significantly superior results in student achievement of lower-level objectives, such as attending and knowledge (Rich, 1981; Rich & Bush, 1978; Salomon & Achenbach, 1974). The same research also indicates that higher-level objectives are best achieved by students experiencing low control interventions and teaching styles.

Thus, accomplishment of an educational objective, by its nature and hierarchical position, can be said to be facilitated by the use of procedures (both interventions and teacher style) that are consistent with the objective. That is, basic, lower-level objectives that are concrete and specific tend to be more readily achieved by students in educational environments that are concrete and specific (e.g., external style; structured and behavior modification interventions). Advanced, higher-level objectives that require more elaborate cognitive and affective processing are achieved more readily by students when the environment encourages interaction and exploration (e.g., internal style; psychoeducational and open education interventions).

Content

"When the school specialist speaks of *content*, he refers to the compendium of information which comprises the learning material for a particular course or a given grade" (Parker & Rubin, 1966, p. 1). The trend regarding educational content seems to be that students are being required to learn more information earlier in their school experience. The increasing emphasis on the acquisition of academic information has reached the point where neither teachers nor students can ignore the fact that prescribed levels of competency are required if school is to be successfully completed. To a great extent curriculum patterns and subject matter areas are predetermined by regulations and policies and therefore cannot be grossly altered to fit the individual needs and interests of students. Thus, the question of content is not whether students will be required to study math, reading, science, and so forth, but what content alternatives are available that will enable disturbed students to be academically successful students.

An obvious alternative is related to content relevance. Relevance refers to consistency between the academic content and the characteristics of the students, at least including the students' learning style, affective needs, and life-style, that will increase interest, motivation, and success. If students can relate to the content and, consequently, experience success, their rate of appropriate involvement will enhance their learning experience. On the other hand, if the content is inappropriate, boredom and frustration may evolve into active or passive behaviors that will create a negative experience.

For disturbed students, content relevance implies cognitive and affective consistency with the personal characteristics of the learner. Although teachers have traditionally been concerned with cognitive content (i.e., intellectual and academic learning experiences), they have typically ignored the affective implications (i.e., feeling, emotions, and acceptance). This discrepancy between cognitive and affective concerns exists because the curriculum content is based on the cognitive requirements of the various subject matter disciplines rather than the affective characteristics of students (Weinstein & Fantini, 1970). For example, a teacher who requires a slow learner to read from a text book that is two grade levels below that which the classroom group is using, even though it may be cognitively appropriate, totally ignores the affective needs of the student. This situation negatively influences the student in several ways: it reduces self-concept, it identifies the student as different, and it is chronologically and developmentally inappropriate.

In addition, the failure to recognize the affective impact on students is evidenced by content about faraway lands, when some students do not understand much of their own environment; by content about etiquette and manners, when some students are malnourished and battered; and by content on vacation trips and whaling ships, when some students are confined to the neighborhood streets. For many students in the regular classroom, such content may have affective relevance, but for many mainstreamed disturbed students the affective irrelevance is accentuated because of their environmental, physical, or psychological limitations. Certainly, life beyond the students' immediate environment must be introduced, but to require attention, performance, and participation, and to be cognitively evaluated on irrelevant content denies the feelings and experiences of many disturbed students (Rich, 1978a).

Joseph (1969) expressed the feeling that the standard curriculum content has typically ignored the real world needs of many disturbed, deprived, and even delinquent students. Rather than deal with personal content issues such as fear, death, and drugs, teachers unfortunately insist that students write essays about "How to Be a Good Citizen," or list the capitals of the 50 states, or read a "nice" story about Dick and Jane (Joseph, 1969).

Aside from the irrelevance of much of the curriculum content, Parker and Rubin (1966) are concerned about an additional problem:

> Where primary emphasis is on content, the learner ordinarily functions in the passive mode. He conditions himself to submit to authority. He accepts the proffered gospel, and he neither selects his conclusions nor assesses their validity. He does not wear a tailor-made suit, but a ready-made one, cut in the fashion of the day. Even here he employs a number of processes—directed toward the sponging-up of bookishness and its consequent exhibition in the preferred manner (p. 2).

The selection or adaptation of curriculum content, then, has direct implications for developing teaching-learning strategies. Although disturbed students are expected to be able to read, use math, and so forth, the content vehicle can be modified to be more consistent with the needs, experiences, and interests of the students. Curriculum content cannot, however, be separated from the curriculum process.

Process

The teaching-learning process employed by teachers to enable students to learn the required content may be more influential on the classroom experience than the content itself. The process, or *how* students are taught or learn is as important as *what* they are taught or learn. "Educators are finding . . . that children learn different amounts of content at different rates at different times (and) that children learn by talking, doing, and teaching as well as by listening" (Turnbull & Schulz, 1979, p. 121). Clearly, the optimal process for learning math, reading, or science will be different for different students, and will vary with different objectives. For example, a student who has poor auditory memory skills will be penalized if a teacher relies heavily on a lecture process; a student who is hyperactive will perform poorly when the task is sedentary; and a student who has difficulty discriminating stimuli will not perform well under highly stimulating conditions. In each of the three examples, inappropriate process procedures create a negative learning experience for the students involved.

In order to promote a positive climate for students, individualized process procedures are required. Depending on the individual student, a number of process factors must be planned and implemented to create the most effective learning experience. Process factors include the students' input modality (how they receive stimuli), output modality (how they transmit what they have learned) instructional setting (the classroom group organization), structure (the degree of instructional freedom), and activity level (the amount of physical involvement). Table 3 graphically lists some of the process options available.

There is no one pattern of process options appropriate for all students. Also, with different content areas and objectives, the process options may have to be changed to fit the student.

Table 3. Curriculum learning process options

Student's input modality	Student's output modality	Instructional setting	Preferred structure	Activity level
Visual	Verbal	Independent	Controlled	Passive
Auditory	↓	One-to-one	↓	↓
Tactile	(Combination)	Small group	(Mixed)	(Mixed)
	↑		↑	↑
Sensory	Physical	Large group	Permissive	Active

Fox et al. (1974) identified a number of educational determinants that relate to the above process options. Each determinant must be viewed in terms of a continuum of amount or degree (e.g., many–some–none; or usually–sometimes–rarely) for different students:

Opportunities for active learning
Individualized performance expectations
Varied learning environments
Flexible curriculum and extracurricular activities
Support and structure appropriate to learning maturity
Rules cooperatively determined
Varied reward system (pp. 73–81).

Each of the above determinants, if employed individually, will enhance the climate, making ". . . it possible to work productively toward important goals, such as academic learning, social development, and curriculum improvement" (Fox et al., 1974, p. 1).

CLASSROOM GROUP DYNAMICS

Even though teacher behaviors and curriculum experiences are critical factors in setting the tone of the classroom learning environment, the impact of the classroom student group cannot be overlooked. According to Morse (1960), "the teacher can ill afford to ignore alignments when they operate to influence learning behavior of the pupil members" (p. 230). In many classrooms, teachers demonstrate a knowledge of both group dynamics and individual student needs through the use of effective intervention, teaching-learning, and management strategies. However, even in the most skillfully led classroom groups, student behaviors and attitudes may emerge that are counterproductive to an effective learning environment. The problem is escalated when teachers ignore or are oblivious to student needs, inadvertently setting the stage for increased student influence. Under such circumstances, the teacher's influence may erode as the students assume more influence. The conflict between inappropriate teaching behaviors and student needs creates a power struggle in which teachers become more concerned with control and discipline, and the students become more concerned with resisting control and exerting influence. For both teacher and students, classroom behaviors are shaped more by the motivation to survive independently than by the motivation to teach or to learn.

These negative classroom conditions can be minimized if teachers recognize critical group characteristics and their effect upon individual students, and then develop appropriate teaching-learning strategies.

The disturbed student who has been mainstreamed into the regular classroom often presents a special case of individual student relationship with an ongoing classroom group.

Group dynamics is included as a part of teaching-learning strategies because "constructive student-student relationships are probably an absolute necessity for maximal achievement, socialization, and healthy development" (Johnson, 1981, p. 5). Student-student relationships are reported to contribute to the development of disturbed students in the following ways:

1. Peer relationships influence educational aspirations and achievement.
2. Peer relationships contribute to the socialization of values, attitudes, and ways of perceiving the world.
3. Peer relationships are prognostic indicators of future psychological health.
4. It is within peer group relationships that students learn the social competencies necessary to reduce social isolation.
5. Peer relationships influence the occurrence or nonoccurrence of potential problem behaviors. . . .
6. Peer relationships provide a context in which children learn to master aggressive impulses.
7. Peer relationships contribute to the development of sex-role identity.
8. Peer relationships contribute to the emergence of perspective-taking abilities [i.e., empathy].
9. Peer relationships influence attitudes toward school (Johnson, 1981, pp. 5–6).

Because the peer group influences the behavior of disturbed students in the classroom, some aspects of group dynamics warrant closer examination. In particular, three group properties typically determine the character of groups: norms, cohesiveness, and goal structure (Johnson, 1981; Schmuck, 1966).

Norms

Norms are standards of behavior that are shared by the classroom group and that serve to regulate student behavior. In varying degrees, everyone is subject to the peer group influence to conform to expectations of behavior. Even though individuals may intentionally engage in behaviors in order to gain peer approval, more often individuals may not be consciously aware of the tremendous psychological pressure that is exerted by the peer group to ensure that individuals conform to group standards and expectations of behavior. For example, what one wears, the clubs one joins, and the expressed motivation for school, teachers, and friends are shaped by group norms (Jackson, 1960). Often this pressure comes in the form of statements or gestures that convey approval or disapproval of an individual student's behavior, whether or not such behavior is productive or appropriate in the eyes of the teacher.

Teachers must be sensitive to the norms of the classroom group. Teachers who encourage students to violate peer norms are inviting a negative, sometimes hostile, reaction. For example, some classrooms have expectations of how often a student may speak out in class. Students who go beyond the norm and speak out more frequently than the accepted rate, particularly to the teacher, may be socially rejected and unofficially labeled "teacher's pet," "brain," or "Miss Know-it-all." Similarly, students who speak out less than the norm requires are usually pressured by the peer group into verbalizing, even if the questions or answers are inappropriate. Of course, the acceptable norm for speaking will vary from class to class, and from student to student. In some classes, particularly if the teacher is disliked by the most popular and powerful students, the norm may be that no student speaks out. Efforts by the teacher to encourage verbal interaction result in blank stares, shrugging shoulders, or inaudible grunts. Under such circumstances, teachers who demand interaction, without understanding the peer group norm structure, are inviting a confrontation. Such a confrontation has no winners, only losers, and the classroom environment grows steadily more negative.

Although younger students are greatly influenced by adult behaviors and expectations, with increasing age the peer group gradually becomes a stronger force. In fact, it is well documented that older children and adolescents, particularly, may intentionally violate school rules or teacher expectations in order to gain or maintain peer approval (Vorrath & Brendtro, 1974). Typically, classroom groups that demonstrate a high rate of work involvement, frequently ask the teacher for guidance, and show a low tolerance for peer distractions do so as the result of group norms. Similarly, such behaviors as aggression, defiance, and academic failure are an indication that classroom norms exist, but are contradictory to the expectations of the teacher and education in general.

Norms that are in opposition to a positive learning climate often go beyond the boundaries of a single classroom and are evidenced throughout an entire school, perhaps the entire community. For example, Brookover and Schneider (1975) found that the academic environments within schools, rather than individual classrooms, had an effect upon academic achievements. Two particular student norms seemed to have contributed significantly to low achievement: 1) students' belief that significant others (e.g., teachers and parents) were pessimistic regarding the students' future academic accomplishments, and 2) students' sense of futility, lack of control, or hopelessness regarding academic accomplishment. Since approved and desired goals were considered unattainable, counterproductive group norms emerged that reinforced toughness and independence. The disturbed student introduced to such a classroom or school may find the situation intolerable. If the student aligns with the teacher, the group will exert pressure to conform to existing group norms; if the student aligns with the group, the teacher may perceive the behavior to be intentional resistance. In either case, the probability of success for the disturbed student is minimized. In the case of negative classroom environments, there is rarely a middle ground; one is typically accepted or rejected.

Johnson and Bany (1970) have provided a list of student behaviors that are symptomatic of group norms associated with negative classroom learning environments:

A hostile, aggressive classroom group is one that subtly defies the teacher and often disrupts instructional activities . . .

1. Murmuring, talking, lack of attention throughout the group when tasks are presented or assigned.
2. Constant disruptions which interfere with carrying out assignments.
3. Subtle defiance, united resistance, and some evidence of solidarity within the group.
4. Overall nonconformity to generally accepted school practices.
5. Solidarity in resisting teachers' efforts, poor interpersonal relations.

A class group that is dissatisfied with conditions in the classroom and frustrated because of pressure stemming from inappropriate teacher control techniques . . .

1. The group applauds disruptive behavior of one or a few individuals.
2. Defiant acts of one or two individuals are approved by group as a whole.
3. The group sometimes reacts with imitative behavior.
4. The group employs scapegoating.
5. The group promotes fights between individuals.
6. Apathetic and indifferent attitudes are shown to school tasks.
7. It is indifferent about completing tasks.
8. The group is apathetic (but exhibits little problem behavior in the classroom), aggressive, and always in trouble on the playground.
9. Members are well behaved when the teacher is present—unruly and aggressive when the teacher is away or does not constantly supervise the group.
10. Some individuals are not tolerated by group—little attempt is made to be a group.

An insecure, dependent class that has not developed a good functioning group . . .

1. The students are easily distracted when any outsider enters the room.
2. They cannot adjust to changes in routine.
3. Members are easily upset by rumors.
4. Changes in the weather upset the class.
5. Newcomers to the class may be resented (Johnson & Bany, 1970, pp. 410–412).

Direct confrontation, using the institutional power ascribed to the teacher, usually results in disaster, increasing the hostility, frustration, or dependency. Equally important, the disturbed student introduced to classroom groups will tend to demonstrate behaviors that are consistent with group norms and therefore may be totally unrelated to the nature of the student's behavioral or psychological problem. The development or continuation of group norms that deter academic achievement, mental health, or social development must be altered.

The establishment of an effective classroom learning environment requires that the teacher support those group norms that are positive and develop a strategy for changing those that are negative. Interestingly, there is very little information available that tells teachers specifically how to bring about change in the classroom norm structure. This is probably attributable to the fact that classroom groups are individually different, forming unique social structures, so that generalizations regarding how a teacher should influence change may be inappropriate, even counterproductive.

Given this tentative and unique nature of group norms and teacher-group relationships, a number of teacher role behaviors seem to be prerequisites to the establishment of a positive climate. Smith, Neisworth, and Greer (1978) identify five teacher characteristics that are essential to a positive learning climate: 1) a positive attitude, 2) a planned instructional approach, 3) the ability to be flexible, 4) maintaining consistency, and 5) showing understanding. Each of the teacher characteristics is directly related to the establishment of an appropriate learning climate. A positive attitude is necessary to reduce students' sense of futility and project an attitude of optimism regarding their academic accomplishments. A planned instructional approach, including the use of individualized educational programs, is required if, in reality, the teacher is to enable the students to learn academic material. Flexibility in expectations and behavior is needed if students are to be considered individuals and not stereotypes that possess equal ability, skill, and motivation. Consistency, or reliability, is necessary if students are going to be able accurately to identify and predict the important rules and standards of the classroom. Also, understanding between human beings, expressed as empathy, concern, or appreciation, goes a long way in promoting a positive classroom environment.

Cohesiveness

The degree of group cohesiveness (attraction toward and unity within a classroom group) has critical implications for the classroom environment. Some classroom groups appear to function as a single unit, moving smoothly from one activity to another, displaying little deviant behavior, and freely cooperating and sharing. In other classrooms it is difficult to shift activities, noise and physical intimidation are commonplace, and individual but selfish behaviors are frequent. In the first example, the group structure would appear to be attractive to the individual members, possessing a rather balanced sociometric structure, lacking significant "stars" and scapegoats. In the second example, there is less group attractiveness, and the group probably possesses well defined status positions or a "pecking order." Schmuck (1966) found that classroom ". . . groups characterized by a nearly equal distribution of liking and influence choices in contrast to those which were distinctly hierarchical had both more cohesiveness and more positive norms concerning the goals of school" (p. 62).

This balanced social structure, or equal distribution of classroom social choices, provides one of the clearest indicators of cohesiveness. Socially balanced classroom groups have a greater capacity to attract new members (including the mainstreamed disturbed student), function more harmoniously as a unit, and create a positive classroom learning environment. By comparison, groups that are polarized into subgroups are repeatedly plagued by interpersonal conflict. Subgroups may take many forms, for example, racial (blacks versus whites), economic (rich versus poor), academic (bright versus slow), and social (popular versus isolates). The continuous competition between subgroups for social-psychological superiority typically results in a negative learning climate. Teachers may unwittingly contribute to the classroom polarization by rewarding members of one subgroup and punishing or ignoring members of the other. Consequently, teachers must be conscious of the distribution of grades, privileges, and responsibilities so that they do not routinely favor one subgroup over another.

Group cohesiveness has rather significant implications for disturbed students mainstreamed into the regular classroom. Obviously, the probability of success is enhanced if the student is assigned to a cohesive classroom group. Since the attitudes of such groups are more positive toward peers, school life, the teachers, academic work, and themselves as students, the disturbed student is placed in a climate that minimizes the exceptionality and maximizes personal and academic success.

On the other hand, groups that lack cohesiveness are apt to create a survival climate. With the distinct hierarchy of power among the class members, the disturbed student is apt to be relegated to an inferior position and become a scapegoat or even alienated. Regardless of the normative role, the disturbed student will be more preoccupied with physical and psychological survival than with learning academically.

Teachers can be instrumental in creating a more cohesive group, thus establishing a more favorable classroom environment.

The teachers with more positive social climates, in contrast to the others, emphasized and were more sophisticated about classroom mental health conditions. They also perceived more linkages between mental health and academic learning concepts than the other teachers. Teachers with more positive climates perceived their pupils' characteristics in a more differentiated manner and emphasized psychological attributes in contrast to physical characteristics more than other teachers. Teachers with positive climates appeared to converse often with a wide variety of students and to reward individual students . . . In contrast, teachers with more negative climates conversed often with only a few students, seldom issued reward statements, and often punished individual students publicly (Schmuck, 1966, p. 65).

Thus, the attributes of a teacher who desires to influence the normative structure of the classroom hold true for influencing the cohesiveness of the group. Those attributes include being positive, planned, flexible, consistent, and understanding. Unfortunately, as obvious as these attributes may seem, a substantial percentage of teachers choose to exercise negative, haphazard, rigid, inconsistent, and intolerant behaviors. The difference in the classroom learning environment for these two teacher extremes is remarkable. For the disturbed student, the results will be equally remarkable in favor of the teacher who, with the group, establishes a positive learning environment.

Goal Structure

Both group norms and cohesiveness can be influenced by the way the teacher encourages or requires that educational objectives be achieved by students in the classroom. The teacher behavior that conveys how students will learn can be described as goal structure. Teacher influence during the early elementary years is particularly important because younger students frequently adopt the teacher's values as their own. It is not until later childhood that the pressure of contradictory group norms noticeably creates classroom conflicts between teachers and students.

According to Johnson and Johnson (1975), three distinctive forms of group structure exist: cooperative, competitive, and individualistic. "Cooperative goal structure exists when students perceive that they can obtain their own goals if, and only if, the other students with whom they work can obtain their goals. A competitive goal structure exists when students feel that they can obtain their own goals only if other students fail to obtain their goals. Individualistic goal structures occur when a student's achievement goals are unrelated to the achievement goals of other students" (Good & Brophy, 1978, p. 301).

These three forms of structure can only exist with the support of consistent teacher behaviors and curriculum experiences. In terms of disturbed students, the cooperative and individualistic structures provide the most appropriate learning climates. The competitive structure, which limits the number of students who can succeed and thus receive rewards, typically places the disturbed student at an educational disadvantage. If learning is perceived as a cooperative or individual effort, then the success of disturbed students will be enhanced; if learning is perceived as a competitive effort, disturbed students will develop a sense of futility.

There is considerable evidence that cooperative learning experiences, compared with competitive and individualistic ones, result in more positive student-student relationships characterized by mutual liking, positive attitudes toward each other, mutual concern, friendliness, attentiveness, feelings of obligation to each other, and desire to win each other's respect. In competitive situations there is a tendency for students to choose their friends on the basis of academic performance, so that high performance students in particular form a coherent and exclusive friendship group; in cooperative situations friendship circles tend to be more fluid and open and are formed on the basis of interests and other variables in addition to academic performances. There is evidence that cooperation, compared with competitive and individualistic learning experiences, promotes more positive relationships across ethnic, social class, sexual, and ability lines. Cooperative learning experiences, compared with competitive and individualistic ones, also promote more positive attitudes toward teachers and other school personnel. Students experiencing cooperative instruction like the teacher better and perceive the teacher as being more supportive and accepting, academically and personally. Such positive perceptions by students of their relationship with the teacher are important for many reasons, not the least of which is that the more positive the relationship between the teacher and the students, the less the teacher has to rely on direct power and coercion to motivate students to comply with classroom norms and role definitions (Johnson, 1981, pp. 7–8).

Teaching behaviors that emphasize cooperative, individualistic, or competitive goal structure therefore have important implications for classroom group dynamics and teaching-learning strategies. Since the competitive structure dominates most classrooms (Johnson, 1981), mainstreamed disturbed students do not tend to perform well. The competitive goal structure pits students against students, increases the failure rate, and works against positive student relations. Disturbed students, who are less adequately prepared than other students to compete, become "losers" when there can only be a limited number of "winners." The individualistic and, more particularly, cooperative goal structures, on the other hand, can facilitate achievement, socialization, and healthy mental development.

STUDENTS' AFFECTIVE NEEDS

No discussion of teaching-learning strategies can be complete without including some reference to the internal psychological, or affective, needs of students. Previously, affective objectives were discussed in terms of legitimate curriculum objectives that need to be addressed in education. In this context, Krathwohl, Bloom, and Nasia (1956) stated that affective objectives are those that deal with "feelings, emotions and acceptance." However, this rather loose definition of affect is difficult to operationalize in the classroom, particularly because teachers are already aware of the fact that students share in the "pain and joy in school" (Schultz, Heuchert, & Stampf, 1973).

A concise statement of student affective needs is difficult to construct because of the diversity of theories and definitions that currently exist. Concepts such as ego development (Llorens and Rubin, 1967), self-concept (LaBenne and Greene, 1969), and self-control (Fagen, Long, and Stevens, 1975) are typical of the affective needs discussed in the literature. Psychosocial factors such as student needs for trust, autonomy, initiative, and identity (Erikson, 1965) have been used to describe mental health crises of childhood and early adolescence. Motivational needs for safety, self-esteem, love, and belongingness (Maslow, 1970) represent affective needs considered important in the development of the human personality. Bloom (1976) regarded these as affective entry characteristics that are "a complex compound of interests, attitudes, and self-views" (p. 75).

In general, the variety of affective needs may be reduced to two basic concerns: positive feelings about one's self and a degree of control over one's environment. In the case of positive feelings, it is important that the student has a self-concept as a worthy and successful individual who possesses a number of good qualities, and who is valued by others. Control is related to exercise of choices over one's own destiny—a degree of power in making decisions that are respected. Both self-concept and self-control have a direct and causal effect on the successful use of teaching-learning strategies and the continued effective growth of students.

Self-Concept

LaBenne and Greene (1969) defined self-concept as an individual's "total appraisal of his (her) appearance, background and origins, abilities and resources, attitudes and feelings which culminate as a directing force in behavior" (p. 10). The authors additionally cite a number of research studies that report a positive relationship between self-concept and both academic performance and classroom behavior. C. M. Charles (1976) drew a similar conclusion, stating that "students who think well of themselves also happen to do better in school" (p. 20). Charles further concluded that good readers have more positive self-concepts than do poor readers. In addition, disturbed students experiencing regular classroom placement have been reported to develop a more positive self-concept than those students assigned to a special class (Calhoun & Elliott, 1977).

Even though the relationship between self-concept and classroom performance is well established, whether or not one causes the other is not clear. For individual disturbed students, feelings of inadequacy, low frustration tolerance, and negative attitudes toward education (including teachers) have resulted in academic failure or disciplinary actions. Students with poor self-concepts, for example, may be unwilling to express themselves verbally or to read aloud for fear of failure or disapproval, they may be unable to sit for long periods to complete numerous academic tasks, and they may be unable to tolerate constant personal control by an autocratic teacher.

Thus, in individual cases, there is reasonable evidence of a causal relationship between self-concept and academic success. For many students, however, both negative self-concept and academic failure arise from a lifelong process of environmental deprivation, parental hostility or apathy, and educational programs without purpose. Even though self-concept development is a lifelong process, "this does not mean that affective needs cannot be more fully attended to throughout the years of school" (Valett, 1977, p. 23).

Teaching strategies that do not attend to self-concept will be ineffective in accomplishing the designated cognitive objectives. Tasks that require more information than the student possesses, that require more work space and time than the student is provided, that require more stringent controls and limitations than the student can manage, and that require an environmental background the student has not experienced are inappropriate for the development of self-concept.

It should be understood that one of the primary functions of the human organism is to maintain consistency with one's concept of self. If a student considers himself or herself agile, attractive, or smart, the student will engage in behaviors designed to protect and maintain those self-conceptions. Similarly, if he or she feels clumsy, ugly, or dumb, behaviors will be evidenced that perpetuate those negative conceptions. The effort to maintain consistency is evidenced in behaviors that are designed to counter any threat to one's self-concept, even though such behaviors may seem to be counterproductive. Teachers who discipline a student by conveying such messages as "big boys don't act like that" or "ladies would never do such a thing" can expect students to react in order to defend their self-concept. They may choose to return verbal abuse, become defiant, get into a fight—anything to recover the damage inflicted upon the self-concept. Students who lose peer group status because of academic failure may resort to similar counterproductive behaviors in order to achieve self-concept consistency.

The case of negative self-concept is accentuated for students who do not enter their educational roles with skills or attitudes comparable to regular class students. Bloom (1977) has indicated that the "latent" or unwritten curriculum is one of competitive and personal comparisons among students. This comparative process teaches students how well they function in relation to other children in the classroom and school. If, then, the learning experiences have been relatively negative through the comparative process, the disturbed student is apt to be academically unsuccessful, to regard himself or herself as inadequate, and to develop a negative view toward learning and school. Figure 1 illustrates the systematic deterioration of self-concept as a result of unsuccessful school experiences.

The case for individualizing teaching-learning procedures based on self-concept is an immediate affective need. It may be necessary to sacrifice some of the traditional cognitive objectives in favor of materials and procedures that enhance a student's sense of adequacy, creating a more positive self-concept.

Self-Control

An individual's ability to direct, control, or regulate his or her own behavior in a way that realistically meets the requirements of a given

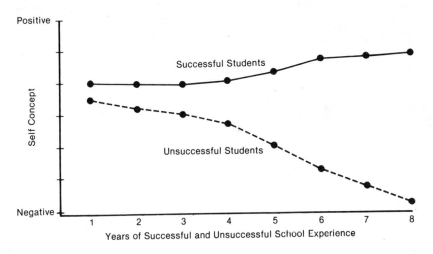

Figure 1. Self-concept of successful and unsuccessful students. Successful students were in the upper fifth on teacher's grades; unsuccessful students were in the lower fifth on the same criterion. Adapted from Bloom, 1976.

situation is evidence of self-control. Educators are aware of the great waste of student potential and the enormous amount of teacher resources and energy necessary to deal effectively with disruptive, defiant, and aggressive behaviors. These types of acting-out student behaviors are signals that students do not have the necessary self-control to function effectively in the typical classroom. This conclusion is particularly appropriate for some special children who have sensory and/or neurological impairment and therefore may have a distorted perception of reality.

However, there is a second side to self-control, namely, the need to determine or control one's own destiny. Rotter (1966) uses the term "internally controlled" to describe an individual who perceives that reinforcement is contingent upon his or her own behavior, and is not the "result of luck, chance, fate, as under the control of powerful others" such as the teacher (p. 2). In short, students with self-control (internally controlled) have developed a degree of personal autonomy, identity, and independence, and do not desire that others manage their lives. It is in this area that educators and students find themselves in conflict.

Fagen, Long, and Stevens (1975) have identified three "basic educational distortions" that have impeded freedom of choice and have contributed to teacher-student conflicts:

1. Externally controlled academic tasks: This particular distortion is evident when the teacher defines the nature of the task without giving consideration to the learner's needs, interests, and abilities. In effect, the teacher decides what is to be done, when and by whom without significant input from the student. . . .
2. Restrictive competition for grades and recognition: This distortion exists when the number of students receiving positive reinforcement is restricted substantially. That is, praise, acclaim, encouragement or affection are offered on a space available basis. . . .
3. Focus on narrow academic products: American education historically has concentrated on tangible signs of productivity. Thus, the classroom focus has been on the correct answer—the pertinent fact—the material outcome (pp. 31–32).

Adequate individualization of the teaching-learning process can effectively contribute to the self-control and independence of students. Obviously, continuous teacher control, with specific expectations regarding both behavior and academic performance, has cast the student into a role of dependency, helplessness, and for some, frustration. Unless "beaten" into a role of submission or dependency, students will inevitably test the environment—home, school, and community— for limits to their own power and control. For example, a student who talks back to a teacher may be attempting to exercise a degree of control or independence over a confining and frustrating educational situation. The exercise of absolute power by the teacher, without the availability of programmatic options, is a basis for conflict.

Teacher behaviors and curriculum experiences must be modified or adapted to accommodate reasonable expectations for self-control. The development of student independence and control can be encouraged through the use of meaningful student input, optional types of materials, and teacher control that is exercised in an amount appropriate for the individual student.

Thus, teacher behaviors, curriculum experiences, and objectives should be used with a thorough knowledge of the disturbed student's individual affective needs. If an educational program is employed unilaterally and inclusively to the classroom group, some students will fail. The students will fail academically, and more importantly, they will fail affectively, feeling less adequate and less independent.

Bloom's (1976) data, which demonstrate a declining concept of self with cumulative years of unsuccessful school experience, are evidence of the relationship between unmet student needs and teaching-learning behaviors. According to Bloom, there are several constraints in education that perpetuate this model for failure: 1) "school learning . . . is largely group learning," 2) "school learning is subject centered," and 3) "students are expected to learn from a set of materials and a teacher" (pp. 20–21). To overcome these constraints, educators must conceptualize "learning which can be related to group or individual learning, to graded subject-centered as well as non-graded less formal learning situations, and which can reflect the style and characteristics of the instructional materials and the instructor" (p. 21).

The application of predetermined teaching behaviors and curriculum experiences designed to achieve the same objectives for all students in the classroom will result in failure for a substantial percentage of the group. An undifferentiated teaching-learning procedure leads one to believe that all students in a classroom group are the same, that they learn in the same way, and that they need to know the same things. Unfortunately, many classroom settings continue to represent external control models in which teachers possess the power to make decisions for students—what they will learn and how they will learn it. Indicative of this pattern is the fact one study revealed that elementary teachers spent more than 90% of their time evaluating, monitoring, lecturing, directing, and criticizing, but less than 10% of their time to encouraging, building on student ideas, and accepting student feelings (Rich, 1973). Under such circumstances, many students will not achieve the prescribed objectives, nor will they develop self-control or a positive self-concept.

LEARNING CLIMATES

During the past few years, educational issues such as "back to basics," accountability, competency testing, discipline, and mainstreaming have been of primary concern to teachers, frequently at the expense of an appropriate classroom learning climate. So much teacher energy has been devoted to meeting individual cognitive, behavioral, and legal requirements that the learning climate and its impact on the performance of both teachers and students have been ignored.

This chapter is based on the belief that appropriate teaching-learning strategies that include learning climates will enhance the teacher's ability to provide better instruction, reduce discipline problems, and enable greater individualized learning for both disturbed and regular class students. Although the focus of this chapter is on individual teachers, disturbed students, and classroom groups, it should be recognized that both teachers and students throughout an entire school building or even an entire school system may be influenced by the administrative leadership philosophy demonstrated by principals, superintendents, and the community in general. Often this influence is so great that it interferes with the most conscientious teacher efforts to alter the existing learning climate. For example, if the philosophy of the administration is essentially custodial, complete with a rule orientation, orderliness, and unquestioned obedience to authority, then the teacher is limited in the types of teaching-learning procedures that may be attempted. On the other hand, administrative leadership that recognizes the importance of a positive learning climate, and supports teachers and students by providing resources, encouragement, and understanding, gives the teacher and students a wider range of alternatives.

Within a school system, a school, or individual classrooms, a number of behaviors and attitudes may be evidenced that are indicative of a negative school climate. Fox et al. (1974) have developed a checklist of school-related problems that are symptomatic of a negative school climate:

_____ High student absenteeism
_____ High frequency of student discipline problems
_____ Weak student government
_____ Student cliques
_____ High faculty absenteeism
_____ Negative discussion in faculty lounges
_____ Crowded conditions
_____ "Lost" feeling of students because the school is too large
_____ Vandalism
_____ Student unrest
_____ Poor school spirit

___ Poor community image of the school
___ Faculty cliques
___ Property theft from lockers
___ High student dropout rate
___ Underachieving students
___ Low staff morale
___ Passive students
___ Faculty apathy
___ Supplies and equipment unavailable when needed
___ Students carrying guns, knives, and other weapons
___ Poor image of the school by staff
___ Dislike of students by faculty members
___ Feeling among students that school has little purpose
___ High incidence of suspensions and expulsions (pp. 2–3).

The presence of one or more of the above conditions identifies the school as having a learning climate that needs immediate and direct attention. When several of the negative conditions exist, teachers and students are chiefly concerned with day-to-day existence, even survival in many cases, with little attention devoted to academic learning or human needs. "It could be said that if schools continue to perpetuate an anti-humane climate in which apathy, failure, punishment, and in-adequate success in achieving the curriculum are characteristic, they may guarantee their own demise, and ultimately that of the American social system" (Fox et al., 1974, p. 3).

Under such negative conditions, students, particularly disturbed students, have little opportunity to succeed. If students have difficulty relating to their peers, their teachers, or the curriculum due to their behavioral or emotional handicapping condition, a negative school climate accentuates the competition between teachers and students and among students, ensuring greater degrees of failure and apathy.

The negative school climate checklist serves only to identify and list school climate problems. However, many schools are positive, showing little evidence of a negative climate. According to Fox et al. (1974), positive climates seem to be attributable to at least eight factors:

1. *Respect.* Students should see themselves as persons of worth, believing that they have ideas, and that those ideas are listened to and make a difference. Teachers and administrators should feel the same way. School should be a place where there are self-respecting individuals. Respect is also due to others. In a positive climate there are no putdowns.

2. *Trust.* Trust is reflected in one's confidence that others can be counted on to behave in a way that is honest. They will do what they say they will do. There is also an element of believing others will not let you down.

3. *High Morale.* People with high morale feel good about what is happening.

4. *Opportunities for Input.* Not all persons can be involved in making the important decisions. Not always can each person be as influential as he might like to be on the many aspects of the school's programs and processes that affect him. But every person cherishes the opportunity to contribute his or her ideas, and know they have been considered. A feeling of a lack of voice is counterproductive to self-esteem and deprives the school of that person's resources.

5. *Continuous Academic and Social Growth.* Each student needs to develop additional academic, social, and physical skills, knowledge, and attitudes. (Many educators have described the growth process as achieving "developmental tasks." Educators, too, desire to improve their skills, knowledge, and attitudes in regard to their particular assignments within the school district and as cooperative members of a team).

6. *Cohesiveness.* This quality is measured by the person's feeling toward the school. Members should feel a part of the school. They want to stay with it and have a chance to exert their influence on it in collaboration with others.

7. *School Renewal.* The school as an institution should develop improvement projects. It should be self-renewing in that it is growing, developing, and changing rather than following routines, repeating previously accepted procedures, and striving for conformity. If there is renewal, difference is seen as interesting, to be cherished. Diversity and pluralism are valued. New conditions are faced with poise. Adjustments are worked out as needed. The "new" is not seen as threatening, but as something to be examined, weighed, and its value or relevance determined. The school should be able to organize improvement projects rapidly and efficiently, with an absence of stress and conflict.

8. *Caring.* Every individual in the school should feel that some other person or persons are concerned about him as a human being. Each knows it will make a difference to someone else if he is happy or sad, healthy or ill. (Teachers should feel that the principal cares about them even when they make mistakes or disagree. And the principal should know that the teachers—at least most of them—understand the pressures under which he or she is working and will help if they can).

The authors do not believe the factors listed above, or the other listings used to describe the school's climate, are all-inclusive. Readers may wish to delete or add items. (Fox et al., 1974, pp. 7–9).

Even though the eight factors are intended to create a positive climate within the school, the factors are equally important to the climate of the individual classroom. The task of establishing an appropriate learning climate in the classroom is not a simple one, nor is the responsibility clearly defined in many situations. The fact that an infinite number of variables have influence on the learning climate can be an overwhelming problem for the teacher. The complex nature of the classroom climate, created by individual needs, high rates of behavior, group dynamics, and prescribed educational objectives, requires both planned and spontaneous actions and reactions on the part of the teacher. Disturbed students introduced to the regular classroom typically increase the complexity of the classroom climate.

The use of planned teaching-learning strategies appropriate to individual student needs is critical to the learning climate. According to Turnbull and Schulz (1979), "A key element to successful mainstreaming . . . is the creation of a positive school environment . . . in which the human differences of all students are accepted and respected" (p. 339).

SUMMARY

This chapter discussed several critical teaching-learning factors that have definite implications for the education of disturbed students. Specifically, five separate components of teaching-learning strategies were addressed: teaching behavior (instructional behavior and teaching style); curriculum experiences (objectives, content, and process); classroom group dynamics (norms, cohesiveness, and goal structure); student affective needs (self-concept and self-control) and the learning climate. Even though the five factors were discussed separately, they should be viewed as interrelated and interdependent influences within the classroom.

Teachers often with low expectations of disturbed students and through the use of stereotypic teaching styles have a significant negative impact on the classroom. Many teachers use an authoritarian or external control style to promote academic achievement and reduce the complexity of the classroom environment. Although such a style may be appropriate for some students and some objectives, it was suggested that alternate teaching styles be employed that will encompass a greater variety of student learning characteristics, including student affective needs for a positive self-concept and for self-control.

The curriculum influence was discussed in terms of objectives, content, and process. An effective teaching-learning strategy is dependent upon the level and type of objectives to be achieved and the development of relevant content alternatives, supported by a process that recognizes individual student experiences and characteristics.

Classroom group dynamics were discussed in terms of three group characteristics: norms, cohesiveness, and goal structure. Group standards of behavior (norms) and degree of attractiveness (cohesiveness) are instrumental in shaping the classroom learning experience. Similarly, cooperative and individualistic, rather than competitive, goal structures create a more supportive environment for disturbed students. It is essential that teachers recognize the effects of these influences, and if they create negative conditions, teachers should intervene by being positive, planned, flexible, consistent, and understanding.

Throughout the chapter, it has been stressed that disturbed students, as well as other students in the regular classroom, require an appropriate classroom learning environment. In other words, teacher leadership behaviors, group influences, and curricular experiences should be productively compatible with the unique needs and characteristics of all students. Although the ongoing classroom environment may be sufficient in many cases, frequent adaptions in teaching-learning strategies are required if the classroom is to promote and encourage a successful school experience for all students.

9

Behavior Management Strategies

The management of inappropriate, disruptive, and interfering behavior among students has been a persistent and critical concern of classroom teachers. No educational issue or problem has created more discussion, frustration, and irritation among teachers than the need to manage educationally interfering behaviors among individual students or the classroom group (Jones & Tanner, 1981). Numerous hours and enormous energy have been expended by teachers in an effort to create and maintain a positive learning environment in the classroom. The time and energy that have been devoted to classroom behavior management have consumed an inordinate amount of teacher attention, thus reducing the teacher's instructional responsibility and minimizing the students' learning experiences. In addition to the physical and emotional drain on teachers, the frequent teacher focus on interfering behavior is a primary factor that has contributed to the failure of many students to achieve educational objectives.

To a great extent, the current managerial dilemma is a consequence of rather traditional and rigid educational practices and expectations that have remained relatively stable in the presence of scientific, technological, and social change. Historically, teachers have been well trained to transmit academic information to large groups of students who were considered to be very much alike. Within such an academic and teacher-centered approach, an orderly, passive learning environment was usually required. Classroom control, therefore, was primarily dependent on students' willingness to submit to authoritarian demands and expectations. Students who failed to comply with the prevailing standards were reprimanded, punished, or otherwise disciplined. Thus, the classroom has historically represented an external control model in which student conformity to standards of conduct was rewarded and disruptive interference was categorically punished through adult intervention.

Disruptive behavior, however, is not the only source of interfering behavior. Often students provide their own internal source of interference through extreme forms of behaviors such as withdrawal, daydreaming, and inattention. Even though such a student does not disrupt the classroom, teachers have a responsibility to intervene and bring the student back to the reality of learning. This precautionary note is included because disruptive behavior is highly visible, demanding, and even provoking, thus consuming an inordinate amount of teacher time and attention. Consequently, teachers tend to ignore or omit managerial techniques for the more behaviorally compliant students even though the students may be engaging in interpersonally interfering behaviors.

This managerial situation has been accentuated during the past few years by the introduction of exceptional students to the regular classroom. Even though individual disturbed students may be no more or less difficult to manage than normal students, at least two critical conditions underscore the need to develop more effective management strategies. First, the fact that handicapped students including the disturbed are being mainstreamed has created a more complex and divergent student population in the regular classroom, increasing the usual range of student needs and characteristics. As a result, the typical classroom may include students from a variety of socioeconomic backgrounds, functioning on different academic and intellectual levels, possessing a broad range of physical and sensory traits, and evidencing an assortment of psychological and behavioral conditions. For example, the regular classroom may contain a large contingent of normal students, as well as some students who are mildly to moderately retarded, learning-disabled, physically impaired, visually or aurally limited, or disturbed. It is unlikely that such a composite of individual students will respond appropriately and uniformly to the repetitive use of a relatively few authority-oriented management procedures used by many classroom teachers.

Second, many handicapped students require managerial techniques that take into consideration the uniqueness of their handicapping conditions. For example, verbal threats, such as "Sit down and keep quiet or I'll send you to the principal," may have little effect on a student who is hyperactive; the teacher's physical closeness, rearranging the classroom, or positive reinforcement may be preferable.

Similarly, techniques such as corporal punishment, extra work, and restricted movement (e.g., time out), all of which are punitive in nature, may not take into account a student's intellectual level, degree of mental health, or ability to understand and perform in accordance with teacher expectations.

With the increasing range and uniqueness of student needs and characteristics included within the regular classroom, teachers can no longer rely on the traditional authoritarian methods of behavior management. Even though some students accept the classroom procedures and respond appropriately to external control, other students do not recognize the value of school or the ascribed authority of educators, or do not possess the skills necessary to respond appropriately. This mixture of traditional expectations and diversified students has resulted in inappropriate management procedures that tend to be overly severe, negative, and self-defeating, forcing a confrontation between teacher and student. To avoid these inappropriate disciplinary procedures and to manage effectively the interfering behaviors demonstrated by a wide variety of disturbed students, teachers should be equipped with a comprehensive repertoire of managerial strategies.

Behavior management strategies refer to corrective interventions on the part of teachers that are intended to prevent or appropriately change student behaviors that are considered incompatible with the accomplishment of educational objectives in the classroom. The managerial strategies discussed in this chapter do not subscribe to a singular theoretical approach but draw from a number of theories, including biophysical, behavioral, psychodynamic, sociological, and ecological theories (Rhodes & Tracy, 1972a). However, the subsequent discussion of management strategies roughly adheres to a sequence from a specific, behavioral focus, to an interpersonal, affective focus, to a general, inclusive environmental focus. This sequence is comparable to the progressive nature of both the theories of causality and the intervention strategies. Aside from some general principles of behavior management, the sequence includes: 1) surface management, 2) interpersonal management, 3) group management, and 4) classroom environmental management.

These categories of behavior management do not include all of the available strategies nor do they imply success unless they are individually, appropriately, and consciously employed. In addition, the intervention strategies (Chapter 7) and the teaching-learning strategies (Chapter 8) have definite implications for behavior management. Introducing a disturbed student to the appropriate intervention and teaching-learning strategies that are designed to reduce inappropriate behavior, increase achievement, and promote positive mental health is the most effective behavior management strategy. In those situations, however, where it is not possible to determine or practical to employ the appropriate intervention and/or teaching-learning strategies, then teachers may take other measures to manage the behavior of disturbed students.

GENERAL PRINCIPLES OF MANAGEMENT

The successful utilization of specific management strategies will be increased if a number of guiding principles are recognized. Although these principles do not constitute a unitary model of all the available techniques and concerns, they are frequently reported as prerequisites to direct behavior management in the literature and by experienced teachers (Long, Morse, & Newman, 1976).

Knowledge of Individual Students

Even though teachers may have command of a variety of management strategies, those strategies will be of limited assistance unless the teacher also has substantial knowledge of individual students. Although a trial-and-error strategy may be appropriate in a limited number of circumstances, the probability of increasing management effectiveness is enhanced by the utilization of techniques that are appropriate for the individual. Matching the appropriate technique with the individual student requires that the teacher be aware of individual academic, psychological, and physical characteristics. Academically, the teacher needs knowledge of the student's functional level, modality strengths and weaknesses, motivational level, and interests in the various subject areas. Psychologically, the teacher needs to be aware of frustration levels, self-concept, degree of acceptance, and attitudes toward the teacher, peers, and education. Physically, the teacher needs to know the individual's strengths and limitations, and the impact of physiological differences on academic and psychological performance.

Practical differences among individuals include, for example, students who are impulsive, who require techniques that are quite different than those needed for students who have low self-concepts. Whereas the former may benefit from structure, the latter typically respond to positive reinforcement. Students from deprived, as opposed to enriched, backgrounds may respond differently to the same technique. For example, reactions may be quite different to a teacher's appeal for academic performance, the use of tangible rewards, or acceptance of authority. Similarly, students who lack verbal skills may respond more favorably to physical and visual techniques than to verbal intervention. The degree of self-control, achievement, motivation, and environmental experiences of individual students also may result in the differential success of various intervention procedures. In short, the management of interfering behaviors should be as individualized as the academic program that has been designed for the individual student.

Tolerance of Selected Behaviors

Teachers should not manage every deviant behavior in the classroom. In fact, some so-called deviant behaviors are not maladaptive at all but constitute individual responses to the learning environment. Behaviors that are a function of individual differences should be tolerated, not managed through teacher intervention. According to Long and Newman (1976), tolerating behavior includes such individualized concepts as "learner's leeway," "behavior that reflects a developmental state," and "behavior that is symptomatic of a disease." Each of the three concepts dictates the need for teachers to recognize the variability.

Learner's leeway simply reflects the teacher's belief that students perform in accordance with their individual characteristics. Certainly not all students will complete the same number of math problems in the same amount of time and with the same degree of accuracy, nor will they drink the same amount of water from the hall fountain, nor can they physically remain still for identical periods of time. Therefore, the teacher should expect individual differences in behavior and provide some leeway in the expression of those differences.

Although most children and adolescents go through the same developmental stages, they do not accomplish the developmental milestones at the same time or at the same rate. High levels of motor activity, for example, are more evident among primary-age children, but show a steady decrease as children get older (Rich, 1978c). Similarly, boys are generally more motor-active than girls. Coordination, lying, tattling, and grooming are examples of other behaviors that may only reflect a developmental stage. If the interfering behaviors are developmental in nature, then maturation is the most effective intervention technique.

Behavior that is symptomatic of a disease is a critical management concern when working with disturbed students. When a teacher says of a disturbed student, "He could act right if he only wanted to," this is an indication that the teacher is not recognizing the pathology of disturbance, that is, the nature of the disease or problem. Certainly if a student came to class with a broken leg, evidenced by a cast and crutches, the teacher would not say "He could walk if he only wanted to." Thus, the physical evidence of a broken leg makes teachers aware of the symptomatic nature of a physical problem. Disturbance, however, is usually determined by behavior, not by physical evidence. This lack of physical evidence creates a suspicion in the minds of teachers that disturbed behavior is voluntary and willful deviance, rather than a symptom of disturbance. If the student is disturbed, the behaviors are not under the voluntary or willful control of the student and therefore should be tolerated as much as possible. Tolerance of symptomatic behaviors does not, however, imply a lack of educational programming. It does imply that a degree of futility will be experienced if direct, spontaneous management is attempted. Therefore, the management of symptomatic behaviors requires a long-term therapeutic plan and program independent of the simple management of behavior.

Focus on Specific Behaviors

Vague, general statements, such as "He's lazy," "He never does what I tell him," or "She's a disruptive child," convey little meaning and are behaviorally inappropriate. Attempting to manage behaviors so globally described does not provide the information necessary to focus on a manageable behavior. Similarly, a teacher who attempts to intervene with numerous behaviors, important as well as trivial ones, is spreading management so thin that it is doubtful that any technique will be successful.

Unfortunately, some teachers have so many rules of conduct that neither the teacher nor the students are aware of them all, and certainly there is no consistency in enforcing them all. Classroom rules should be clear, specific, and limited to a relative few. Each behavioral rule should contribute to the effective maintenance of the learning environment. Rules to regulate behaviors that personally annoy the teacher but that have no visible impact on the learning environment should be avoided

Some students may engage in a series of disruptive behaviors on occasion. For example, a student may arrive late, slam the door, engage another student in conversation, stumble over the trash can, drop a book, and finally be seated rather loudly and clumsily. The teacher may similarly use a series of verbal managements: "You're late . . . don't slam the door . . . no talking . . . watch where you're walking . . . pick up that book . . . sit quietly, please!" Although this example may not reflect a typical classroom scene, certainly elements of the sequence occur daily. In the example, the teacher's attempted management is ineffective for a number of reasons. A primary reason, however, is that the teacher attempts to manage every deviant behavior that occurs within a few seconds. The teacher's effectiveness could have been increased if a single behavior had been selected. In this case, being on time should have been the teacher's focus, because the subsequent behaviors would have been unimportant if the class had not started.

Since it is impossible to manage every deviant behavior, it is important to select specific behaviors that have the greatest threatening, disruptive, or interfering effect. Without a focusing perspective, the teacher is forced into the role of disciplinarian rather than instructional leader.

Develop a Variety of Techniques

Many teachers repeatedly use a relative few behavior management techniques, whether or not the techniques are successful. Sending students to the principal, raising one's voice, telling students to sit down or be quiet, and giving them the "evil eye" are techniques used routinely in most classrooms. With some students such obvious procedures may be effective, but for most students the techniques have become so commonplace and undifferentiating that they are ineffective. Teachers who rely on stereotypic techniques often unconsciously convey to the students whether or not they are serious about managing behavior. Students may know that a particular teacher will not intervene until he or she is standing, or until the teacher's voice reaches a certain decibel level, or until students verbally challenge the teacher's authority. Students usually know when, where, how, and with whom teachers will intervene, and the students have developed stereotypic responses to neutralize anticipated patterns of teacher behavior.

Based on the teacher's knowledge of the students and the desire to manage specific behavior, any number of possible techniques may be attempted until success if achieved. Success with a behavior management strategy does not imply that it will continue to produce the same results. Students change, the activities change, the environment changes, making it necessary to develop other techniques.

Reward Appropriate Behavior First

Deviant behavior, particularly behavior that is disruptive in nature, tends to distract both teacher and students so that the learning environment is destroyed or, at least, temporarily altered. Extreme motor activity, student arguments, and loud obnoxious noises tend to interfere with the teacher's instructional responsibilities and create a contagious distraction within the classroom group. Such disruptive behaviors have a distracting quality that creates negative teacher attention and intervention. To intervene continually with certain types of inappropriate behavior creates an atmosphere of negativism. Such responses also provide attention for the deviant, whereas the student who is performing appropriately goes unnoticed. Therefore, a systematic plan of rewarding appropriate behavior—students who are sitting still, completing their work, and remaining quiet—would serve a more positive function. Students who are disruptive for attention would learn that appropriate behavior is rewarded.

The most disruptive student performs appropriately at times. Even though a student may be out of his or her seat 50 minutes an hour, there are 10 minutes per hour the student is demonstrating in-seat behavior. For every examination, homework assignment, or project, the disruptive student has performed something correctly, either correctly completing one problem, putting his or her name on the paper, or just turning something in to the teacher. Such performances, as minimal as they may be, should not go unnoticed. In short, "catch the children being good" (Tinsley & Ora, 1970) and reinforce the behavior.

Deal with the Present

Reminders of past problems serve no purpose other than to kindle feelings of failure or resentment. Teacher statements such as "This is the third time you've been late," "You did the same thing last week," or "How many times have I had to tell you" are direct signals to the student that the teacher will continue to use past behaviors to evaluate current performance. As problems occur they should be dealt with in the here and now, without bringing past problems into the discussion. Certainly, all problems will not be managed successfully, but focusing on current behavior affords the opportunity for change. Past behavior, on the other hand, is a record of behavior that cannot be altered.

Management for Learning

Most students are willing to accept a teacher's authority and knowledge with reference to academic instruction. However, teacher intervention within the personal realm is viewed with skepticism by many students. Whether or not students eat all their lunch, wash their hands, button their coats, or cut their hair are areas that have created the most serious conflicts between teachers and students. Management strategies that attempt to change personal behaviors only compound the management problems. If changes in personal behaviors are considered necessary for the adjustment of the student in the social-vocational world beyond school, then such issues should be pursued through a course of study, rather than by the individual values and spontaneous judgment of the teacher.

Prevent Rather than Manage

Most teachers know in what situations and under what circumstances a student becomes a management problem. Therefore, it seems pointless to subject a student to a condition that will cause the student to get into difficulty and cause the teacher to have to manage the behavior. A more educationally and mentally sound procedure would be to prevent the problem by moving to the student, providing an interesting activity, restructuring the environment, or utilizing other techniques suggested in this chapter. Once a deviant behavior has developed, the energy and resources necessary to intervene effectively are much greater than those necessary to prevent the behavior.

When to Manage

Classroom teachers obviously have a wide variety of expectations regarding the appropriateness of student behaviors. Whereas some teachers encourage student movement, verbalization, and exploration, other teachers manage the same behaviors. Some teachers manage behavior more frequently if the principal is near the classroom, when the classroom temperature is uncomfortable, or when the teacher has a personal problem. Certainly management is conducted by human teachers with human feelings and will always reflect a degree of idiosyncratic behavior. However, management should not be totally dependent upon the personal or spontaneous whim of the teacher.

To provide some consistency among teachers, Long and Newman (1961) have presented a set of criteria to guide teachers in knowing when to manage behavior:

1. Reality dangers: When children might injure themselves or others (e.g., playing with matches or throwing dangerous objects).
2. Psychological protection: When children are being psychologically injured (e.g., by scape-goating or using derogatory racial comments).
3. Protection against too much excitement: When too much excitement, anxiety, or guilt is developing (e.g., losing control or feeling very unhappy).
4. Protection of property: When children are likely to destroy or damage school property, equipment or the building (e.g., carving on desks or tearing clothing).
5. Protection of an on-going program: When children disrupt the entire lesson or learning environment (e.g., yelling or being obnoxious).
6. Protection against negative contagion: When children are negatively influencing the entire group (e.g., causing tension or spreading gossip).
7. Highlighting an area of school policy: When it is impossible for children to understand school policy or rules (e.g., why it is not possible for everyone to be first in line or how poor communication creates misunderstandings).

8. Avoiding conflict with the outside world: When children interfere with other classrooms or even the public (e.g., disrupting a school assembly or littering on a class trip).
9. Protecting a teacher's inner comfort: When certain types of behavior makes a teacher feel extremely uncomfortable (e.g., cursing or "talking back"). Inner comfort is not the first thing to be considered by a teacher. If it is, he or she may be in the wrong profession. In many cases the teacher may have to learn to be more comfortable with the behavior, rather than manage the behavior. (Adapted from Long & Newman, 1961, pp. 51–52, and Long & Newman, 1976, pp. 310–311)

These general principles of management have been presented as prerequisites for effective intervention with student behaviors. The managerial strategies employed will be more effective if the teacher can answer the following questions affirmatively:

1. Do I have sufficient knowledge of the student to be able reasonably to predict the outcome of a particular intervention?
2. Do the behaviors exceed the conditions for individual learning, developmental stages, or pathology?
3. Have I selected specific behaviors to manage?
4. Have I rewarded the student when the student demonstrated appropriate behavior?
5. Do I plan to ignore past problems and focus on the current behaviors?
6. Does the behavior interfere with the learning environment, rather than cause me personal irritation?
7. Have I taken measures to prevent the inappropriate behavior?
8. Does the behavior constitute a physical or psychological threat to the student or others?

If the answers to the above questions are yes, then the management of behavior can be facilitated with the following variety of management techniques.

SURFACE MANAGEMENT

"Surface management may be defined as dealing with overt behavior that needs to be regulated immediately without regard to underlying causes or motives" (Fagan & Hill, 1977, p. 209). Surface techniques, therefore, are only temporary or "stopgap" methods that are designed to eliminate infrequent deviant behavior and restore the learning environment. When teachers are responsible for large groups of students, it is not always possible to look for underlying causes; instead, immediate action is required. Fights, destruction of property, loss of behavioral control, and violent disruption of the learning environment are examples of behavior that require immediate teacher management. If such behaviors continue to recur, however, then more permanent and well designed solutions should be considered.

The surface techniques described in this section are a composite of intervention procedures reported in the literature (Gnagey, 1965; Long, Morse, & Newman, 1976; Redl & Wineman, 1957). Teachers will recognize many of the techniques from their own personal classroom experience. Other teachers may have used some of the techniques without any conscious awareness that they were doing so, or of their effect on students. At any rate, a list of surface management techniques is presented as a tool for teachers to enlarge the variety of techniques available to them and to increase awareness of their purposes and potential effects.

Ignoring Behavior

Many deviant behaviors are spontaneous and occur frequently, usually motivated by some extraordinary classroom event. The cancellation of a field trip, a fire drill practice, or the introduction of a new pet animal to the classroom are examples of incidents that spark highly contagious disruptive behavior, which typically subsides after a brief period of time. The best management technique under such circumstances is not to manage directly, but to ignore the behavior.

On other occasions, however, student behavior may be more purposeful, designed to test the teacher or solicit attention, even if such attention may be negative in nature. If the teacher is perceived to be the target of the deviance, thereby making the teacher the rewarding agent, planned ignoring of student behavior can produce a positive behavioral change.

Teachers must be careful in the use of planned ignoring. Before employing this technique the teacher must be certain that the behavior is one that can be ignored, that the teacher (not the peer group) is the reinforcer, and that nonreinforcement will produce the desired change. This technique does have the advantages of being unobtrusive, limiting contagion, and permitting the teacher to remain with the instructional activities.

Signal Intervention

The use of physical cues is one of the most frequent forms of intervention currently employed by teachers. A variety of body postures, hand movements, and facial expressions are routinely used to convey approval and disapproval of student behavior. Smiles, winks, and a pat on the back are used to convey approval; frowns, throat clearing, and finger snapping are used to deter behavior. Although signals can be effective during the initial stage of deviance, their usefulness is limited after deviance has moved into advanced stages of behavior and emotions.

The frequent use of signals among teachers is partially responsible for their limited effectiveness. Unfortunately, signals are used indiscriminately in situations where other forms of management would be more appropriate. However, because of the relative ease of signal intervention, which is quick and effortless, signals remain a routine classroom management technique.

If signal intervention is to remain a useful technique, more creative uses must be developed. Special, individualized signals can be designed to communicate with selected students. The signals can be as simple and subtle as tugging the ear, touching the nose, or pulling out a handkerchief. Personal signals are successful if the student knows that the signal is a unique message between teacher and student. Such a technique also has the advantage of remaining a "secret" and does not identify the student in the presence of peers, thus eliminating a potential confrontation.

Entire classrooms can also participate in the development of signals whereby students become managers of deviant behaviors. For example, the class may decide to use the "peace sign" if the noise in the classroom becomes so loud that it is distracting. Any student or the teacher could raise the peace sign, which, when observed, every individual in the class would imitate until the class was quiet. This example was actually witnessed in a class of disturbed students, and the results were amazing—contagion in a positive direction.

Closeness Control

Many students, particularly younger elementary-age children, need the physical presence of an adult to aid them in controlling impulsive, anxious, and even forgetful feelings and emotions. Without this physical assurance, negative feelings and emotions stimulate behaviors that may be unacceptable in the classroom. Even after interfering behaviors are evidenced, movement of the teacher toward the student is typically associated with reduced deviance. Such movement, however, must be interpreted by the student as concern and reassurance and not preparation for punishment.

Older students also respond favorably to teacher movement in the classroom. Again, the movement must be associated with positive concern, academically or emotionally, and not a spying technique to catch students doing something that violates classroom rules. Often teacher movement does little more than remind students that they are off-task, which is sufficient to reduce deviance in many situations.

Teachers who are "glued" to a small area of the classroom (e.g., behind a desk, in front of the chalkboard, or near a relatively few students) tend to have the highest rates of deviance among those students who are the greatest distance from the teacher. In such instances, management usually takes the form of verbal directions or reprimands shouted across the classroom. Such techniques often do more to destroy the classroom learning environment than does the students' deviant behavior. Classroom movement, or closeness control, could be used to reduce the frequency of interfering teacher intervention.

Hurdle Help

This technique combines well with closeness control because it requires individual tutoring to help a student overcome an academic roadblock. This individual hurdle help can be an effective preventive management strategy when students need only minimal information to get them functioning appropriately. For example, a student may not have understood the teacher's directions and therefore is not involved in the lesson. "Instead of asking for help and exposing himself to the teacher's wrath for not paying attention . . . the child is likely to establish contact with neighbors, find some interesting trinket in his pocket, or draw on his desk" (Long & Newman, 1961, p. 56). Providing the student with directions or explanations would get the student back on task, eliminating the deviant behavior. The concept of hurdle help as a management strategy is thus designed to help the student "hurdle" frustrating obstacles within an academic setting.

Teacher Interest

Student performance on various academic tasks often wanes because of a lack of motivation or interest in the particular activity. Typically, the lack of motivation is accompanied by nonperformance, followed by boredom or restlessness. It is in this latter stage that students begin to engage in behaviors that disrupt the classroom.

Before the boredom or restlessness develops into behaviors that are difficult to manage, the teacher should demonstrate interest in the student's assignment or performance. Verbal cues, such as "That's an important assignment you're doing," or "You have a difficult assignment, but I'm sure you can do it," can serve to motivate the student.

Teacher interest is a particularly effective technique for students who have a tendency to seek approval from adults.

Removing Temptations

Classrooms are usually filled with a variety of objects that are designed to enhance learning: globes, bulletin boards, games, and the like. Most students can handle the variety of stimuli that bombards the classroom, even though most of the stimuli may be totally unrelated to the current lesson. Some students, however, particularly those who are hyperactive, brain-damaged, or impulsive, have difficulty separating the relevant from the irrelevant stimuli. The globe may be more attractive than the math assignment, the baseball on the teacher's desk may be more enticing than the reading assignment, or the student's new lunch box may be more visually alluring than the spelling words. In each case an environmental stimulus, unrelated to the lesson, becomes a visual temptation.

Teacher management in the form of stimulus reduction is required for those students who are inclined to be tempted by visual or verbal distractions. The most effective procedure is to remove the temptation—place the globe, the ball, or the lunch box out of sight. Of course, it is not possible, perhaps not desirable, to remove all irrelevant stimulation. Observation, however, may reveal that some students are more inclined to be distracted by specific objects. In these situations, the removal of temptation would help the student focus attention on the lesson and reduce task avoidance behavior.

Altering Instructional Methods

Often students are satiated with a repetitive task or a routine instructional method. Examples of repetitive methods include answering every question box in a textbook, completing a specified number of math problems each day, and limiting the instructional method to lecturing or reading. These stereotypic, monotonous, and repetitive approaches tend to create an attitude of indifference toward learning and negative feelings toward the teacher.

Teacher intervention in this context is related to the teacher's willingnesss to alter the instructional methods and/or requirements. Using a wider variety of input-output procedures may prevent satiation, increase interest, and consequently reduce deviant behavior. For the previous examples of repetition, methodological changes can include using a blend of verbal and written responses, devising a math program that emphasizes utilization rather than paper-and-pencil practice, and organizing exploratory discussion sessions as a substitute for lecturing. After all ". . . the task is not so much to teach children as to provide the conditions under which learning can take place" (Long, Morse, & Newman, 1976, p. 313).

Routine Structure

Whereas some students are bored with the routine of a classroom, other students thrive on the predictive quality of structure. Students who have failed to develop basic trust in themselves, others, or their environment are psychologically threatened by confusion, spontaneity, and unstructured situations. When the classroom setting is unpredictable, these students express their fear and anxiety through withdrawal, hyperactivity, crying, and other behaviors that interfere with their learning.

Unstructured situations are created by many classroom conditions, for example, when teachers change their minds or make exceptions to selected rules or behaviors, when free-time activities or active games are introduced, and when the class schedule is interrupted by announcements, special events, or even a substitute teacher. Structure, at least initially, is a preferable management strategy when students need the security of predictability. A stringent schedule of sequential activities accompanied by teacher consistency and punctuality, and permanent resources (desk, books, etc.) may reduce student apprehension and thus reduce deviant behavior.

Rule Reminders

When emotions are high or events in the classroom generate excitement, students are prone to forget classroom rules. A teacher should be aware of the fact that the escalation of confusion and potent feelings may eventually erupt into behaviors that will require direct management. Before that point, however, it is suggested that the teacher remind the group or individual students of rules that are about to be violated. "Remember, you must remain in your seat," or "The rule is 'keep your hands to yourself,'" should be announced as reminders before such violations occur. Signal interference or closeness control may serve the same function as a verbal reminder.

A rule reminder is a minimal management technique designed to prevent deviance and the need for more dramatic intervention. Just as speed limit signs are posted along the highway to remind drivers of the legal speed, rule reminders are announced by the teacher so that students are cognizant of behavioral limitations. In fact, teachers should routinely remind students of important classroom rules, even when the students are on-task and such violations are not anticipated. These reminders reinforce classroom behavior, provide predictable structure, and convey the message that classroom rules are important.

Positive Removal

There are times when students lose control and become a threat to themselves or others. A frequent disciplinary procedure to control threatening behaviors has been to exclude students from the classroom by sending them to the hall or the principal's office. In less severe cases, some teachers have developed procedures for isolating students in the classroom by using special "time-out" areas. In each case, isolation has a degree of merit, if isolation or exclusion is used as the last available measure to protect people or property.

The issue here, however, is to make the removal of a student as positive as possible by avoiding the purely punitive aspect of exclusion. The teacher's interpretation of the isolation process can be a positive management technique. For example, the teacher could verbally interpret the action as a helping action:

> "I'm sending you to the hall, because you are going to get into trouble. I can't permit that. I don't want you to get into trouble. When you can handle the situation, I want you to come back."

or,

> "People are trying to learn in here and you won't let them. So, I'm sending you outside. When you think you can help people to learn, I'd like to have you back in the classroom."

For both examples, the teacher is excluding the student, but the verbal messages convey the need to help, not punish. Consequently, the student's re-entry into the classroom is based on behaviors or expectations that promote a more positive relationship.

The surface management strategies discussed in this section are presented as tools to assist the teacher in maintaining a learning environment in the classroom. Since the presentation has not followed a comprehensive model, there are both duplications and omissions. In fact, surface management techniques not covered in this section have probably occurred to the reader and been used in the classroom.

Before concluding this section, two points need to be emphasized. First, surface management strategies should be as individualized as the academic program. In fact, some educators believe that the academic program and behavior management cannot be separated. "No plan for reducing inappropriate behavior will be appropriate in the absence of individualized academic instruction. Omission of suitable academic tasks may be one reason for the student's unacceptable behavior" (Browder, 1981, p. 52). Whereas some students may respond appropriately to a specific behavior (or academic) management strategy, other students may become more deviant. Thus a knowledge of the individual student and a variety of behavior management strategies will increase the probability of successful management. Second, surface management strategies are only temporary solutions to behavioral problems. If deviant behaviors occur frequently, then other management techniques must be considered. In addition, some deviant behaviors require techniques that are designed to intervene with the causes of behavior, rather than externally manage surface behavior.

Because of the limitations of surface management, other management strategies are explored in this chapter. Within the classroom a number of critical factors contribute to the deviance of students and therefore must be altered if appropriate behavior is to be increased. The critical classroom factors include interpersonal, group, and environmental sources of deviancy and management.

INTERPERSONAL MANAGEMENT

Interpersonal management refers to psychological or affective techniques that involve both the teacher and the student. Affective techniques, as opposed to academic or behavioral controls, focus on those phases of the classroom experience that are concerned with feelings, emotions, and acceptance (Krathwohl, Bloom, & Masia, 1956). It is well known that students' psychological-affective states, including anxiety, frustration, rejection, and helplessness, are precipitators of deviant or disruptive behaviors. Therefore, "tuning in" to the student's affective state and responding interpersonally can facilitate more positive mental health and reduce the frequency and intensity of inappropriate classroom behavior.

Even though teachers have long known that students' academic, behavioral, and psychological-affective performance cannot be separated, there remains a tendency in education to promote academics, control behavior, and ignore feelings and emotions (Rich, 1978a). This emphasis on academic and behavioral performance partially exists because of the traditional subject-oriented curricular designs and large instructional group responsibility (Weinstein & Fantini, 1970). Interpersonal management requires some alteration in the traditional patterns and beliefs, and emphasizes the need for personal interaction between teacher and student.

The personal characteristics of the teacher, rather than the size of the group, grade level, or knowledge of the academic discipline, are more significant in the effective use of interpersonal management techniques. Obviously, a teacher who is exclusively concerned with teaching subject content and maintaining strict order is less prone to exercise interpersonal management. For those students who require structure, academic-behavioral teaching priorities may be appropriate. However, there are students who need understanding, warmth, and even psychological support from teachers.

Hamachek (1969) has identified five teacher characteristics that facilitate the interpersonal teacher-student dimension:

1. They seem to have generally more positive views of others—students, colleagues, and administrators.
2. They do not seem to be as prone to view others as critical, attacking people with ulterior motives; rather they are seen as potentially friendly and worthy in their own right.
3. They have a more favorable view of democratic classroom procedures.
4. They seem to have the ability and capacity to see things as they seem to others—i.e., the ability to see things from the other person's point of view.
5. They do not seem to see students as persons "you do things to" but rather as individuals capable of doing for themselves once they feel trusted, respected, and valued (p. 343).

Given that many teachers possess these characteristics, there are a number of interpersonal techniques that may be used to manage interfering behavior. However, the employment of interpersonal techniques is also dependent on the rapport the teacher has established with individual students. Rapport, in this context, refers to positive teacher-student relationships, based upon the students' perceptions of the teacher as a caring, fair, courteous, friendly, and trustworthy person (Howard, 1972). Although the use of interpersonal management may serve to build a positive relationship, initial attempts to use these intervention techniques may be relatively unsuccessful in reducing interfering behavior if positive rapport does not exist. The greatest deterrent to interpersonal management occurs when students accurately perceive their teacher as an insensitive taskmaster or censor of behavior, who is only going through the motions of caring.

Every student, normal or exceptional, at times experiences unpleasant and intolerable feelings that make it difficult to function appropriately in the classroom. Typically, large groups of students assembled in schools and classrooms create settings for crises that precipitate negative feelings. Behavioral incidents or crises that can precipitate strong feelings and emotions include: student-student crises (e.g., threats, teasing, or separation), student-teacher crises (e.g., forgetting homework, talking back, or violating a rule), and internal crises (e.g., disappointment, mistakes, or inadequacy). Each of these crises may foster so much anxiety or anger that the student is unable to function in the classroom. In turn, these feelings and emotions may motivate deviant behavior that must be managed in order to preserve the learning environment and protect the students.

In order to manage deviant behavior among students effectively, strong negative feelings must be positively reduced. For the teacher described by Hamachek (1969), there are a number of interpersonal techniques that may be appropriate for individual students.

Listening to Feelings

This intervention technique requires two basic ingredients: interest and time. On the simplest level, listening to feelings is being physically available to a student at a time when the student needs to vent emotions that are about to explode. Sitting close, leaning forward, providing eye-to-eye contact, and showing understanding by nodding or smiling can provide the body language necessary to convey a personal interest in the student.

This passive listening technique does not approve or condemn the circumstances that precipitated the feelings, but it does indicate teacher interest in the student's problem. This sympathetic communication can be used to "drain off" the strong feelings that would otherwise result in deviant behavior (Redl, 1959). In times of crisis, many people are comforted by the fact that a sympathetic ear is available and that feelings do not have to be dealt with alone. Students are no different.

Responding to Feelings

This interpersonal management strategy goes beyond the passive listening to feelings, and adds the dimension of teacher response. To facilitate communication the teacher becomes an active listener, accurately interpreting the meaning of the message sent by the student and responding in a way that reflects the student's feelings.

> In active listening, then, the receiver [teacher] tries to understand what it is the sender [student] is feeling or what the message means. Then he puts his understanding into his own words . . . and feeds it back for the sender's verification. The receiver [teacher] *does not* send a message of his own—such as an evaluation, opinion, advice, logic, analysis, or question. He sends back *only what he feels the sender's message meant*—nothing more, nothing less (Gordon, 1970, p. 53).

The technique of responding to feelings requires that the teacher ". . . discerns the overt as well as the covert or disguised behavior of another person" (Gazda et al., 1973, p. 39). This is particularly important because the verbal message may not convey what the student is feeling. For example, a student who has failed an exam may feel inadequate unless the failure is projected to the teacher by saying, "You said this part of the book wouldn't be required on the exam." Similarly, a student who feels threatened by a peer may want protection, but says, "I don't feel well today; I don't want to go out to recess." Or a student who is not selected to be on a team may elect to reduce the pain by saying, "I really didn't care about being on the team anyway." Each of these examples of verbal messages carries an entirely different meaning than the feeling behind it.

Teacher responses to feelings should reflect the feelings, not the overt message. For the three examples, teacher responses should be something like: "You're saying that it hurts when you don't do well on an exam," "We all need someone to help us when we are afraid," and "It really hurts when we are left out." These examples are based on the teacher's knowledge of the student, an empathic understanding of the problem, and a desire to help the student. Although the three responses may seem trite, they are certainly more facilitative than: "I specifically said that the entire chapter would be on the exam," "You weren't ill 10 minutes ago," and "Then why did you try out for the team?"

Effective responding techniques can reduce the probability of deviant behavior by demonstrating teacher understanding of the student's personal crisis. Strong feelings and emotions that are not reduced but rather increased by responses that condemn, question, or emphasize the negative, often explode into crises that consume extraordinary amounts of time and energy.

Maintaining Communication

In times of crises, students often retreat into a solitary world, not communicating with either peers or the teacher. Attempts to identify the problem or find a solution are negated by the fact that the student is nonverbal and nonresponsive. If, however, teachers involve the student in some form of communication, it can prevent the next level of retreat (Redl, 1959).

A student accused of theft, cheating, or related behaviors may choose this regressive course of action as the least painful, particularly if a student lacks the skills necessary for adequate self-protection. Efforts on the part of the teacher to "grill" the student, point out the unacceptable behavior, or even encourage more appropriate behavior typically fall on deaf ears and motivate the student to increase the personal-emotional distance from the teacher.

Maintaining communication requires that the teacher involve the student in conversation completely unrelated to the situation that motivated the crisis. In short, the teacher should find a psychologically comfortable area in which the student can relax the defenses and engage in appropriate behavior. If the crisis involves peers, then the teacher may want to provide the student a solitary learning responsibility; if the teacher was the source of the crisis, then peer group activities may be more appropriate; or if stealing or cheating was the accusation, then communication involving baseball, dancing, or hobbies may be areas of renewed communication. Even though the teacher may not be able to deal directly with the issue, it is necessary to maintain contact with the student by involving the student in an area or activity that is psychologically safe. At a later time, when communication has been reestablished, the teacher may elect to deal with the original crisis.

Emphasizing Natural Consequences

Many traditional teacher-student disciplinary interactions are based on threats of punishment for noncompliant student behavior. Failing grades, suspension, moral devaluation, and even corporal punishment are common consequences that are administered by teachers for failure to respond appropriately to classroom rules or teacher expectations. However, these examples are not natural consequences, but are forms of punishment that may only occur in school-related environments.

Natural consequences, in the context of interpersonal management, are those negative experiences that logically and functionally occur as a result of behavior. A failing grade is not a natural consequence if a student does not study. The natural consquence is that the student will not learn the information necessary for a vocation. Similarly, fighting physically hurts, the inability to get along with peers causes loneliness, and resentment of authority leads to limited job opportunities.

Many students do not understand the relationship between their behaviors and the natural consequences. Greater emphasis on life situations and adjustment, particularly for older students, is more meaningful since they may perceive school as an irrelevant obstacle in the path to adulthood. The motivation to perform more effectively will be increased for those students who understand that adult success is partially based on correct behavior, but not necessarily related to teacher expectations.

Increasing Verbal Skills

Educational institutions tend to be highly verbal settings where teachers talk a great deal and students are expected to communicate appropriately with both teachers and peers. Many students, however, are physically oriented, lacking the verbal skills necessary to communicate their needs and wishes. This physical orientation is especially common among younger students and students who have experienced restrictive language patterns in their home and community life-styles. If a second-grade boy likes a girl, rather than saying, "I like you," he may knock her books to the ground, inviting a chase. A friendly tap on the shoulder, a shy glance to the floor, and touching, in general, are physical expressions of affection. Similarly, unverbalized anger may erupt into fighting, cursing, or hyperactivity. Often these indirect but deviant behaviors are the result of insufficient verbal skills necessary to convey feelings, resolve differences, or obtain needs.

The management of behaviors precipitated by inadequate verbal skills therefore requires the development of appropriate verbal skills. To implement this intervention technique successfully, teachers need to provide students with more opportunities to communicate, explore feelings, and identify ways of expressing needs. Such a program of verbal skill development will require that teachers talk less and students talk more. If teachers continue to tell students what they did wrong, why they did it, and what is going to be done about it, then students will have limited opportunities to interact or understand their own feelings, behaviors, and consequences. Currently, there is an inverse relationship between student talk and chronological age in elementary school (Karlin & Berger, 1972; Rich, 1978c). In short, as students grow older they talk less and teachers talk more. In terms of teacher-student interaction, this regressive development needs to be reversed. Teachers must also become effective listeners.

Although the interpersonal management techniques reported in this section do not constitute an exhaustive list, the techniques are believed to be important in facilitating adjustment in the classroom. Prerequisites for interpersonal management, such as trust, acceptance, and understanding, are not here discussed at length because they reflect personal teacher characteristics rather than management techniques per se. The presence of positive personal characteristics, however, is related to both the desire to use and the effectiveness of interpersonal techniques.

It is important to remember that interpersonal management is basically a personal learning experience for the student, rather than a disciplinary action. The process of interpersonal teacher-student interaction should emphasize an understanding of feelings and emotions and how they are translated into inappropriate behavior. The management of behavior therefore involves the development of skills necessary to express feelings and emotions in a more acceptable manner.

GROUP MANAGEMENT

Whenever deviant behavior occurs in the classroom, the teacher must decide whether to manage the behavior of individual students or the entire group. Of the two choices, this chapter emphasizes teacher management of interfering behavior demonstrated by individual students. This is an intentional focus because the purpose of this chapter is to assist teachers in managing disturbed students in the regular classroom.

The management of individual students, however, has at least two primary limitations. First, individual management may create a negative ripple effect, that is, result in unintended but inappropriate teacher influence on nondeviant students (Kounin, 1970). Visible teacher management techniques tend to reduce the task-appropriate behavior of students witnessing the intervention, thereby shifting the classroom emphasis from learning to management. Second, deviant behavior may be a function of group norms, rather than of individual interfering behavior. Thus, deviance may be a role behavior acquired by an individual student, but one that is expected and supported by the group as a whole.

If mainstreaming is to be effective, teachers must be cognizant of the fact that disturbed students are also members of the classroom group. Although students may occupy the same physical space and are legally present to learn a prescribed curriculum, they will have a variety of needs, skills, behaviors, and values that can prevent the class from becoming an effectively functioning educational group. Students who defy the teacher, act as the class clown, or are lazy are typically demonstrating role behaviors that have group support, Even though these behaviors are not indicative of academically successful students, nor are they ". . . desirable in the teacher's set of values, some peer recognition of whatever kind may be better than no recognition at all" (Smith, 1959, p. 11). This failure to comply with teacher expectations is partially attributable to the fact that students in general, but particularly older students, are more concerned with peer expectations than with those of the teacher or even the parents.

The classroom group sanctions those behaviors that are consistent with the norms of the group, and the group condemns those behaviors that are not. Although the teacher is exclusively responsible for awarding grades and granting privileges, ". . . it is quite possible for students who have a high degree of social acceptance to influence the distribution of public praise and approval among class members" (Jensen, 1960, p. 107). This is particularly evident among members of smaller subgroups who have developed an identity and goals independent of the total group and the stated purposes of the educational program.

The effective use of group management first requires that the teacher identify classroom behaviors that are symptomatic of group problems. Toward this end, Johnson and Bany (1970) have classified group behavior problems in terms of distinguishing characteristics

Table 1.   Classroom management problems in terms of behavioral descriptors

Distinguishing characteristics	Behavior descriptions
1. Lack of unity	The class lacks unity and conflicts occur between individuals and subgroups as: when groups split; argumentative over competitive situations such as games; boys against girls; when groups split by cliques; minority groups; when group takes sides on issues or breaks into subgroups; when hostility and conflict constantly arise among members and create an unpleasant atmosphere.
2. Nonadherence to behavioral standards and work procedures	The class responds with noisy, talkative, disorderly behavior in situations which have established standards for behaving, as: when group is entering or leaving room or changing activities; lining up; cleaning up; going to auditorium; when group is working in ability groups; engaging in committee work; when group is completing study assignments; receiving assignments; correcting papers; handling work materials; when group is engaged in discussion, sharing, planning.
3. Negative reactions to individual	The class becomes vocal or actively hostile toward one or more class members, as: when group does not accept individuals and derides, ignores, or ridicules children who are different; when group reacts negatively to members who deviate from group code; to those who thwart group's progress; or when a member's behavior upsets or puzzles members of the class.
4. Class approval of misbehavior	The class approves and supports individuals as: when they talk out of turn; act in ways which disrupt the normal work procedures; engage in clowning or rebellious activities.
5. Easily distracted; prone to work stoppage and imitative behavior	The group reacts with upset, excited, or disorderly behavior to interruptions, distractions, or constant grievances, as: when group is interrupted by monitors, visitors, a change in weather;

(Continued)

Table 1. (*Continued*)

Distinguishing characteristics	Behavior descriptions
	when members constantly have grievances relating to others, lessons, rules, policies or practices they believe are unfair; and when settlements are demanded before work proceeds.
6. Low morale and hostile, resistant, or aggressive reactions	The class members engage in subtle hostile, aggressive behavior which creates slow-downs and work stoppages, as: when materials are misplaced, pencils break, chairs upset; when books, money, lunches are temporarily lost; when there are constant requests for assignments to be repeated and explained; when children constantly complain about behavior of others, with no apparent loss of friendship; when children accuse authority figures of unfair practices and delay classwork by making claims.
7. Inability to adjust to environmental change	The class reacts inappropriately to such situations, as: when a substitute takes over; when normal routines are changed; when new members transfer into the class; when stress situations cause inappropriate reactions

From Johnson, L. V., and Bany, M. A. *Classroom management: Theory and skill training.* London: Collier-MacMillan Ltd., 1970, pp. 46–47. Reprinted with permission of Macmillan Publishing Co.

(Table 1). Problems that are inherent in the group will not be effectively managed by intervening with individual students. Many students may deliberately demonstrate deviant behaviors in order to maintain a group role, inviting teacher management that will serve to reinforce the group role. For example, a student considered a subgroup leader may challenge the teacher's authority and even welcome punishment in order to reaffirm peer group leadership status. Disturbed students in the regular classroom constitute an unusual group problem. Often, their special problems are used as a negative source of group identification and status. Students identified as immature, aggressive, or dependent may engage in behaviors that are consistent with their group-recognized roles as "crybaby," "tough guy," or "brown-noser." Direct and individual teacher management with the students involved typically serves to reinforce these role behaviors.

The group and teacher maintenance of such deviant roles, although productive for group status, is counterproductive in terms of personal development and academic achievement. Therefore, management that considers the total classroom group must be implemented. A prerequisite to group management is the teacher's willingness to involve the group in open communication and share some of the power typically allocated to teachers. In short, teachers must develop an atmosphere of understanding and cooperation, rather than one of control and competition (Vorrath & Brendtro, 1974).

The best techniques for managing group behavior are those that are based on cooperative and participatory practices. These practices include:

1. Guiding group toward examination of behavior.
2. Creating in group an awareness of the problem.
3. Helping group clarify problem.
4. Guiding group in diagnosis of the problem.
5. Helping group establish goals and intentions of actions.
6. Helping group improve techniques for resolving conflict and solving problems (Johnson & Bany, 1970, p. 106).

Effective group management is based on the teacher's awareness of the group's psychosocial structure, an accurate assessment of individual behaviors within the group, and a willingness to involve the group in understanding and resolving the problems. Group management, then, is assisting the group in identifying problems and issues that have negative influence on classroom performance, helping the group decide upon solutions and strategies for resolving problems, and facilitating the group in dealing with their own problems. This approach requires that the teacher be open, communicative, and democratic within the context of a problem solving philosophy.

CLASSROOM ENVIRONMENTAL MANAGEMENT

Physical classroom characteristics have been an overlooked dimension of behavior management. Although teachers are aware that classroom factors, such as room size, temperature variations, and general decor, do affect learning and behavior (Drew, 1971), there is little evidence that the physical environment by itself directly causes appropriate or deviant behavior. Therefore, the emphasis on environmental management will be that ". . . physical settings have their own properties which place constraints on some behavior and facilitate, if not require, others" (Proshansky, 1974, p. 553).

Even though teachers should be able to justify the physical arrangement of the classroom, many teachers do not recognize ". . . which aspects of learning and social behavior should be expected to change as a function of the particular environmental design . . ." (Cruickshank & Quay, 1970, p. 265). One way of evaluating the environmental design is to study both the *symbolic* meaning and the *pragmatic* function of the physical classroom arrangement and what the arrangement communicates to students and teachers (Proshansky & Wolfe, 1974). Symbolic meaning refers to the psychological expectation of behavior, whereas the pragmatic function refers to the actual effectiveness of the environment in supporting or reducing specific behaviors.

For the purpose of discussing both symbolic and pragmatic implications of environmental management, two different examples of classroom physical arrangements are considered: traditional and informal. Figure 1 illustrates the physical arrangements of the two classrooms. Certainly the traditional and informal classrooms, as presented, represent only a portion of the possible classroom arrangements that are currently in use. However, the two examples do constitute, with minor variations, arrangements that are the most frequently employed instructional-managerial designs.

Symbolic Meaning

Traditional Classrooms   This more formal design, often referred to as a teacher-centered environment, has been the basic model of classroom arrangement for several centuries. The typical arrangement consists of several rows of student seat-desks, one behind the other, facing the front of the room where the teacher's desk and chalkboard are located. The teacher's primary work station, near the desk, enables the teacher to control the flow of traffic in and out of the classroom, speak directly to students, and maintain visual supervision of the entire group.

This standardized classroom design psychologically emphasizes expected patterns of behavior on the part of teachers and students alike. These expectations include the exercise of authoritative control, a lecture method of intruction, the passive use of space, and the presumed homogeneity of students. "The location of the teacher's desk in the traditional room not only communicate(s) the isolated role of the teacher; it also physically place(s) that space off limits for the use by the children" (Proshansky & Wolfe, 1974, p. 559).

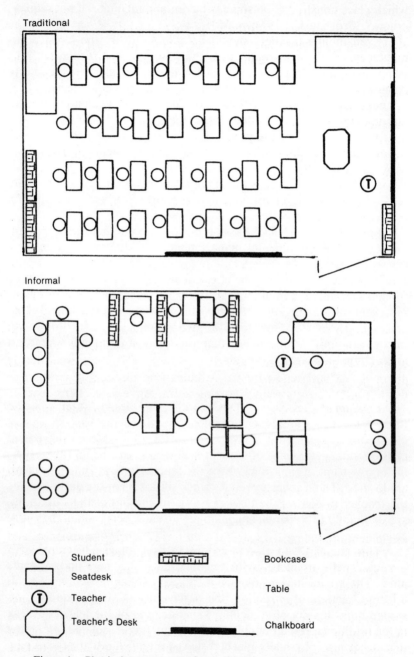

Figure 1.   Physical arrangement of a traditional and an informal classroom.

The uniformity and postion of the students' seating arrangements suggests educational conformity, passive learning, and an orderly standard of behavior. The lack of variability in student work space implies that all students require the same spatial area regardless of the task, perceptual-motor abilities, or psychological needs. Because students face the teacher and not each other, the instructional format is predetermined to consist primarily of teacher lecturing, directing, and questioning; the physical arrangement does not facilitate student communication with anyone other than the teacher.

A student poem reflects one attitude regarding the traditional classroom arrangement:

> . . . It was funny about school.
> He sat in a square brown desk
> like all the other square brown desks
> and he thought it would be red.
> And his room was a square brown room
> like all the other rooms.
> And it was tight and close. And stiff.
> He hated to hold the pencil and chalk,
> with his arm stiff and his feet flat on the floor, stiff
> with the teacher watching and watching . . .
> (Schultz, Heuchert, & Stampf, 1973, p. vi).

In summary, the symbolic meaning of the traditional classroom emphasizes controlled behavior and unilateral communication that is directed and supervised by the teacher. The physical separation of teacher and students reinforces the authoritative role of the teacher and increases the social distance, precluding interpersonal management. The confined, standard student seating arrangement requires passive, isolated learning within the context of reduced motor activity, limited exploratory behavior, and restricted student-student interaction.

Informal Classrooms   The informal classroom arrangement, which approximates an open-space or child-centered environment, conveys a different symbolic meaning than that of the traditional classroom. A visual overview of the informal classroom reveals a nonuniform arrangement of student work areas, a variety of work-size surfaces, and both individual and small group activity settings. The teacher's physical position in the classroom is not well defined, nor does the teacher's desk constitute a physical or psychological barrier.

The informal arrangement precludes a lecture method of instruction because the teacher does not occupy a commanding position that is directly visible to all students. Similarly, many students are out of the visual range of the teachers. The lack of reciprocal face-to-face contact requires that task objectives and activities be different for individuals and small groups. Thus, the teacher functions in the role of facilitator, rather than director or controller.

Noise, movement, and general activity are expected behaviors, because the physical arrangement is predicated on the assumptions of involvement, flexibility, interaction, and individualized programming. Different work surfaces, spatial allowances, and activity settings symbolically suggest that individual differences are accommodated, at least in terms of the physical task requirements and motor needs.

In summary, the informal classroom ". . . is not a single homogeneous space cube; rather it is a network of interconnected and varied micro-environments" (Sommer, 1977, p. 175). Individualized activities, teacher movement and facilitation, and the variety of spatial arrangements add up to a classroom with a great amount of noise, verbal interaction, and physical mobility. The informal classroom is partially predicated on the assumption that an individualized physical environment will reduce environmental constraints that impede student performance.

Pragmatic Functions

The management of interfering behavior can be assisted by a physical classroom arrangement that is consistent with the teacher's instructional-managerial style and the characteristics of the students. No one arrangement is universally preferable; the best arrangement is one that is effective for the individuals involved. Both the traditional and the informal classrooms have managerial advantages and disadvantages.

The traditional arrangement was designed as an orderly, lecture-type environment. Therefore, if the teacher's style is one of maintaining control and of lecturing, then the straight rows of desks are more preferable than random clusters of students (Sommer, 1977). On the other hand, the informal arrangement is designed to implement more individualized, self-directed learning. An interpersonal, facilitating teacher style is more consistent with this later environmental arrangement.

It is important to note, however, that the teacher's style and preference is only one factor in the determination of physical arrangements. Any decision to use a particular arrangement must account for and accommodate the needs of the students who occupy the learning environment. It is this critical relationship between teacher style and student needs that should be used to determine the most appropriate classroom arrangement. These interacting conditions require that the teacher determine ". . . the physical relationship between the child and the teacher, the physical and visual needs of the child, and all other similar factors which may have an effect on physical structure" (Cruickshank & Quay, 1970, p. 264).

Differences in the physical and spatial needs are typified by Fitt's (1974) description of two students:

> Johnny and Susy enter the classroom together. Susy waves expansively at the teacher, throws her sweater vaguely in the direction of her locker, and charges into the room waving frantically at her friend who is already at work across the room. She sprawls at her desk, spreading her arms out onto the two adjoining desks. Meanwhile, Johnny has moved to his locker and has carefully folded his sweater and placed it in one corner of his locker. He walks to his desk with his arms held closely to his sides and sits down, drawing his feet under his chair and stacking his books and papers carefully in the center of his desk (p. 618)

Johnny's physical and spatial needs are obviously more limited than those of Susy. Whereas Johnny may function well in the traditional classroom arrangement. Susy's physical expression would be disruptive and generally inappropriate in the same classroom. In all probability the most conscientious surface, interpersonal, and instructional managerial techniques would be unsuccessful with Susy, unless the physical environment were arranged to meet her needs.

Johnny, on the other hand, may constitute a behavior problem in the informal classroom, particularly if his spatial needs are indicative of related psychological needs for consistency and predictability. The symbolic assumption of openness, movement, and independence may be so psychologically traumatizing that Johnny will be unable to function effectively and may intrapersonally withdraw or attack the informal environment.

Of the management techniques discussed in this chapter, some are more functionally appropriate for the traditional classroom, whereas others are more compatible with the informal arrangement. For example, it is generally assumed that the hyperactive child should be in close proximity to the teacher and work under conditions relatively free of unnecessary stimulation (Fairchild, 1975). These intervention procedures could best be accomplished in the traditional classroom where teacher mobility and environmental stimulation are more limited. The traditional design also enables hearing-impaired students to ". . . see the teacher's face for speech reading development . . ." and aid a student with a mobility handicap ". . . to anticipate obstacles, traffic, and new spatial areas" (Cruickshank & Quay, 1970, p. 263). The use of teacher signal intervention, rule reminders, and routine structuring is also more practial in the traditional class.

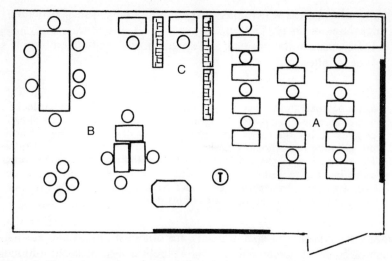

Figure 2. Physical arrangement of a combination traditional and informal class. A, traditional classroom area; B, informal classroom area; C, specialized reduced stimulus area.

The informal arrangement, accompanied by high teacher mobility, has the advantage of personalizing intervention without drawing attention to the student in question. Certainly it is easier to tolerate selected behaviors when students are not expected to conform to an established pattern of passive behavior. Ignoring behavior, spontaneous closeness control, and individual tutoring are similarly consistent with both the symbolic and pragmatic functions of the informal class. Interpersonal management can be conducted within the classroom, and does not require waiting for an appropriate time or going out into the hallway as one might expect in the traditional classroom.

Certainly no one classroom arrangement will adequately deal with every instructional-managerial concern. Each classroom is designed with specific objectives, styles, and behaviors in mind; those that are inconsistent with the environmental design will be less than successful. One answer may be to use a combination of both arrangements: a segment of the class assigned to individual seat desks while the other students are working independently or in small groups. Figure 2 represents such a physically arranged classroom, that is, a combined traditional and informal arrangement, with a specialized reduced stimulus area for hyperactive or distractible students.

Whatever classroom arrangement is used, it should not be based on historical precedents but on a knowledge of the needs, behaviors, and characteristics of the students. The intervention strategy that has been designed for the students and the teaching-learning strategy most appropriate for students should also be used to determine the physical arrangement of the classroom environment.

SUMMARY

This chapter has been devoted to an overview of behavior management strategies that can be used by teachers to control, reduce, or eliminate interfering student behaviors that occur in the classroom. Throughout the chapter it has been stressed that a variety of management techniques are required if teachers expect to maintain an effective learning environment. Whereas some students may respond appropriately to surface management, others may require a more interpersonal approach. Similarly, some students may adjust to individual techniques, whereas others may be fulfilling group expectation and require group management. Different environmental designs also have different managerial effects on different students.

The success of any management strategy is determined by the teacher's knowledge of the student and the employment of a technique that is appropriate to the academic, psychological, and physical characteristics of the student. Management should be as individualized as the academic program—no two students learn exactly the same thing from the same instruction, nor do they respond in the same way to the same management. This concept of individualized management is particularly important for the disturbed student in the mainstream because the student may have unique characteristics that are not appropriate for the traditional types of teacher management.

Section IV
SYNTHESIS

10
A Matching Model

Educators long have been involved in a search to identify *the* teacher operating *the* intervention strategy that is most effective for disturbed students. However, if educators acknowledge that teacher behaviors vary considerably, that interventions represent different methodologies, and that disturbed students demonstrate a variety of characteristics, they must conclude that no single teacher and no single strategy is most effective for all disturbed students. Consequently, the search will be more profitably directed if educators seek to determine *which* teachers, operating *which* strategies, are most effective for *which* disturbed students. A potential answer to this search resides in a synthesis of the characteristics and educational strategies related to disturbance. However, such a synthesis must go beyond simply combining the different factors; it must establish the functional relationships among the factors. Functional relationships or reciprocal interactions represent a matching model by which educational and/or treatment decisions can be made based upon the *congruence* among the factors.

The need for a matching model has been well established in education. For example, Rubin (1973) stated that a teacher's natural style should ". . . be conjoined both with the pupil's natural learning style and with a particular method" (p. 31), and Joyce and Weil (1980) "believe that strength in education resides in the intelligent use of . . . [a] variety of approaches—matching them to different goals and adapting them to the student's styles and characteristics" (p. xxiii).

With regard to disturbed students, Braun, Mathilda, and Lasher (1968) reached a similar conclusion. "Perhaps there are children who could profit more from one style than from another . . . This may indicate that certain aspects of teaching style could be matched with certain developmental stages of children" (p. 617). In the Morse, Cutler, and Fink (1964) study of classes for disturbed students, the researchers found that "there is no doubt that certain kinds of teachers fit better into certain kinds of programs, and that certain children are more ready to respond to one or another program types" (p. 129).

Morse (1977) elaborated on the need to match strategies and disturbed students:

> The main thing is the match of interventions with the type of the problem the youngster has. For example, if we take a child who has a serious neurotic conflict and apply only an external kind of measure of behavioristic approach, I think we are short changing that youngster. On the other hand, there are particular children with whom a behavioristic approach can be useful, such as in a child who has a value disorder or an attitudinal disposition that is alien to societal survival.
>
> I see the main priority as matching the intervention with the type of problem the youngster has. We have to talk about the general personality style of the individual to decide what would be useful for that individual. We talk about individualizing the way we teach reading and everything else. It seems to me just as important to individualize and spot the method that might be used as well as the specific content that will alleviate the problem for an individual (Morse, 1977, p. 158).

Recent developments in the identification of effective educational matching procedures have taken the form of person-environment interaction (Hunt, 1974) or aptitude-treatment interaction (Cronbach & Snow, 1977). Interaction in this sense is the systematic adaptation of instruction based upon student attributes and for which there is a predictable outcome. For example, if a teacher decides a student within a classroom group has a poor self-concept, and the teacher therefore uses encouragement to increase the self-concept of the individual student, an interaction construct is being utilized.

Research specifying differential aptitudes or characteristics and differential treatments has produced results that support the matching or interaction procedure (Cronbach & Snow, 1977; Hunt, 1974; Rich & Bush, 1978; Warren, 1969). In general, the studies have demonstrated that students assessed as functioning on different behavioral or psychological levels perform differently under the influence of different treatments. Reynolds and Balow (1972), in a review of interaction studies, stated that ". . . interactions between pupil characteristics, teaching methods, and material suggest that the teacher would be more or less effective depending on the decisions he made to match the teaching system to the pupil" (p. 364).

In addition to the research results, educators have long known that matching or interaction does exist. To state that interaction does not exist ". . . is to assert that whichever educational procedure is best for Johnny is best for everyone else in Johnny's school. Even the most commonplace adaptation of instruction, such as choosing different books for more capable and less capable readers of a given age, rests on an assumption of [interaction] that seems foolish to challenge" (Cronbach & Snow, 1977, p. 492).

Three exemplary models have been produced based on the interaction effects between different student developmental characteristics and different treatments. These models, which are discussed in the following section, serve as blueprints for the development of a matching model for disturbed students. Even though the interaction models focus on different populations—autistic, culturally deprived, and delinquent students—the concept of interaction is a common denominator.

INTERACTION MODELS

The three exemplary models discussed are *developmental therapy, conceptual level model,* and *interpersonal maturity level* treatments. A generalization that may be made regarding all three models is that specific student characteristics are developmentally arranged to match treatments that are similarly arranged. These two hierarchical continuums can be visualized as vertical parallel constructs that match horizontally (Figure 1). The representation in Figure 1 is much like a ladder with the vertical supports representing student development and treatments, both arranged on a continuum from basic (i.e., low level student development and controlled treatments) to advanced (i.e., high level development and self-determined or independent treatments). The steps, or rungs, represent the points at which there is a match, that is, the points at which specific treatments are most effective for students with specific developmental characteristics.

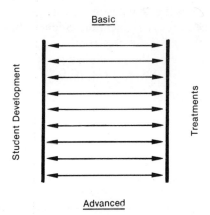

Figure 1.   Matching relationships between student development and treatment.

Developmental Therapy

Developmental therapy (Wood, 1972, 1975; Wood & Swan, 1978) is a therapeutic intervention for young children with serious emotional and behavioral problems, especially those with autistic characteristics. This model contains curriculum experiences in behavior, communication, socialization and (pre)academics that are sequenced according to five distinct stages of therapy. "The teacher's role, the amount of intervention required, the types of activities and materials, the experiences needed, and the type of participation *change* with each stage" (Wood, 1975, pp. 7–8). The five stages of developmental therapy are summarized in Table 1.

Developmental therapy utilizes the hypothetical interaction between therapeutic methods and student development. This interaction is evident when the major premises are analyzed and synthesized.

1. Each therapy stage requires different teacher roles, different techniques, different interventions, and different environments and experiences.
2. Each therapy stage progressively shifts from physical, consistent, and direct methods toward verbal, reflective, and independent methods.
3. Each therapy stage is based on a normal, but delayed sequence of student development.
4. Therefore, each therapy stage is designed to employ therapeutic methods that are congruent with the development of the student.

Wood and Swan (1978) reported that the research on the developmental therapy model has substantiated the hierarchical nature of the stages and the progressive development of disturbed students. "This model illustrates the changes that can occur in children receiving a carefully sequenced, developmentally oriented program. It also underscores the necessity for the classroom design, the curriculum, and the materials to change as the child changes, reflecting new developmental stages" (Wood & Swan, 1978, p. 197).

Conceptual Level

The conceptual level model is a system that describes *how* an individual relates to his or her environment (Harvey, Hunt, & Schroder, 1961). A level within this system is determined by the degree of cognitive complexity (or conceptual structure) that the individual experiences when processing information about the environment (Hunt, 1971). Thus, students who are functioning on the highest conceptual level perceive their environments to be complex and variable, whereas the lowest level students perceive their environments to be relatively simple and concrete. Although conceptual level is considered to be a continuum, Hunt (1974) considers three basic levels: high, low, and very low. Hunt has also equated these levels with developmental states: independent, dependent, and unsocialized. "From a developmental view, the stages can be described in terms of increasing interpersonal maturity and increasing understanding of oneself and others" (Hunt, 1974, p. 22).

An equally important counterpart to individual conceptual level is a "matched environment for development." The basic characteristic of a matched environment can be described as the degree of structure. In unstructured educational environments, students are responsible for determining the conditions under which they learn. However, highly structured environments are "largely determined by the teacher, while the student . . . has little responsibility for what happens in the environment" (Hunt, 1974, p. 24). To achieve maximum results the student's conceptual level or developmental stage must be matched with an environment that contains the appropriate degree of structure (Table 2).

Hunt (1971) considered the matched interactive relationships in Table 2 to be a *contemporaneous* arrangement, that is, an initial match based upon the current conceptual levels of students. In the final analysis, the model is *progressive*; that is, students and their environments should evolve toward higher levels. The conceptual level model "considers developmental progression or growth to be determined *both* by the person's present development stage and by the environment he experiences" (Hunt, 1974, p. 24).

Miller (1981) examined the empirical evidence available regarding the conceptual level model and found that the model was supported by an adequate theory and methods. Even though the model has not been sufficiently tested, Miller contends that the limited research evidence should not detract from the conceptual level theory or its application. Matching the conceptual level of students with commensurately structured environments has produced significant results.

Interpersonal Maturity Level

This model, designated an "I-level" system, has been used primarily in the treatment of delinquents. According to Warren (1969), the essence of I-level treatment is the match between "a sequence of personality (or character) integrations" and treatments that include "workers, settings and methods" (pp. 47, 52).

> This classification system focuses upon the ways in which the individual is able to see himself and the world, especially in terms of emotions and

Table 1.   Summary of developmental therapy stages

Stage I: Responding to the environment with pleasure

General description: *Responding and trusting*

Teacher's role	Arouser and satisfier of basic needs
Techniques	Body language, controlled vocabulary, routine, stimulating activities
Intervention	Constant physical contact; caring, arousing
Environment and experiences	Routine constant; luring rather than demanding; stimulating, arousing activities (sensory)

Stage II: Responding to the environment with success

General description: *Learning individual skills*

Teacher's role	Verbal reflector of success; redirector of old coping behaviors to successful outcomes
Techniques	Routine, consistency, holding limits, redirection
Intervention	Frequent, both physical and verbal
Environment and experiences	Activities leading to self confidence, communication, exploration, and success

Stage III: Learning skills for successful group participation

General description: *Applying individual skills to group procedures*

Teacher's role	Reflector of feelings and progress; encourager; holder of limits
Techniques	Reflector of feelings; predictability; frequent verbal intervention, consistency
Intervention	Frequent, group focus, mostly verbal
Environment and experiences	Focus on rules; focus on group; focus on consequences of behavior; approximate real life as much as group can tolerate; sharing

Stage IV: Investing in group processes

General description: *Valuing one's group*

Teacher's role	Reflector of reality and success; counselor, group leader
Techniques	Reality reflection, individual Life Space Interview, group discussions aimed at problem solving, group planning
Intervention	Intermittent, approximating real life
Environment and experiences	Approximates real life with normal expectations; emphasis on learning experiences, unsimulated normal expectations, role play, field trips, plans developed by children

Stage V: Applying individual and group skills in new situations

General description: *Generalizing and valuing*

Teacher's role	Counselor, teacher
Techniques	Normal expectations; relationships between feelings, behaviors, and consequences; nonclinical

(Continued)

Table 1.   (*Continued*)

Intervention Environment and experiences	Infrequent Normal childhood settings; conversations about real-life experiences; support in solving problem situations; independent skill building

Reprinted with permission of the author from M. M. Wood, *The Rutland Center Model for Treating Emotionally Disturbed Children*, 2nd Ed. Athens, Georgia: Rutland Center Technical Assistance Office, 1972, p. 70.

> motivations; that is, his ability to understand what is happening between himself and others as well as among others. According to the theory . . . successive stages of interpersonal maturity characterize psychological development. They range from the least mature, which resemble the interpersonal reactions of a newborn infant, to an ideal of social maturity which is seldom or never reached in our present culture. Each of the . . . stages, or levels, is defined by a crucial interpersonal problem which must be solved before further progress toward maturity can occur . . . It should be stressed that interpersonal development is viewed as a continuum. The successive steps, or levels, which are described in the theory, are seen as definable points along the continuum (Warren, 1969, p. 52).

Each I-level stage, or level, is matched with the most appropriate treatment (Table 3). Noticeably, the possible treatments progressively shift from well defined environments, to psychological intervention, to "[treatment] unnecessary."

On the basis of a series of research studies of I-level treatment, Warren (1969) reached several conclusions that are applicable to disturbed students and their education:

1. "The theory provides a classification of offenders which can be reliably used and which has relevance to treatment-planning, goal-setting, and program-organization."
2. "The feasibility of developing a range of treatment atmospheres in group home settings [and possibly classrooms] has been shown."
3. "A product of the differential-treatment studies is a set of increasingly elaborate techniques and strategies for working with a delinquent population."
4. "Among the most clear-cut of the findings . . . is that homogeneity (by delinquent subtype) . . . consistently reduced management problems. Significantly fewer serious rule-infractions and peer problems were reported. . . ."
5. "The differential-treatment studies have given support to the view that treatment can usefully be conceptualized as a product of at least four major, coexisting interactions—interactions between

Table 2.   Conceptual level matching model

Developmental stage (level)	Characteristic behavior for stage (level)	Matched environment for development
Unsocialized ◄──► (very low)	Concrete; impulsive; ◄──► poor tolerance for frustration	Accepting but firm; highly structured
Dependent ◄──► (low)	Concerned with rules; ◄──► dependent on authority; categorical thinking	Encourage self-expression within moderate structure
Independent ◄──► (high)	Inquiring; self- ◄──── assertive; questioning; have more alternatives available	Unstructured with emphasis on autonomy

Adapted from Hunt (1974), pp. 22–34.

type of program, type of treatment environment, type of client [student], and type of worker [teacher]." (Warren, 1969, pp. 54–56)

Even though the three interaction models address different populations, using different theoretical bases, and promoting different outcomes, they are operationally consistent. That is, all three models are based on the premise that congruence between the individual and the individual's environment is the most effective educational or treatment arrangement. Further, this congruent arrangement is not conceptualized as a static relationship, but as one that must progress toward higher levels of individual development and environmental complexity.

The matching model proposed for disturbed students and educational environments utilizes the interaction relationships of the three models, as well as the current theory and research on person-environment interaction. This particular matching model has been formulated to increase the effectiveness of educational programs for disturbed students. Although the procedure for estimating the initial match is a nomothetic (from the Greek *nomos,* meaning law) model, it should be conceptualized not as a static product, but as an evolving process or idiographic (from Greek *idio,* or personal) model that facilitates the individual student's progressive development. Neither is the model intended to be limited to disturbed students; related research and theory indicate that the matching concept is applicable to all teaching-learning environments, including regular, special, and higher education (Joyce & Weil, 1980).

Because there are innumerable factors that could be included in a matching model, the factors must be reduced to a relatively few critical ones that can be used to explain differences in educational outcomes. Toward this end, the interdependent factors central to school learning identified by Bloom (1976) are used to outline the matching model. According to Bloom, instructional techniques, learning outcomes, and student characteristics are the most critical factors. Translated into the education of disturbed students, the factors include 1) intervention strategies, 2) teaching styles, 3) management strategies, 4) educational objectives, and 5) developmental behaviors of disturbed students. Other factors discussed in this book, such as the theories of causality and assessment procedures, can tentatively be adapted to the

Table 3.   Classification of delinquents as an aid to treatment

I-level subtype[a]	Characteristics	Treatment
Asocial	Primitive, impulsive, insecure, inadequate, maladaptive, hostile, nontrusting	Clear and concrete structure of low pressure; warmth and acceptance; slow and supportive direction toward conformity
Conformist	Concerned with power, need for structure and social approval, rule-oriented, short-term goals, concrete, superficial	Clear and consistent external structure; develop concern through behavior controls; peer group pressure and involvement; skills to increase adequacy and independence
Antisocial manipulator	Internalized norms, guilt-free, self-satisfied, nontrusting, callous, hostile, counteractive to authority	Encourage socially acceptable manipulative skills; work through childhood trauma; revive capacity to depend on and be concerned about others
Neurotic offender	Intimidated, disturbed, overinhibited, anxious, depressed, withdrawn	Resolution of neurotic conflict through insight into family and individual dynamics; therapy
Subcultural identifier	Internalized values of a deviant subculture, group-oriented, distrustful of authority, views problems as "external"	Stop violations through exclusion; develop skills in obtaining needs; provide an appropriate model; improve in-group value experiences
Situational reactor	Normal individuals who are ego-alien, accidental, and/or nonrepetitive	Varied or unnecessary

Adapted and abridged from Warren (1969), pp. 47–59.
[a] The extent to which an individual has an integrated, or consistent, level of interpersonal maturity (I-level); some variations have been omitted.

model, but the interaction relationships are somewhat speculative and only partially documented.

SUMMARY OF MATCHING FACTORS

Intervention Strategies

Chapter 7 included a discussion of five educational intervention strategies (structured, behavior modification, psychoeducational, environmental, and alternatives) and three variations (engineered class, reality therapy, and open education). Three supportive, noneducational interventions (physiological, psychoanalytic, and expressive therapy) were also discussed.

The sequence of interventions presented is not random, but a logical progression that essentially follows the sequence of the theories of causality. That is, the most basic level on the hierarchy begins with a specific, physiological intervention, evolves through behavioral, psychological, and environmental interventions, and terminates on the most advanced level, represented by a complex, student-determined intervention.

As a general summary statement, successive steps along the intervention hierarchy place increasingly less emphasis on the individual as the source of disturbance, with a corresponding decrease in intervention control over the individual student. Thus, the interventions evolve in succession from stringent, preplanned, and highly controlled methods to flexible, student-planned, and low control methods.

Teaching Styles

Chapter 8 included a discussion of teaching styles as a part of teaching-learning strategies. The construct used to describe teaching styles was a hierarchical continuum of teacher control. Although teaching style terminology may vary (e.g., authoritarian-democratic, direct-indirect, command-decision), the continuum reflects the degree to which the teacher makes decisions for the students. Thus, teachers who make essentially all of the decisions for students are exercising external control, whereas teachers who permit students to make all decisions are demonstrating an internal control style.

Of course, teachers rarely, if ever, totally demonstrate an external or internal teaching style. More often teacher styles represent a blend of the two extremes, typically demonstrating different degrees of external-internal control. For example, Flanders (1965) has expressed this blend in terms of an I/D (indirect/direct) ratio, which expresses the percentage of teacher verbal interaction that is indirect. Thus, an individual teacher style may fall anywhere along the continuum from 0.00 (direct) to 1.00 (indirect).

The extent to which teachers control students, or make decisions for them, correlates with the intervention strategies. That is, the degree of external-internal teaching control style should parallel the progressive sequence of the intervention strategies. For example, the structured intervention, which requires stringent schedules, specifically preplanned methods, and behavioral limitations is more consistent with the external teacher control style. On the other extreme, open or countertheory alternatives, which place emphasis on student freedom and choice, are more consistent with internal control teaching styles. Thus, the hierarchical progression from structured to alternative interventions should be accompanied by a hierarchical progression in teaching styles from external to internal control.

Management Strategies

Chapter 9 included a discussion of four basic management strategies: surface, interpersonal, group, and environmental. Although there was no hierarchy identified in the discussion, the frequency with which specific management strategies are employed to manage students correlates with both interventions and teaching styles. Certainly, individual teachers use all four management strategies, regardless of the intervention, but the frequent, pervasive, and routine use of specific management strategies yields a progressive continuum. Just as the ratio of external-internal teaching behaviors yielded a teaching style continuum, dependence on particular management strategies yields a management continuum.

Environmental management, which minimizes the human element yet maximizes the physical dimensions of management, is considered to be the most basic strategy. For example, Wood (1975) and Cruickshank et al. (1961) emphasized the necessity for establishing controlled environments in order to manage seriously disturbed students. Thus, environmental management is the basic ingredient to physical intervention.

Surface management, which represents the second step on the continuum, is designed to control the overt behavior of individual students. This management strategy is used extensively by teachers with external control styles operating behaviorally oriented programs. The emphasis is not on why behaviors are occurring, but what behaviors, and to immediately alter the behaviors to be consistent with the teacher's expectations for that classroom setting. Thus, surface management is designed to produce behavior change among students without particular regard for the psychological motivation.

Interpersonal management, the third step on the continuum, deals with feelings, expression, and, generally, the cause or "why" of disturbed characteristics. This is a preferred management strategy for teachers with an internal control style or who employ psychologically oriented interventions. Although behavior change typically takes longer under interpersonal management than under surface management, there is the underlying belief that permanent behavior change cannot be externally maintained but must be accompanied by student motivation, values, or understanding. Even though interpersonal management may have more lasting effects, it is more time-consuming and difficult to employ in a large class.

Group management has a definite sociological orientation and therefore represents the highest level on the continuum. Effective group management is a complex strategy that requires that the teacher possess sophisticated skills, awareness, and multiple, yet concurrent, techniques. Not only does the teacher have to know about the effects of the environment, the overt behaviors, and the psychological conditions regarding individual students, but the teacher must be able to analyze and synthesize these pieces of information in order to understand the dynamics of the classroom group. Group management, then, must consider the group as a whole as well as the function of individual students within the group.

This management continuum (i.e., environmental, surface, interpersonal, and group) represents a hierarchy that is based on a correlation with both intervention strategies and teaching styles. Independently, however, the management continuum generally represents strategies that range from an individual to a group focus, from overt behavior to psychological causes, and from a basic to an advanced process.

Educational Objectives

Chapter 8 listed, on a hierarchical continuum, the major cognitive, affective, and psychomotor educational objectives (Table 2 in Chapter 8). This hierarchy will be listed again as a component of a matching model (Table 4, this chapter). Therefore, repetition at this point has limited value. The critical summative issue to be reinforced here is that the hierarchical positions of the different objectives should be congruent with the corresponding components of the matching model. That is, basic objectives are best achieved in basic educational strategies (interventions, teaching style, and management), whereas more advanced objectives are best achieved in educational strategies that *commensurately* evolve toward a higher level.

Developmental Behaviors

Chapter 5 discussed the theoretical and practical rationale for ranking student behaviors on a developmental hierarchy. Developmental behaviors were listed in Figure 3 of Chapter 5 and will be listed again in Table 4, this chapter; therefore, they are not repeated here. The primary implication of the developmental hierarchy is that the most effective educational strategies are those that are congruent with the developmental level of students. Because a function of education is student growth, however, both educational strategies and developmental behaviors should systematically and commensurately progress toward higher levels.

This summary of interaction factors has emphasized two critical concepts: continuums of hierarchical strategies and development, and the horizontal congruence among the continuums. These relationships among the continuums constitute a matching model.

A MATCHING MODEL

The following matching model is presented as a guide for initially determining which educational strategies are most effective for which disturbed students. A functional procedure seems necessary, because many educators continue to insist dogmatically on the use of a single educational strategy, in particular a specific intervention and/or teaching style, in an era of individualized programs for disturbed students. However, many teachers of disturbed students have made strategy adjustments. The realistic and practical demands of the classroom have made it necessary for teachers to borrow bits and pieces from all of the available strategies, altering the strategy to fit the student or the objective or the crisis. Thus, teachers by necessity have become eclectic, using the best of what is available from all of the educational strategies. Most teachers tend to recognize that no one strategy has all of the answers for educating disturbed students. At this point in time, however, these individual, eclectic classroom modifications are too infrequently implemented and often only intuitively conceptualized.

In lieu of this intuitive, eclectic conceptualization, a matching model (Table 4) is presented to plan more effectively educational experiences for disturbed students. The matching model is based on two premises: 1) that the five factors individually represent a progressive continuum from basic to advanced levels, and 2) that the interaction among the factors is the most productive when the factors functionally match, that is, represent person-environment congruence or consistency. Table 4 is to be read horizontally to determine the match between

Table 4. A matching model

Continuum hierarchy	Intervention strategies	Teaching style	Management strategies	Educational objectives			Developmental behaviors
				Cognitive	Affective	Psychomotor	
Basic	Structured→	External control	Environmental	Knowledge	Receiving	Imitation	←Unsocialized
	Engineered class →				Responding	Manipulation	Hyperactive
		.20^a	Surface				↓ Impulsive
	Behavior modification→			Comprehension		Precision	←Protective
		.40		Application			↓ Withdrawn
	Reality therapy→	.60	Interpersonal	Analysis	Valuing	Articulation	↓ Dependent
				Synthesis			↓ Ritualistic
	Psychoeducational→	.80	Group		Organization	Naturalization	←Defining
				Evaluation	Characterization		↓ Negativistic
	Open education→						↓ Aggressive
		Internal control					↓ Assertive
Advanced	Countertheory→						←Self-controlled

^{a} Approximate percentage of internal control.

and among the factors. For example, the structured intervention strategy and environmental management under the direction of a teacher with an external control style are most effective with unsocialized students who are attempting to achieve basic educational objectives such as receiving and imitation. At the next levels the engineered class and behavior modification interventions emphasizing surface management are also directed by teachers with external control styles, although tempered with some internal control behaviors. The combination of educational strategies is most effective with students who are developmentally demonstrating protective behaviors and who are attempting to achieve knowledge, responding, and manipulation objectives. This arrangement is consistent with teachers who prefer to lecture. "Since the rate of transmission of information is slow in discussion classes [e.g., psychoeducational and open], we would expect lecture classes to be superior in helping students acquire knowledge of information" (McKeachie, 1962, p. 1126). In short, students functioning on the more basic levels are ". . . lacking important basic skills, who need direction and protection until they can acquire them" (Joyce & Harootunian, 1967, p. 95).

The advanced continuum extremes indicate grossly different matched factors. Self-controlled or assertive students who are attempting to achieve higher level objectives such as evaluation and characterization are best facilitated by open or alternative environments accompanied by teachers with internal control styles and group management.

Matching combinations falling between the two extremes would require proportionate shifts among the factors. For example, students whose problems are primarily psychological in nature (indicated by behavior such as negativism) require a psychoeducation intervention, a teacher with an intermediate external-internal control style, interpersonal management, and educational objectives that emphasize analysis, valuing, and articulation.

As disturbed students achieve the hierarchical educational objectives and/or behavior changes to a more advanced level, the intervention strategy, teacher style, and management strategies need to shift accordingly. This progressive shift may involve phasing out tangible rewards, eliminating a rule or limit, introducing the student to a problem solving group, providing more independent study, or, as Garner (1976) has suggested, combining aspects of different strategies, because some disturbed students may need both behavioral and psychological intervention.

According to the matching model, a significant educational issue is to facilitate the movement of students who are functioning on the basic levels to more advanced levels. Thus, students who have teachers with external control styles must gradually and progressively be introduced to teachers with internal control styles. Similarly, intervention and management strategies must evolve from direct, controlling, and preplanned treatments toward indirect, flexible, and individually determined experiences. The educational objectives students are to achieve must also progress from basic, low level accomplishments to advanced, high level achievement. This progressive movement, of course, is dependent upon the developmental change among students. Ideally, both the educational strategies and the developmental behaviors will commensurately evolve toward more advanced levels. Practically, however, either or both may stagnate at a specific level. Teachers may not change, objectives may remain constant (with only the content changing), and specific intervention and management strategies may be dogmatically employed. Under such conditions, students will not progress, or if they do it will be in spite of the educational strategy. Thus, it is imperative that educational strategies progressively change at a rate that leads the student much like the proverbial carrot before the donkey's nose.

Aside from the problem that some teachers may not alter the educational strategies, the organization of schools also fosters a great deal of inconsistency and often a developmental regression. For example, a disturbed student who is promoted to a higher elementary grade may experience a more controlling teacher, lower level objectives, and a more extensively preplanned intervention than the student experienced the previous year. Secondary schools also are inconsistent because of the variety of classes, and consequently educational strategies, that students experience on a daily basis. For the matching model to be longitudinally effective, the school principal, in particular, must be cognizant of the experiences provided in different classrooms and assign disturbed students so that the potential for progressive development is maintained. The alternative is an increase in student failure, repetitious disruptions, and the continuation of disturbance.

Obviously, all five of the factors will not consistently match all of the time. Therefore, the match must be considered with flexibility, that is, as a narrow range or spread across the table, rather than as specific points. Also, it may be necessary to eliminate a factor that is not necessary or that is consistently mismatched with the remaining factors. It should be remembered that this is a model or representation, a theoretical conception rather than an empirically precise cause-and-effect relationship. Nonetheless, a matching model is needed to enable educators initially to develop a system by which different disturbed students are introduced to the most appropriate educational strategies from those that are available.

MODEL DOCUMENTATION

Models are not created from a void, but developed from a body of related knowledge. Hence, this matching model was developed from the theoretical literature and research results regarding disturbance, educational strategies, and, in particular, person-environment interaction.

The theoretical literature regarding the model factors and person-environment interaction was discussed in preceding pages, with the conclusion that different disturbed students perform differently (better or worse) when they experience different educational strategies. Therefore, the emphasis of this section is on the research that is available regarding the effects of specific student-educational strategy combinations.

The majority of research studies confirm the fact that the matching concept is an effective educational procedure. Cronbach and Snow (1977), for example, reviewed hundreds of studies and arrived at one conclusion: person-environment interaction does exist. However, the primary difficulty in documenting this particular matching model is the fact that different researchers and practioners use different terms to describe similar concepts. For example, the discussion of teaching styles in Chapter 8 included a variety of style terms such as direct-indirect and authoritarian-democratic. The underlying premise of all of the style terms is related to the degree of control exercised by the teacher. Therefore, teacher style was described as an external-internal control continuum that was functionally consistent with the literature on teacher styles, even though the nomenclature was not the same.

Thus, the documentation of this matching model is dependent upon the translation of different terms into concepts that represent similar functions. The interaction effects between different components of educational strategies and normal students are well documented. The following exemplary studies attest to the validity of the matching concept.

Janicki and Peterson (1981) found that students with an external locus of control (low developmental level) performed better in direct instructional situations. Students with an internal locus of control (high developmental level), on the other hand, performed better in small group situations where they had more freedom of choice. Although locus of control and developmental levels are not equatable concepts, there is sufficient evidence to assume that both are highly related developmental constructs (e.g., Rotter, 1966). Both locus of control and developmental behaviors, then, are similarly influenced by instructional style.

Rich and Bush (1978) found that "direct teachers who employ more structured learning environments appear relatively more facilitative for students low in SED [social-emotional development] than for students high in SED. Similarly, indirect teachers who employ less structured environments appear relatively more facilitative for students high in SED than for students low in SED" (p. 456). This research, which was based on Hunt's (1974) conceptual level interaction model, found that teaching styles and student characteristics have a joint influence on student outcomes, particularly achievement, time at attention to task, and preference for teaching styles.

Solomon and Kendall (1976) found that students that were creative and independent performed better in open environments, whereas students who were classified as undisciplined (probably hyperactive and/or impulsive) performed better in traditional classes. This led these researchers to conclude that "the child's characteristics may help to determine the type of class from which he would derive the greatest benefit" (p. 623).

With reference to preschool students, who are typically functioning on a lower developmental level, Karnes and Teska (1975) affirmed the need to provide structured intervention strategies. "It appears clear that the more structured programs with specific instructional objectives and particular techniques designed to meet those objectives have produced more measurable change in children than have the more unstructured programs . . ." (p. 238).

On the basis of a mass of interaction research data, Brophy and Good (1974) arrived at a specific conclusion regarding student characteristics and educational strategies. Students ". . . with high control needs [compulsive and/or anxious students] preferred more structured situations with the teacher in a position of control. Subjects with low control needs [independent and/or non-conforming students] selected settings in which the teacher's position of control was less obvious" (p. 246).

Brophy and Good went on to equate high and low control needs with learning styles, in particular convergent (organized, deductive problem solving) and divergent (generating alternative solutions) thinking. "In general . . . data from several sources suggest that both convergent teachers and convergent students prefer a well-organized, businesslike, achievement oriented classroom with a clear-cut structure established primarily by the teacher. In contrast, divergent teachers and students are less achievement and structure oriented, preferring instead a teaching approach involving minimal structure, highly personal interactions, and encouragement of everyone to follow his own interests" (p. 251).

All of the reported research studies and reviews either claimed or alluded to the fact that matched strategy-student combinations produced significantly better results. Research with both normal and exceptional children, using a variety of strategies including teacher style, has yielded some consistent patterns. Structured and external control strategies and styles have demonstrated significantly superior results in enabling students to achieve basic level objectives such as knowledge and receiving (e.g., Bennett, 1976; Salomon & Achenbach, 1974). Students of secondary school age, however, are reported to both prefer and achieve advanced level objectives in educational environments that emphasize internal control (e.g., Hamachek, 1969; Scheuer, 1971). This distinction was recognized earlier by Anderson (1959), who maintained that "democratic" environments better achieved social-emotional goals, whereas "authoritarian" environments were more effective when the objectives were simple and concrete.

Three different aspects of the matching model have been partially supported by research results. First, in a study of classroom climates for the disturbed (Rich, 1969), it was found that direct (external control) and indirect (internal control) teachers had a differential effect on aggressive and withdrawn students. Whereas withdrawn students instructed by direct teachers demonstrated greater achievement, aggressive students achieved similar gains with indirect teachers. The alternate or mismatch arrangement (i.e., direct-aggressive and indirect-withdrawn) produced significantly lower achievement scores.

Second, in a follow-up of the previous study (Rich, 1979a), classroom verbal patterns among direct and indirect teachers and aggressive and withdrawn students were investigated. In this study, the mismatch between students and teachers produced the most dramatic effects. In particular, aggressive students demonstrated a higher rate of aggressive and dominant behaviors toward both teachers and peers when they were instructed by direct teachers. In short, the teacher-student mismatch produced a greater rate of deviancy.

Third, the relationship between student locus of control and achievement on two levels of reading objectives was expected to produce interaction effects. In a study to test this hypothesis (Rich, 1981), although all expected differences were not significant, they were in the expected direction. That is, students with an internal locus of control outperformed their external counterparts on advanced level objectives (analysis and synthesis), whereas students with an external locus of control performed better on basic objectives (knowledge or recall).

Finally, Hunt (1974), Warren (1969), and Wood (1975) have produced an enormous amount of data in support of their particular interaction models. Because the matching model for disturbed students is theoretically and conceptually equivalent to the functional matches among the hierarchical factors in these three models, their research also tentatively validates this matching model.

The research documentation presented in support of the matching model does not justify its unquestioned acceptance. Certainly, there is also research available that fails to support the validity of the interaction factors presented (e.g., Fraser & Rentoul, 1980; Hessler & Sosnowsky, 1979). However, most of the objections are based on the inadequacy of the research methodology rather than on the concept of person-environment interaction. Of course, additional research on the matching model is necessary before definitive claims can be made regarding its effectiveness as a practical educational tool. Therefore, future research should evaluate the hierarchical factors in the context of interaction effects.

A matching model is needed as a classroom guide in the education of disturbed students. This, or a similar model, is necessary if educators are to introduce disturbed students to the most appropriate educational strategy. This matching model has been presented as a procedure by which the best fit can be accomplished among certain teachers, certain disturbed students, and certain educational strategies.

CLASSROOM ADAPTATION OF THE MODEL

On the simplest level, a classroom teacher may have a large group of homogeneous students, that is, students who are functioning on the same developmental level, who are attempting to accomplish the same objectives, and who progress at the same rate. Under such a condition, the teacher can employ the same style, the same intervention, and the same management strategy with all of the students. Obviously, such homogeneity rarely, if ever, exists. Certainly, if disturbed students were like normal students there would be no need for identification, classification, or mainstreaming in the first place. Yet disturbed students do exist; therefore, teachers need to make classroom adaptations of the model in order to maximize the educational experiences for students. This is not to say that the total educational experience of every disturbed student should be adapted. However, those learning or behavioral experiences that are most critical to the development of that student should be individualized or adapted to produce more successful experiences. For example, the teacher may elect to adapt a specific portion of the academic program or skill area in which the student is experiencing failure, or adapt management strategies if the primary problem is behavioral in nature, or adapt the teaching style to accomplish a particular objective.

Educators can cope with individual differences in a number of ways. They range from Procrustean methods that involve little adaptation, through intuitive and little tested rules for adaptation, up to, in principle, tested rules derived from theory.

The least responsible solution is to fix the curriculum and method of instruction and to "adjust" the student body to the method, selecting at the outset and making it easy for the discouraged student to drop out.

We may distinguish between two broad kinds of adaptation. One is to choose different educational goals for different persons, and the other is to choose different educational means toward the same goals. The former serves to develop the person's capacity for self-expression in work and leisure. It cannot be the only policy, however. The easy escape of shunting some students into a "non-academic" curriculum cannot be tolerated, so long as proficiencies formerly considered "academic" are necessary for most kinds of success and participation in society. Educators have to invent methods to open opportunity to persons who would not attain traditional goals in traditional ways. Teachers have adapted methods by various tactics: diversifying reading materials to suit children with different skills and interests, setting out a range of projects calculated to appeal to different pupils, providing individualized remedial work, and so on.

Adaptations differ with respect to their scale, and with respect to their tactics. The most far-reaching choice is that between institutions run along different lines, as between a Montessori preschool and a permissive one. This preselects the child's total school experience during a period of a year or more. At a second level are choices of "stream" within a single school. Differentiation of students into fast, slow, and intermediate tracks affects the rate at which material is introduced, the standards upheld, and to some extent the content introduced.

Some plans set up alternative series of lessons or projects, or alternative curricula, to which a student can be "assigned" or self-assigned for a period of time. Another possibility is microadaptation where the path of instruction is modified minute by minute as the instruction proceeds. It takes one form in the computer, where very small units of instruction are available in considerable variety and capable of being assembled in myriad sequences. It takes a different form in clinical work, where an experienced instructor who has a highly developed theory of individual differences analyzes closely the moment-by-moment performance and shapes his interactions with the learner accordingly. . . .

In another kind of adaptation, weekly or monthly assignments are individualized. Variants of this are found in Individually Prescribed Instruction, Project PLAN, and other schemes reminiscent of the Dalton and Winnetka plans of a generation ago. Decisions are based largely on detailed measures of the student's achievement to this point. The basic concept is that each unit of instruction lays a base of proficiency on which the next unit can build. Conversely, one can specify the proficiencies needed to master a new unit, and then, after taking inventory of what the student can do, put him through remedial work. Mapping hierarchies of subskills and elementary concepts in the subject matter has undoubted value. . . .

The long-range requirement is for understanding of the factors that cause a student to respond to one instructional plan rather than another. These plans should differ in more than the amount of time devoted to specific drills. The range of instructional procedures open to the educator is enormous—individual projects, workbooks, teacher-monitored prob-lem-solving, group projects, discussion, etc. New media extend the range of methods and also extend the capability of the school to administer flexible and diversified programs. There is no reason to assume that an eclectic mixture of all methods will serve every kind of student. There must be some kinds of students who respond best to group discussions, and others who do much better by themselves. The same is to be said of all the parameters of instruction: level of comprehension required by the presentation, rigor of supervision, presence of competition, etc. (Cronbach & Snow, 1977, pp. 522–524).

As Cronbach and Snow have suggested, the particular routes that teachers choose to adapt educational experiences in order to match students are numerous. Teachers are typically knowledgeable about individualized techniques such as diagnostic-prescriptive teaching, modularized instruction, and learning centers (e.g., Charles, 1976). There is even a wealth of information regarding the individualization and adaptation of educational materials (e.g., Anderson, Greer, & Odle, 1978).

Thus, the lack of knowledge and sometimes skill are not the pri-mary reasons that teachers often resist implementing individual edu-cational matches between strategies and students. Rather, teacher at-titudes, motivation, "burn-out," and available time seem to be the primary deterrents to individual adaptations. Of these, time is the most frequently and publicly echoed reason: "With 30 students, I just don't have the time."

Unquestionably, time is a relevant factor that impinges on both teachers and students. Since time is such a precious quantity, it seems that effective utilization of time should be a priority concern of edu-cators, but this does not seem to be the case. For example, Gump (1971) found that elementary teachers spent 17 to 33 percent of the time allocated for instruction "out of the academic area" (p. 162). Similarly, Smith et al. (1979) found that 26 percent of an elementary teacher's time was devoted to management transition, which included activities such as taking attendance, making announcements, and man-aging behaviors. These studies indicate that less than 75 percent of an instructional period is actually used for instruction.

What occurs during that 75 percent of instructional time? Typically, the time consists of lecturing, individual student seatwork activities, and individual teacher-student interactions that are limited to a small percentage of the class.

This type of time utilization is most effective in achieving basic level objectives, but detrimental to the accomplishment of advanced objectives. In fact, Durkin (1981) found that instruction above the "knowledge" objective level amounted to only 45 minutes out of a total of 11,587 minutes (.003%) of instructional time. These kinds of results led Coleman (1966) to conclude that many high school students effectively used only 10 minutes out of each school day.

Although less dramatically, Jackson (1968) concluded "in several different ways students . . . are required to wait their turn and to delay their actions. No one knows for certain how much of the average student's time is spent in neutral, as it were, but for many students in many classrooms it must be a memorable portion" (p. 15). The more students wait, the greater the anxiety, boredom, frustration, and, in general, deviant or disruptive behavior.

Matching strategies and students is not a panacea to the time utilization issue. Evaluating, implementing, and periodically evaluating the match will require teacher time. It is believed, however, that such a match will ultimately require less teacher time and waste less student time. For example, Rich (1973) found that teachers who were matched with students according to the model spent less than 5 percent of their time managing off-task student behaviors, whereas teachers in mismatched arrangements spent more than 25 percent of their time managing off-task behaviors. From the students' perspective, they spent significantly more time on task and demonstrated higher achievement scores when matched with teachers. Both teachers and students also had more positive feelings about the matched arrangement. Thus, the matched arrangement not only utilizes time more effectively, but it may also change attitudes, increase motivation, and reduce burnout.

SUMMARY

This chapter discussed a matching model, or person-environment interaction concept, for educating disturbed students. The matching model was based on the premise that interaction congruence among five critical factors would produce significantly better results with regard to the education of disturbed students. The factors included student developmental behaviors and components of the educational strategies (interventions, teaching styles, management strategies, and educational objectives). Each factor was arranged on a hierarchical continuum from basic to advanced, so that horizontal consistency represented matched relationships.

Three existing matching models, developmental therapy (Wood, 1975), conceptual level (Hunt, 1971, 1974), and interpersonal maturity (Warren, 1969), were presented as prototypes for the matching model. The theoretical rationale, operational procedure, and research support for each of the models was presented.

The theory and application of the matching was documented through the literature and research that is currently available. The conclusion reached was that the matching model is an effective procedure for assigning disturbed students to the most appropriate educational arrangements. As a precaution, however, the model should be implemented tentatively, because many aspects of the model have not been adequately tested.

Finally, it was suggested that the model is an individualized education procedure that can be a vehicle for more effectively utilizing teacher and student time, increasing achievement, and producing more positive attitudes. In the final analysis the matching model is a systematic procedure for functionally and effectively educating disturbed students in the mainstream.

11
Future Directions

What can be said about the decade of the 1980s—and beyond—regarding disturbed students? Although no one knows for certain, speculative projections can be presented based on a mixture of past and current trends, contemporary literature, the author's personal beliefs, and some intuitive crystal ball gazing. All of these sources can be synthesized to yield a tentative picture of disturbance for the immediate future. These projections are presented in a manner that parallels the organization of this book: background, characteristics, educational strategies, and synthesis.

Any discussion of possible future directions must be prefaced by a single critical factor: economics. Education and human services, in general, are greatly influenced by inflation, tax rates, and in particular, government appropriations. Services that at one time were supported by substantial economic resources are now being negatively affected by broadly based austerity budgets. Many state and local education agencies, for example, have reduced their operating budgets to levels that only provide for essential or basic programs. The numbers of teachers, counselors, and other related personnel are being reduced, supportive programs such as art and music are being eliminated, capital expenditures and administrative costs are being pared, and special education and related services are being curtailed.

The financial resources available for the education of handicapped students have been maintained chiefly because of state and federal legislation that has mandated services and resources. However, this base of support is in jeopardy. Several states have amended or are in the process of amending legislation previously enacted on behalf of handicapped students.

Some categories of handicapping conditions are being eliminated, definitions of the different conditions are being rewritten with more specificity (thus limiting the number eligible), and financial appropriations are being reduced. On the federal level, there has been considerable discussion regarding the repeal of PL 94-142, or at least certain aspects of the law such as related services requirements and the excess cost formula (*Update*, 1981.).

In addition to the reduction of funds, proposed federal legislation (e.g., The Elementary and Secondary Consolidation Act of 1981) threatens to eliminate PL-142 or combine it with several of the so-called "title" programs mandated by the Elementary and Secondary Education Act of 1965. This type of legislation would not only drastically reduce the amount of funding for services to handicapped and disadvantaged children, but it would provide the money in a block grant to state and local governments without specifying the recipients. At best, advocates for the poor would would be pitted against advocates of the handicapped in lobbying for the limited amount of money at the local level. Although this proposed legislative action does reduce the involvement or interference of the federal government in local government, it does not reduce the possibility of mismanagement, political infighting and inefficiency. Whether individual state and local level leaders have the political stability, administrative resources, and financial maturity to disseminate appropriately these additional monies is questionable. Because it will take years, if ever, for many state and local government personnel to develop the competence to manage effectively this additional responsibility, it is expected that federal block funding proposals will experience a relatively short existence. Even though a U.S. Senate compromise measure temporarily, at least, preserved PL 94-142, the first half of the 1980s will witness reduced appropriations for human services and piecemeal efforts to decentralize the administration of specialized educational programs. However, it is expected that this type of economic and political maneuver will be reevaluated and reserved to a large degree by the close of this decade.

What implications do these economic conditions have for the education of disturbed students? Aside from the fact that there will be less money available, there appear to be at least three major effects:

1. *Fewer* students will be officially identified as disturbed
2. *More* of the students who are identified as disturbed will be educated in the regular class
3. Specialized assistance to regular class teachers will be *reduced* (e.g., resource teachers, psychological and counseling services, and specialized materials).

These economic effects indicate that regular class teachers will be expected to do more, but with fewer resources. This rather pessimistic condition does achieve mainstreaming, but for the wrong reason. Rather than mainstreaming disturbed students based on the concept of the most appropriate educational environment, many will be assigned to the regular classroom because it is the cheapest possible program available or the "least expensive environment." The alternative, of course, may be no program for mildly and moderately disturbed students.

Special education teachers will also be confronted with problems that arise from economic austerity. Aside from the fact that there will be fewer special education teachers, those who are employed will be expected to educate more students and those who have more severe handicapping conditions, such as autistic children. Also this will have to be accomplished without the customary resources such as teacher aides and specialized equipment.

This pessimistic, economically austere condition will probably exist through the first part of this decade. However, if economic conditions stabilize (with reduced inflation, increased employment, and greater national productivity), and they are expected to do so, then Americans will witness a return to the humanitarian and educational ideals that achieved prominence in the 1960s and 1970s. A cyclic pattern of economic need and plenty has been persistent throughout the history of the United States, and there is no evidence to indicate that the future will be any different. Even though the economic implications for disturbed students and education in general are somewhat grim at the present, one may be optimistic regarding the near future.

BACKGROUND

Historical Developments

Service to handicapped individuals may have at least temporarily peaked during the decade of the 1970s. A humanitarian philosophy emerged during the twentieth century that ultimately resulted in civil rights legislation, programs for the poor and disabled, and finally the education of all handicapped children. Riding this wave of humanitarianism, educators such as Dunn (1968) and Blatt (1970) challenged the necessity of proliferating segregated services (e.g., special classes and institutions), maintaining that many of these placements were dehumanizing, ineffective, and unjustifiable. This philosophical position was supported by the fact that many students in segregated placements, particularly the special class, demonstrated relatively few positive gains. "These results eroded confidence in one of the fundamental assumptions in special education, that is, that a specially trained teacher working with small groups of exceptional children could make a significant difference . . .'' (Kirk & Gallagher, 1979, p. 483). As a consequence of this humanitarian philosophy, research data, and litigation and legislation on behalf of the handicapped, mildly and moderately disturbed students were placed in the regular class with increasing frequency.

Unfortunately, the decade of the 1980s may witness a regression in this placement philosophy. With decreased funding and the possibility that protective legislation (due process, least restrictive environment, etc.) may be repealed or at least amended, it is doubtful that the majority of school personnel will voluntarily embrace the concept of mainstreaming for disturbed students. An alternative, of course, is exclusion, particularly at the secondary level. The following student's case may become representative of the schools' solution to disturbed students:

> In three years, I never attended one assembly program and rarely went to homeroom and cut a lot of other classes, too. Actually, I got away with most of this because I suppose that no one noticed that I was absent or didn't care whether I was there or not. From time to time, though, all of this would catch up with me, and I would be placed in detention hall or would be expelled for several days. I never understood this kind of contradiction either: I would have thought that the authorities would want to make certain we came to school, not send us home as a measure to improve attendance (Wawrzyniak, Smith, & Brown, 1981, p. 403).

It well may be that the above case is symptomatic of an even deeper underlying problem that may resurface after a decade of legal mandates and parent involvement. For adolescents in particular, however, "the misuse of exclusionary practices such as continuous suspension, ignored truancy, and the inappropriate use of homebound instruction and shortened school must be stopped" (Grosenick & Huntze, 1980, p. 136).

On the positive side, there are many teachers, supported by administrators and other school personnel, who believe that mainstreaming is the only reasonable solution to the education of disturbed students. Many of those who believe in this educational philosophy will survive the decade of the 1980s, but not without frustration, failure, and often indifference. However, they will have helped disturbed students, and they will be joined by a growing number of dedicated teachers as the humanitarian philosophy regains the momentum that has been temporarily delayed.

Theories of Causality

The different theories of causality have provided a complex framework for determining the etiology of disturbance. Whereas the earliest scientific theories were entrenched in biophysical explanations, other theories evolved which placed greater emphasis on other causes of disturbance. In particular, the ecological theory and environmental explanations began to achieve a significant degree of acceptance during the 1970s. However, the skills and technology necessary to evaluate students and the interaction with their environments have not been sufficiently developed. Even though there are scientific data to support the theory that disturbance is a function of multiple personal and environmental factors, the practical process of determining the effects on individual students is a major limitation. The future, however, will undoubtedly witness a more intense effort to understand and categorize in systematic fashion the cumulative effects of the environment not only on disturbed students, but on all aspects of human variance.

In the meantime, there is a trend to reestablish the primacy of the biophysical cause of disturbance (Wender & Klein, 1981). For example, autism is often classified as "other health-impaired" (a biophysical disorder) rather than "seriously emotionally disturbed" (a psychological problem). The escalating use of drugs, diet, and other physiological treatments is also evidence of a shift back to an earlier scientific period. Aside from the fact that biophysical causes are more palatable than psychological or social ones, particularly for parents, this narrowly defined explanation implies definitively prescribed treatments that primarily involve medical decisions, rather than educational accountability. Thus, because of the specific, palatable, and prescriptive nature of biophysical causes, it is expected that this explanation of disturbance will increase in popularity during the 1980s.

Other theories of causality (i.e., behavioral, psychodynamic, sociological, and countertheory) will probably maintain, at best, a status quo existence during the 1980s. Although there are individuals that espouse one or another of these theories, their influence on educators and the public in general is sporadic, unorganized, and consequently unheeded. The 1980s, then, probably will witness a dual emphasis on the possible causes of disturbance: biophysical and environmental.

CHARACTERISTICS

Defining Disturbance

The most critical problems in defining disturbance are that the available definitions represent different theories, different diagnostic procedures, and, in the final analysis, different expectations of behaviors (Fink & Glass, 1973). Consequently, the behavioral and psychological characteristics of students defined as disturbed vary from state to state and even from classroom to classroom. Even definitions that have broad based acceptance (e.g., PL 94-142) can be so loosely or stringently interpreted that everyone or no one could be defined as disturbed.

In addition to the continuation of this amorphic defining process, three probable directions are on the horizon for the 1980s:

First, there are those who believe that labeling students is a dehumanizing process and that definitions have only two purposes: to comply with legislation and receive money for the excess costs of education. Because both of these reasons are in jeopardy, at least at the federal level, there will be a renewed effort among the humanists and countertheorists virtually to eliminate labels and therefore definitions of disturbance.

Second, there is a movement toward the identification of specific behaviors, rather than definitions per se, as the vehicle for defining disturbance. For example, Wood and Lakin (1979) suggested "that greater use be made of [behavior] rating scales to provide more comparable descriptions of groups of subjects" (p. 42). Similarly, Kauffman (1981) stated the belief that "although the best possible definition should be earnestly sought, the clear description of behavioral characteristics appears to be a more productive goal" (p. 21).

Third, there is an increased emphasis on the development of operational definitions of disturbance (Wood, 1979). Operational definitions would not simply define the student as disturbed, but specify the critical conditions (setting, behaviors, etc.) under which the targeted characteristics were demonstrated. This approach to a definition would have an advantage in that initial program planning could evolve from the definition.

It is doubtful that the problems relating to definitions will be resolved during the 1980s. In all probability the current definitions will continue to be used, chiefly for the convenience of educators. However, the trend toward specifying behaviors as an alternative to definitions will certainly gain momentum in the immediate future.

Classification of Disturbance

Classifying of disturbance is similar to the defining of it in that both activities suffer from the same problems and share the same trends. One distinct difference, however, is that the most widely accepted classification systems are psychiatrically and/or medically oriented. Consequently, educators' dependence on medical syndromes and treatments have caused these systems to be of little value in the classroom.

During the 1970s there was a concerted effort by a few individuals (e.g., Quay, 1972; Quay & Peterson, 1979) to develop a classification system that was more appropriate for education. However, even these systems continue to maintain an obvious terminology link with the medical classification systems.

With more disturbed students receiving their primary, if not exclusive, treatment in educational settings, it is apparent that classification systems must do more than simply produce terms that categorize syndromes of behaviors—they must first of all provide information that is educationally relevant. The possibility of this occurring in the 1980s is remote. Educators, unlike psychiatrists, do not have sufficient experience, expertise, or even interest in developing a classification system that categorizes and prescribes for behavioral, psychological, and environmental problems. On the other hand, educators are competent in the areas of instruction and management. Therefore, the projected classification trend is toward the development of systems to be used by teachers that include appropriate instructional and managerial procedures.

Developmental Behaviors

The developmental behaviors discussed in this book represent a theoretical ranking of age-appropriate behaviors that is equated with the severity of disturbance. The inclusion of a chapter on this topic typifies a trend that is growing rapidly. For example, Clarizio and McCoy (1976), Kauffman (1977, 1981), and Shea (1978) included detailed discussions of behaviors and their relationship to disturbance. In short, behaviors are becoming the exclusive criterion for defining, classifying, treating, and evaluating disturbance. However, behavior as such should not be the sole criterion, but rather the relationship between behavior and some functional estimate such as human growth and development or developmental psychology.

When behavior is evaluated as an isolated concept, as it has been in the past, several negative identification conditions are created. In particular, there has been an overidentification of males, acting-out behaviors, minority group members, and adolescents. Unfortunately, these past trends may also be the trends of the future, because schools continue to be conceptualized as environments where quiet, orderly, and obedient behaviors are considered normal, whereas disruptive behaviors are considered symptomatic of disturbance. Educators in the future, however, need to reevaluate this narrow behavioral perspective. The mere fact that noxious behaviors command the most attention is no justification for inadequately programming for nice, quiet, and compliant students who also may be disturbed.

Assessment of Characteristics

Over the past decade there was (and there will continue to be) a great deal of public concern over the inefficient and inappropriate use of economic and human resources in education. Consequently, the term "accountability" became a popular expression used to identify a process for holding educators more responsible for what happens in schools. The assessment of disturbance has been a part of this movement, and it will continue at an even more stringent level. Not only will there be increased accountability in the assessment of disturbance but also in the assessment of all significant classroom behaviors.

> The teaching profession is dedicated to the task of changing behavior—changing behavior demonstrably for the better. What can one say, then, of educational practice that does not include reliable and forthright measurement of the behavior change induced by the teacher's methodology? I believe this: *It is indefensible* (Kauffman, 1981, p. 284).

The assessment of characteristics was discussed in terms of three major types of procedures: tests, observations, and judgments. Of these, tests have come under sharp attack, particularly when the results are used to make critical decisions regarding the future of students. The use of intelligence and personality tests, for example, has been greatly limited in many states. Even standardized achievement tests and competency tests have a great many critics. Thus, the future of tests in the role of assessment is uncertain, but probably their use will be curtailed even more in the 1980s.

Observation, on the other hand, is clearly the assessment procedure of the future. The ability to use direct observational and accurate recording procedures will be required of teachers and other school personnel. Observation in this context does not include the global estimates so often expressed by teachers such as "Mary did not do well today" and "Johnny gets into trouble every day." Rather, observation competencies include scientific principles of measurement, so that the recorded data can be used to communicate in specific terms with students, parents, and others; to evaluate students' progress; and to make decisions regarding the effectiveness of the education strategies.

Judgment represents the best and the worst assessment procedure (Salvia & Ysseldyke, 1978, 1981). As unreliable and biased as some teachers' judgments are, the act of teaching cannot and should not be a purely scientific process. Despite all the fallacies present in individual judgments, it is necessary to recognize that not every significant characteristic of students—or of teachers—can be measured. Nonobservable characteristics such as feelings, values, and opinions are an important part of education and human relations. Thus, judgment is and will continue to be an important dimension of assessment. However, judgment should be tempered by honesty, openness, introspection, and observational data.

EDUCATIONAL STRATEGIES

Intervention Strategies

Eight specific educational intervention strategies, including their unique methodologies, were identified and discussed. Of these interventions, the data collected over the past two decades indicate that the behavioral methodology is the most frequently employed with disturbed students. Advocates of other educational interventions, equally as vehement as the behaviorists, appear to be losing ground in the "war for the child" (Garner, 1976). This intervention trend is expected to continue through the decade of the 1980s.

On a practical level it is difficult to understand why educators engage in such rigidity, accepting one intervention and excluding other intervention alternatives. Even though there may be as many reasons as there are teachers, there is one factor that affects all teachers: teacher training programs. Colleges of education often develop curriculum experiences that are devoted to the perpetuation of a single orientation, with minimal tolerance for alternative theories and interventions. This kind of dogmatic philosophy does not recognize the unique needs of individual students—or teachers. When prospective teachers are inundated with behaviorism or humanism, for example, their competence and possible even desire to implement an alternative intervention is minimized. Therefore, there is a trend toward an eclectic orientation in teacher training and ultimately in the implementation of eclectic interventions. The development of this trend, however, will be dependent on the degree to which teachers and, indirectly, parents and students express dissatisfaction and constructive solutions to teacher trainers, administrators, and the public.

The trends toward the increased use of behavioral interventions and the possibility of eclectic interventions are somewhat contradictory. Whereas the first is a matter of record, the second is an optimistic projection that may be only partially realized. In the immediate future, behavioral interventions undoubtedly will continue to flourish. However, over a more extended period of time the value of variable or eclectic interventions should be more fully realized.

Teaching-Learning Strategies

The classroom represents such a complex, interwoven variety of educational factors that it is difficult to single out specific future directions. Consequently, speculations regarding the future of a teaching-learning strategy may omit, minimize, or inaccurately project some trends.

If it is true that the past is the best predictor of the future, then a great many future educational conditions will be carried over from the past decade. For example, it is suspected that the following conditions will continue to represent teaching-learning strategies, particularly with reference to disturbed students:

Traditional curriculum experiences (i.e., basic skills instruction, basic objectives and standard materials)

Authoritarian instruction (i.e., inflexible external control teacher style, expectations of student compliance, and passive learning environments)

A lack of confidence in students (i.e., low expectations, punitive discipline such as corporal punishment and suspension, and academic failure)

These conditions will probably continue because there are relatively few indications that the need for change is recognized or even desired. "The harsh reality in most schools seems to be . . . that no one really wants to know what is going on" (Knoblock & Goldstein, 1971, p. 13). This kind of public apathy combined with internal school conditions (e.g., large classes, limited resources, and academic competency testing) militates against any substantive change in the near future. Although many teachers recognize the need for change, their efforts actually to influence educational conditions are typically sporadic, unorganized, and generally ineffective. The energy and enthusiasm that teachers typically demonstrate during the first few years of teaching often begin to diminish under the pressure of mounds of paperwork, numerous meetings, administrative requirements, and an endless procession of students.

Yet teachers are agents of change! This role has been minimized, even scoffed at by many parents, administrators, students, and teachers themselves. Although the impact of some teachers has been minimal, even negative, the vast majority of teachers have had some positive effects of the vast majority of students. However, if teachers expect to continue to have a persistent positive impact on disturbed students in the classroom, then several new directions appear necessary.

1. Curriculum experiences should include both cognitive and affective objectives. Historically, education has emphasized the teaching and learning of basic cognitive skills, particularly the "three Rs." Although the past few decades have witnessed more diversified curriculums, the trend is to go back to these basic objectives. However, cognitive skills represent only a part of the learner's needs; affective skills are also important, particularly for disturbed

students (Weinstein & Fantini, 1970). The reduction of deviant behavior, the development of human resources, and the facilitation of emotional health require a curriculum for affective education. For example, social behaviors (Stephens, 1981), self-control (Fagen, Long, & Stevens, 1976), and self-concept (Canfield & Wells, 1976) are critical student skills that are necessary to reduce disturbance.

2. There needs to be a greater cooperative effort between schools and community resources, particularly parents. Although it may be true that many parents are inflexible, uncooperative, or uninterested, the same may be said for many teachers. This kind of closed, negative, and often hostile attitude leaves the disturbed student in the middle, or on the battleground, in the conflict between parents and teachers. This condition, when it exists, cannot prevail. Educators must begin to think of parents as program resources: as providers of information, educational assistants, and homebound instructors. The education of disturbed students must go beyond the school or home and include both. This same cooperative effort should prevail with regard to other personnel involved in the education and treatment of disturbance, such as physicians, psychologists, and social workers.

3. Educators, particularly principals, need to develop ways to prevent teacher burnout. The negative attitudes, complaining, and frustration expressed by teachers is at least partially the result of separation, loneliness, and powerlessness. When teachers are "trapped" in a room with 30 students, when they are evaluated on the orderliness and quietness of their classrooms, and when they have limited opportunities to communicate with other adults, burnout is a likely result.

> How paradoxical it is that so many teachers do not see themselves as resources within their own classrooms, but rather as keepers of the peace, curriculum and school tradition. It is this keeper role too that needs to be changed . . . (Knoblock & Goldstein, 1971, p. 14).

In order to begin to deal with the teacher burnout problem, more effective communication within schools needs to be developed. Teachers need the opportunity to be more flexible, to obtain validation for what they are doing, to be curriculum planners, and, perhaps most important, to receive positive feedback from adults, not just students.

Behavior Management Strategies

Historically, the management of disruptive student behaviors has been conceptualized as a secondary educational process that infringes upon instructional time. Consequently, most management strategies were relatively routine, emphasizing authority-oriented techniques that focused on surface behaviors. Although this emphasis may have been effective when the classroom represented a relatively homogeneous group of achievement-oriented students, today's classrooms contain a greater diversity of students. Historical management strategies, consequently, have become less effective.

Behavior management can no longer be considered a secondary educational process. Management should be as much of a student learning experience as the academic curriculum experiences. The management trend of the future should be the employment of a wider variety of strategies that are specifically designed for individual students. Although authoritarian techniques may continue to be the primary strategy, increased emphasis on alternative management strategies should gain momentum during the 1980s.

A Matching Model

A matching model was constructed as an alternative to the intuitive, infrequent, and dogmatic implementation of specific educational strategies with all disturbed students. The essence of the matching model is that there is a functional interaction or congruence among the characteristics of disturbance and educational strategies, including interventions, teaching styles, management strategies, and educational objectives. In short, certain characteristics and educational strategies interact to produce more effective and efficient combinations of congruent arrangements.

Although this particular matching model may witness limited implementation, there is a growing body of knowledge that supports the concept of person-environment interaction. Although the specific effects of different combinations have not been clearly and unquestionably demonstrated, there is sufficient evidence to warrant the belief that matching models of some sort will be more widely accepted in the near future. The inability of traditional educational programs to educate students with diverse characteristics will mandate the need for research, administrative assignments, and classroom adaptations that are designed to functionally match characteristics and educational strategies.

Future Directions

This chapter has identified past educational practices as well as emerging trends that will be evident in the future. These trends are consistent with the projections made by Stainback and Stainback (1980): "(a) placement of exceptional children in normal settings; (b) direct and functional methods of identifying programming needs; (c) individualization of instruction; (d) education as a primary treatment approach; and (e) increasing concern for quality programming" (p. 240). Unfortunately, economic conditions rather than educational needs will largely determine the extent to which these trends become a reality. Although many teachers, parents, administrators, and other professionals are seeking relevant solutions to complex problems involving disturbed students, the limitations imposed by dwindling resources, traditional attitudes, and dehumanizing practices will deter substantive changes. Charles Dickens' opening sentence in *A Tale of Two Cities* can be used in retrospect at the end of this decade to summarize the 1980s for disturbed students: "It was the best of times, it was the worst of times."

References

Achenbach, T. M. *Developmental psychopathology*. New York: Ronald Press, 1974.

Adams, R., & Biddle, B. *Realities of teaching*. New York: Holt, Rinehart & Winston, 1970.

Ahmann, J. S., & Glock, M. D. *Evaluating pupil growth*. Boston: Allyn & Bacon, 1959.

American Psychiatric Association. *Diagnostic and statistical manual of mental disorders (DSM)*. Washington, D.C.: American Psychiatric Association, 1951 (2nd ed., 1968; 3rd ed., 1980).

American Psychological Association. *Standards for educational and psychological tests and manuals*. Washington, D.C.: American Psychological Association, 1966.

Anderson, R. C. Learning in discussions: A resume of the authoritarian-democratic studies. *Harvard Educational Review*, 1959, *29*, 201–215.

Anderson, R. M., Greer, J. G., & Odle, S. J. (Eds.) *Individualizing educational materials for special children in the mainstream*. Baltimore: University Park Press, 1978.

Andrews, J., & Bartolini, P. *Need hierarchies and programming considerations for emotionally disturbed children*. Unpublished manuscript. Syracuse, N.Y.: Syracuse University, 1964.

Azrin, N. M., & Holz, W. C. Punishment. In W. K. Honig (Ed.), *Operant behavior: Areas of research and application*. New York: Appleton-Century-Crofts, 1966.

Bakan, R. Malnutrition and learning. *Phi Delta Kappan*, 1970, *51*, 527–530.

Baker, A. M. The efficacy of the Feingold K-P Diet: A review of pertinent empirical investigations. *Behavioral Disorders*, 1980, *6*, 32–35.

Bakwin, H., & Bakwin, R. M. *Behavior disorders in children* (4th ed.). Philadelphia: W. B. Saunders, 1972.

Baldwin, A. L. *Theories of child development*. New York: John Wiley & Sons, 1967.

Bandura, A. Vicarious processes: A case of no-trial learning. In L. Berkowitz (Ed.), *Advances in experimental social psychology* (Vol. 2). New York: Academic Press, 1965.

Bandura, A. Psychotherapy based on modeling principles. In A. E. Bergin & S. L. Garfield (Eds.), *Handbook of psychotherapy and behavior change*. New York: John Wiley & Sons, 1971.

Bender, L. *A visual motor gestalt test and its clinical use*. New York: The American Orthopsychiatric Association, 1938.

327

328   References

Bellak, L., & Bellak, S. *Children's Apperception Test*. Larchmont, N.Y.: C.P.S., 1965.

Bennett, N. *Teaching styles and pupil progress*. Cambridge, Mass.: Harvard University Press, 1976.

Bills, R. E. Personality changes during student centered teaching. *Journal of Educational Research*, 1956, *50*, 121–126.

Blackham, G. J. & Silberman, A. *Modification of child and adolescent behavior* (3rd ed.). Belmont, Calif.: Wadsworth Publishing Co., 1980.

Blatt, B. Some persistently recurring assumptions concerning the mentally subnormal. *Training School Bulletin*, 1960, *57*, 48–59.

Blatt, B. *Exodus from pandemonium*. Boston: Allyn & Bacon, 1970.

Bloom, B. S. (Ed.) *Taxonomy of educational objectives. Handbook I: Cognitive domain*. New York: David McKay Co., 1956.

Bloom, B. S. *Stability and change in human characteristics*. New York: John Wiley & Sons, 1964.

Bloom, B. S. *Human characteristics and school learning*. New York: McGraw-Hill, 1976.

Blum, G. *Blacky pictures: A technique for the exploration of personality dynamics*. Ann Arbor, Mich.: Psychodynamic Instruments, 1967.

Bower, E. *Early identification of emotionally handicapped children in school* (2nd ed.) Springfield, Ill.: Charles C Thomas, 1969.

Braun, S. J., Mathilda, S. H., & Lasher, M. G. Teachers of disturbed preschool children: An analysis of teaching styles. *American Journal of Orthopsychiatry*, 1969, *39*, 609–618.

Brookover, W. B., & Schneider, J. M. Academic environments and elementary school achievement. *Journal of Research and Development in Education*, 1975, *9*, 83–91.

Brophy, J. E., & Good, T. L. *Teacher-student relationships: Causes and consequences*. New York: Holt, Rinehart & Winston, 1974.

Browder, D. The critical need for inservice training in behavior management. *Education Unlimited*, 1981, *2*(5), 49–53.

Buck, J., & Jolles, I. *House-Tree-Person*. Los Angeles: Western Psychological Services, 1966.

Buckley, N. K., & Walker, H. M. *Modifying classroom behavior*. Champaign, Ill.: Research Press, 1970.

Bureau of Education for the Handicapped, U.S. Office of Education. *Annual report*. Washington, D.C.: U.S. Government Printing Office, 1975.

Burke, D. Counter theoretical interventions in emotional disturbance. In W. C. Rhodes & M. L. Tracy (Eds.), *A study of child variance*. Vol. 2: *Interventions*. Ann Arbor, Mich.: University of Michigan, 1972.

Buros, O. K. (Ed.) *Seventh mental measurements yearbook*. Highland Park, N.J.: Gryphon Press, 1972.

Bush, A. J., Kennedy, J. J., & Cruickshank, D. R. *An empirical investigation of teacher clarity*. Paper presented at the annual meeting of the American Educational Research Association, New York, April 1977.

Buss, A. H. *Psychopathology*. New York: John Wiley & Sons, 1966.

Calhoun, G., & Elliott, R. N. Self concept and academic achievement of educable retarded and emotionally disturbed pupils. *Exceptional Children*, 1977, *43*, 379–380.

Canfield, J., & Wells, H. C. *100 ways to enhance self-concept in the classroom*. Englewood Cliffs, N.J.: Prentice-Hall, 1976.

Cartwright, C. A., & Cartwright, G. P. *Developing observational skills*. New York: McGraw-Hill, 1974.

Cattell, R., Coan, R., & Belloff, H. *Jr.-Sr. High School Personality Questionnaire*. Indianapolis: Bobbs-Merrill, 1969.

Charles, C. M. *Individualizing instruction*. St. Louis: C. V. Mosby, 1976.

Cheney, C., & Morse, W. C. Psychodynamic interventions in emotional disturbance. In W. C. Rhodes & M. L. Tracy (Eds.), *A study of child variance*. Vol. 2: *Interventions*. Ann Arbor, Mich.: University of Michigan, 1972.

Chorover, S. L. Big brother and psychotechnology. *Psychology Today*, 1973, 7, 43–69.

Clarizio, H. F., & McCoy, G. F. *Behavior disorders in children* (2nd ed.). New York: Thomas' Y. Crowell, 1976.

Coan, R., & Cattell, R. *Early Childhood Personality Questionnaire*. Champaign, Ill.: Institute for Personality and Ability Testing, 1970.

Cohen, E. G. Sociology and the classroom: Setting the conditions for teacher-student interaction. *Review of Educational Research*, 1972, 42, 441–452.

Coker, H., Medley, D. M., & Soar, R. S. How valid are expert opinions about effective teaching? *Phi Delta Kappan*, 1980, 62, 131–134.

Coleman, J. C. *Abnormal psychology and modern life*. Glenview, Ill.: Scott, Foresman & Co., 1964.

Coleman, J. S. *Equality of educational opportunity*. Washington, D.C.: U.S. Government Printing Office, 1966.

Combs, A. Humanistic education: Too tender for a tough world? *Phi Delta Kappan*, 1981, 62, 446–449.

Cooper, J. O. *Measurement and analysis of behavioral techniques*. Columbus, O.: Charles E. Merrill, 1974.

Cott, A. Megavitamins: The orthomolecular approach to behavior disorders and learning disabilities. *Academic Therapy*, 1972, 7, 245–258.

Cronbach, L. J., & Snow, R. E. *Aptitudes and instructional methods*. New York: Irvington Publishers, 1977.

Cruickshank, W. M., Bentzen, F. A., Ratzeburg, F. H., and Tannhauser, M. T. *A teaching method for brain-injured and hyperactive children*. Syracuse, N.Y.: Syracuse University Press, 1961.

Cruickshank, W. M., & Quay, H. C. Learning and physical environment: The necessity for research and research design. *Exceptional Children*, 1970, 37, 261–268.

Cullinan, D., & Epstein, M. Administrative definitions of behavior disorders: Status and directions. In F. H. Wood & K. C. Lakin (Eds.), *Disturbing, disordered or disturbed? Perspectives on the definition of problem behavior in educational settings*. Minneapolis, Minn.: University of Minnesota, 1979.

Curran, T. J., & Algozzine, B. Ecological disturbance: A test of the matching hypothesis. *Behavioral Disorders*, 1980, 5, 169–174.

Dale, E. *Building a learning environment*. Bloomington, Ind.: Phi Delta Kappa, 1972.

Dave, R. H. *Taxonomy of educational objectives: Psychomotor domain*. New Delhi, India: National Institute of Education, 1970.

Des Jarlais, D. C. Mental illness as social deviance. In W. C. Rhodes and M. L. Tracy (Eds.) *A study of child variance*. Ann Arbor, Mich.: University of Michigan, 1972.

Despert, J. L. *The emotionally disturbed child—Then and now*. New York: Robert Brunner, Inc., 1965.

Dizney, H. *Classroom evaluation for teachers.* Dubuque, Ia.: William C. Brown Co., 1971.

Drew, C. J. Research on the psychological-behavioral effects of the physical environment. *Review of Educational Research,* 1971, *41,* 447–465.

Dunn, L. M. Special education for the mildly retarded—Is much of it justifiable? *Exceptional Children,* 1968, *35,* 5–22.

Durkheim, E. *The division of labor in society.* New York: The Free Press, 1965.

Durkin, D. Schools don't teach comprehension. *Educational Leadership,* 1981, *21,* 453–454.

Edwards, A. *Edwards Personality Inventory.* Chicago: Science Research Associates, 1966.

Erikson, E. H. Youth and the life cycle. *Children,* 1960, *7,* 43–49.

Erikson, E. H. *Childhood and society* (2nd ed.). New York: Norton, 1963.

Erikson, E. H. Youth and the life cycle. In D. E. Hamachek (Ed.), *The self in growth, teaching, and learning.* Englewood Cliffs, N.J.: Prentice-Hall, 1965.

Erikson, E. *Identity, youth and crisis.* New York: Norton, 1968.

Fagan, S. A., & Hill, J. *Behavior management.* Washington, D.C.: Psychoeducational Resources, 1977.

Fagen, S., & Long, N. J. A psychoeducational curriculum approach to teaching self-control. *Behavioral Disorders,* 1979, *4,* 68–82.

Fagen, S., Long, N., & Stevens, D. *Teaching children self-control: Preventing emotional and learning problems in the elementary school.* Columbus, O.: Charles E. Merrill, 1975.

Fairchild, T. N. *Managing the hyperactive child in the classroom.* Austin, Tex.: Learning Concepts, 1975.

Feagans, L. Ecological theory as a model for constructing a theory of emotional disturbance. In W. C. Rhodes & M. L. Tracy (Eds.), *A study of child variance.* Vol. 2: *Interventions.* Ann Arbor, Mich.: University of Michigan, 1972.

Feingold, B. F. Hyperkinesis and learning linked to the ingestion of artificial food colors and flavors. *Journal of Learning Disabilities,* 1976, *9,* 551–559.

Fenichel, C. Psycho-educational approaches for seriously disturbed children in the classroom. In P. Knoblock (Ed.), *Intervention approaches in educating emotionally disturbed children.* Syracuse, N.Y.: Syracuse University Press, 1966.

Fine, M. J. *Intervention with hyperactive children.* Jamaica, N.Y.: SP Medical & Scientific Books, 1980.

Fink, A. H., & Glass, R. M. Contemporary issues in the education of the behaviorally disordered. In L. Mann & D. A. Sabitino (Eds.), *The first review of special education* (Vol. 2). Philadelphia: JSE Press, 1973.

Fink, A. H., Glass, R. M., & Guskin, S. L. An analysis of teacher education programs in behavior disorders. *Exceptional Children,* 1975, *42,* 47–48.

Fitt, S. The individual and his environment. *School Review,* 1974, *82,* 617–620.

Fitts, W. *Tennessee Self Concept Inventory.* Nashville, Tenn.: Counselor Recordings and Tests, 1965.

Flanders, N. A. *Teacher influence, pupil attitudes, and achievement.* Washington, D.C.: U.S. Government Printing Office, 1965.

Fox, R. S., Boies, H. E., Brainard, E., Fletcher, E., Huge, J. S., Martin, C. L., Maynard, W., Monasmith, J., Olivero, J., Schmuck, R., Shaheen, T.

A., & Stegeman, W. H. *School climate improvement: A challenge to school administrators.* Bloomington, Ind.: Phi Delta Kappa, 1974.

Fox, R., Luszki, M. B., & Schmuck, R. *Diagnosing classroom learning environments.* Chicago: Science Research Associates, 1966.

Fraser, B. J., & Rentoul, A. J. Person-environment fit in open classrooms. *Journal of Educational Research,* 1980, *73,* 159–167.

Freud, A. *The ego and mechanisms of defense.* New York: International Universities Press, 1946.

Freud, A. *Psychoanalysis for teachers and parents.* Boston: Beacon Press, 1935.

Gadow, K. D. *Children on medication: A primer for school personnel.* Reston, Va.: The Council for Exceptional Children, 1979.

Gajar, A. Educable mentally retarded, learning disabled, emotionally disturbed: Similarities and differences. *Exceptional Children,* 1979, *45,* 470–472.

Gallagher, P. A. *Teaching students with behavior disorders: Techniques for classroom instruction.* Denver, Co.: Love Publishing Co., 1979.

Garner, H. G. A truce in the "war for the child." *Exceptional Children,* 1976, *42,* 315–320.

Gazda, G. M., Asbury, F. R., Balzer, F. J., Childers, W. C., Desselle, R. E., & Walters, R. P. *Human relations development.* Boston: Allyn & Bacon, 1973.

Geer, B. Teaching. *International Encyclopedia of the Social Sciences.* New York: Macmillan, 1968.

Glass, G., & Smith, M. Meta-analysis of research on class size and achievement. *Educational Evaluation and Policy Analysis,* 1979, *1,* 2–16.

Glasser, W. *Reality therapy: A new approach to psychiatry.* New York: Harper & Row, 1965.

Glasser, W. *Schools without failure.* New York: Harper & Row, 1969.

Glavin, J. P. Persistence of behavior disorders in children. *Exceptional Children,* 1972, *38,* 367–376.

Gnagey, W. J. *Controlling classroom misbehavior.* Washington, D.C.: National Education Association, 1965.

Goertzel, V., & Goertzel, M. *Cradles of eminence.* Boston: Little, Brown, 1962.

Good, T. L., & Brophy, J. E. *Looking in classrooms.* New York: Harper & Row, 1978.

Goodman, P. No processing whatever. In R. Gross & B. Gross (Eds.), *Radical school reform.* New York: Simon & Schuster, 1969.

Gordon, I. J. *Studying the child in school.* New York: John Wiley and Sons, 1966.

Gordon, T. *Parent effectiveness training.* New York: Peter H. Wyden, Inc., 1970.

Gough, H. *California Psychological Inventory.* Palo Alto, Calif.: Consulting Psychologists Press, 1969.

Gropper, G. L., Kress, G. C., Hughes, R., & Pekich, J. Training teachers to recognize and manage social and emotional problems in the classroom. *Journal of Teacher Education,* 1968, *19,* 477–485.

Grosenick, J. K., & Huntze, S. L. *National needs assessment in behavior disorders: Adolescent behavior disorders.* Columbia, Mo.: Department of Special Education, University of Missouri, 1980.

Gross, R., & Gross, B. (Eds.) *Radical school reform.* New York: Simon & Schuster, 1969.

Group for the Advancement of Psychiatry. *Psychological disorders in childhood: A proposed classification.* New York: Group for the Advancement of Psychiatry, 1968.

Gump, P. V. What's happening in the elementary classroom? In I. Westbury & A. A. Bellack (Eds.), *Research into classroom practice.* New York: Teachers College Press, 1971.

Gump, P. V. Operating environments in schools of open and traditional design. *School Review*, 1974, *82*, 575–593.

Hall, C. S. *A primer of Freudian psychology.* New York: World Publishing Co., 1954.

Hall, R. V., Hawkins, R. P., & Axelrod, S. Measuring and recording student behavior: A behavior analysis approach. In R. A. Weinberg & F. H. Wood (Eds.), *Observation of pupils and teachers in mainstream and special education settings: Alternative strategies.* Minneapolis, Minn.: University of Minnesota, 1975.

Hallahan, D. P., & Kauffman, J. M. Labels, categories, behaviors: ED, LD, and EMR reconsidered. *Journal of Special Education*, 1977, *11*, 139–149.

Hamachek, D. Characteristics of good teachers and implications for teacher education. *Phi Delta Kappan*, 1969, *50*, 341–345.

Haring, N. G., & Phillips, E. L. *Educating emotionally disturbed children.* New York: McGraw-Hill, 1962.

Hartman, H. Psychoanalysis as a scientific theory. In S. Hook (Ed.), *Psychoanalysis: Scientific method and philosophy.* New York: New York University, 1959.

Harvey, O. J., Hunt, D. E., & Schroder, H. M. *Conceptual systems and personality organization.* New York: John Wiley & Sons, 1961.

Hathaway, S., & McKinley, J. *Minnesota Multiphasic Personality Inventory.* New York: Psychological Corporation, 1967.

Havighurst, R. J. Life-span developmental psychology and education. *Educational Researcher*, 1980, *9*(10), 3–8.

Hawes, R. M. Reality therapy: An approach to encourage individual and social responsibility in the elementary school. *Elementary School Guidance and Counseling*, 1969, *4*, 120–127.

Herbert, M. *Emotional problems of development in children.* London: Academic Press, 1974.

Hessler, G. L., & Sosnowsky, W. P. A review of aptitude-treatment interaction studies with the handicapped. *Psychology in the Schools*, 1979, *16*, 388–394.

Hewett, F. M. *The emotionally disturbed child in the classroom* (1st ed.). Boston: Allyn & Bacon, 1968.

Hewett, F. M. *Education of exceptional learners.* Boston: Allyn & Bacon, 1974.

Hewett, F. M., with Forness, S. R. *Education of exceptional learners* (2nd ed.). Boston: Allyn & Bacon, 1977.

Hewett, F. M., & Taylor, F. D. *The emotionally disturbed child in the class: The orchestration of success* (2nd ed.) Boston: Allyn & Bacon, 1980.

Hilgard, E. R., & Bower, G. H. *Theories of learning* (3rd ed.) New York: Appleton-Century-Crofts, 1966.

Hobbs, N. Helping disturbed children: Psychological and ecological strategies. *American Psychologist*, 1967, *22*, 1105–1115.

Hobbs, N. *Futures of children*. San Francisco: Jossey-Bass, 1975.

Hollister, W. G., & Goldston, S. E. *Considerations for planning classes for the emotionally handicapped*. Reston, Va.: The Council for Exceptional Children, 1962.

Holt, J. *How children learn*. New York: Pitman Publishing Corp., 1967.

Holtzman, W. *Holtzman Inkblot Technique*. New York: Psychological Corp., 1966.

Horton, D. *Comparison of behavior problem rankings*. Mimeographed. Memphis: Memphis State University, 1973.

Howard, A. W. Discipline is caring. *Today's Education*, 1972, *61*, 52–53.

Hunt, D. E. *Matching models in education: The coordination of teaching methods with student characteristics*. Toronto, Ontario, Canada: Ontario Institute for Studies in Education, 1971.

Hunt, D. E. Learning styles and teaching strategies. *Behavioral and Social Science Teacher*, 1974, *2*, 22–34.

Ilg, F. L., & Ames, L. B. *Child behavior*. New York: Dell Publishing Co., 1960.

Illich, I. *Deschooling society*. New York: Penguin Books, 1973.

Jackson, J. M. Structural characteristics of norms. In N. B. Henry (Ed.), *The dynamics of instructional groups*. Chicago: National Society for the Study of Education, 1960.

Jackson, P. W. *Life in classrooms*. New York: Holt, Rinehart & Winston, 1968.

Janicki, T. C., & Peterson, P. L. Aptitude-treatment interaction effects of variations in direct instruction. *American Educational Research Journal*, 1981, *18*, 63–82.

Jensen, G. The sociopsychological structure of the instructional group. In N. B. Henry (Ed.), *The dynamics of instructional groups*. Chicago: National Society for the Study of Education, 1960.

Jersild, A. T. *When teachers face themselves*. New York: Teachers College, Columbia University, 1955.

Johnson, D. W. Student-student interaction: The neglected variable in education. *Educational Researcher*, 1981, *10*(1), 5–10.

Johnson, D. W., & Johnson, R. *Learning together and alone: Cooperation, competition and individualization*. Englewood Cliffs, N.J.: Prentice-Hall, 1975.

Johnson, J. A. The etiology of hyperactivity. *Exceptional Children*, 1981, *47*, 348–354.

Johnson, J. L. *Definitions and explanations: Observing and recording behavior*. Unpublished manuscript, Syracuse University, 1968.

Johnson, L. V., & Bany, M. A. *Classroom management: Theory and skill training*. New York: Macmillan, 1970.

Jones, R. S., & Tanner, L. N. Classroom discipline: The unclaimed legacy. *Phi Delta Kappan*, 1981, *67*, 494–497.

Joseph, S. M. (Ed.) *The me nobody knows*. New York: Avon Books, 1969.

Joyce, B., & Harootunian, B. *The structure of teaching*. Chicago: Science Research Associates, 1967.

Joyce, B. & Weil, M. *Models of teaching*. Englewood Cliffs, N.J.: Prentice-Hall, 1972. (2nd ed., 1980).

Kagan, J., & Moss, H. A. *Birth to maturity: A study in psychological development*. New York: John Wiley & Sons, 1962.

Kameya, L. I. Behavioral interventions in emotional disturbance. In W. C. Rhodes and M. L. Tracy (Eds.), *A study of child variance*. Vol. 2: *Interventions*. Ann Arbor, Mich.: University of Michigan, 1972.

Kanner, L. *Research on emotionally disturbed children*. Paper presented at the meeting of the Society for Research in Child Development, Pennsylvania State University, March, 1961.

Kanner, L. Emotionally disturbed children: A historical review. *Child Development*, 1962, *32*, 92–102.

Kanner, L. *Childhood psychosis: Initial studies and new insights*. Washington, D.C.: V. H. Winston, 1973.

Karlin, M. S., & Berger, R. *Discipline and the disruptive child*. West Nyack, N.Y.: Parker Publishing Co., 1972.

Karnes, M. B., & Teska, J. A. Children's response to intervention programs. In J. J. Gallagher (Ed.), *The application of child development research to exceptional children*. Reston, Va., The Council for Exceptional Children, 1975.

Kauffman, J. M. *Characteristics of children's behavior disorders*. Columbus, O.: Charles E. Merrill, 1977 (2nd ed., 1981).

Kauffman, J. M. An historical perspective on disordered behavior and an alternative conceptualization of exceptionality. In F. H. Wood & K. C. Lakin (Eds.), *Disturbing, disordered or disturbed? Perspectives on the definition of problem behavior in educational settings*. Minneapolis, Minn.: University of Minnesota, 1979.

Kauffman, J. M., and Lewis, C. D. *Teaching children with behavior disorders: Personal perspectives*. Columbus, O.: Charles E. Merrill, 1974.

Kavale, K., & Hirshoren, A. Public school and university teacher training programs for behaviorally disordered children: Are they compatible? *Behavioral Disorders*, 1980, *5*, 151–155.

Kazdin, A. E. *The token economy*. New York: Plenum, 1977.

Kelly, T. J., Bullock, L. M., and Dykes, M. K. Behavioral disorders: Teachers' perceptions. *Exceptional Children*, 1977, *43*, 316–318.

Kenniston, K. *All our children: The American family under pressure*. New York: Harcourt Brace Jovanovich, 1977.

Kessler, J. W. *Psychopathology of childhood*. Englewood Cliffs, N.J.: Prentice-Hall, 1966.

Kirk, S. A., & Gallagher, J. J. *Educating exceptional children* (3rd ed.). Boston: Houghton Mifflin Co., 1979.

Knoblock, P. Open education for emotionally disturbed children. *Exceptional Children*, 1973, *39*, 358–365.

Knoblock, P., Barnes, E., Apter, S. and Taylor, S. *Preparing humanistic teachers for troubled children*. Syracuse, N.Y.: Syracuse University Press, 1974.

Knoblock, P. & Goldstein, A. P. *The lonely teacher*. Boston: Allyn & Bacon, 1971.

Knopf, I. J. *Childhood psychopathology: A developmental approach*. Englewood Cliffs, N.J.: Prentice-Hall, 1979.

Kohl, H. R. *The open classroom*. New York: Vintage Books, 1969.

Kohlberg, L. The cognitive-developmental approach to moral education. *Phi Delta Kappan*, 1975, *61*, 670–677.

Kohlberg, L., LaCrosse, J., & Ricks, D. The predictability of adult mental health from childhood behavior. In B. Wolman (Ed.), *Manual of child psychopathology*. New York: McGraw-Hill, 1972.

Koppitz, E. M. *The Bender gestalt test for young children*. New York: Grune & Stratton, 1964.

Koppitz, E. M. *Human Figure Drawing Test*. New York: Grune & Stratton, 1968.

Kounin, J. S., An analysis of teachers' managerial techniques. *Psychology in the Schools*, 1967, *4*, 221–227.

Kounin, J. S. *Discipline and group management in classrooms*. New York: Holt, Rinehart & Winston, 1970.

Kozol, J. *The night is dark and I am far from home*. Boston: Houghton Mifflin, 1975.

Krathwohl, D. R., Bloom, B. S., and Masia, B. B., *Taxonomy of educational objectives. Handbook II: Affective domain*. New York: David McKay Co., 1956.

LaBenne, W. D., & Greene, B. I. *Educational implications of self-concept theory*. Pacific Palisades, Calif.: Goodyear Publishing Co., 1969.

Landsman, M., & Dillard, H. *Evanston Early Identification Scale*. Chicago: Follett Educational Corp., 1967.

Lee, L. C. *Personality development in childhood*. Belmont, Calif.: Wadsworth Publishing Co., 1976.

Levy, F. Hyperkinesis and diet: A double-blind crossover trial with a tartrazine challenge. *The Medical Journal of Australia*, 1978, *1*, 61–64.

Lewin, K., Lippitt, R., & White, R. K. Patterns of aggressive behavior in experimentally created social climates. *Journal of Social Psychology*, 1939, *10*, 271–299.

Lindholm, B. W., Touliatos, J., & Rich, A. Racial differences in behavior disordered children. *Journal of School Psychology*, 1978, *16*, 42–48.

Lipsitt, L. P. A self-concept scale for children and its relationship to the children's form of the manifest anxiety scale. *Child Development*, 1958, *29*, 463–472.

Llorens, L. A., & Rubin, E. Z. *Developing ego functions in disturbed children*. Detroit: Wayne State University Press, 1967.

Long, N. J., Morse, W. C., & Newman, R. G. (Eds.) *Conflict in the classroom: The education of emotionally disturbed children* (2nd ed.). Belmont, Calif.: Wadsworth Publishing Co., 1971 (3rd ed., 1976).

Long, N. J., & Newman, R. G. Managing surface behavior of children in school. In N. J. Long, W. C. Morse, & R. G. Newman, (Eds.), *Conflict in the classroom: The education of emotionally disturbed children* (3rd ed.). Belmont, Calif.: Wadsworth Publishing Co., 1976.

MacFarlane, J., Allen, L., & Honzik, M. *A developmental study of the behavior problems of normal children*. Berkeley, Calif.: University of California Press, 1954.

Madaus, G. F., Woods, E. M., & Nuthall, R. L. A causal model analysis of Bloom's taxonomy. *American Educational Research Journal*, 1973, *10*, 253–262.

Mahoney, M. J. *Abnormal psychology: Perspectives on human variance*. San Francisco: Harper & Row, 1980.

Marshall, H. H. *Positive discipline and classroom interaction*. Springfield, Ill.: Charles C Thomas, 1972.

Maslow, A. H. *Motivation and personality* (2nd ed.). New York: Harper & Row, 1970.

Maurer, C. G. Of puppets, feelings, and children. *Elementary School Guidance Counselor,* 1977, *12,* 26–32.

McKeachie, W. J. Procedures and techniques of teaching: A survey of experimental studies. In N. Sanford (Ed.), *The American college: A psychological and social interpretation of higher learning.* New York: John Wiley & Sons, 1962.

McKeachie, W. J. Research on teaching at the college and university level. In N. L. Gage (Ed.), *Handbook of research on teaching.* Chicago: Rand McNally Co., 1973.

Mehrabian, A. *Public places and private spaces.* New York: Basic Books, Inc., 1976.

Merton, R. *Social structure and social theory.* New York: The Free Press, 1957.

Meyer, W. J. *Developmental psychology.* New York: The Center for Applied Research in Education, 1964.

Miller, A. Conceptual matching models and interaction research in education. *Review of Educational Research,* 1981, *51,* 33–84.

Million, T. *Theories of psychopathology.* Philadelphia: W. B. Saunders Co., 1967.

Morse, W. C. Diagnosing and guiding relationships between group and individual class members. In N. B. Henry (Ed.), *The dynamics of instructional groups.* Chicago: National Society for the Study of Education, 1960.

Morse, W. C. The education of socially maladjusted and emotionally disturbed children. In W. M. Cruickshank & G. O. Johnson (Eds.), *Education of exceptional children and youth* (3rd ed.). Englewood Cliffs, N.J.: Prentice-Hall, 1975.

Morse, W. C. Crisis intervention in school mental health and special classes for the disturbed. In N. J. Long, W. C. Morse, & R. G. Newman (Eds.), *Conflict in the classroom: The education of emotionally disturbed children* (3rd ed.). Belmont, Calif.: Wadsworth Publishing Co., 1976.

Morse, W. C. Serving the needs of individuals with behavior disorders. *Exceptional Children,* 1977, *44,* 158–164.

Morse, W. C., Cutler, R. L., & Fink, A. H. *Public school classes for the emotionally handicapped: A research analysis.* Reston, Va.: The Council for Exceptional Children, 1964.

Morse, W. C., & Smith, J. M. *Videotape training packages in child variance, Workshop 5: Alternative views.* Ann Arbor, Mich.: University of Michigan, 1978.

Morse, W. C., & Smith, J. M. *Understanding child variance.* Reston, Va.: The Council for Exceptional Children, 1980.

Morse, W. C., Smith, J. M., & Acker, N. *The biophysical approach: A self-instructional module.* Ann Arbor, Mich.: University of Michigan, 1977.

Morse, W. C., Smith, J. M., & Acker, N. *The sociological approach: A self-instructional module.* Ann Arbor, Mich.: University of Michigan, 1978.

Morse, W. C., Smith, J. M., & Won, H. *The behavioral approach: A self-instructional module.* Ann Arbor, Mich.: University of Michigan, 1977.

Mosston, M. *Teaching: From command to discovery.* Belmont, Calif.: Wadsworth Publishing Co., 1972.

Moyer, K. E. The physiology of violence. *Psychology Today,* 1973, *7,* 35–38.

Moyer, K. E. The physiology of violence: Allergy and aggression. *Psychology Today*, 1975, *9*, 77–79.

Murray, H. A. *Thematic Apperception Test*. Cambridge, Mass.: Harvard University Press, 1943.

National Society for Autistic Children, *Working definition of the syndrome of autism*. Mimeographed. Washington, D.C.: National Society for Autistic Children, 1977.

Neill, A. S. *Summerhill: A radical approach to child rearing*. New York: Hart, 1960.

Newcomer, P. L. *Understanding and teaching emotionally disturbed children*. Boston: Allyn & Bacon, 1980.

Odle, S. J., & Galtelli, B. The individualized education program (IEP): Foundation for appropriate and effective instruction. In J. W. Schifani, R. M. Anderson, & S. J. Odle (Eds.), *Implementing learning in the least restrictive environment: Handicapped children in the mainstream*. Baltimore: University Park Press, 1980.

O'Leary, K. D., Becker, W. C., Evans, M. B., & Saudargas, R. A. A token reinforcement program in a public school: A replication and systematic analysis. *Journal of Applied Behavior Analysis*, 1969, *2*, 3–13.

O'Leary, K. D., & O'Leary, S. G. (Eds.) *Classroom management: The successful use of behavior modification*. New York: Pergamon Press, 1972.

Olson, J., Algozzine, B., & Schmid, R. E. Mild, moderate and severe EH: An empty distinction? *Behavioral Disorders*, 1980, *5*, 96–101.

Parker, J. C., & Rubin, L. J. *Process as content: Curriculum design and the application of knowledge*. Chicago: Rand McNally Co., 1966.

Parsons, T. *The social system*. New York: The Free Press, 1951.

Patterson, G. R., Reid, J. B., Jones, R. R., & Conger, R. E. *Social learning approaches to family intervention*. Vol. 1: *Families with aggressive children*. Eugene, Or.: Castilia Publishing Co., 1975.

Pauling, L. Orthomolecular psychiatry. *Science*, 1968, *160*, 265–271.

Peck, R. F., & Havighurst, R. J. *The psychology of character development*. New York: John Wiley & Sons, 1960.

Phillips, D. C., & Kelly, M. E. Hierarchical theories of development in education and psychology. *Harvard Education Review*, 1975, *45*, 351–375.

Phillips, L., Draguns, J. G., & Bartlett, D. P. Classification of behavior disorders. In N. Hobbs (Ed.), *Issues in the classification of children* (Vol. 1). San Francisco: Jossey-Bass, 1975.

Phillips, E. L., Weiner, D. N., & Haring, N. G. *Discipline, achievement, and mental health*. Englewood Cliffs, N.J.: Prentice-Hall, 1960.

Piers, E., & Harris, D. *The Piers-Harris Children's Self-concept Scale*. Nashville, Tenn.: Counselor Recordings and Tests, 1969.

Pimm, J. B. *Early detection of emotional disturbance in a public school setting: A three year follow-up*. Paper presented at the annual meeting of the Canadian Psychological Association, Ottawa, 1967.

Pimm, J. B., & McClure, G. *Ottawa School Behavior Check List*. Ottawa, Canada: Pimm Consultants Ltd., 1969.

Pope, L. Motor activity in brain-injured children. *American Journal of Orthopsychiatry*, 1970, *40*, 783–794.

Porter, R. B., & Cattell, R. B. *Children's Personality Questionnaire*. Champaign, Ill.: Institute for Personality and Ability Testing, 1959.

Premack, D. Reinforcement theory. In D. Levine (Ed.), *Nebraska symposium on motivation*. Lincoln, Neb.: University of Nebraska Press, 1965.

President's Commission on the Mental Health of Children. *Report on the mental health of children*. Washington, D.C.: U.S. Government Printing Office, 1969.

Proshansky, E., & Wolfe, M. The physical setting and open education. *School Review*, 1974, *82*, 557–574.

Proshansky, H. M. Theoretical issues in environmental psychology. *School Review*, 1974, *82*, 541–556.

Prugh, D. G., Engel, M., & Morse, W. C. Emotional disturbance in children. In N. Hobbs (Ed.), *Issues in the classification of children*. San Francisco: Jossey-Bass, 1975.

Quay, H. C. Patterns of aggression, withdrawal, and immaturity. In H. C. Quay & J. S. Werry (Eds.), *Psychopathological disorders of childhood* (1st ed.). New York: John Wiley & Sons, 1972.

Quay, H. C. Measuring dimensions of deviant behavior: The Behavior Problem Checklist. *Journal of Abnormal Child Psychology*, 1977, *5*, 277–287.

Quay, H. C. Classification. In H. C. Quay & J. S. Werry (Eds.), *Psychopathological disorders of childhood* (2nd ed.). New York: John Wiley & Sons, 1979.

Quay, H. C., & Peterson, D. R. *Manual for the Behavior Problem Checklist*. Privately printed, 1979. (Available from D. R. Peterson, School of Professional Psychology, Busch Campus, Rutgers University, New Brunswick, NJ 08903).

Randhawa, B., & Fu, L. Assessment and effect of some classroom environment variables. *Review of Educational Research*, 1973, *43*, 303–321.

Rathbone, C. H. (Ed.) *Open education: The informal classroom*. New York: Citation Press, 1971.

Redl, F. The concept of the life space interview. *American Journal of Orthopsychiatry*, 1959, *29*, 1–18. (a).

Redl, F. The concept of a therapeutic milieu. *American Journal of Orthopsychiatry*, 1959, *29*, 721–734. (b).

Redl, F., & Wineman, D. *The aggressive child*. Glencoe, Ill.: The Free Press, 1957.

Reimer, E. *School is dead: Alternatives in education*. Garden City, New York: Doubleday, 1971.

Reinert, H. R. *Children in conflict: Educational strategies for the emotionally disturbed and behaviorally disordered* (2nd ed.). St. Louis: C. V. Mosby, 1980.

Report to the President from the President's Commission on Mental Health. Washington, D.C.: U.S. Government Printing Office, 1979.

Reynolds, M. C., & Balow, B. Categories and variables in special education. *Exceptional Children*, 1972, *38*, 357–366.

Rhodes, W. C. A community participation analysis of emotional disturbance. *Exceptional Children*, 1970, *36*, 309–314.

Rhodes, W. C. Overview of intervention. In W. C. Rhodes & M. C. Tracy (Eds.), *A study of child variance*. Vol. 2: *Interventions*. Ann Arbor, Mich.: University of Michigan, 1972.

Rhodes, W. C. The illusion of normality. *Behavioral Disorders*, 1977, *2*, 122–129.

Rhodes, W. C., & Head, S. *A study of child variance*. Vol. 3: *Service delivery systems*. Ann Arbor, Mich.: University of Michigan, 1974.

Rhodes, W. C., & Paul, J. L. *Emotionally disturbed and deviant children: New views and approaches.* Englewood Cliffs, N.J.: Prentice-Hall, 1978.

Rhodes, W. C., & Tracy, M. L. (Eds.) *A study of child variance.* Ann Arbor, Mich.: University of Michigan, 1972. (a).

Rhodes, W. C., & Tracy, M. C. (Eds.) *A study of child variance.* Vol. 2: *Interventions.* Ann Arbor, Mich.: University of Michigan, 1972. (b).

Rich, H. L. *An investigation of the social and emotional climate in a class of emotionally disturbed children.* Unpublished doctoral dissertation, Syracuse University, 1969.

Rich, H. L. *The effect of teaching styles on student behavior as related to social-emotional development.* (Final report to the U.S. Office of Education, Department of Health, Education and Welfare). Memphis: Memphis State University, 1973.

Rich, H. L. Behavior disorders and school: A case of sexism and racial bias. *Behavioral Disorders,* 1977, *2,* 201–204.

Rich, H. L. Affective considerations in the use of instructional materials. In R. M. Anderson, J. G. Greer, & S. J. Odle (Eds.), *Individualizing instructional materials for special children in the mainstream.* Baltimore: University Park Press, 1978. (a).

Rich, H. L. A model for educating the emotionally disturbed and behaviorally disordered. *Focus on Exceptional Children,* 1978, *10* (Whole number 3). (b).

Rich, H. L. Teachers' perceptions of motor activity and related behaviors. *Exceptional Children,* 1978, *45,* 210–211. (c).

Rich, H. L. Classroom interaction patterns among teachers and emotionally disturbed children. *The Exceptional Child,* 1979, *26,* 34–40. (a).

Rich, H. L. The syndrome of hyperactivity among elementary resource students. *Education and Treatment of Children,* 1979, *2,* 91–100. (b).

Rich, H. L. Establishing the learning climate. In J. W. Schifani, R. M. Anderson, & S. J. Odle (Eds.), *Implementing learning in the least restrictive environment: Handicapped children in the mainstream.* Baltimore: University Park Press, 1980. (a).

Rich, H. L. Managing interfering behavior. In J. W. Schifani, R. M. Anderson & S. J. Odle (Eds.), *Implementing learning in the least restrictive environment: Handicapped children in the mainstream.* Baltimore: University Park Press, 1980. (b).

Rich, H. L. Educationally handicapped children's locus of control and reading achievement. *Exceptional Children,* 1981, *48,* 244–248.

Rich, H. L., Beck, M. A., & Coleman, T. W. Behavior management: The psychoeducation model. In R. L. McDowell, G. W. Adamson, & F. H. Wood (Eds.), *Teaching emotionally disturbed children: Instructional strategies.* Boston: Little, Brown, in press.

Rich, H. L., & Bush, A. J. The effect of congruent teacher-student characteristics on instructional outcomes. *American Educational Research Journal,* 1978, *15,* 451–457.

Rimland, B. *The cause and treatment of autism.* Paper presented at a meeting of the Southeast Missouri Chapter of the National Society for Autistic Children, Cape Girardeau, Mo., October, 1979.

Rimland, B. Psychogenesis versus biogenesis: The issues and the evidence. In S. C. Plog & R. B. Edgerton (Eds.), *Changing perspectives in mental illness.* New York: Holt, Rinehart & Winston, 1969.

Rogers, C. R. Persons or science? A philosophical question. *American Psychologist,* 1955, *10,* 267–278.

Rogers, C. R. *Personality Adjustment Inventory.* New York: Association Press, 1961.

Rogers, C. R. *Freedom to learn.* Columbus, O.: Charles E. Merrill, 1969.

Rorschach, H. *Rorschach Inkblot Test.* New York: Grune & Stratton, 1966.

Rosenthal, R., & Jacobson, L. *Pygmalion in the classroom.* New York: Holt, Rinehart & Winston, 1968.

Ross, A. O. *Psychological disorders of children: A behavioral approach to theory, research, and therapy* (2nd ed.). New York: McGraw-Hill, 1980.

Rotter, J. B. Generalized expectancies for internal versus external control of reinforcement. *Psychological Monographs,* 1966, *80,* (1, Whole number 609).

Rubin, L. J. Matching teacher, student, and method. *Today's Education,* 1973, *62,* 31–35.

Rubin, R. A., & Balow, B. Prevalence of teacher identified behavior problems: A longitudinal study. *Exceptional Children,* 1978, *45,* 102–111.

Russ, D. F. A review of learning and behavioral theory as it relates to emotional disturbance in children. In W. C. Rhodes & M. L. Tracy (Eds.), *A study of child variance.* Ann Arbor, Mich.: University of Michigan, 1972.

Ruttenberg, B. A., Kalish, B. I., Wenar, C., & Wolf, E. G. *Behavior rating instrument for autistic and other atypical children.* Chicago: Stoelting Co., 1980.

Sagor, M. Biological bases of childhood behavior disorders. In W. C. Rhodes & M. L. Tracy (Eds.), *A study of child variance.* Ann Arbor, Mich.: University of Michigan, 1972.

Salomon, M. K., & Achenbach, T. M. The effects of four kinds of tutoring experience on associative responding. *American Educational Research Journal,* 1974, *11,* 395–504.

Salvia, J., & Ysseldyke, J. S. *Assessment in special education and remedial education.* Boston: Houghton Mifflin, 1978 (2nd ed., 1981).

Sanford, R. N. (Ed.) *The American college.* New York: John Wiley & Sons, 1962.

Sarason, S. B., Lighthall, F. F., Davidson, K. S., Waite, R. R., & Ruebush, B. K. *Anxiety in elementary school children.* New York: John Wiley & Sons, 1960.

Scheuer, A. L. The relationship between personal attributes and effectiveness in teachers of the emotionally disturbed. *Exceptional Children,* 1971, *37,* 723–731.

Schmuck, R. Some aspects of classroom social climate. *Psychology in the Schools,* 1966, *3,* 59–65.

Schultz, E. W., Heuchert, C., & Stampf, S. M. *Pain and joy in school.* Champaign, Ill.: Research Press, 1973.

Schultz, E. W., Hirshoren, A., Manton, A. B., & Henderson, R. A. Special education for the emotionally disturbed. *Exceptional Children,* 1971, *38,* 313–319.

Semmel, M. I., Gottlieb, J., & Robinson, N. M. Mainstreaming: Perspectives on educating handicapped children in the public school. In D. C. Berliner (Ed.), *Review of research in education.* Washington, D.C.: American Educational Research Association, 1979.

Shea, T. M. *Teaching children and youth with behavior disorders.* St. Louis: C. V. Mosby, 1978.

Sivage, C. A. The organizational context of mainstreaming. *The Directive Teacher,* 1980, *2,* 16–17.

Skinner, B. F. Two types of conditioned reflex and a pseudo-type. *Journal of General Psychology*, 1935, *12*, 66–77.

Skinner, B. F. *The behavior of organisms*. New York: Appleton-Century-Crofts, 1938.

Skinner, B. F. *Science and human behavior*. New York: Macmillan, 1953.

Skinner, B. F. *Contingencies of reinforcement: A theoretical analysis*. New York: Appleton-Century-Crofts, 1969.

Sleator, E. K., & Sprague, R. L. Pediatric pharmacotherapy. In W. G. Clark & J. del Guidice (Eds.), *Principles of psychopharmacology* (2nd ed.). New York: Academic Press, 1978.

Smart, R., Wilton, K., & Keeling, B. Teacher factors and special class placement. *Journal of Special Education*, 1980, *14*, 217–229.

Smith, D. L., McWilliams, L., Clark, P., Putnam, J., Meadows, K., & Graves, A. *Pupil activity accounting: A pilot study*. Unpublished manuscript, 1979. (Available from D. L. Smith, College of Education, Memphis State University, Memphis, TN 38152).

Smith, H. C. *Sensitivity to people*. New York: McGraw-Hill, 1966.

Smith, L. M. *Group processes in elementary and secondary schools*. Washington, D.C.: National Education Association, 1959.

Smith, R. M., Neisworth, J. T., & Greer, J. G. *Evaluating educational environments*. Columbus, O.: Charles E. Merrill, 1978.

Solomon, D., & Kendall, A. J. Individual characteristics and children's performance in 'open' and 'traditional' settings. *Journal of Educational Psychology*, 1976, *68*, 613–625.

Sommer, R. Classroom layout. *Theory into Practice*, 1977, *16*, 174–175.

Spivack, G., & Spotts, J. *Devereux Child Behavior Rating Scale*. Devon, Pa.: Devereux Foundation, 1966.

Springer, N. Value of good food. In R. Perske, A. Clifton, B. McLean, & J. Stein (Eds.), *Mealtimes for severely and profoundly handicapped persons: New concepts and attitudes*. Baltimore: University Park Press, 1977.

Sroufe, L. A. Drug treatment of children with behavior problems. In F. D. Horowitz (Ed.), *Review of child development research* (Vol. 4). Chicago: University of Chicago Press, 1975.

Stainback, S., & Stainback, W. Some trends in the education of children labelled behaviorally disordered. *Behavioral Disorders*, 1980, *5*, 240–249.

Stennett, R. G. Emotional handicaps in the elementary years: Phase or disease? *American Journal of Orthopsychiatry*, 1966, *36*, 444–449.

Stephens, T. M. Teaching social behavior—The schools' challenge in the 1980's. *The Directive Teacher*, 1981, *3*, 1, 10.

Stern, G. C. Environments for learning. In N. Sanford (Ed.), *The American college: A psychological and social interpretation of higher learning*. New York: John Wiley & Sons, 1962.

Stouffer, G. A. W. Behavior problems of children as viewed by teachers and mental hygienists. *Mental Hygiene*, 1952, *36*, 271–285.

Strauss, A. A., & Kephart, N. C. *Psychopathology and education of brain-injured children*. Vol. 2: *Progress in theory and clinic*. New York: Grune & Stratton, 1955.

Strauss, A. A., & Lehtinen, L. E. *Psychopathology and education of brain-injured children*. New York: Grune & Stratton, 1947.

Swanson, H. I.., & Reinert, H. R. *Teaching strategies for children in conflict: Curriculum, methods and materials*. St. Louis: C. V. Mosby, 1979.

342   References

Swap, S. M. Disturbing classroom behavior: A developmental and ecological view. *Exceptional Children*, 1974, *41*, 163–172.

Swap, S. M. The ecological model of emotional disturbance in children: A status report and proposed synthesis. *Behavioral Disorders*, 1978, *3*, 186–196.

Thomas, A., & Chess, S. *Temperament and development.* New York: Brunner/Mazel, 1977.

Thomas, R. M. *Comparing theories of child development.* Belmont, Calif.: Wadsworth Publishing Co., 1979.

Thompson, R. F. *Foundations of physiological psychology.* New York: Harper & Row, 1967.

Thorndike, E. L. *Animal intelligence.* New York: Macmillan, 1911.

Thorpe, R., Clark, W., & Tiegs, E. *California Test of Personality.* Monterey, Calif.: California Test Bureau, 1953.

Tinsley, D. G., & Ora, J. P. Catch the child being good. *Today's Education*, 1970, *59*, 24–25.

Torres, S. (Ed.) *A primer on individualized education programs for handicapped children.* Reston, Va.: The Council for Exceptional Children, 1977.

Travers, R. M. W. *Essentials of learning.* New York: Macmillan, 1963.

Turnbull, A. P., & Schulz, J. B. *Mainstreaming handicapped students: A guide for the classroom teacher.* Boston: Allyn & Bacon, 1979.

Update, Newsletter of the Council for Exceptional Children, *12*(4), 1981.

Urban, W. *Draw-a-Person.* Los Angeles: Western Psychological Services, 1963.

Valett, R. E. *Humanistic education.* St. Louis: C. V. Mosby Co., 1977.

Victor, J. B., & Halverson, C. F. Distractability and hypersensitivity: Two behavior factors in elementary school children. *Journal of Abnormal Child Psychology*, 1976, *3*, 83–94.

Vinter, R., Saari, C., Vorwaller, D., & Schafer, W. *Pupil Behavior Inventory.* Ann Arbor, Mich.: Campus Publishing Co., 1966.

Vorrath, H. H., & Brendtro, L. K. *Positive peer culture.* Chicago: Aldine Publishing Co., 1974.

Walker, D. K. *Socioemotional measures for preschool and kindergarten children.* San Francisco: Jossey-Bass, 1973.

Walker, W. *Walker Problem Behavior Identification Scale.* Los Angeles: Western Psychological Services, 1970.

Warren, M. Q. A case of differential treatment for delinquents. *The Annals of the American Academy of Political and Social Science*, 1969, *381*, 47–59.

Watson, J. B. *Behaviorism.* Chicago: University of Chicago Press, 1924.

Wawrzyniak, J. J., Smith, J., & Brown, G. B. Epilogue. In G. B. Brown, R. L. McDowell & J. Smith (Eds.), *Educating adolescents with behavior disorders.* Columbus, O.: Charles E. Merrill, 1981.

Weinstein, G., & Fantini, M. D. *Toward humanistic education: A curriculum of affect.* New York: Praeger Publishers, 1970.

Wender, P. H., & Klein, D. F. The promise of biological psychiatry. *Psychology Today*, 1981, *15*(2), 25–41.

Werry, J. S., & Quay, H. C. The prevalence of behavior symptoms in younger elementary school children. *American Journal of Orthopsychiatry*, 1971, *41*, 136–143.

Wickman, E. W. *Children's behavior and teachers' attitudes.* New York: The Commonwealth Fund, 1928.

Wilson, E. O. *On human nature.* New York: Bantam Books, 1979.

Wirth, S. Effects of a multifaceted reading program on self-concept. *Elementary School Guidance Counselor,* 1977, *12,* 33–40.

Wood, F. H. Defining disturbing, disordered and disturbed behavior. In F. H. Wood & C. K. Lakin (Eds.), *Disturbing, disordered or disturbed? Perspectives on the definition of problem behavior in educational settings.* Minneapolis, Minn.: University of Minnesota, 1979.

Wood, F. H., & Lakin, C. K. (Eds.) *Disturbing, disordered or disturbed? Perspectives on the definition of problem behavior in educational settings.* Minneapolis, Minn.: University of Minnesota, 1979.

Wood, M. M. (Ed.) *The Rutland Center model for treating emotionally disturbed children* (2nd ed.). Athens, Ga.: Rutland Center Technical Assistance Office, 1972.

Wood, M. M. Developmental therapy. In M. M. Wood (Ed.), *Developmental therapy: A textbook for teachers as therapists for emotionally disturbed young children.* Baltimore: University Park Press, 1975.

Wood, M. M., & Swan, W. W. A developmental approach to educating the disturbed young child. *Behavioral Disorders,* 1978, *3,* 197–209.

Wood, F. H., & Zabel, R. H. Making sense of reports on the incidence of behavior disorders/emotional disturbance in school aged populations. *Psychology in the Schools,* 1978, *15,* 45–51.

Woody, R. H. *Behavioral problem children in the schools.* New York: Appleton-Century-Crofts, 1969.

Wright, H. F. Observational child study. In P. H. Mussen (Ed.), *Handbook of research methods in child development.* New York: John Wiley & Sons, 1960.

Zbinden, G. Experimental and clinical aspects of drug toxicity. In S. Garattini & P. Shore (Eds.), *Advances in pharmacology* (Vol. 2). New York: Academic Press, 1963.

Zilboorg, G., & Henry, G. W. *A history of medical psychology.* New York: W. W. Norton, 1941.

Zimbardo, P. G., Pilkonis, P. A., & Norwood, R. M. The social disease called shyness. *Psychology Today,* 1975, *8,* 69–72.

Zubin, J. Classification of the behavior disorders. In P. R. Farnsworth (Ed.), *Annual Review of Psychology,* 1967, *18,* 373–406.

Index

Humanistic psychology, 35, 37
Hyperactive behavior
  and behavior management strate-
      gies, 254
  biochemical factors, 28
  characteristics of, 127–129
  as a developmental factor, 30
  and diet therapy, 208
  and drug therapy, 205
  early classification of, 12
  and external control, 228
  generalization of, 33
  matching models, 302, 306
  providing structure for, 267
  and proximity to teacher, 283
  psychoanalytic theory of, 37
  removal of irrelevant stimuli for,
      226
  and structured intervention
      strategy, 16, 176, 178–180
  and teaching-learning process, 234
  and verbal skills, 274

Id, 36–37, 108–109, 209
Impulsive behavior
  and acting-out behavior, 161
  as characteristic of autistic beha-
      vior, 127
  characteristics of, 129–130
  as developmental factor, 30
  and developmental levels, 126
  external control with, 228
  and intervention strategies, 188
  matching models, 302, 306
  and proximity to teacher, 264
  and psychoanalytic theory, 37
  and removal of irrelevant stimuli,
      266
  use of structure with, 256
Inattentiveness, 81, 208, 254
Individual educational program, 21,
    58, 239
Individualization
  of academic instruction, 268
  in behavior management strategies,
      257
  matching models, 301, 309–310
  in structured intervention, 179
  in teaching-learning strategies,
      234, 245–246, 248
Infanticide, 4–6

Institutions, 39, 44–45
  historical development of, 16, 18
  as placement for children with
      autistic behaviors, 20
Instruction
  clarity of, 218
  expectations, 219–222
  movement (transition) of, 218–219
Internal control, 322
  matching models, 302–304, 307
Interpersonal maturity level model,
    293–296
Intervention strategies, 171–211
  future directions for, 321
  historical development of, 15–18
  matching models, 302, 304, 308
  related to teaching-learning strate-
      gies, 216
Interpersonal management, 269–274
  matching models, 299–300, 302–303
Intrapsychic theory, 37–39
Itard, J., 16

Judgments
  assessment procedure, 146–147
  future directions for use of, 320
Judiciary, role in intervention strate-
    gies, 204

Labeling, 14, 57, 67, 70–71, 75, 91,
    195
  advantages and disadvantages, 58,
      62, 69, 97
  future directions in use of, 318
  objections to, 13
    by countertheorists, 190
  as outgrowth of science era, 10
  use by educators, 12, 42
Labeling theory, 39, 42
Larry P. v. Riles (1972), 20–21
Learning disabilities, 9, 59, 139, 159,
    193, 254
Learning theory, see Behavioral
    theory
Least restrictive environment, 20, 58,
    69, 193
  future directions for, 315–316
  legislation and litigation affecting,
      21
Lebanks v. Spears (1973), 21